Little to Eat and Thin Mud to Drink

Little to Eat and Thin Mud to Drink

Letters, Diaries, and Memoirs from the Red River Campaigns, 1863–1864

Gary D. Joiner, General Editor

Voices of the Civil War
Peter S. Carmichael, Series Editor

The University of Tennessee Press / Knoxville

The Voices of the Civil War series makes available a variety of primary source materials that illuminate issues on the battlefield, the home front, and the western front, as well as other aspects of this historic era. The series contextualizes the personal accounts within the framework of the latest scholarship and expands established knowledge by offering new perspectives, new materials, and new voices.

Cloth: First printing, 2007.
Paper: First printing, 2015.

Library of Congress Cataloging-in-Publication Data

Little to eat and thin mud to drink : letters, diaries, and memoirs from the Red River campaigns, 1863-1864 / Gary D. Joiner, general editor. — 1st ed.
p. cm. — (Voices of the Civil War)
Includes bibliographical references and index.

ISBN-13: 978-1-62190-195-2

1. Red River Expedition, 1864—Personal narratives.
2. United States—History—Civil War, 1861–1865—Personal narratives.
I. Joiner, Gary D.
II. Series: Voices of the Civil War series.

E476.33.L57 2007
973.7'36—dc22 2006017294

To Professor Ludwell Johnson,
the dean of all historians of
the Red River Campaign.

THEIR GLORY SHALL NEVER DIE. THEIR EPITAPHS ARE WRITTEN IN THE HEARTS OF MANKIND AND WHEREVER THERE IS SPEECH OF NOBLE DEEDS, THEIR NAMES SHALL BE HELD IN REMEMBRANCE.

—Inscription on the Confederate Monument
at Scott Cemetery in Scottsville, Texas

CONTENTS

ILLUSTRATIONS

Figures

Maps

Foreword

When a Neanderthal hunter hurled a spear at a rival warrior, he understood, better than some of his more scholarly and erudite descendants, that war was fundamentally a political act about who rules whom. Professional historians, especially those who work in cultural and social history, have struggled to grasp this truism from the Middle Paleolithic period and insist that battles and generalship—the very violence of war and the command decisions that caused it—are not worth studying even though they are interested in questions about how power is exchanged and negotiated. State-sanctioned conflicts offer a perfect opportunity to see how people simultaneously challenge and accept the very order of their society. A predictable and unthinking disdain for all things military, especially in regard to the Civil War, infects members of the academy who consider books on strategy and tactics to be hopelessly pedestrian. A Harvard history professor, for instance, in describing his plans for teaching a Civil War class, advised students that he would ignore the military aspects of the conflict, saying, "I make every effort to head off the would-be colonels who think the course is going to be a study of the battles. If you want to go up one hill and down the next, this course is not for you."

Many academics continue to dismiss military history as the province of buffs or warmongers, but it is striking that military historians have been quick to adopt an interdisciplinary approach. Since the early 1980s, social and cultural history have figured prominently in Civil War scholarship as part of a broadening of the field that reveals the multifaceted ways in which society and war interface. The result is a rich body of secondary literature that captures the dynamic relationship between home front and army, civilians and soldiers, and battlefield and politics. Gary D. Joiner's *Little to Eat and Thin Mud to Drink* is inspired by the belief that the fighting and maneuvering of armies take on deeper meaning when contextualized within the social and political issues of the times. Through an array of carefully selected primary sources, Joiner and his collaborators allow the reader to see how a variety of people made sense of one of the most significant campaigns in the Trans-Mississippi Department. This important volume further demonstrates that the impact of military operations extended beyond the battlefield as the presence of Union armies brought ruin to Southern plantations, shattering morale among Confederate civilians while causing embarrassment to the Lincoln administration and Republicans for their partisan designs for the campaign. For slaves, the presence of a Union army brought the promise of liberation. An unidentified Vermont soldier, whose narrative is published in this volume, recalled that a runaway working in the Union camp was ignorant of the "intricate condition of the Politics" that had caused the war; nevertheless, the Union soldier was impressed that the ex-slave "had along known that it ment [*sic*] freedom."

No campaign has been as richly documented in a single volume before Joiner's *Little to Eat and Thin Mud to Drink*. This innovative approach, so successfully employed by the editor, allows the reader to confront a variety of perspectives on a single instance of history, pushing us to see that there is not a single narrative of truth but, rather, an array of impressions and interpretations that evoke the chaos and confusion consuming people at the very moment they tried to give order to events. Joiner, a noted and award-winning author on the Red River Campaign, deserves high praise for creating a new genre of campaign studies—one that, I hope, will be copied by future contributors to the Voices of the Civil War Series so that we may better appreciate the war's great campaigns from the ground level.

Peter S. Carmichael
University of North Carolina at Greensboro

Acknowledgments

No author or editor can claim that a work is solely his or hers, and that is certainly the case with this work. Collaborative efforts are complex pro-jects, with each contributor performing individual tasks and usually re-quiring the resources of different institutions or individuals. It is impossible to thank and give credit for all those who have helped us, either directly or indirectly over the past several years.

The editors gratefully acknowledge the assistance of several individuals and institutions who have provided critical information. Archivists are the guardians of masses of material that rarely see the light of day. They are the historian's greatest ally. I have been fortunate to work with some of the best, particularly DeAnne Blanton at the National Archives and Records Administration in Washington, D.C.; Sherry Pugh at Jackson Barracks in New Orleans; Laura Connerly, formerly the archivist at Louisiana State University in Shreveport; and Tara Zachary Laver, assistant curator of manuscripts at Hill Memorial Library at Louisiana State University in Baton Rouge. This book would not have been possible without them.

Thanks must also go to Ed Bearss, Chief Military Historian Emeritus of the National Park Service; Terry Winschel, historian at Vicksburg National Military Park in Mississippi; Anne Bailey, professor of history at the Georgia College and State University, Milledgeville; Arthur Bergeron, archivist at the U.S. Army Military History Institute at Carlisle Barracks, Pennsylvania; Steve Bounds, manager of the Mansfield State Historic Site in Louisiana, and Scott Dearman, interpretive ranger at Mansfield State Historic Site. All of these people have helped in many ways that even they may not realize.

Scot Danforth, acquisitions editor with the University of Tennessee Press, and Dr. Peter Carmichael, series editor of the Voices of the Civil War series, have both been instrumental in encouraging the general editor to bring this project forward. Lastly, although great care has been taken to eliminate them, any errors in the research and analysis are solely the editors'.

Gary D. Joiner
December 2005

General Editor's Note

The editors have made every effort to retain the composition, grammar, punctuation, and style of the diarists and letter writers. Parenthetical marks are original to the manuscripts, and passages that were originally underlined have been italicized here. Insertions by the editors are in brackets. Where words or lines are missing, spaces were inserted to indicate damaged or unintelligible areas.

The use of explanatory notes is essential in a work of this nature. They are included to explain information the authors believed was common knowledge or to place passages in context. Where appropriate, the editors have cross-referenced notes for comparison between authors. This approach allows the reader to see the points of view of combatants and civilians in their own context.

Each chapter and, where applicable, each individual document list the editors who worked on it.

Introduction

Gary D. Joiner

The great stories of history, particularly those of military campaigns, are almost always told from the top down. Events are seen in light of the knowledge of outcomes, brilliant or poor planning, dynamic leadership, political and social forces, the vagaries of weather, or the preparedness of forces. This God's-eye view allows the historian to examine events and personalities from the lofty perspective of hindsight. Most often this occurs after the participants or other authors have described the course of action. Subsequent works seek to add to the body of knowledge or reflect on some heretofore unexplored facet of the subject. All good historians and writers of history stand upon the shoulders of others. Sometimes, however, the voices of less recognizable or previously unknown people add information that alters the perceptions of events or significantly changes the understanding of them. These accounts become particularly important when historical sources are scarce and records are incomplete.

The Civil War in the Trans-Mississippi theater is the least explored and researched area of the conflict for several reasons. The region was far from Virginia and the nexus of power. Given that the capitals of the United States and the Confederacy were only 100 miles apart, it is not surprising that the history of the war centers on the East. The press coverage in the eastern theater was, by close proximity and degree of importance, the most intensive. Reporters filed stories with less frequency as distance to the West increased, and the means of delivering the information to the various newspapers was less assured. The public's attention to events west of the Appalachians was tenuous at best after the fall of Chattanooga. By 1864, the Northern press reported anything that even hinted at victory as a self-fulfilled prophecy that the Union would win. When things went wrong, the press was not as quick to describe the degree of failure, and, sometimes, the event simply disappeared. The Red River Campaign in Louisiana and its northern component in Arkansas, the Camden Campaign, are prime examples of this.

Union forces conducted a three-pronged offensive to take Shreveport, Louisiana, during the spring of 1864. The town was the Confederate capital of Louisiana, the headquarters of the Trans-Mississippi Department and the headquarters of the Army of Western Louisiana. Union land forces exceeded forty-two thousand men and officers. The U.S. Navy and the U.S. Army Quartermaster Corps committed more than one hundred vessels to the effort, making the long treacherous trek up a river that was inhospitable, shallow, twisting, and snag-filled. The main column of the army moved overland across the swamps of southern Louisiana, then northward through flat sandy cotton fields, and finally through a pine-barren wasteland. A second column accompanied the fleet to the Alexandria in the center of the state and then split, some remaining with the fleet while others joined the main column. A third column descended from Little Rock and Fort Smith in Arkansas in an attempt to link up with the others. Over four hundred miles separated the northern and southern pincers. Through an astounding series of blunders, the Union forces frittered away their superiority.

The Confederates could muster no more than twenty-five thousand men and had no more than twelve thousand on the field of battle at any given time during the campaign. Their forces stretched from the coastal marshes of southern Louisiana to Matagorda Bay in Texas, and from near the Mississippi River to the south central portion of Oklahoma. The Confederates thwarted the Union forces at the battles of Mansfield (Sabine Crossroads) and Pleasant Hill in Louisiana, and in a series of bloody engagements in Arkansas, including a needless battle at Jenkins' Ferry.

The twin campaigns ended the military field careers of the Union commanders and saved the Trans-Mississippi region from further invasions. The actions also were known for the high levels of animosity among the Union and Confederate commanders toward officers within their own ranks. The Red River Campaign might have only been remembered regionally had Congress not highlighted its actions in an investigation and had not a handful of writers pursued research and written about the expeditions.

Most of the Confederate reports and orders from the region were destroyed or lost at the end of hostilities. The basis for all study of the Red River Campaign exists in Union and surviving Confederate orders and letters in *The War of the Rebellion: A Compilation of the Official Records of the Union and Confederate Armies*, the *Official Records of the Union and Confederate Navies in the War of the Rebellion*, and congressional testimony and analysis found in the *Report of the Joint Committee on the Conduct of the War: The Red River Expedition*.[1] Historical accounts of substance covering the campaign are few. The first scholarly attempt to chronicle the campaign was published in 1958 and was reprinted in 1993. This work, *Red River Campaign: Politics and Cotton in the Civil War*, is the doctoral dissertation of Professor Ludwell Johnson at Johns Hopkins University.[2] William Riley Brooksher's *War along the Bayous: The 1864 Red River Campaign in Louisiana* brought another examination of the subject along the lines of that from Professor Johnson.[3] More recently, I have published two studies of the campaign. The first of these, *One Damn Blunder from Beginning to End: The Red River Campaign of 1864*, came out in 2003.[4] Aside from covering the campaign in Louisiana and Arkansas, it describes in detail the Confederate efforts to defend the region. This book received the Albert Castel Prize in 2004 for best historical book on the western theatre and the A. M. Pate Award for excellence in research and writing in the Trans-Mississippi theater in 2005. The second book, a more exhaustive study of the campaign, is titled *Through the Howling Wilderness: The 1864 Red River Campaign and Union Failure in the West* and was published by the University of Tennessee Press in 2006. This volume attempts to expand the knowledge of the campaign and its aftermath.

While researching sources for a dissertation and *One Damn Blunder*, I found several accounts of the Red River Campaign that had never been published, widely disseminated, or analyzed. These sources, from a variety of individuals, represent new voices in the story of events in Louisiana and Arkansas in 1863 and 1864. The diarists, essayists, and letter writers are from widely diverse backgrounds, and each person's viewpoint is often radically different from the others. This book is an effort to portray what common soldiers, midlevel officers, commanders, and civilians experienced during the largest military campaign west of the Mississippi in the Civil War. These new voices shed light on the campaign and life in Louisiana during that period of the war.

Soldiers writing to their loved ones and friends from the scene of battle or from a place of relative safety soon afterward often convey the emotion of the battlefield more vividly than even the same individuals writing autobiographical passages at a later date. Both Confederate and Union accounts are included in this volume, and these provide a true sense of what they believed and observed and the rumors that they heard. Trans-Mississippi accounts, especially Confederates letters, are very rare, but several accounts are included in this volume. Some deal with famous commanders, but the majority are from men on the front line. Any errors on their parts are from lack of information on the scene, not faulty scholarship. Relatively few Union letters from the Red River Campaign exist, but this volume includes seven. The writers witnessed and participated in the campaign from different units and held varied levels of knowledge of events. The authors span the gamut from highly educated to barely literate, and their writing styles range from tragedy to cynical humor. Together they provide a powerful sense of the action and chaos of the Civil War battlefield.

Also included in this volume are personal diaries, which were very popular in the nineteenth century. Examining the daily events of a single person offers insight into what he or she believed and experienced. Often diaries contain the same generic information, whether soldiers or civilians wrote them. When people are away from their homes and families, some themes act as threads. Boredom, the sameness of weather over weeks or months, melancholy, and angst for those left behind are all common recurring entries. Some diarists minimalized their hardships by writing sparsely or detailing events other than what modern readers might find interesting. Once past the mundane, the writers offer a keen insight into their world.

James A. Jarratt was a sergeant in the Confederate Consolidated Crescent Regiment. His company led the charge at the Battle of Mansfield. Jarratt spent his adolescence near the battlefield and hunted doves on it as a teenager. His description of the battlefield, including very specific details, has proved to be absolutely accurate. All of his descriptions have been verified from a period engineer's map or from contemporary on-the-ground surveys. During that battle, Jarratt and a small cadre captured some of the guns of Nims' Union artillery battery located at the very center of the Union line.[5] Writing in 1906, he reflected on the sad state of affairs of veterans and how history was incorrectly being taught to the youth of that day. The most important piece of information he relays is that the commander of the Louisiana Division, Brigadier J. J. A. Alfred Mouton, did not die near the beginning of the Confederate charge at Mansfield, as had been thought. Instead, he led his troops throughout the assault and died in a last volley of Union troops before they surrendered.

This alters the common view of the attack and explains how the Confederate left wing was able to continue their attack and take the initial Union positions. Jarratt, an excellent writer, conveys his thoughts in a very organized manner.

As a counterpoint, this volume includes an account by an anonymous Union soldier from Vermont, who was an artillerist in the very battery that Jarratt and his men captured. This soldier barely escaped. His essay was evidently prepared as a speech before a veterans' association, perhaps the Grand Army of the Republic or the Military Order of the Loyal Legion of the United States. He directs his very bitter expressions regarding the campaign at the Union commander of the expedition, Major General Nathaniel Prentiss Banks. This writer appears less educated than Jarratt, but is no less compelling.

Representing a minority viewpoint from a Southern officer is a letter by Lieutenant Edward Cunningham, a member of the staff of Lieutenant General Edmund Kirby Smith, commander of the Department of the Trans-Mississippi. Smith's staff was very protective of him and almost uniformly took his side in the bitter war of words between the commanding general and his district commander, Major General Richard Taylor. A month after the Red River Campaign ended, Lieutenant Cunningham wrote a scathing letter about Taylor to his uncle in Virginia. Several times in his narrative Cunningham defends Smith's actions to the detriment of Taylor. Some of his comments so closely paralleled Smith's views that they could have been penned by the general himself. Although he does not specifically state his location during the campaign, it is obvious that Lieutenant Cunningham accompanied Smith to Arkansas. His description of events during the Camden Campaign is much more specific than his knowledge of actions in Louisiana.

Lengthy diaries from the Trans-Mississippi are very rare items. Those that offer detail of combat are even rarer. Private Julius Knapp of the 116th New York Volunteer Infantry kept a diary for the entire year of 1864. As part of Emory's Division, Knapp participated in the final stage of fighting at Mansfield on April 8 and at Pleasant Hill the following day. Perhaps of more importance, Knapp describes the movements of Banks's army during the campaign better than any other source found to date, including official records. As a private, he heard all the rumors coursing through the column and dutifully reported those he believed to be true. He is very much an eastern soldier, and his attitudes reflect his regionalism. The editor has chosen to include all Knapp's entries from January 1 through the end of May of 1864. Although the remainder of the diary contains many interesting comments, it falls outside the scope of this volume and will be retained for publication in a future work. This block of time in 1864 allows the reader to observe the 19th Corps and its activities in southern Louisiana; the preparation for the campaign; and the rigors of marching, fighting, and retreating. It also provides insight into daily life and the decompression following an arduous expedition. Another interesting aspect of this diary is that the author was the principal musician, the drummer, for the regiment. No other such diary has come to light for action west of the Mississippi River. For continuity, entries prior to the campaign are included in Appendix 4.

Major General Richard Taylor was the most popular Confederate commander west of the Mississippi River. Educated at Harvard and Yale, son of President Zachary Taylor, and brother-in-law of Jefferson Davis, Taylor was a dynamic speaker and writer. He instilled pride in his men, and they were fiercely loyal him. Taylor's orders to his troops following the campaign have been printed in various versions; however, editors or newspaper publishers sanitized most of them. The version of the order included in this volume is the one that appeared in the *Washington (Arkansas) Telegraph* shortly after the conclusion of the campaign. It is filled with Taylor's pride and compassion for his men and withholds nothing.

General Camille Armand Jules Marie de Polignac, a French prince who came to the South to fight for a cause in which he believed, was one of Taylor's favorite commanders. Polignac was sent west, where he received command of a brigade of Texans. The hard-living, generally uneducated Texans did not know what to make of their diminutive leader: he wore his hair in curls and sported a perfectly waxed moustache. The Texan ear did not grasp the fine distinctions of the French tongue. They had trouble pronouncing his name and generally referred to him as "General Polecat." The prince had to gain the respect of his men, and several of his officers worked against his authority. In a letter written in the fall of 1863, Polignac defends his honor against some of these Confederate officers, who believed he was a usurper trying to gain fame. Shortly after this, the prince became immensely popular with his men and captured the imagination of the Confederate nation.

The commander of the Consolidated Crescent Regiment, Colonel James Beard, was another very popular leader in Taylor's Army of Western Louisiana. A native of Shreveport, the dashing Beard was a local planter, a devoted family man, and natural leader. Beard's Consolidated Crescent Regiment had fought in western campaigns since Shiloh and had been reformed several times. It was the first regiment to lead the charge at the

Battle of Mansfield and suffered the loss of half its number in the first fifteen minutes of fighting. Among those who fell was the gallant Colonel Beard. Included in this volume is a letter that Beard wrote to his wife shortly before the Battle of Mansfield.

Captain Joshua L. Halbert of the 15th Texas Infantry Regiment was part of Stone's Brigade in the Louisiana Division at the battles of Mansfield and Pleasant Hill. Halbert's regiment was closer to the center of the Confederate line at Mansfield than that of Colonel Beard and James Jarratt's Consolidated Crescent Infantry Regiment. From Halbert's position, he was able to see the charge of Texans under General Polignac, as well as the charge of the Texas Division. He describes in detail the first phase of the battle, as well as the fighting at Pleasant Hill. He wrote this letter at Mansfield on April 13, 1864.

After the Battle of Pleasant Hill, General Taylor ordered his favorite cavalry commander, Texan General Tom Green, to cut off any chance of the Union fleet retreating to Alexandria. Green was a graduate of the University of Virginia, a hero at the Battle of San Jacinto in the Mexican War, a former clerk of the Texas Supreme Court, and was considered a national hero in Texas. General Green and his men went to Blair's Landing, where in one of the strangest battles of the Civil War, Texas cavalry dueled with a Union ironclad monitor and a timberclad warship. Few casualties resulted, but Green was among them. In 1918, W. T. Shaw, who was with Green at Blair's Landing, wrote a letter describing Green's death.

Lucien Flournoy settled in northwest Louisiana at an early age. Members of his family were founders of the village of Flournoy and the town of Greenwood in Caddo Parish. Flournoy wrote a letter to his uncle about the Battle of Monnett's Ferry and the artillery-versus-naval-vessel action known as the Battle of Cane River Landing a few days after they occurred. He was a witness to the naval action. His letter is the best Confederate account known to exist.

Confederate private R. A. Knox wrote a note to his father describing what had occurred to that point in the campaign. His short letter describes his knowledge of past events as well as his predictions of the future moves of the Confederate and Union forces.

Zachariah Howell enlisted in Company A of the 25th Louisiana Infantry. Entering the war as a private, Howell eventually rose through the ranks to become second lieutenant. He participated in battles at Perryville, Kentucky, and Murfreesboro, Tennessee, and aided in the attempts to relieve General Pemberton's army in Vicksburg. He did not serve in the Red River Campaign until the end, when he was assigned to duty in

Shreveport, where he eventually surrendered. He was in Shreveport when he wrote to his second wife, Isabella Jane Whitworth Howell, detailing the army news.

Another private, Barclay E. Ballard, a member of the 36th Texas Cavalry Regiment, wrote a letter on May 20, 1864, to his sister, Araminta, informing her of the death of their brother, George, at the Battle of Yellow Bayou. As one would expect, this poignant letter describes their brother's death and burial.

Private Jefferson Morgan served with Company E, 35th Texas Calvary Regiment. He wrote a series of letters to his wife, Amanda Ann Sportsman Morgan, who was living at their home in Ellis County, Texas. The correspondence covers the period from November 1863 through July 1864. The letters are included to describe the hopes and fears of a typical Confederate soldier, if such a person existed. Morgan did not fight at Mansfield or Pleasant Hill, but his unit was present for the Battle of Blair's Landing. Just prior to the campaign, his unit headed north from Matagorda Bay. Morgan contracted measles during the journey and never fully recovered. His rustic eloquence spoke of his personal concerns at home and of his health. Following his death, his friend, D. W. Fields, wrote to Amanda Morgan, describing her husband's devotion to her, and this letter is also included in this volume.

F. B. Harris of the 4th Texas Cavalry Regiment wrote a letter to a friend the day following after the close of the Red River Campaign, describing with much humor and introspection the battles of Mansura and Yellow Bayou. Harris is very straightforward in his description of how difficult the campaign was on the few cavalrymen who were sent to slow down the Union column as it attempted to flee to safety. Another veteran of the 4th Texas Cavalry, Moritz Maedgen, wrote to a wounded comrade about the actions following the Battle of Pleasant Hill. He depicts the final battles of the campaign and also describes the naval actions and building of Bailey's dam in Alexandria. Moreover, Maedgen displays humor in his retelling of events, obviously attempting to raise the spirits of his convalescing friend.

D. E. Causland was a member of Company H, 4th Confederate Engineers, based in Shreveport. As part of this unit, he was responsible for all pontoon bridges, dams, earthworks, and fortifications. Company H manned the last Confederate engineering outpost west of the Mississippi River in 1865, a pontoon bridge unit in Camden, Arkansas. Causland wrote his commander, Captain Smith Kirby, that he did not how he could retrieve the pontoon train, due to flooding. Causland wrote the letter just over three months from the date Shreveport surrendered. Although not in the timeline of the Red River Campaign, the letter is included in this volume because it portrays the mind-set of the engineers at the close of hostilities.

Elizabeth Jane Samford Fullilove was the wife of Thomas Pope Fullilove, who entered Company D of the 6th Louisiana Cavalry some time after the fall of Vicksburg in 1863. In 1915 she wrote her memoirs, describing their farmwork in preparation for the war and the angst she felt knowing her husband was fighting. Their farm was in Preston, Louisiana, near both Mansfield and Pleasant Hill, and she describes the movement of the troops and wagons as they passed in front of her house on their way to the battlefield.

Union sergeant William H. Scarborough of Company B of the 96th Ohio Infantry Regiment wrote a letter to his parents on March 27, 1864. His regiment was part of the 13th Army Corps. At the time of his writing, the Union column had just reached Alexandria. He describes the march, the beauty of the countryside, and the architecture of the buildings.

A soldier known only as "Thomas" wrote to his wife during the fighting at Pleasant Hill on April 9. He believed it would be his last. His regiment was under heavy fire with no possibility of advancing and little opportunity to retreat. He apologized for the poor penmanship, due to having to write on the top of his cap. Thomas placed his letter as being written "In the line of battle on Pleasant Hill or God Knows Where." It describes the intensity of fighting and the desperation of the Union forces.

An immigrant soldier, Wilson Novyus, wrote his niece from Grand Ecore on April 15, 1864. Novyus was a private in the 161st New York Infantry regiment of Dwight's Brigade of Emory's Division in the 19th Corps. In his letter, he describes the close-quarters fighting in the third and final phase of the Battle of Mansfield, the retreat and fighting at Pleasant Hill, and the news of the death of Confederate General Green at the Battle of Blair's Landing. At the time of the writing, the Union was entrenching at Grand Ecore, and their commanders were uncertain whether to attempt to withstand a siege or to evacuate to Alexandria.

F. W. Pearce was an ordinance sergeant with the 2nd Maine Cavalry Regiment. He wrote a letter to his brother, Varney, from Alexandria on April 21, 1864. In this brief account, the author describes his journey up the Red River, skirmishes with Confederates, his observation of the river's water level, and his impressions of General Banks.

A brief letter from an unidentified soldier named "Jim" to his parents was penned in May 1864 at the end of the campaign. He was a member of the 30th Maine Infantry Regiment. He describes work on Bailey's Dam, the Battle of Mansura, and his knowledge of the amputation of the leg of his commander, Colonel Francis Fessenden, after the Battle of Monett's Ferry.

Hugo Voigt, a private in Company C of the 29th Wisconsin Volunteer Infantry Regiment, wrote his friend, Charles, on May 4, 1864, from Alexandria. Voigt's regiment was part of the Second Brigade, Third Division, commanded by Brigadier General Robert A. Cameron, 13th Army Corps. This small division formed the second line of defense at the Mansfield. Voigt is very pragmatic, relaying the destruction of his small corps and the fighting the following day at Pleasant Hill. His is rustically eloquent and sentimental.

Among the Union letters is one from Thomas Hayden of the 38th Massachusetts Volunteer Infantry Regiment, a component of Grover's Division of the 19th Corps. There is some mystery as to who this soldier is since there were two men named Thomas Hayden in the 38th Massachusetts. This division served as a reserve and remained at Alexandria until the retreat following the Battle of Pleasant Hill. At that time, they moved forward to Grand Ecore. Written to his friend, Jim, on May 4, 1864, from Alexandria. The letter vividly describes his regiment's ascent up the river on the steamer *Mittie Stevens* and the Union army's retreat from Grand Ecore. He is witty and sarcastic, with a strong dose of truth.

An unidentified soldier of the 19th Corps, named "Delamaster," wrote his cousin a letter less than a week after the campaign. He is an enthusiastic supporter of General Banks and places the blame for the Union loss on low water rather than poor generalship. His views of the battle outcomes differ from those of the other Union letter authors and diarists. Delamaster's writing and beliefs reflect those of many of his New England compatriots.

Rufus C. Kemp of the 165th New York Zouaves wrote three letters included in this volume. The first, penned in January 1864, briefly depicts the life of the common soldier of the 19th Corps leading up to the campaign. The second, written immediately after the Battle of Pleasant Hill, assures his family that he is alive and well. The third, written in June while the regiment was awaiting orders, describes camp life following the campaign. Kemp is a typical stoic soldier from an elite unit.

D. R. Wallace, a surgeon or administrator with the Corps d'Afrique, wrote a very compassionate letter to the wife of an attaché in his division concerning her husband's wounds and medical care. This is a very rare example of the type of medical care afforded to Union troops in the field while serving in the Red River Campaign.

William H. Whitney of Cambridge, Massachusetts, was a member of the 38th Massachusetts Infantry Regiment. Included in this volume is a letter Whitney wrote during the campaign and others written after the fighting while he was in Morganza, on the Mississippi River below the mouth of the Red River. He provides an eloquent account of the actions of the 19th Corps. He is also pro–General Banks, but not enthusiastically so. His account is circumspect. Whitney reveals a good grasp on external events and the Red River Campaign's place in events of the day.

Female accounts of the Civil War, particularly west of the Mississippi River, are exceedingly rare. Included are portions of a diary penned by Sidney Harding, a twenty-two-year-old plantation daughter, whose family fled in 1863 to Keachi, a safer place in DeSoto Parish, Louisiana. Harding was the daughter of a wealthy St. Mary Parish plantation owner, W. S. Harding, who died in the late 1850s. The diary chronicles the hardships of travel, the discovery that Union forces burned her St. Mary Parish home, and the realization that her place of refuge was very close to Shreveport, the objective of the same Union forces. Melancholy and denial permeate the diary, because Harding had great trouble coping with the changes in her life. As troops flooded in from Texas prior to the Battle of Mansfield, they marched by her log cabin. She visited the battlefield a few days after the event and described visiting and taking in wounded soldiers.

The death of a single individual sometimes strikes a profound chord outside the immediate family. This is apparent in the death of Acting Volunteer Lieutenant Joseph P. Couthouy, commander of the USS *Chillicothe*. Couthouy was the most senior naval casualty suffered during the Red River Campaign. Vessel paymaster J. H. Hathaway, Massachusetts senator Charles Sumner, and Lieutenant Commander Frank Ramsey of the USS *Choctaw* wrote letters and reports concerning Couthouy's death and the disposition of his body. Also included in this account is a portion of the deck log of the *Chillicothe*.

The recollections of a small boy following the Battle of Mansfield are presented here in the form of J. E. Hewitt, who later became the publisher and editor of the local newspaper in Mansfield. His account of the surprising friendship between his maternal uncle, Captain J. H. Garrett, commander of Company K, 27th Louisiana Infantry Regiment, and Colonel John Reid of the 130th Illinois Infantry Regiment is remarkable.

The memories of the terrible struggle of the Civil War linger, particularly in the South. A victory such as the Battle of Mansfield was long celebrated, and even today the church bell at Christ Memorial Episcopal Church in Mansfield rings at 4 P.M. on April 8, as it has each year since the battle. Shortly after the conflict two maiden sisters wrote the lyrics of a song about the battle, using the tune of "Kingdom Coming." It was played during the 100th anniversary commemoration of the battle. Victor Mansfield de Polignac, the son of the Prince de Polignac, rededicated the monuments on the battlefield on April 8, 1964, and the Mansfield High School band played this song in his honor. The song and the story of its origins are included here.

The first-person narratives in this volume bring the Red River Campaign into focus. They are not only from the annals of veterans' associations and official reports, but, more important, from people who witnessed the battles and their aftermath from a very intimate perspective. In most cases, these events changed their lives or at least created vivid memories that they carried with them always.

A project such as this is best conducted using the talents of several individuals. Each brings a fresh approach to historical research and is an expert in his or her own right. The art of annotating and citing narrative documents requires a depth of knowledge approaching the level of the original writer. Some documents are extraordinarily difficult to interpret due to poor handwriting or the intimate familiarity the writer has with his or her environment. Diaries and letters often contain cryptic passages not intended to fool future readers but inserted because the writer knew, for example, the location of a cotton gin, even though no trace of it now exists. If a place or event is used as a marker, it becomes a major challenge for the historian to determine the accuracy of the writer's information and place it in the greater context of the story. Sometimes, as in the James A. Jarratt narrative, identification of such markers adds credibility to the writer's views or observations. This detective work is perhaps the most interesting aspect of the historian's craft. This volume is edited and annotated by a team of dedicated researchers with intimate knowledge of the Louisiana, Texas, and Arkansas region.

Notes

1. U.S. War Department, *War of the Rebellion: The Official Records of the Union and Confederate Armies*, 128 vols. (Washington, DC, 1890–1901); U.S. War Department, *Official Records of the Union and Confederate Navies in the War of the Rebellion*, 31 vols. (Washington, DC, 1895–1929); U.S. Congress, *Report on the Joint Committee on the Conduct of the War, 1863–1866*, vol. 2, *Red River Expedition* (Millwood, NY, 1977).
2. Ludwell Johnson, *The Red River Campaign: Politics and Cotton in the Civil War* (Kent, OH, 1993).

3. William Riley Brooksher, *War along the Bayous: The 1864 Red River Campaign in Louisiana* (Washington, DC, 1998).
4. Gary D. Joiner, *One Damn Blunder from Beginning to End: The Red River Campaign of 1864* (Wilmington, DE, 2003).
5. See chap. 1 n. 77.

JAMES A. JARRATT AND THE CONSOLIDATED CRESCENT REGIMENT IN THE RED RIVER CAMPAIGN OF 1864

Edited by Gary D. Joiner

ALTHOUGH RELATIVELY LITTLE IS KNOWN OF JAMES A. JARRATT, his command of the English language and his articulate writing indicate he was an educated man. Biographical information on Jarratt is limited to official government documents, city directories, and obituaries. His service record states that he was a resident of Sabine Parish; he entered service as a private with the 11th Battalion of Louisiana Infantry at Mansfield, Louisiana, and was promoted to corporal. After the unit was combined with others, he was promoted to sergeant and was mustered out as a sergeant in Company B of the Consolidated Crescent Regiment, Louisiana Infantry.[1]

The 1920 Decennial Census lists Jarratt as a resident of Shreveport living at 624 Pierre Avenue.[2] He was born on August 16, 1840, in Zebulon, in Pike County Georgia.[3] Jarratt's family moved to Sabine Parish in western Louisiana while he was young.[4] In his narrative, he states that during the Civil War his father lived fifteen miles from the village of Pleasant Hill in DeSoto Parish, which at that time was located just north of the Sabine Parish boundary. Today the town is in Sabine Parish, but the site of the original village and the battle remain in DeSoto Parish. Jarratt married Mary Lou Patterson in 1866, and the couple eventually had five children. In the 1870s, Jarratt and his family moved to Shelby County, Texas, where he became a blacksmith and a sawmill worker. Sometime in the late 1800s his first wife died and Jarratt remarried, this time to Martha Kile. Jarratt also had five children in this marriage. He lost a leg in an accident at the mill on December 22, 1891.[5] Around 1900, he moved back to DeSoto Parish; then in 1902 he moved to Shreveport, where he lived until his death April 14, 1921, at the age of eighty-one.[6] His obituary lists him as a minister and indicates that he died "after a long illness."[7] He is buried in Greenwood Cemetery in Shreveport, Louisiana.[8]

Jarratt's account is the only extended first-person narrative from a nonofficer Confederate participant and one of the few from a participant in the battles of Mansfield and Pleasant Hill. His insight makes the author unique because he had lived in Sabine Parish, immediately south of DeSoto Parish, where the battles of Mansfield and Pleasant Hill were fought. Jarratt states that as a boy he hunted on the very fields where the heaviest action occurred on April 8, 1864. He described landowners and their properties with the ease of familiarity. This knowledge at times puts him at odds with conventional historical accounts; therefore, he adds new insight to some of the events of the Red River Campaign—albeit the word "new" is perhaps an odd term to use for an account written in 1906. Jarratt self-published his thirty-one-page tract with hope of having it copyrighted and published on a larger scale.[9] This never occurred, and the number of printed copies is unknown. Only one surviving copy is known to exist; Jarratt inscribed that copy to Kate Beard, the widow of his regimental commander, Colonel James H. Beard. Jarratt was twenty-four years old when he fought at Mansfield and sixty-six when he wrote his account. His voice was one of bitterness at the treatment of Confederate veterans by their own states. He was determined to right the inaccuracies being told later generations.

The Louisiana Consolidated Crescent Infantry Regiment came into existence on November 2, 1863, at Simmesport, near the mouth of the Red River. It is also known as the Louisiana 24th Infantry Regiment. As its name implies, it was a consolidation of prior units too weak in manpower to continue as viable organizations. These included the Crescent Infantry Regiment, the 11th Infantry Regiment, and the Confederate Guards Response (12th or 16th Louisiana) Infantry Battalions.[10] The regiment was organized into fourteen companies, and it served until May 19, 1865, as one of the last of Confederate field units to surrender.[11]

The Consolidated Crescent Regiment's parent units saw heavy action prior to November 1863. The Confederate Guards Response Infantry Battalion was raised in New Orleans and saw action at Shiloh (April 6–7, 1862), Farmington (May 9, 1862), Fort Bisland (April 13–14, 1863), Irish Bend (April 14, 1863), and Stirling's Plantation (September 29, 1863).[12] The Louisiana 11th Infantry Battalion saw service at the Battle of Fort Beauregard (May 10–11, 1863).[13] The original Louisiana Crescent Infantry Regiment participated in battles at Shiloh (April 6–7, 1862), the Corinth Campaign (April–June 1862), Georgia Landing (October 27, 1862), Grand River (February 16, 1863), and Fort Bisland (April 13–14, 1863).[14]

Colonel James H. Beard (killed at Mansfield on April 8, 1864) originally commanded the Consolidated Crescent Regiment. Its field officers were Colonel Abel W. Bosworth (killed at Mansfield April 8, 1864), Major Mercer Canfield (killed at Mansfield April 8, 1864), Lieutenant Colonel Franklin H. Clack (mortally wounded at Mansfield April 8, 1864), Lieutenant Colonel Arthur W. Hyatt (killed at Mansfield April 8, 1864), Major Hugh W. Montgomery (transferred on October 17, 1864), and Major James J. Yarborough.[15] William B. Spencer (captured on April 1, 1864), and later Abram H. Thigpen, commanded Company B.

The Consolidated Crescent Regiment, along with the 18th and 28th Louisiana Infantry regiments, was assigned as a part of Brigadier General J. J. A. Alfred Mouton's brigade. In March 1864, Mouton received command of the small Louisiana Division, and the Crescent Regiment served as part of the brigade under the command of Colonel (later Brigadier General) Henry Gray. Following Mouton's death at Mansfield, the division came under the command of Brigadier General Camille Polignac. This configuration lasted until a reorganization of Trans-Mississippi units in September 1864. At that time, the Consolidated Crescent Regiment was under the 2nd Louisiana Brigade (still commanded by Gray), Second Division (still commanded by Polignac), 1st Corps, Trans-Mississippi Department.[16]

The regiment fought at Mansfield on April 8, 1864, where it suffered 49 percent casualties. It was the only Louisiana regiment during the Civil War that suffered the loss of all three of its field officers in a single battle.[17] At Pleasant Hill on April 9, 1864, it saw limited fighting and was part of the reserves. The regiment also served as reserves at the Battle of Yellow Bayou on May 18, 1864, and finally served in an action on the Atchafalaya River near Simmesport on June 8, 1864.

Following the Red River Campaign, the unit returned to Alexandria and was then transferred to Shreveport. After garrison duty in Shreveport, the regiment held positions near Alexandria. In May 1864, the Consolidated Crescent Regiment moved to Mansfield, where it disbanded on May 19, 1865.[18]

James A. Jarratt wrote his account in 1906 with the intent of correcting, from his point of view, historically inaccurate accounts of the Battle of Mansfield and the Red River Campaign. He describes the battle action from the infantry soldier's stance, not the perhaps not-so-perfect hindsight of the historian or the field commander. He adds details of the Battle of Mansfield that have never been seen in print in any other account of the action. Jarratt did make some errors, but these can be attributed more to his rank and view of the action rather than malicious intent. Fellow veterans of Company B endorsed his account of the actions of his unit, adding to its authenticity.

Reminiscences of a Great Struggle by Heroes of the Confederacy

[inscribed: Kate H. Beard, from J. A. Jarratt]

An Endorsement

We, the undersigned, are personally acquainted with J. A. Jarratt and unhesitatingly endorse the enclosed write-up, as we were in the Confederate army with him, and know him to be a man of honor and one to be relied on in every particular, who would not knowingly misrepresent anything.

C. C. PHILLIPS.
F. A. LEONARD.
J. J. GARDNER.
DR. M. O. STRIBLING.

FIG. 1.1. Portrait photograph of James A. Jarratt from the frontispiece of his self-published work, circa 1906. Copy in the collection of Russell and Mary Margaret Schulze, Houston, Texas.

Dedication

This little history is dedicated to the memory of Company B of the consolidated Crescent Regiment. The following members are still alive and perhaps more that I have not been able to Find:

J. J. Yarbrough.	J. A. Jarrett.
Abe Thigpen.	Jim Hunter.
F. A. Leonard.	John Thomas.
J. J. Gardner.	Nat Phillips.
C. C. Phillips.	Frank Parsons.
Green Jackson.	Jim Parsons.
Ran Allen.	Abner McCraw.
Dorle Moats.	Billy McCraw.
John Matthews.	Alas Devals.

John Fike.	J. B. Williams, Sr.
Jack Williams.	John Durham.
Josh Billingsly.	Larkin Palmer.
Mose Franklin.	Tip Lee.
Dock Etheridge.	Moat Mathews.

Our Orderly Sergeant, Jemeson Williams, may be alive. The above are members of two companies that were consolidated into one company at the consolidation of Captain Jordan's Company from Pleasant Hill and Shelly, or Captain Yarbrough's Company from Mansfield, La.

J. A. JARRATT

Reminiscences

I was at Camden, Ark, on the 7th day of May, 1906, the anniversary of the battle that was fought between the Federal forces under General Steel[e] and the Confederate forces under General Smith.[19] And as the people of Camden met on that day for the purpose of decorating the graves of the Confederate dead, I was present and watched the proceedings of the decorators. It was truly a gala day for the young and they seemed to enjoy it immensely, for there was not much if any seriousness manifested among the crowd. I thought that as the poor old living soldier that spent four years of the best part of his life battling for the Lost Cause in a great many instances was passing through this life unnoticed or uncared for, that it was a pity that we were not all killed, so that we could have our graves decorated by the lively youth of this day and time. We now find that Governor Blanchard is being heavily criticized for vetoing the bill passed by the Legislature appropriating $100,000 for the purpose of erecting a monument in memory of the Louisiana Confederate dead that lost their lives at Vicksburg, Miss.[20] when their poor old living soldiers are only receiving the pitiful sum of $2.50 per month as a pension, and to get that small amount they have to subscribe to being a pauper.[21] The battle ground at Vicksburg will remain where it is when the last old Confederate soldier will lave long since answered the last roll call. I say first take care of the living, and after they are provided for, then build your monuments in memory of all the Confederate dead. While looking on, my mind reverted back to the 8th of April, 1864, when General Taylor with his little heroic band of not much if any more than 3,000 (actually engaged) stopped the advance of the Federal forces under General Banks numbering about 40,000 all told, gave them a severe thrashing and started them back with a large portion of their train and artillery left in possession of General Taylor and his victorious army, and as I was in that battle I will endeavor to give to the public what I saw and know of that campaign, believing that it will be of interest to the public in this day and time.[22]

I was in Company B of the Crescent Regiment. The old Crescent Regiment was from New Orleans, but as it had dwindled down to what we might term a remnant, it had been consolidated with Shelly's and Clack's Battalions.[23] Before the consolidation Shelly's Battalion was under the command of Lieutenant Colonel Beard, who was promoted to Colonel, and placed in command of the consolidated Crescent Regiment. Lieutenant Colonel Clack (of Clack's Battalion) was placed in the regiment as Lieutenant Colonel, and Major Canfield as Major. None of the regimental officers of the old Crescent Regiment was retained except Lieutenant Wall, who was Adjutant. Here I will say that I have never seen one word in print about one of the best Colonels that wore the Gray. The noble, generous and highminded Colonel Beard, who on the 8th of April, 1864, gave his life for the cause we all loved so well.[24] There are several things that are necessary to be combined in a man to make a good officer first he has to have a clear and well balanced brain, a kind, sympathetic and loving heart, that will make him study the comfort of the lowest down private in his command, and still retain the dignity of a commander. Many good men were failures as officers, because they would allow their sympathies to cause them to do things that their better judgment forbade. When Colonel Beard was on duty he knew no man, only as a soldier; off duty he was kind and generous and sympathetic. Many times have I seen him walking in the rear of his regiment, while on the march, with some poor, ragged, footsore private riding his horse. While I was in the ranks there was not a private nor officer that I loved better than I did the noble Colonel Beard, and yet I had never received any special favors from his hands. He was a handsome and fine-looking man, endowed with enough pride to hold him in his proper position as an officer and man.

Comrades, let your memory go back,
When we stood in Moses' field in rank,
And see our gallant Colonel as he sits his steed,
Ere long on his handsome form bullets will feed.

See him there with sword drawn,
Before no enemy did he ever fawn,
In that day he sacrifice[d] his life
For our homes in that unholy strife.

Many of our comrades too did go,
To the land that none of us know,
They will meet at roll call upon high,
Where there is neither sorrow, moan or sigh.

Then weep not o'er our precious dead,
For their blood they did freely shed,
Battling with our common foe,
To keep them away from our very door.

We saw them falling by our side,
While we passed on with the rising tide,
Then we hear the cry, they flee, they flee,
So the victory was ours as we could see.

Sleep on, comrades, with the noble Colonel Beard,
For no enemy had you ever feared,
Your noble forms have gone back to dust,
But the soul, the life, will never rust.

It was intended by the Federal authorities that General Banks was to march up the west side of Red River to Shreveport, where he was to form a junction with General Steel[e] and his army that was to march down through Arkansas; and then both armies were to march out into Texas and have the wheat crop cut, to be delivered to the Federal Government.[25] And there is no doubt but what their plans would have been carried out had it not been for General Taylor. For all know, that know anything about that campaign, that General Banks had no idea of meeting with any serious opposition before he arrived at or near Shreveport.[26] As I did not keep a memorandum of our proceedings, there no doubt will be some mistakes in this write-up, but what I saw and heard in that memorable campaign has been indelibly impressed upon my mind, and no time can erase it while I live in this world. When we started on the retreat in the lower part of the State, General Taylor had quite a small force at his command, and no cavalry except a small regiment commanded by Colonel Vincent, which was called the Second Louisiana Cavalry. We had retreated up through the Opelousas country, striking the piney woods country at the edge of Red River bottom opposite Alexandria, where we took the road leading to Fort Jesup. When we arrived at the forks of the road in the piney woods near Carroll Jones' house, one road leading to Alexandria, the other (the one we came up) we struck camp.[27] The Federals then having arrived at or near Alexandria. Our little band of cavalry was then camped at Magnut's

Hill between the infantry and the Federals.[28] On account of the carelessness of Colonel Vincent, he was surprised at night by the Federals and nearly or quite all of his regiment was captured.[29] It was then that the real hard times on the infantry began. Not having any cavalry to protect our rear, we had to do picket duty ourselves. Our regiment was accordingly thrown down some distance towards the Federals, to try to hold them in check until our artillery, baggage wagons and our herd of old poor Texas beeves could make their escape up through the piney woods. We were held there for four days, with but little to eat. When we started on our weary march through that desolate long leaf piney woods, there was only one thing that we could say that we had a plenty of, and that was pine knots.[30] Our beeves were so poor that they would break down and refuse to go any farther, and when we would get to them they would charge us, and as weary as we were, they would get a move on us. They would then kill them and issue the beef out that evening. When we started up through that piney woods we thought that our officers put an unnecessary hardship upon us. There was a skirmish line thrown out on each side of the road and those skirmishers had to keep ahead of the men that were walking in the road, and a part of the army would form a line of battle and there wait until the first line had marched by and formed another line. This proceeding was kept up until we arrived at Pleasant Hill, when we were relieved by being reinforced with General Green's cavalry.[31] When we were coming up through the piney woods we struck camp one evening, and I felt like I was bound to have something to eat. I went to a man in our company by the name of Joe Ferguson[32] and said to him: "Joe, I am starved out and I have got to have something to eat." His reply was: "Jimmie, there is not a hog in this whole country that has got one eye of grease in him. I told him that I did not say anything about a hog, but come and we will go down to Captain Patan's headquarters and see if we can't lift something down there.[33] Captain Patan was our brigade commissary man. We went down there and found the Captain with his staff sitting at a table eating. On one side of a wagon about twenty feet from the wagon. I saw the back gate of the wagon was out, and a tub of bacon was sitting just inside. The bacon was cut up in pieces about eight or ten inches square. It was then about dusk. I told Joe there was our chance. I slipped up by the wagon, reached around and got a piece of that bacon, handed it to Joe, when he slipped it under his coat, and we left for our camp fire undiscovered. When we got back we began to cut slices and toast it before the pine knot fire, dropping the grease on our bread. I have been at many good dinners and suppers during my life, but that was the best meal I ever ate in my life. The toasting of that bacon could be smelt all over the camp, and there were many half-starved soldiers crowded around, wanting to know where we got that bacon. After we were relieved by General Green we left Pleasant Hill, arriving at Mansfield on the evening of the 7th of April.[34] We were marched up the Kingston road about four or five miles and camped for the night on a little stream called Bouchest.[35] I was told that on the evening of the 7th of April General Taylor was sitting on his horse in front of old man Cunningham's Hotel, when Mr. Cunningham asked him if he did not think it was best to leave Mansfield. General Taylor's reply was: "No. This time tomorrow General Banks' army will be on the retreat, for I intend to give them battle, but I will fight with a halter around my neck, that is, against orders."[36] And subsequent events proved what General Taylor said was true, for he was courtmartialed and removed to Galveston and General Buckner succeeded him in command.[37] If General Banks had been victorious, General Taylor would have been hung as a traitor, and yet no one but General Taylor and his little band of heroes saved Shreveport and all of the adjacent country by not obeying Kirby Smith. At the close of the war General Kirby Smith would have fared badly if he had fallen into the hands of General Taylor's men that fought Banks's army at Mansfield.

On the 8th of April we left our baggage in camp and were marched back to Mansfield early in the morning. When we arrived in Mansfield we were drawn up in line and as many cartridges as our boxes would hold were issued to every man. It was then for the first time that we knew that we had fighting to do. And many of our men who were then in high spirits would be numbered with the slain before the sun should set beneath the western horizon. Some of them had families there in Mansfield and bid them farewell that morning, never to meet again in life. Among them was our senior Captain Fields, who bid his wife and children adieu for the last time.[38] Why history calls this battle the battle of Sabine Cross Roads it is hard to tell, for the battle was over before the Sabine Cross Roads was reached.[39] There was a cavalry skirmish at the Sabine Cross Roads on the evening of the 7th of April, but nothing like a battle.[40] This skirmish took place to keep the Federals from reaching the Moss place (where General Taylor expected to fight) before General Taylor was ready for them. General Taylor had selected the Moss place as the place for the battle, which is about or near three miles from Mansfield.[41] The Mansfield and Pleasant Hill road ran square through the field but a little distance from the mouth of the lane on the left of the road the field turned to the right and ran nearly diagonally with the road. After passing out of the Moss lane[42] you passed through a skirt of woods near one-quarter of a mile wide, when you came to another field on the right of the road, and about two hundred yards from the corner on the right of the road was the house[43] (owned by Mr. Hunnicut. It is now owned by Mr. Whit Porter).[44] There was a field at that time that started on the left of the road in front of this house and the field[45] on the right joined with the next place which was then owned by Mr. Phincher. This field on the left contained about ten acres, and ran down to a hollow[46] that crossed the road. On the left of the road there was then a small oak grove,[47] and Mr. Phincher's house[48] was on the little hill, and a lane from there to the edge of the woods which was about one-quarter of a mile from Mr. Phincher's house.[49] Up back of the house was a gin house,[50] with a gin house lot of near five acres, and between the ten acres and Moss' field was a strip of woods[51] from (two to three hundred yards wide, getting wider and wider after starting in front of Mr. Whit Porter's house.[52] From the beginning of the Moss lane next to Mansfield to the end of the second lane[53] was nearly if not quite a mile and a half. I can not give the exact distance at this late date but once upon a time as a boy I had hunted other game there besides Yankees, and I did not find near as much danger attached to killing doves in Moss' field as I found in after years killing Yankees in the same field. The beginning of the Moss lane was not much if any over two miles from Mansfield. Mr. Willard Allen[54] lived about four miles from Mansfield, and a Mr. Chapman[55] lived about five miles, and the Sabine Cross Roads was over six miles from Mansfield.[56] When we got near to the mouth of Moss' lane we turned to the left, passing by the Moss house, which was about a quarter, or perhaps more, from the road.[57] After our regiment passed the house two or three hundred yards we were halted and brought to a rest. We did not rest but a little while before we heard firing diagonally across the field, near the far corner, and in a few minutes two of our cavalry came into the field at or near the far corner at full speed with four or five Federals in hot pursuit, firing at our men with their six-shooters.[58] These Yankees ran up in about two hundred yards of our regiment before they saw us, when they wheeled and ran back, with many bullets after them, but not one was hit.[59] One horse was killed, but the rider was taken up behind one at his comrades and they all made their escape apparently untouched. But one of their bullets struck our Sergeant Major (a Mr. Best) on the knee, shattering the knee cap, which necessitated amputation, but he preferred death to amputation, so he died, that

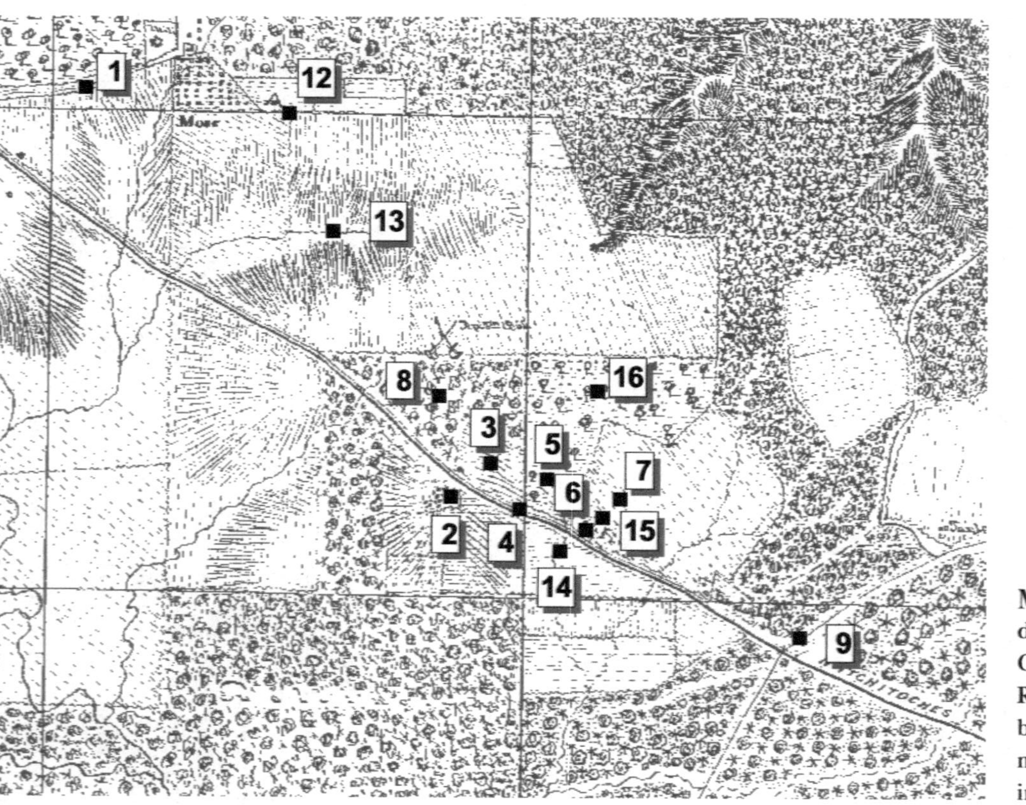

Map 1.1. Mansfield battlefield, drawn shortly afterward by Confederate engineer Major Richard Venable. The numbers indicate specific places mentioned by James A. Jarratt in his narrative.

being the first blood that was spilt at the Mansfield fight.[60] He was raised at or near Mansfield and was a nice clever young man.

When those Yankees started their firing our company was ordered out as skirmishers and as our Captain (J. J. Yarbrough) was absent, Colonel Beard placed Captain Collie (an old Crescent Captain) in command of our company.[61] This Captain had been left out at the consolidation. This was a great mistake made by Colonel Beard, as all of our lieutenants were present, First Lieutenant Thigpen, Second Lieutenant Jackson and Third Lieutenant Zachary.[62] All of our Lieutenants as well as the whole company resisted this act, so Captain Collie could not deploy the company. Colonel Beard saw the mistake that he had made at once, and as he was always ready to right a wrong, he removed Captain Collie and Lieutenant Thigpen deployed the company. We could see the Federal skirmishers being deployed, on the opposite side of the field which was near half a mile off.[63] Skirmish fire now became general. There was just about enough danger in it to make it interesting, and as soon as we saw that there was not much danger in the bullets whistling by us, we became lively and began to laugh and joke with each other. At first I took my position behind a stump in the corner of the cross fence that near crossed the field, but I soon found that it was an unsafe place as they could see the stump and the puffs of smoke from my gun showed them that there was an enemy behind that stump, so they fired at the stump, and if any part of the body should he exposed that part was liable to be struck.[64] There were nine balls that struck the stump while I was behind it. I soon got out in the open field in full view but kept on the move back and forth. When I would see a puff of smoke from one of their guns, I would turn and move in the opposite direction from the way I had been going. I think that we played hide and seek with those Yankees for near or quite two hours. We could hear them coming up the road, with their regular huz zaum[65] which made it appear to us that there was an innumerable host coming to give us battle. No doubt but what General Taylor was watching their every movement from some position that none knew, for he well knew that if he was to be victorious that he would have to strike just at the right moment and take them by surprise. We saw that they were forming a line of battle behind the fence on the opposite side of the field from us.[66] There was a hollow or drein[67] that ran down through the field, so when we got into that drein[68] we were comparatively safe, until we began to ascend the hill, and when we arrived in full view of the Yankees we were not far from them.[69] The time had arrived and now the order came for us to charge.

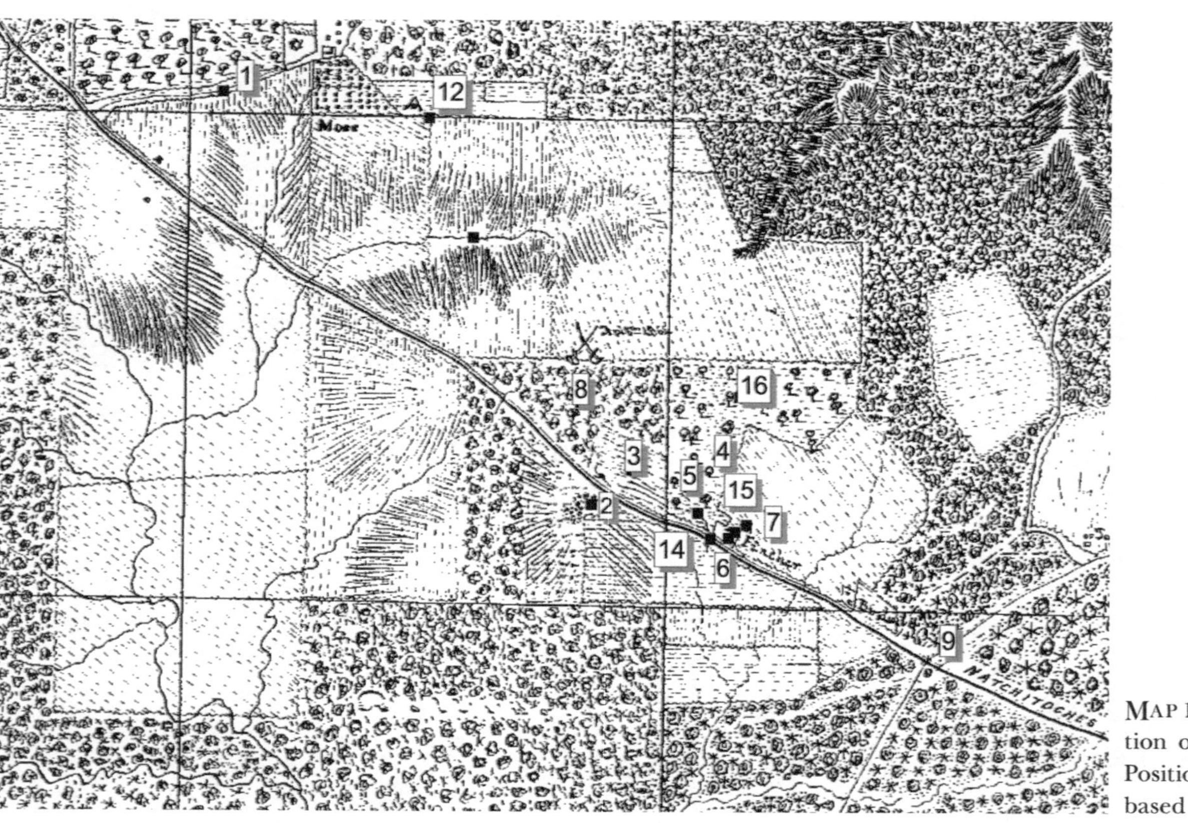

MAP 1.2. Inset of a portion of map 1.1. Note: Position numbers are based on map 1.1.

Attention, my brave lads,
We heard our Colonel cry,
The enemy is across the field,
And their host is drawing nigh,
We see their dark forms at the fence,
As they are placed in line,
Their murderous weapons we now see,
Glistening in the sunshine.

Chorus—Charge is the order that is given,
Just at the bugle call,
Rout the enemy from their post,
Though all of you should fall.

On, on we go at double quick,
Across that fatal field,
With not an object in front of us,
Our bodies now to shield,
On, on my heroic lads,
Our Major doth cry,
Your noble Colonel is now dead,
So rout the enemy or die.

Chorus—Charge is the order that is given,
Just at the bugle call,
Rout the enemy from their post,
Though all of you should fall.

O'er the fence now we go,
Behind which the enemy stood,
And fire between the rails,
The volley that spilt so much blood.
The cry now comes down the line,
They run, they run, they run,
Many of our brave comrades have fallen,
But the battle now is won.

Chorus—Charge is the order that is given,
Just at the bugle call,
Rout the enemy from their post,
Though all of you should fall.

When the order was given to charge, instead of our company taking our position on the right of the regiment, we were pushed on ahead as skirmishers, which would place us at the fence before the regiment ascended the hill.[70] Fortunately for our company there was a gap down in the fence, and it happened to be about twenty steps to the left of the Yankees that were in front of our regiment. The Yankees had not completed their line of battle, so there were no Yankees at that particular place.[71] All of our company with one accord made for that gap, and just as some of us jumped over the fence the Yankees fired on our regiment, and it looked as if they had killed the whole regiment, for all that was not killed fell to the ground to escape the next volley. The first volley killed Colonel Beard and mortally wounded Colonel Clack.[72] Major Canfield was not struck.[73] The color-bearer was shot down, and some of our men were hit with as many as eleven balls. While the Yankees were re-loading, Major Canfield rode around, got down off of his horse, picked up the colors and ordered the regiment forward with him and the colors in the lead. All that could arose and started forward with the Rebel Yell. In the meantime the most of the Yankees had reloaded and gave our regiment another volley, but their aim was not so good, as they were becoming demoralized by such a hot fire from our company on their left flank. But they got our brave little major, and no braver man ever lived or died on a battle field.[74] With our company firing down the fence on their left flank and the remainder of our regiment at the fence, the Yankees not having time to reload, they became panic-stricken, and there became a perfect rout. The Rebel Yell was more than they could stand. There were two pieces of artillery that had taken position in the road on the hill in front of Mr. Hunnecut's house and was then firing down through the woods.[75] I had got out about fifteen or twenty steps into the woods when I heard the word retreat. I looked around and saw C. C. Phillips and Joe Ferguson not far from me, and asked them what it was.[76] They told me retreat. We went back to the fence where our company was and I told them that I was ready to go on, but would never go back across that field. About that time I saw the Twenty eighth Louisiana regiment[77] was in line at the fence and was throwing down the fence preparatory to goin[g] on, and judging from like perfect order that they maintained there was but few if any of them that had been killed, while all of our regimental officers had either been killed or wounded, and nearly half of our men.[78] The skirmishers of the Twenty-eighth Regiment had gone on before, so I pushed on with them. When I left our company I went near or quite fifty yards into the woods when I came up with some skirmishers behind a large tree. There were five or six of them, and they were selecting a leader when I came up, and as I had sergeant stripes on my arms they selected me. I did not know one of them. The artillery on the hill had now ceased firing, and we pushed on, loading and shooting as we went forward from tree to tree. The firing of small arms was going on in every direction, which told us that the battle was raging in every part of the army.[79] When we came out into the road at the top of the hill in front of where Mr. Whit Porter lives, we saw the two pieces of artillery that had been stationed on the hill had started to make their escape, but one of their horses had been killed about twenty-five yards from the top of the hill, and several Yankees were trying to cut him loose, and nearly or quite all of them were killed there in the road.[80] The lane down below the artillery was packed with fleeing infantry, and on the right of the lane, in the field, there was a nice line of cavalry drawn up to protect the rear of the then retreating infantry, who were panic-stricken, leaving everything behind them that would interfere with their flight.[81] Stone's Battalion of Texas troops came over the hill on the right, in fine order, and charged this line of cavalry, which routed them, and all shots fired after that by the Yankees were while they were on the run.[82] When my little squad got to the two pieces of artillery, one of the men jumped up on one of the cannon and hallowed "Hurrah for Texas." I told him that I wanted him to understand that there was one Louisianian among them. His reply was "I will recollect you as long as I live." I then told him to get down and go to fighting, for there was no time to ride cannon. He remarked "Just as you say." I said "down with you then," and he was off in an instant and made as good time loading and shooting as any man could, until we got about one hundred yards below there when he was passing a gully that ran into the ditch from the field, when he spied a Yankee lying down in the gully.[83] He raised his gun, cursed the Yankee and said "I'll get you." I knocked his gun up and told him to go on and shoot them that were shooting at us. I made the Yankee get up and hustle back to the rear without his gun. Our little Texan went on a few steps and after shooting, he was reloading his gun when a ball struck him on the head, killing him instantly. We were then between our men and the fleeing Yankees, so it would be hard to tell who killed that brave little Texan, but it was more than likely that it was a Confederate ball that put an end to his life. I had now fired my last cartridge, and seeing a Yankee lying flat on his back out in the middle of the road I went up to him and was taking some cartridges out of his cartridge box when he opened his eyes. I told him to go to sleep, that I was just getting some cartridges to kill some more of them with. When I was ascending the little hill that Mr. Phincher's house was on, I saw a Yankee go behind a log cabin that was in the rear of the house, when I shot at him.[84] I went up there to see if I hit him. When I got there I saw a Yankee lying flat on the ground dead. I do not know whose bullet killed him. While there I saw the Yankees in a plum Orchard at the edge of the woods taking position with a battery.[85] About that time I heard an order to rally around the colors. I started back to obey orders when I met Colonel Gray (who was in command of Mouton's Brigade, General Mouton was then acting Major General). I told Colonel Gray that the Yankees were taking position near the woods with their battery, and would it not be best to let us push on. His remark to me was to form around the colors and he would ride up on the hill and see. So I went down to the colors. When Colonel Gray got near the top of the hill on his old bald-face black horse a cannon ball passed over his head.[86] There was not more than two or three shots fired from that battery. When Colonel Gray started back to the colors there was a volley fired up in the woods near and back of the ten-acre field that we had passed.[87] When Colonel Gray heard it he cried out: "Here they are boys, give them hell." We all wheeled and made for the fence around the gin house lot as we could see the Yankees running for the gin house.[88] When we got to the fence we began firing on them, and every one of them that tried to run the gauntlet was killed, so the others surrendered. It was said that there were fifteen hundred surrendered in that crowd. I was there and saw them lay down their arms, and was one of the guards that started to the rear with them. When I got about one hundred yards from where I started with them, I passed in ten feet of General Mouton lying dead. The volley that we heard fired was the volley that killed General Mouton. Those Federals had been cut off up in the woods where they were in line of battle, and did not know that the engagement had resulted in such an overwhelming victory for the Confederate forces, and when they started to retreat, arriving at the fence near the corner of the ten-acre field they saw General Mouton and shot and killed him, not after they surrendered but before.[89] The Louisiana history says that on the 8th of April General Taylor drew up his forces at the Sabine Cross Roads, three miles from Mansfield. When the facts are that Sabine Cross Roads is six to eight miles from Mansfield, and General Taylor's troops did not get to the Cross Roads on the 8th of April.[90] History also says: "As the Louisianians approached the Federal lines they had to meet a deadly fire from the Federal artillery," when in fact there was not one killed by that deadly artillery (which consisted of only two pieces) before the Federal infantry had been routed, and as the Federal line was between the artillery and the Confederates, and the Confederates were on lower ground than the Federals, they had to fire over the heads of their own men.[91] Consequently they fired a good deal above the heads of the Confederates. The Confederates were over halfway across the field on their charge before the artillery opened fire. The first ball or shell that passed over us I was near Joe Ferguson and he looked up and said: "Jimmie, what in the hell is that, is it a two-horse wagon?" I have my doubts about one man being killed by that artillery, as I was under the first ball that was fired by it, and continued on until the two pieces that history says did so much damage was captured. History says that General Mouton was one of the first to fall, when the facts are General Mouton was killed between one-quarter and half a mile in front of where the Crescent Regiment was nearly all killed.[92] History says after the Federals had laid down their arms they picked them up and killed General Mouton. It then says not one of them, however, survived this act of treachery. And yet I know that near or quite fifteen hundred survived. If all of the Louisiana History is as false as the account of the Mansfield fight that it gives, we are teaching our children fiction instead of history, something that should not be done. I know that there is but little truth in its account of the Mansfield battle.

I have never been completely reconstructed yet, but I am willing to give the devil his due, as the old saying is. Any Northern man that comes to my house and says any disparaging words about the Confederacy or its soldiers, he is shown the door in quick order. After passing by General Mouton I saw so many were going back as guards I turned and tried to catch up with the firing line. When I got to the edge of the woods where the Pleasant Hill road left the field I found that the road was packed and jammed with ambulances, wagons and artillery, their drivers had tried to turn them around to make their escape but they had locked and jammed them together to such an extent that it was hard to get them loose.[93] When I got there every team had a Confederate driver and each one was doing his best to get his team extricated with their heads towards Mansfield. I did not overtake our men until I got to the branch near Mr. Chapman's, near or quite five miles from Mansfield.[94] They had halted and were gathering together the scattered men, as it was nearly dark.[95] Lieutenant Jackson saw me and called to me. I went to him and there I found that Lieutenant Thigpen and Lieutenant Zachary had been wounded. Our company went into the fight with about forty men, and nineteen had been either killed or wounded. When I got to Lieutenant Jackson I dropped down on the ground completely exhausted and dropped off to sleep. I was shortly aroused by a volley being fired a few hundred yards on ahead. I jumped up and my exclamation was: "My God, have I got to fight tonight?" But the report soon came to us that Stone's Battalion was marching on by the right flank and another regiment (Yankees) was doing the same thing about fifty yards apart, each thinking that the other were friends. When they found out their error each fired at the other, without doing any damage. Our regiment (or what was left of them) then fell back to Mr. Allen's and spent the night, in his yard. So ended my part and my knowledge of the Mansfield fight, and I did not get in one mile of the Sabine Cross Roads where history says I was first placed in line before the fight. I was talking to an old Federal soldier at Mansfield several years ago, and told him that I fired fifty-two rounds at the Mansfield fight. He told me that was nothing, that he knew a Federal soldier to fire five hundred rounds in one fight. I told him that there was nothing surprising about that, as the Confederates stood their ground and the Federal soldier could stand in the same tracks and shoot as much and as long as he pleased, but I had to shoot my game on the wing, and after shooting once I had to load and run to catch up before I could shoot again. He said no more. On the morning of the 9th of April we were ordered on in pursuit of the Yankees with Captain Clayburn[96] of the old Crescent Regiment in command of the regiment, and Lieutenant Jackson in command of our company. Our Captain, J. J. Yarbrough, was absent. He was now our senior captain and had he been at his post he would have been in command of the regiment instead of Captain Clayburn. The next morning we were marched down to Dr. Wilson's place, three miles from Pleasant Hill.[97] We had now been reinforced with Walker's and Churchill's Divisions and General Banks had been reinforced with Smith's Division (said to number ten thousand men).[98] The Louisiana troops were held in reserve at Dr. Wilson's place and Green's Cavalry, Walker's and Churchill's troops were to do the fighting. Late in the evening we were ordered forward at double quick, which we were expected to do for two miles. I imagine now that I can see Captain Clayburn trotting on ahead on his horse, going into the fight by the right flank, with his men scattered on the road for a mile behind him. There was a plenty of the privates more capable of commanding a regiment than he was. When we got under fire near Mrs. Rebecca Jordan's old place we were down on the right of the road at the edge of a pine thicket. I saw that the Twenty-eighth Louisiana Regiment was in good order, so I went up to the captain on the right of the regiment and asked for permission to fight in his company which he agreed to, and assigned me my position. Lieutenant Johnson from Mansfield did the same thing.[99] We then started on through the pine thicket driving the scattering Federals before us. It was then getting late, and in the pine thicket it looked to be about dusk. By some means the Twenty-eighth Regiment got a little ahead of the Eighteenth, and as the Eighteenth could not tell whether we were Confederates or Yankees, they fired on us which stampeded the Twenty-eighth Regiment and every man went where he pleased (or I did.)[100] I took an old road and came out in the Pleasant Hill road in front of Mrs. Jordan's house, where I found the color-bearer of Stone's Battalion (Robert Hamel, an old schoolmate of mine) standing in the road begging the men not to run.[101] He would beg a while, curse a while and then whistle. When he saw me he hallowed to me to come to him. While I was going to him a little lieutenant ran up to me and said: "Don't run, don't run." I told him that I was not on the run, and would go as far as he would. He then said "Rally around the colors," so I went up to the colors. Our little lieutenant rallied about fifty men and started down towards Pleasant Hill with the intention of cleaning up all of Bank's army. We went on down the road near one hundred and fifty yards, arriving in a little sink in the road, when our commander called a halt, and saw that he did not have over a dozen men. We all sat down m the ground, as the Minie balls were keeping time over our heads. Just over the next rise the Yankees had made a breastwork of logs, and we were not over one hundred yards from them, but we were not seen by them and we could not see them.[102] Our little commander decided that it would be foolishness for us to try to capture Banks with such a small force, so we decided to fall back in good order. It was then nearly dark.[103] Our artillery had taken a position in front of Mrs. Jordan's house and was shelling Pleasant Hill, but when they saw us coming up the road they took us to be Yankees and fired on us, but they shot quick and over shot us, and we tried to crawl into the ground out on the side of the road. When they saw they had dispersed us they began to shell Pleasant Hill again. Then Robert Hamel took up the colors, walked out in the road and hallowed to them if they wanted to fire on the Confederate flag to blaze away, so they allowed us to go by them. The Louisiana troops were so badly scattered that some of the officers stood on the side of the road after dark and every once and a while would yell: "All that belong to Mouton's Brigade fall in here," and that is the way we were gathered together. Walker's and Churchill's Divisions were in the same situation. My father lived about fifteen miles from Pleasant Hill, and there was only one house between his place and Pleasant Hill; it was woods all the way, with a large bottom near my father's house. The next day after the Mansfield fight he came to look for me, and found me all right; he stayed until he saw that I was safe through the Pleasant Hill fight and went on home that night. On the road he met up with a Colonel belonging to Churchill's Division with a small squad of men. He asked my father if he could direct him so he could get to Mansfield without falling into the hands of the Yankees.[104] He said that the Confederates were badly whipped.[105] It was hard for my father to make him believe that General Taylor was then in possession of the battle field. General Taylor

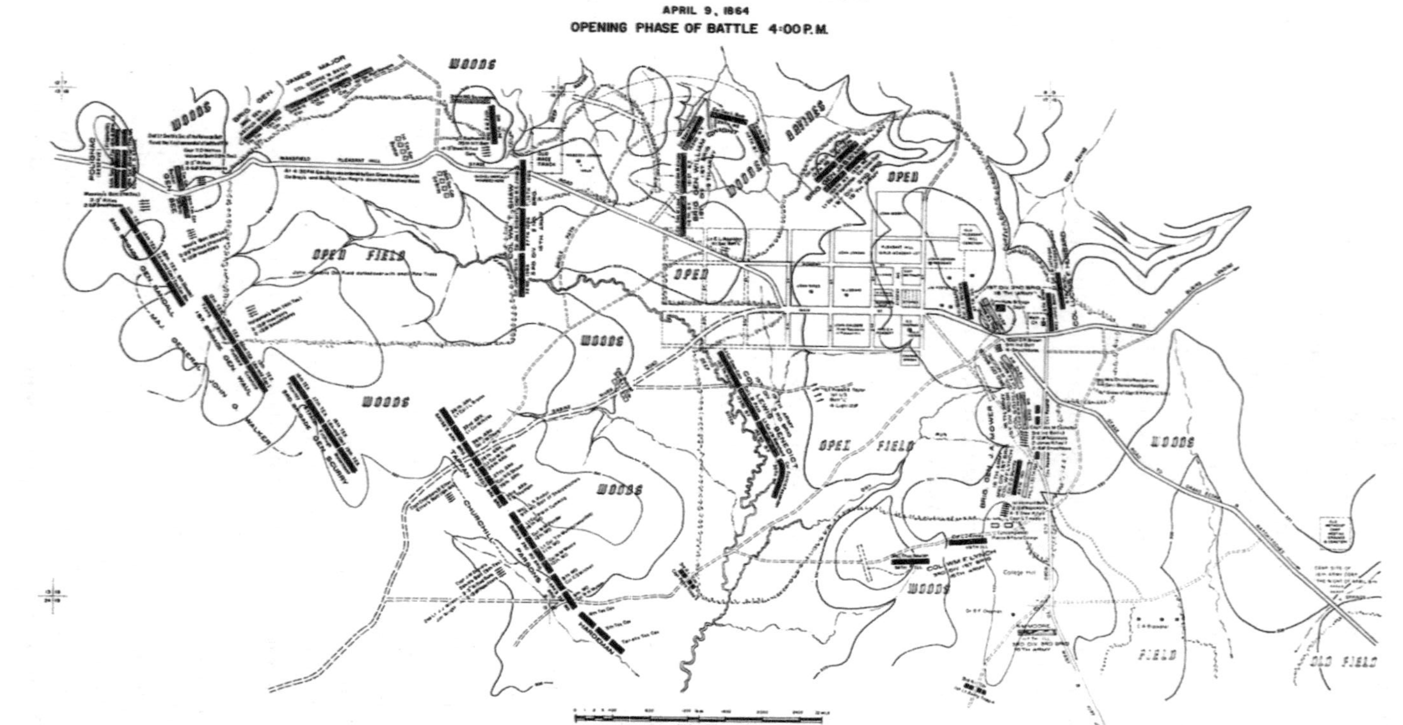

Map 1.3. Battle of Pleasant Hill. Copy at Mansfield State Historic Site. Cartography by Terry Waxham.

did stay on the battle field that night. About 9 o'clock the next day a large Missourian walked up to my father's house with two little Yankees that he had captured and had kept them in the woods with him all night. He said that while the Confederates were whipped, he had done his part towards capturing Banks' army. My father gave them their breakfast, hitched up his hack and carried them to Mansfield.

After night had stopped the engagement, Banks began his retreat. He had trees cut down across the road at every place that he thought it would delay the Confederates in their pursuit.[106] That looked very much like the retreat of a victorious army, and merely going to his supplies, and to get water. We pushed on after them when daylight came. The Yankees told the citizens as they passed that they had met up with one hundred thousand drunken Texans at Mansfield. Banks with his army went to Grand Ecore to gather their shattered forces under the protection of their gunboats in Red River. After the Pleasant Hill fight General Green with his cavalry crossed Bayou Pierre at Jordan's Ferry, and over on Red River he needlessly exposed himself and was killed.[107] His death was a severe blow to the Confederate forces. General Taylor ordered General Polignac to take the Louisiana troops and go below Natchitoches, and he would go and try to get Kirby Smith to let him keep Walker's and Churchill's Divisions, and if he succeeded he would send a courier to him with orders to go on and cross Old Cane River at Manet's Ferry, and take his position on the hill commanding the ferry and he would follow on after the Federals and attack them in the rear.[108] If he could not prevail on Smith to let him have the troops, for General Polignac to fall back and he would order General Bee to take a position across the ferry and General Polignac to attack them in the rear.[109] If Kirby Smith had granted General Taylor's request, Banks with his whole army and all the gunboats in Red River, would have been captured; but instead of doing so, he had Dick Taylor arrested for bringing on the fight at Mansfield.[110] It would have been a hard matter to have convinced the Louisiana troops at that time that Sm[it]h was not a traitor. Instead of allowing General Taylor to keep Walker's and Churchill's Divisions, he rushed them up into Arkansas and got them whipped by General Steel[e], which was a blunder made by General Smith of the worst kind, and I believe that it was caused by envy at General Taylor's success.[111] If we had have captured that army and gunboats it might have prevented General Sherman from making his noted raid through Georgia, for a large portion of Banks' army joined Sherman.[112] That was the last we saw of Dick Taylor.

When Banks started for Alexandria we stepped back a few miles and let him pass. General Bee had taken position on the hill opposite Manet's

Ferry. It was a very strong position and should have been held by General Bee. General Polignac followed on in the rear of the Federals, and when the Federals arrived at the ferry they found that their retreat was blocked. The Louisiana troops were drawn up in line of battle in their rear and we were loading our guns preparing for an attack in their rear. General Bee happened to be a drone, for he only fired one volley with his battery and beat a hasty retreat, which opened the way for Banks so we did not attack him in the rear.

After Banks crossed Cane River at Manet's Ferry with his army the Confederates rushed the St. Mary's Battery down to the mouth of Cane River where it empties into Red River, for the purpose of attacking the gunboats and the transports that were in Red River under the command of Commodore Porter.[113] St. Mary's Battery consisted of two twelve-pounders and two twenty-four-pound Howitzers under the comma[n]d of Captain Carney.[114]

One of the gunboats under the command of Commodore Porter sprung a leak, and he saw that he could not save it, so he blew it up about seven miles above where our battery had taken position on the bank of the river.[115] The Federal fleet came in sight of our men in the evening and the negroes that the Federals had taken from the planters on the river could be heard singing. They had no idea that their singing would be turned into mourning in so short a time. The Federal fleet consisted of three gunboats and two transports.[116] When they got in range of our guns the fight opened in earnest, and lasted for nearly or quite one hour. One gunboat passed and one transport was captured.[117] When the fighting began, the negroes must have gone down in the boiler room. When one of our balls struck the end of one of the boilers, bursting it, two hundred and twenty negroes were scalded to death, the hide peeling off of them like a boiled potato.[118] The captain of the transport was killed. The casualties on our side were quite small. Two of the gunboats and one transport went back up the river out of range of our guns and shelled our men at intervals until midnight, when Commodore Porter saw that he would have to run the gauntlet or surrender. So he made all necessary preparations and made a break for liberty. His two gunboats made their escape, but the transport was sunk. The captain was killed but none of our men were hurt. We never knew how many we killed on the side of the Federals. I am indebted to my old friend, Dr. Stribling, for the above information, he being surgeon of St. Mary's Battery.

General Horton was temporarily placed in command in General Taylor's place.[119] We followed on after Banks until he stopped at Alexandria, and as we did not have force enough to attack him, General Horton contented himself in harassing him all that he could.[120] Consequently we were marched on below Mansura Prairie, and there halted on the road to await the coming of the Federals. After they succeeded in getting their gunboats over the falls at Alexandria they took up the line of march down Red River, neither stepping to the right or the left. When they arrived at Mansura Prairie they found General Horton with his artillery drawn up arrests their front. There we had an artillery duel which lasted a short time, when General Horton moved his little army off to one side and let the Federals pass.[121] It was now General Horton's plan to attack the Federals at Yellow Bayou, after a part of the Federal army had crossed. On the day before at Mansura Prairie General Polignac had started to charge the Federals with this little squad, and the small arms began to he heard all around. General Horton rode up to General Polignac and in no mild language asked him where he was going. General Polignac replied: "Charge them, General, charge them." General Horton ordered him to get his men out of there and do it quick. This highly incensed our little French General, as he came over here to make a name for himself as being a military hero, and General Horton had stopped him in short order. General Horton told General Polignac that he intended to fight the next day at Yellow Bayou, and that he would dismount his cavalry and bring on the fight, and for him to have his men in supporting distance at 10 o'clock the next day. General Horton carried out the plan, but he had insulted the little French General, and he had turned over the command to Colonel Gray without giving him any definite instructions as to the time he was to be on hand, so when we arrived General Horton had brought on the fight and got his men whipped before we arrived.[122] When we did get there we found General Horton with his dismounted cavalry coming out of the woods on the retreat. I was close to Colonel Gray when General Horton rode up to him and asked him where Polignac was. When Colonel Gray told him, Horton did some pretty stout cursing. We were ordered to fall back about two hundred yards, in a ditch, and if the Yankees pursued, as soon as they came out into the field we were to be ordered to fire. But the Federals had no intention of pursuit. All they wanted was to reach a place of safety. Our regiment came very near being stampeded after they got in the ditch. One man in the ditch rested his gun on a small stump; the stock slipped off the stump, the stump striking the hammer, causing the gun to fire, the ball striking him under the chin, coming out at the top of his head, killing him instantly, which came near routing out regiment. The Federals had now made their escape, which ended the fighting of the Crescent Regiment for the war. Captain Clayburn was still in command of the regiment. We were then ordered to Shreveport for the purpose of reorganization. Colonel Boswell, the old Crescent Colonel, was placed in command and Colonel Hyat was made Lieutenant Colonel, and our Captain, J. J. Yarbrough, was promoted to Major, Lieutenant Thigpen was promoted to Captain of Company B, and Lieutenant Jackson First Lieutenant, Lieutenant Zachary Second Lieutenant, and Nat Phillips was elected Third Lieutenant, and in that condition we were found at the surrender.[123] After remaining at Shreveport for about one month, we were marched back to Alexandria. We crossed Red River and struck camp about one mile above Alexandria. While we were camped there Sam Winbush was brigade wagon master, and he was given a detail of men to go into the country after some corn.[124] Among his men was Robert McDonald, a member of Captain Selph's company from Sabine Parish.[125] When they were returning with the corn they came upon a nice lot of good-sized fat shoats, and Sam Wimbush told McDonald that if he could catch one in a fair race that he could do so.[126] McDonald was off of the wagon in an instant, and the race begun, over the logs, round and round they went, over and under the bushes. It was not long before the shoat began ha, ha, ha, when McDonald said "I've most got him, ha, ha, ha, I've most got him," was the cry then until McDonald caught him and stuck him, which put an end to the race and the life of the shoat. We did not do anything at Alexandria but courtmartial and shoot deserters. General Buckner was then in command with his headquarters at Alexandria.[127] I carried one young man down to Alexandria to go before the courtmartial that was then being held. While going down I told him not to try to get away then, but when he got back to camp to make a break at night, for it would be far better to take the chance of one or two men hitting him on the run than to be tied to a stake and shot, for they would be sure to do that. He did not think so, and he was shot the next Friday. We spent the winter of 1864–5 opposite Alexandria. We built our winter quarters in the bend of a large pond, the lower row of quarters being about one hundred yards front the bend of the pond. One night when I was sergeant of the guard some of the men drove a large hog down close to the pond in the bend as far away from the camp as they could get and killed it, and while they were skinning it some of the men in our company found it out and got their guns and stretched out from one side of the horseshoe pond to the outer and marched down on those that were skinning the hog and forced them to take to the water. The pond at that place came up to their armpits, but they thought it was the guard, and they had rather take to the water than be taken to the guardhouse for killing the hog. Our men had possession of the hog and began to finish the process of skinning, when I found out what had been done. It was reported to me by one of the men that had expected to get some of that hog to eat for breakfast the next morning. So to carry out the fun I took a squad of the guard and stretched out from pont[128] to pond and, went down on the robbers and made them take to the water. I took the hog and carried it up to the guard-house and went and reported to Colonel Hyat what I had done. He asked me if I knew any of the men, and of course I did not know them, so he told me to send him a shoulder and keep the balance. I merely did like a great many do now—I robbed according to law and came out all right, but I did better than the robbers now, for I divided with my victims, but the men that did the killing got wet and lost all.

At the surrender we were camped a short distance from Natchitoches. If General Taylor had obeyed Kirby Smith we would have all been marched to Shreveport and Banks would have gotten all of his forces together and captured General Smith, Taylor and the whole army, and then marched out into Texas. So the salvation of Shreveport, Mansfield and all of this part of North Louisiana should be credited to General Taylor and his Louisiana troops, for

Three thousand Confederates in eighteen sixty-four
Whipped thirty thousand Federals if no more,
And sent them back the way they came
Crowned with a crown of utter shame.

General Taylor with his little heroic band
In Moss's field had taken their stand,
To save this country from a foreign foe
Who were then invading our very door.

English, French, Italians and Germans too
Of other nations there were more than a few;
Many foreigners had invaded our soil
To crush out the hardy hand of toil.

We believed then and we believe now
That we were right when we took the vow
To stand by our homes until we should die,
So to hurl our foe back we did try.

Many of our brave comrades that day fell,
When we charged that host and whipped them well;
They killed Colonel Beard and the brave Canfield,
But we retained possession of the battle field.

With many of our brave commanders lying dead,
On that fatal field where so much blood was shed,
While we lost our cause in the end,
We still thank God our country we did defend.

No power on earth can blot out the stain
That fell on a great nation's honored name,
When they hired foreigners to shed a brother's blood,
That they might rob them of their manhood.

I do not say that there was thirty thousand or more that were actually engaged at Mansfield on the Federal side, but there were not over three thousand of the Confederate forces actually engaged at Mansfield, and I doubt there being that many.[129] I do say that we charged the front of the Federal army with so much vim and carried everything before us to such an extent that we hurled them back with such force upon their advancing comrades that all became panic-stricken, and nothing but darkness saved the Federal army. The Crescent Regiment went in the fight with about four hundred men, and one hundred and ninety-five were killed and wounded.[130] At the first burial, I was told, here were fifty-two placed in one grave. The Crescent Regiment bore the brunt of the fight; no others suffered so much, and North Louisiana should see that not one of those surviving heroes should be neglected. This write-up has been given entirely from memory, and there is no doubt but what there are some errors, but it is the way I have got it as an active participant in that memorable campaign.

When General Lee surrendered in Virginia we were camped between Natchitoches and Grand Ecore. Our command became demoralized at once, and the men began to desert rapidly, and every one that could took a horse or mule. The officers did all they could to check the stampede. Colonel Hyat was in command of the Crescent Regiment at that time, and there were so few remained that Colonel Hyat took his turn in standing guard over the few mules that were left to us. While the general exodus was taking place, Lieutenant Zachary was appointed Lieutenant of the Guard in Natchitoches, and I went into Natchitoches. Lieutenant Zachary carried me around and showed me a lot of fine Confederate horses and told me that he would place any man that I might select to be placed on guard over these horses, and as the Federals would be in command in a few days, he advised me to take two or three of those horses that night and pull for home, but my honor forbade. I had cast my lot with the Confederacy and would go down with her. In a few days afterwards we were disbanded by

Colonel Hyat, and he gave me one mule and several of us joined together (Sam Wimbush and F. A. Leonard were among the crowd) and hitched our mules to a wagon and started for home.[131] That night we camped at Marthaville and my mule took sick and died. So I arrived at home after four years of Confederate service with worse than nothing to begin life with. But I can truthfully say I passed through without any serious stain upon my character, as a gentleman and soldier.

Notes

1. National Archives and Records Administration (NARA), Washington, DC, Microscopy M378, Roll 15. The record is also found in the National Parks Service Soldiers and Sailors system.
2. U.S. Dept. of Commerce, Fourteenth Decennial Census (1920), Caddo Parish, Louisiana, unpublished tabulations in NARA. Hereinafter cited as 14th Decennial Census.
3. U.S. Dept. of Commerce, Seventh Decennial Census (1850), Chambers County, Alabama, unpublished tabulations in NARA.
4. U.S. Dept. of Commerce, Eighth Decennial Census (1860), Sabine Parish, Louisiana, unpublished tabulations in NARA. Hereinafter cited as 8th Decennial Census. According to the 8th Decennial Census, Jarratt was listed as a resident of Sabine Parish and living with his parents and siblings. In 1860, the nearest post office was listed as Many in Sabine Parish. In 1870, the nearest post office was listed as Pleasant Hill. The 1860 cen sus recorded his father's name as P. P. Jarratt, forty-five years of age. His Christian name was Pascal, but was sometimes listed as Paschal or Paschol. His occupation was listed as an engineer. Pascal Jarratt enlisted in Con federate service in Company H of the 2nd Louisiana Infantry Regiment in 1861 and was discharged later that year with a surgeon's Certificate of Mobility. He was forty-seven years old at the time. His place of birth was the state of Georgia. He was recorded as a property owner, with real estate assessed at $2,460 and a personal estate assessed at $1,200. Pascal Jarratt's wife was Martha E. Campbell Jarratt, thirty-five years of age in 1860, also born in Georgia. The 1860 Census listed the following children living at home: John C., male, age twenty-one, born in Georgia; James A., male (the author), age nineteen, born in Georgia; Mary J., female, age sixteen, born in Georgia; Martha E., female, age fourteen, born in Georgia; Louisa, female, age ten, born in Georgia; Paschal, male, age eight, born in Alabama; Willie, female, age six, born in Alabama; Francis, female, born in Louisiana; and Neal, male, age one, born in Louisiana.
5. The application is found in microscopy CP1.72 in the Louisiana State Archives, Baton Rouge.

6. *Shreveport Times,* Oct. 30, 1944, obituary of B. K. Jarratt (Bush Kile Jarratt was the son of James A. Jarratt); *Shreveport Times,* April 15, 1921, obituary of Rev. J. A. Jarratt. Much of the information that was not compiled from official records came from e-mail correspondence with Eric C. Demler, James A. Jarratt's great-great grandson. The editor is greatly indebted to Demler for this valuable information.
7. Obituary, B. K. Jarratt; obituary, Rev. J. A. Jarratt.
8. Obituary, B. K. Jarratt; obituary, Rev. J. A. Jarratt.
9. On the frontispiece is written "copyright applied for."
10. Stewart Sifakis, *Compendium of the Confederate Armies: Louisiana* (New York, 1995), 123. Hereinafter cited as *Compendium: Louisiana.*
11. Arthur W. Bergeron Jr., *Guide to Louisiana Confederate Military Units 1861–1865* (Baton Rouge, 1989), 147. Hereinafter cited as *Guide to Louisiana Units.*
12. Sifakis, *Compendium: Louisiana,* 122.
13. Ibid., 90.
14. Ibid., 123.
15. Sifakis, *Compendium: Louisiana,* 123–24; Bergeron, *Guide to Louisiana Units,* 146–47.
16. Sifakis, *Compendium: Louisiana,* 124.
17. Ibid.
18. Bergeron, *Guide to Louisiana Units,* 147.
19. The Battle of Jenkins' Ferry was actually fought on April 30, 1864. Jarratt is referring to Union Major General Frederick Steele, commander of the Department of Arkansas and Confederate Lieutenant General Edmund Kirby Smith, Commander of the Department of the Trans-Mississippi. The Camden Campaign was the northern portion of the Red River Campaign. The Battle of Jenkins' Ferry was the final battle in that campaign. In that action the Confederate Arkansas, Missouri, and Texas divisions that had fought at Pleasant Hill (the Texas Division also participated at Mansfield) attempted to halt the retreat of the Union column. The battle ended with the Federal column escaping across the Saline River and the three Confederate divisions, suffering high casualties, were unable to stop them. Following the battle, Kirby Smith released the three divisions to Richard Taylor in Louisiana. The divisions returned to the Red River Valley, but the fighting had moved far below Alexandria. They arrived too late to assist in trapping the Union forces there. The removal of the three veteran divisions to Arkansas proved to be the worst mistake made by the Confederate command and Kirby Smith personally during the entire campaign.
20. Gov. Newton Crain Blanchard held office in Louisiana from 1904 to 1908. Jarratt wrote the account in 1906. The memorial would be created

thirteen years later. Construction of the Louisiana Monument began on July 10, 1919, and the memorial was dedicated on October 18, 1920. It was finished at a final cost of $43,500. Louisiana governor John W. Parker transferred the memorial to the federal government. It contains an eighty-one-foot Doric column, topped by a brazier of granite with eternal flame. The monument stands on the highest point in Vicksburg National Military Park at 397 feet above sea level. "Louisiana" is displayed on the front of the memorial, and a list of the organizations involved in the Campaign and Siege of Vicksburg appears around its base along the sides. Information provided by Vicksburg National Military Park, Vicksburg, Mississippi.

21. J. A. Jarratt requested a pension application to the State of Louisiana. The application is found in microscopy CP1.72 in the Louisiana State Archives, Baton Rouge.
22. Jarratt may be referring to Louisiana troop contingents. The Confederates had more than 8,800 soldiers on the field at the Battle of Mansfield. Although the Union forces numbered in excess of 40,000 in the campaign, approximately 30,000 were engaged in the Louisiana portion. Of that total, less than half were on the field at Mansfield during various stages of the battle.
23. Shelley's Battalion was the 11th Infantry Battalion, commanded by Lieutenant Colonel Jacob D. Shelley, who resigned August 3, 1863. Major James H. Beard, who was promoted to lieutenant colonel on the same day, then took command. The companies were A and D (from DeSoto Parish), B and C (from Natchitoches Parish), E (from Sabine Parish), F (from Catahoula Parish), and G (from Natchitoches and perhaps Texas) (Bergeron, *Guide to Louisiana Units,* 164). Clark's Battalion was the 12th Infantry Battalion, also known as the Confederate Guards Response Battalion, commanded by Lieutenant Colonel Franklin H. Clack, promoted from major in September 1862. The unit's major was Mercer Canfield. The companies were A and E (from Rapides Parish), B and C (from Orleans Parish), D (from St. Martin Parish), and F (from Lafourche Parish) (Bergeron, *Guide to Louisiana Units,* 164–65).
24. See Theodore P. Savas, "A Death at Mansfield: Colonel James H. Beard and the Consolidated Crescent Regiment," *The Red River Campaign: Union and Confederate Leadership and the War in Louisiana* (Shreveport, 2003), 68–103. Gary D. Joiner, *One Damn Blunder from Beginning to End: The Red River Campaign of 1864* (Wilmington, DE, 2003), 95–99.
25. There is no evidence in the literature of the Red River Campaign that the intent of the Union forces was to capture Texas wheat fields, harvest the grain, and remove it to northern markets or for use to feed Union armies. If any crop was to be confiscated, it would be cotton. Although Banks had no intention of following orders from anyone except President

Lincoln, Lieutenant General Ulysses S. Grant expressly forbade him to enter Texas. Banks responded to the demand by sending an informal letter to the chief of staff in Washington telling him of his intentions. U.S. War Dept., *War of the Rebellion: The Official Records of the Union and Confederate Armies,* 128 vols. (Washington, DC, 1880–1901), ser. 1, vol. 34, pt. 1:179–80. Subsequent citations of the *Official Records* are abbreviated *OR,* followed by series number, volume number, part number and page reference.

26. Jarratt is correct. See U.S. Congress, *Report on the Joint Committee on the Conduct of the War, 1863–1866,* vol. 2, *Red River Expedition* (Millwood, NY: Krauss Reprint, 1977), 10, 30, 60, 400 (hereinafter cited as *JCCW*).
27. Carroll Jones was a wealthy mulatto Creole and a friend of Richard Taylor. Jones set up supply depots along the western back roads of Louisiana for Taylor. Gary B. Mills, *The Forgotten People: Cane River's Creoles of Color* (Baton Rouge, 1977), 215 n.
28. All period sources and subsequent histories refer to this as Henderson's Hill.
29. The Second Louisiana Cavalry arrived on the night of March 21 after riding hard or skirmishing for six straight days with little sleep. They encamped at Henderson's Hill, a toe-shaped ridge that rose above the confluence of Bayou Rapides and Bayou Cotile. McNutt's Hill is the eastern portion of the same ridge. The weather turned ugly and cold, and they were pelted by rain and hail. Trying to keep dry, Vincent's pickets were not vigilant. See Richard Taylor, *Destruction and Reconstruction: Personal Experiences in the Civil War* (New York, 1995), 157.

    Union Brigadier General Joseph A. Mower led a Union force of approximately one thousand men, including a light artillery battery and the lead elements of Banks's column belonging to Brigadier General Albert Lee's cavalry division as he hunted for the Rebel cavalry. Rapidly marching twenty-five miles in seven and one-half hours, Mower and his men ended their march in "knee-deep mud." See Richard H. Zeitlin, *Old Abe the War Eagle: A True Story of the Civil War and Reconstruction* (Madison, WI, 1986), 53.

    Mower and his men captured several Confederates, including officers, and obtained the password used that night by Vincent's cavalry detachment encamped on the hill. Mower "borrowed" a Confederate officer's coat and took his regiments to the hill, led by the veteran 8th Wisconsin Volunteer Infantry Regiment. Mower, dressed in the gray officer's coat over his uniform, gave the password during the driving storm. Just before dawn, the exhausted cavalrymen were surprised to see a thousand rifles aimed at them. Mower captured 350 Confederate cavalrymen and 400 horses while suffering no losses. See *OR,* ser. 1, vol. 34, pt. 1:315–16, 334–35, 463–64, 501; Taylor, *Destruction and Reconstruction,* 157; Joseph P.

Blessington, *The Campaigns of Walker's Texas Division* (New York, 1875), 178; James K. Ewer, *Third Massachusetts Cavalry in the War for the Union* (Maplewood, MA, 1903), 137–39; Joiner, *One Damn Blunder,* 54.

30. A Union cavalryman, in the same region but traveling westward from Grand Ecore on the Red River, wrote that the area was "a howling wilderness." See Ewer, *Third Massachusetts Cavalry,* 142. A reporter for the *Philadelphia Press* accompanying the Union column wrote that he had "ridden for fifty miles into the heart of this pine country, and from the beginning to the end of the journey there was nothing but a dense, impenetrable, interminable forest, traversed by a few narrow roads, with no signs of life or civilization beyond occasional log-houses and half-cleared plantations." Later he added, "Such a thing as subsisting an army in a country like this could only be achieved when men and horses can be induced to live on pine trees and resin." See J. Cutler Andrews, *The North Reports the Civil War* (Pittsburgh, 1985), 506–7.

Jarratt's column was traveling northward from west of Alexandria in Rapides Parish to Pleasant Hill in southern DeSoto Parish, en route to Mansfield, where the Confederates made their stand. The Union column, traveling slower, approached along the El Camino Reale, the old Spanish Royal Road. Banks's men left that road at White's Store, today the village of Robeline. It then moved northwest to Crump's Corners, today the village of Belmont. At that point, the column moved north on the same road used by the Taylor and his army, but more than a day behind.

Jarratt's account underscored the problems Taylor had due to lack of cavalry. The Confederate army was unaware of the size of the Union force arrayed against them or the exact route their opponents took. This problem remained until the arrival of Texas cavalry reinforcements. Even then, Taylor was unsure of the number of his opponents. He believed that the 10,000 veterans loaned by Major General William T. Sherman remained with the fleet. This proved to be a crucial intelligence error.

31. Confederate Brigadier General Tom Green arrived with several regiments of Texas cavalry on April 5. Green was one of the best cavalry officers on either side west of the Mississippi River and one of the most popular. As a boy, Green saw action against the Mexicans at the Battle of San Jacinto during the Mexican War. Before the Red River Campaign, he led the cavalry attack at the Battle of Val Verde in New Mexico and led some of his men as Marines aboard a gunboat and successfully captured the steamer *Harriet Lane* in Galveston Bay. See Ralph A. Wooster, *Civil War Texas* (Austin, 1999), 8, 17, 19; B. P. Galloway, ed., *Texas, The Dark Corner of the Confederacy: Contemporary Accounts of the Lone Star State in the Civil War,* 3rd ed. (Lincoln, NE, 1994), 177, 184–85, 187; Odie Faulk, *General Tom Green: A Fightin' Texan* (Waco: Texian Press), 1963.

32. This is Joe M. Ferguson of Company O from Winn Parish. See Compiled Service Records of Confederate Soldiers Who Served in Organizations from the State of Louisiana, National Archives and Records Administration, Microscopy 320, Rolls, 376, 377, 378, 379, and 380. Hereinafter cited as CSR.
33. There is no reference to a Captain Patan, Patin, or Patton in the Consolidated Crescent Regiment muster rolls. Jarratt either misspelled the name or the officer was not listed.
34. The Consolidated Crescent Regiment marched the twenty miles to Mansfield and the additional four to five miles to their camp on April 7. He was unaware how close the Union army was to the Confederate column. Tom Green fought a delaying action at Wilson's farm, three miles north of Pleasant Hill on April 7. This encounter gave Taylor's army enough time to march to Mansfield, encamp, and rest for the fighting on April 8.
35. Jarratt means Bayou Bon Chasse. The name is a combination of the French word for "good" and the Caddoan Indian word "chasse" meaning hunting. Although no Confederate engineer's map exists showing the encampment, local oral tradition places the camp just west of Louisiana Highway 175 north of Mansfield, and north of the stream on high, dry bluff land. The village of Kingston is located northwest of this position, and the intersection of the road leading to it is just north of this bluff. This campsite was quite large, holding Walker's Texas Division and Mouton's Louisiana Division. The Kingston road was the easternmost of three roads leading from Mansfield to Shreveport. The reason Taylor picked the battle-field south of Mansfield was the existence of these roads. He could not bottle up the Union army north of the place he picked. See Taylor, *Destruction and Reconstruction*, 159; oral interview with Scott Dearman, interpretive ranger at Mansfield State Historic Site, October 26, 2003.
36. The hotel stood near the northwest corner of Mouton Street and Washington Street, facing south on Washington Street in Block No. 1 of the original town plat of Mansfield. Mouton Street was named for the popular governor Alexandre Mouton, father of Brigadier General Alfred Mouton. The building is identified on the 1885 Sanborn Fire Insurance Company map of the Town of Mansfield.

    The conversation may be apocryphal, but the context is correct. Friday, April 8, had been decreed by the Confederate States Congress in Richmond to be "a day of fasting, humiliation, and prayer," and that "military exercises were to be 'suspended' and a 'strict observance' was to be enjoined upon all troops serving in the department." See *OR*, ser. 1, vol. 34, pt. 2:1057.

    Taylor met with Kirby Smith on April 6 and received no clearly defined orders. Taylor, frustrated, decided to go against the wishes of the

Confederate Congress and his department commander, knowing that if he lost the upcoming battle, that blame would rest on him alone. He tried to bring Smith around to his view. Taylor wrote his commander concerning the need to do *something,* "Action, prompt, vigorous action, is required. While we are deliberating the enemy is marching. King James lost three kingdoms for a mass. We may lose three States without a battle." See *OR* ser. 1, vol. 34, pt. 1:522.

37. Jarratt is incorrect here. He was quoting a widespread rumor, but it did not occur. Like most myths, there is a kernel of truth at its core. Relations between Taylor and Smith became worst after the Battle of Pleasant Hill. On June 5, Taylor wrote a letter that blamed Smith for Taylor's inability to capture the fleet and Banks's army. In the letter, Taylor asked for relief of command. Smith put Taylor under arrest five days later and sent a message to President Davis regarding his actions. The same day, June 10, the Confederate Congress passed a joint resolution praising Taylor. Troops loyal to Taylor almost came to blows with troops loyal to Smith. Soon after, Taylor was promoted to lieutenant general and given command of the Department of Alabama, Mississippi, and East Louisiana. He surrendered that department at the end of the war. See *OR,* ser. 1, vol. 34, pt. 1:540–48, 597.

38. Captain Seth R. Field of New Orleans. One of the four obelisk monuments to Confederate heroes of the battle is dedicated to Field. The inscription reads "Captain Seth Robert Field Fell at Battle of Mansfield April 8, 1864 Aged 29 Years." Field commanded Company A of the Consolidated Crescent Regiment. See Bergeron, *Guide to Louisiana Units,* 146.

The last meeting between Fields and his wife and child (only a baby is mentioned) before the battle was reported in the *Houston Daily Telegraph* in April 1864 and also appeared in the *New Orleans Times* on May 4, 1864. Field saw his colonel grab the regimental colors during the charge and watched him fall. Two other officers in succession picked up the fallen banner to lead the attack and they were also killed. Field then picked up the banner and moved forward. He fell in a hail of bullets making him the fourth officer in his brigade to fall leading the opening charge. During the charge, six color bearers were killed. After the battle Field's widow came to the scene, found his body, took him back to Mansfield, and had him buried. She then returned to help the wounded. See Arthur W. Bergeron Jr., "A Colonel Gains His Wreath: Henry Gray and His Louisiana Brigade at the Battle of Mansfield, April 8, 1864," in *The Red River Campaign: Union and Confederate Leadership and War in Louisiana* (Shreveport, LA, 2003), 1–25. Theodore P. Savas, "A Death at Mansfield: Colonel James H. Beard and the Consolidated Crescent Regiment," in *The Red River Campaign: Union and Confederate Leadership and War in Louisiana*

(Shreveport, LA, 2003), 68–103. Unidentified article "Last of the Mohicans," in the archives of the Mansfield State Historic Area, Mansfield, LA.

39. Jarratt described another road he knew of as Sabine Crossroads. This road intersects the Shreveport-Natchitoches Stagecoach Road (today it is Louisiana Highway 175) 4.87 miles southeast of the initial Union battle line on Honeycutt Hill. The Battle of Mansfield occurred along the Shreveport-Natchitoches Stagecoach Road. The road Union forces referred to as Sabine Crossroads lies 1.2 miles south of the initial Union line and 3.67 miles northwest of the road to the one to which he referred. Jarratt's familiarity with the area causes confusion for the reader at this point. His family had lived in northern Sabine Parish for several years prior to the Civil War. If he had occasion to travel to Logansport on the Sabine River to cross into Texas, he would have used the southernmost of the two roads. It was, for him, the legitimate Sabine Crossroads intersection. This would not be the case for someone traveling south from the town of Mansfield. See Map Record Group 77, folio Z 34-4, NARA. This is one of a series of Confederate defense maps by Confederate Major Richard Venable, who was the chief topographic engineer for the Department of the Trans-Mississippi. The road Jarratt refers to as Sabine Crossroads is today a dead-end oil field road. The other road is also closed to through traffic. The north side is a residential driveway. The south side is a dead-end parish (county) road named Addison Road leading to an antebellum home. Traces of the original track of the roads are still evident in places.

40. This skirmish was one of a series fought on April 7. Tom Green's Texas cavalry began to slow the leading cavalry elements of the Union column led by Union Brigadier General Albert L. Lee to buy time for Richard Taylor to set his trap south of Mansfield. Shortly after noon, Green and four regiments of cavalry formed line of battle about three miles north of the village of Pleasant Hill at a sharp curve in the road near Wilson's Farm. Green fought a brief but sharp skirmish, then had his men melt into the woods at their rear. Green formed his men again at Carroll Jones's mill near Ten Mile Bayou, about seven miles north of Wilson's farm and approximately halfway between Pleasant Hill and Mansfield, where a short skirmish occurred. As dusk fell on April 7, Green and his men re-treated again to the hills south of Chapman's (or, incorrectly, Chatman's) Bayou. The skirmish that Jarratt refers to was a probe by Union cavalry. Green's troopers halted them. Jarratt either had no knowledge of the action at Wilson's Farm or ignored it in his narrative. See *OR*, ser. 1, vol. 34, pt. 1:450, 616; *JCCW*, 58–59, 194; Joiner, *One Damn Blunder*, 86–89.

41. Taylor, *Destruction and Reconstruction*, 159; See Map Record Group 77, folio Z 34-2, NARA (hereinafter cited as Venable Z 34-2).

42. The position is marked as "1" on map 1.1. The base map for this figure is Venable Z 34-2. Subsequent citations for positions Jarratt mentioned are referred to in map 1.1, followed by the position number. Map 1.2 is a closer view of map 1.1, showing the concentration of locations Jarratt identified in greater detail.
43. Map 1.1, position 2.
44. The family spelled the name Honeycutt, verified by conversation with Stephen L. Tebo, a direct descendent of the Honeycutt family (oral interview on October 22, 2003). The Porter family sold the farm, known at the time of the battle as Honeycutt Hill, to the Civil War Preservation Trust, which turned it over to the State of Louisiana. Today 134 acres of the farm are part of the Mansfield State Historic Site. An additional forty-two-acre tract that was part of the farm was acquired through a historical easement from Dr. Andrew Porter in 2003. This tract is an integral part of the battlefield and will remain in private hands with oversight and custodial duties operated by the Civil War Preservation Trust and the Friends of the Mansfield Battlefield.
45. Map 1.1, position 3.
46. Map 1.1, position 4.
47. Map 1.1, position 5.
48. Map 1.1, position 6.
49. The family spelled the name Fincher. This is the spelling found on Venable Z 34-2. The Fincher House still exists and is a private residence. It is one of only three original structures remaining on the battlefield. The other two are the Allen House and a Scot-Irish single pen or "dog trot" style house, which today serves a hay barn. See Venable Z 34-2.
50. Map 1.1, position 7.
51. Map 1.1, position 8.
52. Whit Porter bought the Honeycutt farm after the Civil War. His descendents still own portions of the battlefield. The residence mentioned by Jarratt is the location of the park manager's residence (a later brick structure). It is located along the spine of Honeycutt Hill to the south of Louisiana Highway 175.
53. Map 1.1, position 9.
54. Map 1.1, position 10.
55. Map 1.1, position 11.
56. See note 20.
57. Quarter-mile.
58. The Consolidated Crescent Regiment was part of the left wing of the Confederate army. It was positioned at the edge of the large field with the forest at their backs. The Rebel pickets were either part of Brigadier

General Tom Green's Texas Cavalry Corps or members of the Second Louisiana State Guards Battalion, led by Lieutenant Colonel Henry M. Favrot. A diary in the collection of Semmes Favrot of New Orleans suggests that it was probably the latter. The Union troopers were part of Brigadier Albert Lindley Lee's cavalry division of the 19th Corps.

59. Union cavalry pursuing Confederate cavalry pickets would have crossed the field, descending a shallow slope then rising on the other side, only then finding themselves very close and in sight of the massed Rebel line. The Rebels were formed near the top of the opposite face of the hill. This explains why the Union troopers came so close to the Confederate line.
60. Sergeant Major William Best; unpublished casualty list of the Consolidated Crescent Regiment for the Red River Campaign compiled by Steve Bounds, site manager of the Mansfield State Historic Site.
61. Captain David Collie Jr., who commanded Company K of the 24th (Crescent) Regiment from October 27, 1862, and then Company N of the Consolidated Crescent Regiment. See Bergeron, *Guide to Louisiana Unit,* 131, 147.
62. Lieutenant Abram H. Thigpen. See Bergeron, *Guide to Louisiana Units,* 147; Lieutenant William R. Jackson and Lieutenant Irian E. Zachary of Natchitoches Parish. See CSR, Microscopy 320, Rolls, 376, 377, 378, 379, and 380.
63. A portion of the 8th New Hampshire Infantry Regiment.
64. Venable Z 34-2. The cross fence extended south from a smaller fenced lot with a garden and small orchard. Gray's Brigade formed a line of battle in the trees behind the fence located on the north side of this lot. Jarratt's description does not include a mention of West's battery of four guns positioned on the south side of this lot and to the southwest of the brigade and Nettle's (Val Verde) battery of four guns positioned southeast of the brigade. This means that the infantry were in place early in the day, perhaps as late as noon, before their artillery support was stationed near them. Map 1.1, position 12.
65. The constant noise of a column on the march.
66. These troops were the Second Brigade of the 13th Corps under Colonel Joseph W. Vance. The regiments were the 130th Illinois Infantry, led by Major John B. Reid; the 48th Ohio Infantry, under Lieutenant Colonel Joseph W. Lindsey; the 83rd Ohio Infantry, headed by Lieutenant Colonel William H. Baldwin; and the 96th Ohio Infantry, led by Lieutenant Colonel Albert H. Brown. Farther back in the column and approaching the Rebels was the brigade artillery composed of the Indiana Light Artillery, First Battery, commanded by Captain Martin Klauss, and the Chicago Mercantile Battery, commanded by Lieutenant Pinkney S. Cone. See *OR*, ser. 1, vol. 34, pt. 1:464; *JCCW*, 61; Joiner, *One Damn Blunder*, 96–97.

67. Drain. It has been described in other period descriptions as a ravine.
68. Map 1.1, position 13.
69. Traces of the drain still exist as a boggy area following a heavy rain. The feature runs almost due east to west and is deceptively shallow. The slope is almost nonexistent on the northern side and is very gentle toward the Union line at the top of the ridge of Honeycutt Hill. Troops marching forward through the shallow impression were protected from hostile fire coming from the top of the hill due to a gentle hump midway to the crest.
70. The order to charge was given at approximately 4 P.M. Taylor had counted on Banks being impetuous; however, he had no idea that the Union commander was not at the front of his column with the troops, but several miles back behind the wagon supply train. Taylor had anticipated a headlong charge down the road at his center. Additional regiments reinforced the Union forces, and Taylor believed the Confederates had to act or they would lose the initiative. There is some question as to whether Taylor ordered the Louisiana Division under Mouton to attack or whether he told Mouton they would soon attack. The reason for the confusion is the order in which the Confederate units began their charge. Rather than having the entire line moving in unison, as the Texas Division would do, Mouton advanced his regiments in echelon, staggering their lines. This resulted in high casualty rates from the Union units focusing on specific regiments as they came close to their positions. This was not a tactic that Taylor usually employed. Mouton's men had been waiting for their chance for most of the day, and their charge was magnificent, as both sides recorded. The division's officers rode their horses in order for their men to more easily see them, and this act of bravery led to catastrophic results. See *OR*, ser. 1, vol. 34, pt. 1:564; Joiner, *One Damn Blunder*, 98–99; Ludwell Johnson, *The Red River Campaign: Politics and Cotton in the Civil War* (Kent, OH, 1993), 134–35.
71. Jarratt is apparently referring to a gap created on the far left of Vance's Brigade, where Colonel Frank Emerson's First Brigade arrived and extended the Union line south to and past the road. Brigadier General Albert L. Lee's cavalry regiments held each wing of a compact "L" formation. This implies that Jarratt's Company B, charging in front of the Louisiana Division, was aiming at the exact center of the Union line. This line of approach had two results. First, an increasingly wide margin separated Company B from the remainder of the regiment. Gray's Brigade aimed their march at the center of Vance's Union troops. Company B, advancing forward of the main body of the Consolidated Crescent regiment as skirmishers, did not guide on them and vice versa. Second, Company B's line of march toward the gap placed them in line of the crest of Honeycutt Hill, where, after traversing a band of trees, they encountered the position of Nims's Battery at the very center of the Union line.

72. Colonel Franklin H. Clack. See Bergeron, *Guide to Louisiana Units,* 147.
73. Major Mercer Canfield. See Bergeron, *Guide to Louisiana Units,* 147.
74. Jarratt's narrative describes the company at this point being actually in the Union line, facing east, immediately west and on the flank of Vance's Brigade. Facing the brigade to fire upon them, the men of Company B had trees to their front, rear, and on their right flank, and the bulk of the Confederate charge to their left and rear. This put them at great risk from both sides.
75. The Union commanders had actually placed two cannon in and six astride the road. Jarratt only saw two remaining as the Union soldiers moved the others back as the rout began. The two batteries were the 2nd Massachusetts Battery, led by Captain Ormand F. Nims, with six guns, and the 6th Missouri Horse Artillery Battery, commanded by Captain H. H. Rottakan, with two guns. Two guns of the 2nd Massachusetts were set up in the road and four to the north, all in line. The 6th Missouri were lined up south of the road extending to the 2nd Massachusetts battery line.
76. Private Charles C. Phillips, of companies B and later O, from Natchitoches Parish. See CSR Microscopy 320, Rolls, 376, 377, 378, 379, and 380.
77. The 28th Louisiana Infantry Regiment was commanded by Colonel Henry Gray from Coushatta, Louisiana.
78. Jarratt's estimate of casualties was correct. The Consolidated Crescent Regiment lost at least 195 of 400 men committed to battle at Mansfield, yielding a minimum of 48.75 percent loss of strength. Some sources estimate more than 200 casualties. See Johnson, *Red River Campaign,* 135; Mary L. B. Bankston, *Camp-Fire Stories of the Mississippi Valley* (New Orleans, 1914), 152–53; John Dimitry, *Louisiana,* vol. 10 of *Confederate Military History* (Atlanta, 1899), 140–41; Napier Bartlett, "The Trans-Mississippi" *Military Record of Louisiana: Including Biographical and Historical Papers Relating to the Military Organization of the State* (New Orleans, 1875), 13, 42; *OR,* ser. 1, vol. 34, pt. 1:564. The regiment lost seven standard-bearers. Mouton's Division lost one-third of its effective strength in the battle. The Consolidated Crescent Regiment became the only Louisiana combat unit to lose all three of its field officers in a single battle during the war. See Bergeron, *Guide to Louisiana Units,* 147.
79. By this point in the fighting, Richard Taylor had committed the First or Texas Division under Major General John G. Walker. Walker's men charged in line, not echelon, yielding fewer casualties among their troops. The left wing of the Union line was either collapsing or near that point in Jarratt's narrative.
80. The two remaining guns of Ormand Nims's 2nd Massachusetts Battery. Although Jarratt did not know it, the battle had raged all around the six-gun battery. The first attack on the battery came from the Union left, on

the south side of the road. This attack was made by Walker's Texas Division. See Richard Irwin, *History of the Nineteenth Army Corps* (New York, 1892), 306. The second onslaught was from the Union right. This was the charge in which Jarratt participated (see chap. 2). By the time Jarratt and his companions reached the battery, three guns had been taken, one was apparently moved down the road, and the remaining two were stalled due to a lack of horses or mules.

81. The cavalry units protecting the withdrawal were the 3rd Massachusetts Cavalry and the 31st Massachusetts Mounted Infantry Regiment. See Ewer, *Third Massachusetts Cavalry*, 133–86.
82. The Second Brigade of the Second, or Louisiana, Division led by Lieutenant Colonel Robert D. Stone. Composing it was the 15th Texas Infantry, led by Stone; the 17th Texas Consolidated Cavalry Regiment, Dismounted, led by Colonel James R Taylor; the 22nd Texas Cavalry Regiment, Dismounted, led by Major George W. Merrick; the 31st Texas Cavalry Regiment, Dismounted, led by Major Frederick J. Malone; and the 34th Texas Cavalry Regiment, Dismounted, led by Lieutenant Colonel John H. Caudle. The Second Brigade was in the line of battle immediately to the right of the Consolidated Crescent Regiment. The line of attack placed its troops beside the wayward course taken by Company B of the Consolidated Crescent Regiment.
83. Map 1.1, position 14.
84. Map 1.1, position 15.
85. The 1st Indiana Battery with six guns and the Chicago Mercantile Battery, also with six guns. The plum orchard is position 16 on map 1.1.
86. This passage is confusing in its great degree of detail. An examination of map Z 34-2 provides some insight. The two Union batteries were placed due north of the Fincher house and in a plowed field adjoining the plum orchard. Although not shown on the map, the description included a cotton gin yard behind the Fincher house. North of the plum orchard was another plowed field of about ten acres. This was on the lower slope of the southern face of Honeycutt Hill. This small field was bordered on two sides by the band of trees that held the original Union line and through which Jarratt and his small band traversed. Jarratt must have retraced his steps along the road to rally to the colors. Gray must have been at or near the lower end of the ten-acre field and very close to the Fincher house and the cotton gin. He would have retraced his route on horseback to the top of the field, but not into the tree line. While in the open field or the road, the Union guns were in line of sight of him and at that time fired upon the colonel.
87. This volley was fired by troops still holding their positions near the original Union line, probably remnants of Vance's Brigade or the right wing of Emerson's Brigade.

88. This would place Gray's men along the road, west of the residence and gin house, behind the Union battery, and south of the plum orchard. The retreating Union troops would be north of the road, coming out of the dense woods and running across the open ground of the plum orchard and the ten-acre field. Gray's men were effectively behind the Union line, creating a crossfire with the main Confederate force pursuing the then crushed Union right wing.
89. This passage contradicts all published accounts of the timing and location of Mouton's death. It is by far the most detailed description of the location and timing of the general's demise. Jarratt's description has credibility, due to the signatures of other members of Company B who attested to his account (see the beginning of the narrative). Other accounts have Mouton shot in the back by Union soldiers that had surrendered, and most accounts describe the place of his death as near the drain Jarratt describes. Jarratt's account means that the Confederate charge had leadership after Colonel Beard and the other officers were killed and that Mouton survived until his forces had crested Honeycutt Hill.
90. See note 20. The first phase of the battle was fought on Honeycutt Hill, about three miles from the town of Mansfield as it was in 1864.
91. Jarratt is incorrect. He only saw two guns of Nims's Battery in the road and the guns of the Chicago Mercantile and 1st Indiana batteries near the Fincher house. Union forces deployed a total of twenty-eight field pieces—a section of the 6th Missouri Horse Battery (two guns); the 2nd Massachusetts Battery (six guns); Battery G, 5th U.S. Artillery (six guns); another section of the 6th Missouri Horse Battery (two guns); the 1st Indiana Battery (six guns); and the Chicago Mercantile Battery (six guns).
92. See note 56.
93. This was the head of the Union Cavalry Division's supply train. This train blocked any chance of an orderly retreat by Union forces engaged at Mansfield and prevented reinforcements from assisting them. Union materiel losses in the battle were at least 156 wagons, possibly as many as 250, and approximately 1,000 horses and mules. See Irwin, *History of the Nineteenth Army Corps,* 306; *OR,* ser. 1, vol. 34, pt. 1:452; Taylor, *Destruction and Reconstruction,* 164; Johnson, *Red River Campaign,* 140–41.
94. This is Chapman's Bayou, incorrectly listed on USGS 7.5 minute topographic maps as "Chatman's Bayou."
95. Jarratt's participation in the flank attack near the Fincher house was near the end of the first phase of the battle. While he helped take prisoners to the rear, the second phase, which was a short stand by Cameron's Division of about twenty minutes' duration, was fought at Sabine Crossroads (the northern road that Jarratt did not recognize). He returned to the front, now at Chapman's Bayou, near the end of the third and final phase of fighting on April 8.

96. This was Captain William C. C. Claiborne Jr., whose father was the first governor of Louisiana and one of the heroes of the Battle of New Orleans in 1815.
97. This was Wilson's Farm, the site of a short, sharp engagement between Green's Texas cavalry and the Union column on April 7.
98. This was Major General John G. Walker's First or Texas Division, which had fought at Mansfield, and Brigadier Thomas J. Churchill's Division, divided into two small divisions of Arkansans under Brigadier General James C. Tappan and Missourians under Brigadier General Mosby M. Parsons. At the time of the fighting on April 9, none of Taylor's forces knew that Union Brigadier General Andrew Jackson Smith's 16th Corps was on the field at Pleasant Hill. Richard Taylor believed they were on the Red River guarding Admiral David Dixon Porter's fleet. See Joiner, *One Damn Blunder*, 107–21.
99. This was First Lieutenant Joseph B. Johnson of Company K. See CSR Microscopy 320, Rolls, 376, 377, 378, 379, and 380.
100. These regiments were the 18th Louisiana Infantry and the 28th Louisiana Infantry, sister regiments to the Consolidated Crescent Regiment in Gray's Brigade.
101. This was the house of Rebecca Jordan. It stood about three hundred feet north of the Shreveport-Natchitoches Stagecoach Road (Louisiana Highway 175) and approximately eleven hundred feet from the western edge of the village of Pleasant Hill as it was in 1864. See map 1.2. The map is in the collection of the Mansfield State Historic Site, Mansfield, Louisiana. The house no longer exists, nor does the road traversed by Jarratt. The color bearer was possibly Private F. M. Hamil of Company I from Rapides Parish (as listed on the regimental records). See CSR Microscopy 320, Rolls, 376, 377, 378, 379, and 380. There is no Robert Hamel listed in the rolls of the Consolidated Crescent Regiment; however, Jarratt obviously knew the man very well.
102. The Union unit was probably the 153rd New York Infantry Regiment of Dwight's Brigade, which had taken up position on the western edge of the village of Pleasant Hill and immediately south of the stagecoach road. See map 1.2.
103. Jarratt's regiment saw limited fighting at Pleasant Hill. The battle began at approximately 4 P.M. on April 9, and, as was the case the previous day, darkness halted fighting. Whereas the Battle of Mansfield was a stunning victory for the Rebels, Pleasant Hill was a tactical stalemate. The two sides mutually separated as darkness fell, leaving a no-man's-land between them. That night, Banks decided to retreat to Grand Ecore, on the Red River near Natchitoches, where Porter's fleet could supply him. The deciding factor at Pleasant Hill was the presence of Smith's ten thousand veterans from Major General William T. Sherman's command. The

Confederate right wing charged passed them, not noticing the Union 16th Corps. This changed the momentum as Smith's men attacked, forcing a fiercely fought stalemate.

104. See note 7. There is no indication of which direction from Pleasant Hill that Jarratt's father lived. Since he was listed as living in Sabine Parish and met one of the officers in Churchill's Division (which held the Confederate right flank) asking for directions, it may be surmised that he lived west or southwest of the village.

105. Churchill's Division bore the brunt of A. J. Smith's attack. In the confusion after the battle, it can be easily inferred that the men believed that the Confederates had lost the battle. This emphasizes the confusion after the battle. The tactical tie resulted in large numbers of men from both sides remaining on the field, uncertain of which side won and neither being able to tend to the wounded in the no-man's-land until the next day.

106. Rather than taking the Blair's Landing Road from Pleasant Hill, which was the shortest route to the Red River and Porter's gunboats, Banks chose the route he had taken from Natchitoches. This was against the advice of his senior tactical commanders. Johnson, *Red River Campaign,* 162–63.

107. This was the Battle of Blair's Landing. See Joiner, *One Damn Blunder,* 137–45.

108. This was Monett's Ferry.

109. Brigadier General Hamilton Bee commanded a brigade in the Cavalry Corps. Bee attempted to trap the Union force at Monett's Ferry (sometimes written as Bluff) on the lower end of Cane River Island. He performed poorly, allowing the Union force to escape. In Bee's defense, he had inadequate numbers of troops with which to work and Polignac was not in direct contact with the cavalry and was too far away to offer assistance.

110. Jarratt is incorrect here. Taylor was present for the duration of the campaign but was arrested by Smith in June, on the same day that he was granted the "Thanks of the Confederate Congress" and promoted to the rank of Lieutenant General. The arrest was obviously rescinded. Taylor then assumed command of the Department of Alabama, Mississippi, and Eastern Louisiana, based in Selma. Rumors were rampant within the army during the last phases of the Red River Campaign regarding the rancor between Lieutenant General E. Kirby Smith and Richard Taylor. Some troops supported Smith, but Taylor was overwhelmingly popular. Some units even came to blows over their ardor. See Joiner, *One Damn Blunder,* 173–74; Johnson, *Red River Campaign,* 279–83.

111. This portion of the fighting is usually referred to as Steele's Camden Campaign. Jarratt is incorrect in his belief that the Battle of Jenkins' Ferry and the Camden Campaign was a Confederate defeat. The primary objective

of the Union column, to take Shreveport, was not achieved. At Jenkins' Ferry, the Union force crossed over the Saline River to withdraw from the field, leaving it to the Confederates. The Union army left behind most of the wounded, and its baggage train littered the battlefield and the road by which it escaped. Jarratt believed the campaign was a defeat because he could only see the effects the missing Confederate divisions had on Taylor's attempts to destroy or at least to hem in Banks. See Joiner, *One Damn Blunder*, 123–36; Johnson, *Red River Campaign*, 170–205.

112. Jarratt is incorrect. Sherman's ten thousand men under A. J. Smith never reached him. They were diverted to Tennessee, where they saw action at Franklin and Nashville. The bulk of Banks's army was sent to Virginia, where they participated in Sheridan's Shenandoah Valley Campaign.

113. St. Mary's Battery was the 1st Louisiana Battery, also known as St. Mary's Cannoneers. Captain Florian Corney commanded it until his death on April 26; Captain Minos T. Gordy replaced him. See Bergeron, *Guide to Louisiana Units*, 17–18. Commodore Porter was actually Rear Admiral David Dixon Porter.

114. Cornay.

115. This was the USS *Eastport*. It had actually struck a torpedo (mine) laid earlier by the Confederate navy based in Shreveport. See Joiner, *One Damn Blunder*, 148.

116. The gunboats were the *Cricket*, *Fort Hindman*, and the *Juliet*. The transports were actually pump boats *Champion No. 3* and *Champion No. 5*. See Joiner, *One Damn Blunder*, 148–50.

117. This was the USS *Champion No. 5*.

118. This was the USS *Champion No. 3*. At least 100 slaves were verified killed. See U.S. War Dept., *Official Records of the Union and Confederate Navies in the War of the Rebellion*, 31 vols. (Washington, DC, 1895–1929), vol. 26:26, 76.

119. This was Major General John A. Wharton. Wharton took command of the Cavalry Corps following the death of Tom Green.

120. Wharton's actions at the rear of the Federal column are credited with saving the town of Natchitoches from the torch by A. J. Smith's men.

121. Jarratt is describing the Battle of Mansura. Taylor positioned his men in the town. Realizing that the Federal force was much too large to stop, he ordered his men to move east and north of the road upon which the Federal column was traveling. He then tried to draw the Union troops into battle. The Rebels then had their backs to the town of Marksville, and Banks's men spread out across their Avoyelles Prairie, with Lake Pearl at their backs. Several participants described the battle as being a magnificent display by both sides in an almost paradelike setting. There were very few casualties. Taylor simply had too few men to make a difference. See Homer B. Sprague, *History of the 13th Infantry Regiment of Connecticut Volunteers, During the Great Rebellion* (Hartford, CT, 1867), 212.

122. The Prince de Polignac did not relish being under the command of cavalry general Wharton, whom he considered to be an inferior commander. The prince believed Wharton lacked leadership ability and was inadequate in positioning troops and committing them to battle in the proper order. Jarratt's description of events at Norwood Plantation, or the Battle of Yellow Bayou, is remarkably correct. See *OR*, ser. 1, vol. 34, pt. 1:304, 320, 329, 337, 348–49, 357, 364, 367, 594, 624, 631; Taylor, *Destruction and Reconstruction*, 191; Johnson, *Red River Campaign*, 275; Joiner, *One Damn Blunder*, 171–72; Jeff Kinard, *Lafayette of the South: Prince Camille de Polignac and the American Civil War* (College Station, TX, 2001), 165–68.
123. These officers were Colonel Abel W. Bosworth, Lieutenant Colonel Arthur W. Hyatt, Major James J. Yarbrough, Captain Abram H. Thigpen, Lieutenant William R. Jackson, and Lieutenant Irian E. Zachary. There is no record of a Nat, Nate, or Nathaniel (with initial "N" as a first or middle name) Phillips with the Consolidated Crescent Regiment's muster rolls. This is the only name in Jarratt's list that does not appear; therefore, he either has the name incorrectly written, or, for some unknown reason, the name was not added to the list. See Bergeron, *Guide to Louisiana Units*, 147; CSR Microscopy 320, Rolls 376, 377, 378, 379, and 380.
124. This was Sergeant Sam J. Winbush, the Consolidate Crescent Regiment's Quarter Master Sergeant.
125. Private Robert B. McDonald of Captain W. J. Self's Company D.
126. A shoat is a young pig just weaned.
127. General Simon B. Buckner, who surrendered the Trans-Mississippi Department to Federal authorities on May 26, 1865. See John D. Winters, *The Civil War in Louisiana* (Baton Rouge, 1963), 425–26.
128. Pond.
129. The number of three thousand Confederates engaged at Mansfield was probably the number that Jarratt observed, considering that he was positioned on the Rebel left wing nearer the end than the center. Some estimates place as many as four times that number of Confederates on or near the field. Richard Taylor stated that he had fifty-three hundred infantry, three thousand cavalry, and five hundred artillerymen, for a total of eighty-eight hundred combatants on the field. He did not include the Louisiana militia, unexchanged or unparoled veterans, or the Arkansas and Missouri troops of Churchill's Division, which were at Keachi and unavailable for the battle. See Taylor, *Destruction and Reconstruction*, 162.
130. Jarratt is correct. Unpublished casualty records at the Mansfield State Historic Site record at least 193 casualties.
131. Officially the Consolidated Crescent Regiment disbanded in Mansfield on May 19, 1865. See Bergeron, *Guide to Louisiana Units*, 147.

A Vermont Soldier's Experience at the Battle of Mansfield

Edited by Gary D. Joiner

An unidentified Union soldier from Vermont details his experiences as a member of the 2nd Battery, Massachusetts Volunteer Light Artillery (Nims's) in a narrative that he apparently prepared as a speech before a veterans' organization such as the Grand Army of the Republic or the Military Order of the Loyal Legion of the United States. The author's description of the Battle of Mansfield, with his unit occupying the very center of the Union line, acts as an almost perfect counterpoint to that of James A. Jarratt.[1] Considering the number of combatants engaged in the Civil War, it is rare to have two accounts from opposite sides of a battle, by men who faced one another. This is particularly true in the Trans-Mississippi theater. Although not as articulate as Jarratt, this Vermont soldier writes with feeling and honesty and is equally opinionated. Also like Jarratt, he sees the action from ground level without the knowledge a commander would possess in explaining the events of the battle. This gives the narrative a feeling of urgency, even through the intervening years.

The 2nd Battery, Massachusetts Volunteer Light Artillery was recruited by Major Moses G. Cobb in Quincy on July 31, 1861. The battery was the first artillery unit from Massachusetts to be mustered into the service for three years. It was armed with six bronze guns which had been rifled at Alger's Foundry in South Boston to fire 10.5-pound Schenkel shells. On August 8, 1861, the battery went to Washington, but while en route was diverted to Baltimore, Maryland. Major Cobb was unable to lead the battery, and Captain Ormand F. Nims, who was also instrumental in recruiting it, received command of it.

During November and December of 1861, the unit was assigned to an expedition on the eastern shore. On February 25, 1862, the battery was then assigned to duty with Major General Benjamin F. Butler in the Department of the Gulf. It arrived at New Orleans and was ordered to Baton Rouge on June 2, where it joined with General Thomas Williams's Brigade. Shortly thereafter, they cooperated with Admiral David G. Farragut's fleet from June 20 to July 26, 1862, in an early operation against Vicksburg. The battery almost depleted its manpower during this period, with only 21 out of the 140 men able to report for duty.[2] A detail of 30 men from the 9th Connecticut Infantry Regiment was secured to man the guns. The battery was ordered on August 5 to assist in defending Baton Rouge from a Confederate attack under General John C. Breckenridge. The battery, commanded by Lieutenant Trull, was very active in this engagement, changing its position four times. Its next duty post was in the vicinity of New Orleans, where it remained until December 17, 1862. The unit then returned to Baton Rouge, where it spent the winter of 1862–63. Immediately prior to reposting in Baton Rouge, the new commander of the Department of the Gulf, Major General Nathaniel Prentiss Banks reorganized the Union forces in Louisiana. This unit formed part of the Fourth Division (Grover's) of the newly created 19th Corps.

The battery was first engaged on March 13, 1863, as part of a combined arms operation assisting Admiral Farragut to force past the batteries at Port Hudson. Returning to Baton Rouge on March 20, it was sent to Donaldsonville, Louisiana, a week later, and from there the battery marched to Brashear City (Morgan City), where it joined the Bayou Teche Expedition as a part of the Second (Kimball's) Brigade of the Fourth Division. The Federal forces in southern Louisiana were sent on expeditions with limited orders and no clear set goals. The column in which the battery operated reached Opelousas on April 20 and Alexandria on May 12. A flotilla under Rear Admiral David Dixon Porter fleet was in possession of the town. Without explicit orders for at least ten days, the entire expedition returned down the Red River via Simmesport to Bayou Sara on the Mississippi River on May 24. The battery then joined in the advance on Port Hudson. It operated during the siege until the surrender of the Confederate garrison on July 9, after which it was ordered to return to Baton Rouge.

General Banks conducted another operation along Bayou Teche in the autumn of 1863. The battery left New Orleans on September 18, arriving at Brashear City via railroad the following day. The force moved westward in an ill-conceived overland attempt to invade Texas. A week later, the march continued to Bisland and then to Opelousas, with constant action against the Rebels almost every day. Opelousas was reached October 21, and the battery was reassigned to Brigadier General Albert Lindley Lee's Cavalry Division of the 19th Corps.

Again with no clear orders, the column left Opelousas on November 1. Two sections of the battery were dispatched forward to Vermilionville (Lafayette). The remaining section under Lieutenant William Marland was attacked at Carrion Crow Bayou (Carencro) on November 2, and at Grand Couteau (the Battle of Bayou Bourbeau) on the November 3. The section had a desperate fight at Bayou Bourbeau, fleeing the battlefield at a gallop and being saved only by maintaining a furious fire until they crossed a bridge to the safety of the opposite bank.[3] The column advanced to New Iberia on November 17, where the battery remained until January 1864. It was then sent to winter quarters at Franklin in St. Mary Parish.

The battery joined the Red River expedition on March 13, 1864, still part of the Cavalry Division of the 19th Corps. The long column of about 20,000 men and equipment, using a single road, marched along the same route it had followed in the Teche expedition, reaching Alexandria on March 21. Still suffering under Banks's lackluster leadership, the force resumed the march up the river on March 28. It arrived at Natchitoches on April 3. Banks made perhaps the worst mistake of his military career by moving the column inland away from the protection of the U.S. Navy's guns. The force veered west and then north to the village of Pleasant Hill. The lead elements engaged Confederate cavalry at Wilson's Farm on April 7.

On April 8 the column, strung out over twenty miles along a single road, found two Confederate divisions waiting for them on a field three miles south of Mansfield, Louisiana. This column was forced to fight since its baggage train blocked the only means of escape. Nims's Battery was placed astride the road at the apex of the Union line, which was formed in the shape of an "L" to match the Confederate line. The Union forces were completely routed. The 2nd Battery lost three men killed or mortally wounded, sixteen officers and men wounded and five captured, all its guns, and eighty-two horses.

Without artillery, the survivors retreated to Pleasant Hill and from there to Grand Ecore. Although the river levels were falling, boats transported the men to New Orleans, arriving on April 22. On May 10 the battery was transferred to nearby Carrollton and reequipped with four light guns that were later exchanged for three-inch rifles. Captain Nims was sent north on July 27 on recruiting duty, and two days later, the members who had not reenlisted embarked for Boston. These veterans were mustered out in Boston on August 16, 1864. At this point, presumably, the author was mustered out of Federal service.

The battery re-formed with recruits and reenlisted men and was ordered to Morganza, Louisiana, where it remained until the following spring. On March 7, 1865, the battery sailed to Barrancas, Florida to join Major General Steele's expedition against Mobile. Captain Nims had resigned, and Captain Marland commanded the battery. The unit assisted in the capture of Fort Blakely, which surrendered on April 9, the same day that General Robert E. Lee surrendered at Appomattox. The battery then was sent on an expedition to Claiborne, Alabama. The unit's last battle was at Daniels' Landing on April 11, 1865. Late in May, the battery went to Columbus, Mississippi. Railroad carried the men back to Mobile, and from there, boats transported them to Vicksburg, where they arrived on June 4. On July 22 the battery's guns and equipment were turned over to the Federal authorities, and the men were placed on vessels bound for Massachusetts. The unit was mustered out on August 11, 1865.

The Red River Expedition to Shreveport and Back

In giving this narrative[4] I do not propose to follow historic facts, but to give my own personal experience + observation which came under my eye, as one of the organization, as the history of the late War has been treated at length by the ablest writers, yet still ~~personal~~ incidents + personal observation are often of more interest to a gathering like this than the dry facts of history. In the organization of the Red River Expedition it is a question whether the interest of the Government and the advancement of our arms was the main object or private speculation and precuniary motives of men in high places, making a cover of the army movements, to conduct a vast scheme of Cotton Stealing made legitimate by Government sanction.[5] Gen. Butler had been removed from command of the department of the Gulf, and in his place Gen N. P. Banks had been established.[6] Why this change was made has never been fully explained unless it was from the hugh and cry from the copper-heads[7] and rebel simphathizers ~~from~~ in the north, for surely a more noble, patriotic and efficient officer never drew sword in the union cause than Gen. B. F. Butler any private in the command who had a grievience, could come to him and have it righted. No copper-head was handled with gloves.

He was not afraid of them. Bold, fearless, and just he administered the affairs of the government as one, who knowing his duty, sought to preform it honestly, regardless of the remarks which were made. His orders to subsist your self on the country as far as possible, ment to the private Soldier, not to go hungry, while there were chickens in a rebel hen roost.[8]

Not so with his successor Gen'l N. P. Banks. Coming into office by political preforment[9] and wire pulling. But he was beset by the shrewd political speculators, So there-fore his administration was but a series of Catering to unprincipled army followers. The culmination of which was the *Red River Expedition.* Some said the motive of this was to occupy Texas, and that the *objective* point was Galveston.[10] But started on a Round about way up the Red River. Because of the large amount of cotton stored on its banks and for that reason the expedition was suplied with extensive wagon trains, bagging, Rope and other facilities for transportation.[11] These facts are well known and all can draw their own conclusions.

But, wether or no, our battery was ordered to report, at Franklin, Mar. 12th, 1864, where we found the Expedition.[12] Consisting of the cavelry division. under Gen'l A. L. Lee to whose command we were assigned.[13] This division was made up of 6,000 cavelry and 4 Battery's of artillery, —two of the regular army, the Chicago Merchantile Battery of 4 pound

Howartziers, and Nims 2nd Battery of light artillery. [In this last named Battery I rode the forward horse on one of the guns].[14]

The Infantry division was made up of the 19th army corps under Gen'l Franklin, and the 13th army Corps under Gen'l Ransom.[15] The cavelry started one day in advance of the main body of the army with, Nims Battery and the Chicago. Merchantile Battery.[16] This division operated with cavalry and was commanded by Gen'l Lee whose orders were to clear the way for, the main body of the army, and its combersome wagon train, the use of which we did not find out untill we arived at Alexandria, where the wagons and mules were verry handy to bring in the cotton from outlaying plantations.[17] On the first day out we encountered a small force of Rebel Cavelry with a 4 pound steel gun, which disputed our right of way. But a few shells from our guns and a gallant charge from an Indiana Reg. of cavelry, put them to flight.[18] From this time out we were constantly harrased by a force in our front, which was constantly receiving reinforcements.[19] we were attacted useualy at night or crossing some "bayou" or some reviene, any where they could make an ambush. And *30* days of harder marching and fighting cannot be found in the whole record. That little steel gun that was such a nuicence at first we captured on the 3d day out at Pictous-Plantation.[20] The Capt. in charge was shot through the hips, he was carried to the house where he soon died.

At "Carrion Crow Bayou," we arrived just after dark. here we had quite a skirmish with the Rebs. who crossed the river burning the bridge after them.[21] The artillery went into possition and shelled the woods, across the river. The Cavalry, fording the stream under cover of our guns, drove them along, and we went into camp for the night.[22]

In coming up to this Bayou I noticed about half a mile back, a Sheep nibbling the grass in front of a Planters door. This was the first one that I had seen in the Department of the Gulf. But I had not forgotten the taste of mutton. And who could blame a Vermonter for wanting a roast of good fat mutton after haveing been fed on Salt horse and hard-tack, with the exception of an occasional chicken from a rebel hen roost. Well at any rate at about nine o'clock I called the attention of a comrade to the facts of seeing a sheep, which he disputed insisting that it must have been a goat. To settle the dispute we went back (of course) to see who was right. I was for the creature had hair wool instead of hair. The planter had now come out and, seeing what we were about, begged that we would not take it arguering that it was a blooded sheep and far too valuable to be killed and served to private soldiers. Say also that we could have any thing else that we could find about the place. But no! mutton we came for and mutton we must have. (by the way who ever heard of a Soldier disapointing his palate for the whim of a Jonnie Reb. All protestation was in vain. We shouldered our sheep and picked our way back to camp, under cover of the gloom of night. And were soon seated around the camp-fire with a ~~brace~~ Dozen or more of genial comrads discussing the relative merrits of course and fine wool Sheep. the last bone was scarsely picked, when there came a blast from *Gradys* bugle "Boots & Saddles" and in seven minuets from the first sound we were again in action.[23] The rebels having been reinforsed were down upon us again vainly endevering to catch us napping.

And so it was through out our whole march we drove a constantly increasing forse before us untill our arriveal at Sabine Cross roads.[24] Here our final engagement and defeat occured. Our march from Carrion Crow bayou to Grandecore was simply a repitition of the last few days march.[25] Constantly Skirmishing. some days makeing little progress, and others makeing long marches, getting into camp late at night, and on the march at day-light. We had but little rest, and I can well say it was 30 days of the hardest service that fell to my lot since my enlistment of *three years*. ~~Our march (thus far) had been~~ thus far had been across the country to strike Alexandria six miles from the Red-River. We found a Division of the 16th Corps. and one division of the 17th Corps under command of Brig. Gen A. J. Smith, had been detatched from Shermans army, in Missouri and had came to Alexandria on the 16th and occupied the place without any opposition. On their way up the river they had captured Fort De Russy, carried it by assault, takeing 260 prisoners and 10 heavy guns.[26]

Our loss was slight. They joined our army hear and were with us untill after the final engagement.

Portors fleet of gunboats had also arrived from down the river with a lot of transports, the use of which we did not understand at first, but afterwards came in play to carry off loose cotton.[27] The army lay at Alexandria for a week or more. I believe there was a state election held in which Gen. Banks assisted but we of the cavalry division saw little of this for we were always on the go. Scouting or forageing around the country for a radius of 30 miles.

The Army broke camp at grandecore on the 6th of April. Advancing in direction of Wilsons farm.[28] here we had a Skirmish with the rebs. and marched 21 miles to crumps hill.[29] We advanced again on the morning of the 7th for plesant-hill. Still Skirmishing with the enemy, finding some resistance. We at length arrived at "Wilsons farm." We met a large force of Rebel cavalry, and went into action.[30] We send a messenger back, after the battle to ascertain how near the Infantry was and were reported not a

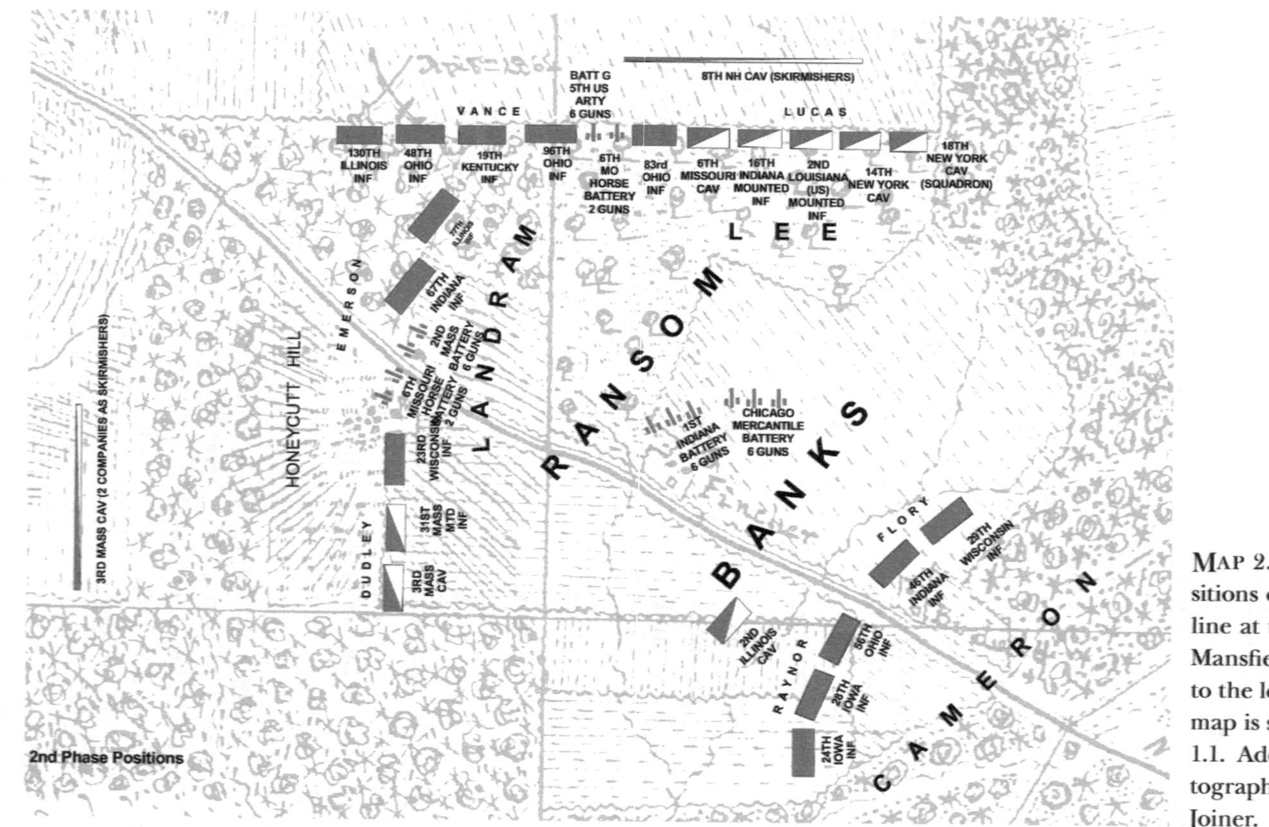

MAP 2.1. Initial positions of the Union line at the Battle of Mansfield. North is to the left. The base map is same as Map 1.1. Additional cartography by Gary D. Joiner.

great way behind. Also requested that our wageon train (consisting of 190 wageons) to the rear of the Infantry so it would be protected by it.[31] But Gen. Franklin of the 19th corps ordered that we take care of our own train and keep it well up with the cavalry. On the 8th we advanced and found the Enemy in large force. Their was fighting during the day. We pressed them back to Sabine Cross Roads, where the rebs were reported in large numbers in our front. Word was sent back for a brigade of Infantry which soon arrived commanded by Col. ——and also a division of the 13th Corps under Gen. Ransom.[32] We were posted on a hill near the road, at the left of a belt of timber suported by the 23d Wisconsin Infantry on the left and the 67th Indiana on the right, joined by the 77th Illinois, the 130th Ill, 48th Ohio 19th Ky. 76th and 83d, makeing in all about 2,500 Infantry.[33] The Cavalry and mounted Infantry under Gen'l Lee were posted on the flanks and rear, haveing Col. Dudleys Brig. on the left, and Lucus on right.[34] Also skirmishers deployed in front of this Infantry.[35]

We could see the enemy massing in solid columns in a field back of the woods. There was sharp skirmishing on the right. At 2.30 we went in battery and shelled the woods. The enemy paid little attention to this until 3 o clock P.M. when they advanced in line of battle across the open field in front of us and made a charge up the hill.[36] We met them with duble shot canister, which did fearful execution an Indiana regiment of cavelry made a double counter charge which was the finest cavalry charge I ever saw.[37] Charging through their lines and back again closing up and retiring in good order [what few was left of them] his *was* equal to the charge of the famus 600.[38]

The enemy fell back to the woods reformed and advanced again with overwhelming numbers in two lines. With Shot and Shell we drove them back in confusion but recovering they again advanced untill unable to stand our heavy fireing they broke about 200 yards from our front.[39]

While the battle rageing the Shells Shreeking and the omnious buz of the minne ball. and all the well known sounds we all have heard and whose familiar sounds we do not care to hear again.

There occured an incedence of Personal bravery of the colored man which I feel bound to relate. He was connected with our battery in capacity of cook + had been with us for a number of months. He was a contraband we had picked up in our travels and I must say we found him as faithful as it was possible for man to be.[40] Ever caring for us we were never alowed to want good cooked rations, under any circumstances. And many was the nice dish he could fix for the Boys. It was about 4 P.M. of the fight while we were under the heaviest fireing. Our horses were most all disabeled and the ground strewn with dead and wounded, and many of our own comrads, were also dead and dying. That "Henry" appered on the field with a well cooked Kettle of Coffee and lunch, looking as unconcerned as ever, Said it was about time I had some grub inside of us. The brave fellow had not forgoten us, and had the commanding General been as faithful to his duty as this poor nigger this Story never would have been told. And when I asked him if he was not afraid of being hit he answered that "if *you* are willing to stay for *me I* ought not to be afraid to work for *you.*["] The poor fellow had sented freedom but was igront of the intricate condition of the ~~political~~ Politics which brought this all about He had along known that it ment freedom—

By overwhelming numbers they ~~drove us from~~ succeeded in turning our left flank our horses disabled we were forced to abandon our position. Leaving 3 (three) of our guns on the hill.[41] We found ourselves uterly whipped with the main body of the army from 6–8 miles in our rear. We fell back to the edge of the woods where we attempted to reform but the roads were filled with flying men from the field. We went back through the woods untill we met the 19th Corps under Gen'l Franklin to late to render us aid.[42] We passed through their lines, they closing up and receiving the advancing shock of the Rebs. so gallantly that they were effectualy checked, and fell back.[43] The fighting was now over for the night.[44]

We had lost our guns and baggage-train and most of our horses.[45] In fact I found myself entirely cleaned out. My valiese was strapped on the off Horse and contained all my traps and he lay dead on the field. I succeeded in getting away with old *Bill* who had born me faithfully for most three years and he was badly hurt, his jaw was shot away by a musket-Ball.

We retreated back that night to Pleasant-hill where we arrived at about day light. Completely exhausted from want of food haveing eaten nothing since the morning before, except what "Henry" brought us on the field. At Pleasant hill we found A. J. Smith with a part of the 16 and 17 Corps actualy frothing at being kept back in the rear and haveing our army defeated in detail. When with proper generalship on the part of the commanding officer we would have won an easy Victory and marched into Shreevesport 12 miles distant from Sabine-Cross roads found a junction with Porters fleet where we could command a position which we could hold against any odds that could be brought to bear against us.[46]

That night the 19th Corps fell back to pleasant hill pressed hard by the Enemy. Gen. Smith taking Command a Spirited engagement ensued on the morning of the 9th,[47] when the Rebs were defeated and drove back with terrible loss in fact their loss was so heavy in the last 2 days fighting that they did not deem it proper to follow us longer.[48] And our return to Alexandria where our transports lay, our journy down the Red River to New Orleans again had few if any incedences worth note.[49]

Notes

1. See chap. 1.
2. The drastic number of losses were not due to battle casualties. The unit lost four enlisted killed or mortally wounded, and twenty-six were killed by disease. See William F. Fox, *Regimental Losses in the American Civil War* (Dayton, OH, 1985), 470. The loss of so many men while on campaign was probably due to desertion, although some men may have been furloughed.
3. See Richard Lowe, *The Texas Overland Expedition of 1863* (Fort Worth, 1996), 80–100. David G. Edmonds, ed., *Yankee Autumn in Acadiana: A Narrative of the Great Texas Overland Expedition through Southwestern Louisiana, October–December 1863* (Lafayette, LA, 1979), 296–308.
4. This account of the Red River Campaign is an undated manuscript, MSS 83422, Louisiana and Lower Mississippi Valley Collections, Louisiana State University Libraries, Baton Rouge. A version of this manuscript, with analysis by Sally Power, appeared in *Louisiana History* 40, no. 2 (1999): 355–64. The author of the manuscript is unknown, but was from Vermont. He was a member of Captain Ormand Nims's 2nd Massachusetts Light Artillery Battery attached to the Cavalry Division of the 19th Corps. Note on transcription: The text of the account was transcribed literally, with the following emendations of punctuation and style. The author's spelling and capitalization have been rendered as written. Notation has been made where accidentally repeated words and passages have been omitted. All uses of the long S have been modernized. Punctuation has been retained with the exception of line breaks and hyphenations at end of lines. Strikeouts and superscripts have been rendered as such. Paragraph breaks have been retained as written, but catchwords, where they occur, have not. Punctuation has been added where the author omitted it when it occurred at end of lines. The late Stone Miller of Louisiana State University's Special Collections prepared a preliminary transcription. The editor has used the conventions set by Sally Power in her treatment of this manuscript and, where appropriate, used her citations. Additional information has also been added, and in some cases parenthetical information has been deleted from citations. Annotations and analysis are by Gary D. Joiner.
5. Text from "our arms" to "Government sanction." Repeated in document. "Private speculation and pecuniary motives" refers to the openly allowed cotton stealing carried on by the Union army (illegally) and the Union

Navy, legally sanctioned by the Naval Prize Law. In the week ending March 24, 1864, Admiral Porter and his "jack tars" confiscated, from an area extending outward approximately ten miles from Alexandria, 2,129 bales of cotton, twenty-eight barrels of molasses, and eighteen bales of wool for transshipment to the prize court at Cairo, Illinois.

6. Major General Benjamin F. Butler and Major General Nathaniel Prentiss Banks.
7. Copperheads were Northern Democrats who opposed the Union war policy and favored a negotiated peace. The author, by his writing, is evidently a pro-radical abolitionist and likely a Republican.
8. John D. Winters, *The Civil War in Louisiana* (Baton Rouge, 1963), 330. During the campaign, as was usual, orders prohibited straggling, foraging, private plunder, arson, and the destruction of private property. The 13th and 19th Corps strictly enforced this. It was not true of the 16th Corps, under Brigadier General Andrew Jackson Smith. This command was not under the direct control of General Banks, but was on loan from Major General William T. Sherman for this campaign. These men had begun Sherman's philosophy of Total War in the Meridian (Mississippi) Expedition immediately prior to the Red River Campaign. Creating even greater plundering were the marines of the Mississippi Marine Brigade, who created such havoc and distrust among the other Union units, that they were sent back to patrol the Mississippi River and did not ascend the Red River above Alexandria. See Gary D. Joiner, *One Damn Blunder from Beginning to End: The Red River Campaign of 1864* (Wilmington, DE, 2003), 38, 41, 68, 79.
9. Performance
10. This was not the case. Although the Union desperately wanted to plant the flag on the mainland of Texas, Banks had troops on some of the barrier islands. He had also attempted two invasions of Texas in 1863 at Sabine Pass and an abortive invasion across southern Louisiana.
11. Phillip Cuccia, "'Gorillas' and White Glove Gents: Union Soldiers in the Red River Campaign," *Louisiana History* 36 (1995): 413–31. Brigadier General Albert L. Lee's cavalry division was followed by three hundred wagons. Seven hundred additional wagons followed Major General William Buell Franklin's three divisions of infantry. This was an extraordinary number of wagons to accompany a single column of about thirty thousand men.
12. Winters, *Civil War in Louisiana*, 330. The first to arrive at Alexandria on March 19 were one hundred men from Lee's Cavalry.
13. Brigadier General Albert Lindley Lee of Kansas.
14. *Official Army Register of the Volunteer Force of the United States Army for the Years 1861–65*, 8 parts (Washington, 1865), pt. 1, 140. Ormand F. Nims was discharged on January 7, 1865.

15. General Franklin and Brigadier General Thomas Edward Greenfield Ransom.
16. The batteries were the 2nd Massachusetts Battery, with six guns; the 6th Missouri Horse Artillery Battery, with two guns; the 1st Indiana Battery, with six guns; and the Chicago Mercantile Battery, also with six guns.
17. This unknown soldier mirrors the opinions expressed by the Joint Committee on the Conduct of the War, which investigated the campaign beginning in December 1864. See U.S. Congress, *Report on the Joint Committee on the Conduct of the War, 1863–1866,* vol. 2, *Red River Expedition* (Millwood, NY, 1977).
18. This was the 16th Indiana Mounted Infantry under Lieutenant Colonel James H. Redfield. This was the only Indiana mounted regiment serving in the Cavalry Division on the campaign.
19. The Confederate forces keeping watch on the advancing Union column was Vincent's Cavalry Brigade under Colonel William G. Vincent. The brigade consisted of the 2nd Louisiana Cavalry led by Major Winter O. Breazeale and the 4th (7th) Louisiana Cavalry commanded by Colonel Louis Bush.
20. This plantation would be located approximately halfway between Brashear City (Morgan City in St. Mary Parish) and Opelousas in St. Landry Parish. A search of records yielded no plantation by that name, but it may be the author's spelling of "Pictus," of which at least one plantation was named, but not on this route.
21. This is Carencro in Lafayette Parish, a short distance north of the city of Lafayette. The origin of the name is Carrion Crow.
22. For a thorough examination of the skirmish at Carrion Crow Bayou, see Lowe, *Texas Overland Campaign,* 80–100; Edmonds, *Yankee Autumn,* 190–94.
23. "Boots and Saddles" was a bugle call formerly used in the U.S. Cavalry to summon soldiers to mount.
24. The Union called the largest battle of the Red River Campaign "The Battle of Sabine Crossroads"; the Confederacy referred to it as "The Battle of Mansfield."
25. Grand Ecore in Natchitoches Parish was the port of the town Natchitoches. It was at Grand Ecore that General Banks turned his army inland away from the protective guns of the Mississippi River Squadron's vessels.
26. This was a force of ten thousand men that General Sherman loaned to General Banks for this expedition. Brigadier General Andrew Jackson Smith led these men. The author most likely saw the 3rd Division of the 16th Corps under Brigadier General Joseph A. Mower and Brigadier General Thomas Kilby Smith's 2nd (Provisional) Division of 17th Corps. These men guarded the navy's assets. Deep animosity existed between Sherman's Westerners and the eastern troops of the 19th Corps. They had fought in the Meridian Campaign in Mississippi immediately prior

to the Red River expedition. Fort DeRussy was the large Rebel fort located in Avoyelles Parish. Mower's troops took this lower anchor of the Red River defenses with comparative ease.

27. Winters, *Civil War in Louisiana,* 331; Ludwell H. Johnson, *Red River Campaign: Politics and Cotton in the Civil War* (Kent, OH, 1993), 101–2; Joiner, *One Damn Blunder,* 59–62. Porter seized cotton from warehouses in Alexandria and marked it "U.S.N. Prize." Naval personnel went into the interior to confiscate all cotton wherever it was found regardless of the loyalty of its owners. The army owned the troop transports and most of the supply vessels. The navy's contingent were "fighting hulls" and vessels to support them. The Union used a total of at least 103 vessels on the campaign. See Appendix 2.

28. Banks headed his army inland along the old Spanish Royal Road, against the advice of his senior commanders. He used a single road to march a column consisting of over thirty thousand men, one thousand wagons, and ninety artillery pieces. The route led away from the river at Grand Ecore and headed westerly through the town of Natchitoches and continued west (along the modern Louisiana Highway 6) to the town of Robeline. At Robeline, then a crossroads called White's Store, the route moved northwest (along the modern Louisiana Highway 120) to Belmont (then called Crump's Corners) and the intersection of the Shreveport-Natchitoches Stagecoach Road (the modern Louisiana Highway 175.) At this point, the road headed northerly through the village of Pleasant Hill, extended to Mansfield, and beyond that, Shreveport.

29. The author lists the actions in reverse. The first enemy action on the western route from Grand Ecore occurred at Crump's Corners on April 6. Wilson's Farm was a sharp delaying action by the Rebels on April 7. Wilson's Farm lies about three miles north of the village of Pleasant Hill. The newly arrived Texas Cavalry Corps under Brigadier General Tom Green instigated both of these actions.

30. For detailed descriptions of Lee's cavalry actions, see Winters, *Civil War in Louisiana,* 330; Johnson, *Red River Campaign,* 124–45; Joiner, *One Damn Blunder,* 55–98.

31. General Albert Lee, commanding the Cavalry Division, repeatedly requested that his supply train be moved back with the infantry's train. Both Banks and Franklin refused. They rode about seven miles behind the most forward cavalry units and had no clear picture of the changing situation. See *JCCW,* 30, 58–59; Richard Irwin, *History of the Nineteenth Army Corps* (New York, 1892), 300. Lee's cavalry had approximately three hundred wagons assigned to it.

32. This was the Colonel Frank Emerson's First Brigade and Colonel Joseph W. Vance's Second Brigade of the Fourth Division of the 13th Corps under Colonel William J. Landrum.

33. See map 2.1.
34. This was the Cavalry Division's Fourth Brigade commanded by Colonel Nathan A. M. "Goldlace" Dudley and the First Brigade under Colonel Thomas J. Lucas.
35. This was the 8th New Hampshire Infantry, which was also designated the 2nd New Hampshire Cavalry for the campaign. See John M. Stanyan, *A History of the Eighth Regiment of New Hampshire Volunteers Including Its Service as Infantry, Second N.H. Cavalry, and Veteran Battalion in the Civil War of 1861–1865, Covering a Period of Three Years, Ten Months, and Nineteen Days* (Concord, NH, 1892), 382–457.
36. The charge began at approximately 4 P.M. See U.S. War Dept., *War of the Rebellion: The Official Records of the Union and Confederate Armies,* 128 vols. (Washington, DC, 1880–1901), ser. 1, vol. 34, pt. 1:564 (hereinafter cited as *OR,* followed by series number, volume number, part number, and page reference).
37. An observer from Nims's Battery would believe that the barrage was mowing down the front lines of Confederate infantry. A participant at the forefront of the charge in the Louisiana Consolidated Crescent Regiment stated that at the opening cannon fire, the line was in a shallow depression under the brow of Honeycutt Hill and that the men immediately dropped down. This would have appeared from a position on the hill as sweeping destruction. See chap. 1 in this volume.

    The author is referring to the 16th Indiana Mounted Infantry under Lieutenant Colonel James H. Redfield. There are no other accounts of any of the cavalry units making a countercharge.
38. The author is referring to the charge of the British Light Brigade at Balaclava during the Crimean War and Alfred, Lord Tennyson's poem. The first stanza reads:

    Half a league half a league
    Half a league onward
    All in the valley of Death
    Rode the six hundred:
    "Forward the Light Brigade
    Charge for the guns" he said
    Into the valley of Death
    Rode the six hundred

39. See chap. 1 in this volume. The author is describing a point in the charge in which the Consolidated Crescent Regiment lost six standard-bearers and all three of its officers before regrouping. There is no reference in the literature of the Rebel line breaking, reforming, and advancing in a second charge. The Consolidated Crescent Regiment lost at least 195 of its 400 men in this charge.

40. Runaway slaves who attempted to attach themselves to Union columns.
41. From the author's position, he would have been able to see south of the road along the ridge of Honeycutt Hill and not through the woods on his right. The Union line was in the shape of a compact "L." Both flanks were turned back into the center, with the Union right wing (in the woods) holding out slightly longer than the left wing, which was attacked a few minutes after the Rebel charge hit the right wing.
42. General Franklin, commander of the 19th Corps.
43. The author is describing a brief attempt to hold the Confederates at bay while the survivors of the first attack made their way to the rear. The units holding this line at the intersection of Sabine Crossroads were Cameron's Division. The second line held for approximately twenty minutes before it collapsed.
44. The author does not describe the third and final phase of the battle, which ended with nightfall. The Union line held on top of a ridge above Chapman's Bayou, a small creek about three miles from the original line. The Confederates pushed the Union troops beyond the water, the last source for at least seven miles. This ended Banks's hopes of pushing the Rebels back. The third phase of the Battle of Mansfield (or Sabine Cross Roads by the Union) is named in Union reports as the Battle of Pleasant Grove, referring to a peach orchard in the yard of Mr. Chapman, for whom the stream was named.
45. Cuccia, "'Gorillas' and White Glove Gents," 416. All of the leading supply wagons were captured, plundered, or burned.
46. Shreveport was about forty miles from Mansfield. The author may be referring to the planned rendezvous with the fleet near Springfield Landing, northeast of Mansfield. The general mentioned is General Andrew Jackson Smith, commanding the contingent from General Sherman's forces. Smith was so angry at Banks for his actions of April 8 and 9 that he wanted him arrested and removed from command and replaced by William B. Franklin. Smith assured Franklin that he would have the full support of the 13th, 16th, and 17th Corps. General Franklin considered this, but changed his mind, telling the angry veteran commander, "Smith, don't you know this is mutiny?" Since mutiny was an offense that resulted in hanging upon conviction of the crime, the generals dropped the conversation. See *OR*, ser. 1, vol. 34, pt. 1:34, 309.
47. The Battle of Pleasant Hill began approximately at 4 P.M. on April 9, 1864, almost exactly twenty-four hours after the beginning of the Battle of Mansfield.
48. The Battle of Pleasant Hill, fought on April 9, was considered a tie turned into a strategic defeat for the Union forces when General Banks

decided to abandon the battlefield and, for the second time in two days, his dead and wounded. The army retreated to Grand Ecore. General Edmund Kirby Smith, commanding the Confederate Department of the Trans-Mississippi, removed three divisions from pursuing Banks's column and moved them to Arkansas. This left only the Louisiana Division and Texas cavalry to oppose the much larger force. The author apparently did not know this.

49. The author does not refer to the desperate flight of the army back to Grand Ecore; the plight of the Union army and navy, trapped at Alexandria due to low water; and the battles of Mansura and Yellow Bayou during the retreat of the Union forces before the campaign ended on May 22.

Lieutenant Edward Cunningham: A Kirby Smith Loyalist Complains about Richard Taylor

Edited by Gary D. Joiner

A survey of the primary source literature of the Civil War in the West yields few documents in which Edmund Kirby Smith is purported to be a better soldier or a even a better person than Richard Taylor. Taylor believed Smith was more an armchair general with antiquated ideas on the conduct of modern warfare than a dynamic field commander. Although he respected his subordinate, Smith was jealous of Taylor's family connections (son of Zachary Taylor and brother-in-law of Jefferson Davis) and resented his disregard for authority.

Some pro-Smith accounts do exist. Most of Smith's staff was very loyal to him and vigilantly defended his honor. One staff member with family ties to the commanding general penned a personal letter that clearly illustrates this loyalty. Lieutenant Edward Cunningham was a member of Kirby Smith's staff prior to the first Battle of Manassas in 1861. When Smith moved to the Trans-Mississippi in 1863, Cunningham was his aide-de-camp. He was made chief of artillery at Shreveport in 1864.

Kirby Smith received a shoulder wound at First Manassas. He recuperated about thirty miles from the battlefield at Cunningham Manor, the estate of Richard Cunningham, uncle of Edward Cunningham.[1] Richard Cunningham and Kirby Smith remained close, and the younger Cunningham kept his uncle informed of Smith's actions. While still in Virginia, the elder Cunningham sent hams, butter, and foodstuffs to Smith in the field.[2]

Edward Cunningham was transferred to New Orleans in late 1861.[3] He went to Tennessee after the fall the Crescent City, where he joined Smith again. Smith made Cunningham adjutant and increased his responsibilities. Cunningham spent time around Knoxville before accompanying Smith on his invasion of Kentucky. Following a difficult and disappointing campaign, Cunningham, then a first lieutenant, came to Louisiana with Smith in late February 1863. As Smith's aide-de-camp,[4] he issued Smith's correspondence and orders.

Cunningham accompanied Smith to Arkansas during the Camden Campaign, the northern portion of the Red River Campaign, and was present at the Battle of Jenkins' Ferry. He was an able, although biased, narrator of the campaigns. Just over a month following the culmination of the twin Union defeats, Cunningham wrote a letter to his uncle in Virginia describing the course of fighting and the attending political fallout from Smith's and Taylor's actions. It remains an eloquent defense of Smith's motives.

Letter from Lieutenant Edward Cunningham, Aide-de-Camp to Lieutenant General Edmund Kirby Smith and Chief of Artillery at Shreveport, to His Uncle, Richard Cunningham in Virginia

SHREVEPORT, LA., June 27, 1864.[5]

MY DEAR UNCLE: I stated in my letter to you, written about two weeks since, that I would inclose some orders and an address from General Taylor to his troops. I neglected to do so at that time, but send them now.[6] General Taylor has been relieved from the command of the District of West Louisiana and ordered to Natchitoches, there to await the pleasure of the President.[7] The circumstances under which he was relieved it is not my business to tell. All that is generally known is that General Taylor requested to be relieved. I do not wish to be regarded as writing in a mischief-making or partisan spirit.[8] An effort will very probably be made by General Taylor's friends at Richmond to excite dissatisfaction against General Smith, or even to have him relieved from command.[9] As they will no doubt take issue on the conduct of the campaign, rather than directly upon any point of difference which may exist between General Smith and General Taylor, I shall endeavor to give you an account of the course of events, together with the reasons, as far as I understand them, for which the principal movements of troops were made. This explanation may enable you to appreciate correctly any discussions of this subject which may come under your notice. Here let me say you cannot depend upon the truth of many statements you may hear. General Taylor's friends will doubtless get their information from him and those around him here, among whom there is a disposition to criticize, misrepresent, and condemn everything done by or connected with General Smith.[10] General Taylor is a very bad man. You understand that I speak deliberately sentiments. I have held with good reason for more than twelve months, but which for obvious reasons I have never made known except to General Smith and some of his friends, who could see as much as I. I have been as cautious and particular as I know a person occupying my position should be about such matters.

About the 1st of February last it became evident, from the movements of the enemy at New Orleans, Little Rock, and Fort Smith; that a combined offensive movement was preparing against the Trans-Mississippi Department.[11] The Red River Valley was to be the theater of operations. This appeared both from the enemy's movements and from reports from his lines.[12] The Northern papers stated that Sherman's force, which had just returned from its expedition through Mississippi, would also be sent for a time to this side of the river, and that Sherman, Banks, and Steele would make a combined movement on Shreveport.[13] Accordingly, every preparation was made for concentrating the troops. Green's division of cavalry was ordered from the Texas coast to Alexandria, while depots of subsistence and forage were placed on the important lines connecting Arkansas, Louisiana, and Texas.[14] Troops of all arms were ordered to be mobilized as well as possible and held in readiness to move with celerity to any point where they might be needed. This was a critical juncture. It was expected that Sherman would move from Vicksburg or Natchez. Instead of that, however, he sent only two divisions (one of the Sixteenth and one of the Seventeenth, in all about 10,000 men) to the mouth of Red River.[15] From that point this command moved to De Russy, when it again took transports and joined Banks at Alexandria on March 18.[16] General A. J. Smith commanded the two divisions.[17] It preceded Banks three or four days.[18] It landed at Simsport[19] March 12. At that time the distribution of our force was as follows: In Louisiana General Taylor had two divisions of infantry and 1,500 or 2,000 cavalry in detachments; Walker's division, consisting of Randal's, Waul's, and Scurry's brigades, was posted from Fort De Russy down the Bayou De Glaize to Simsport; Mouton's division, consisting of Polignac's and Gray's brigades, was divided—one brigade near Alexandria and the other on its way to Alexandria from Trinity, the junction of the Ouachita, Little, and Tensas Rivers.[20] Banks was organizing his expedition at Berwick Bay.[21] Colonel Vincent, with the Second Louisiana Cavalry and a battery, was near Opelousas watching him.[22] General Liddell, with a brigade of cavalry and several batteries, was near Monroe watching the approaches from Natchez and Vicksburg. Green's cavalry, although ordered to move two weeks before this, did not leave the vicinity of Hempstead, Tex., till March 15, and did not reach General Taylor till between the 1st and 5th of April.[23] The strength of the column which landed at Simsport was, as it usually is, overestimated.[24] General Walker, whose force compared to it as four to ten, fell back up the Bayou De Glaize to a point near Fort De Russy, and thence moved to Evergreen, about 30 miles south of Alexandria, where he was joined by General Taylor with Mouton's division. Meanwhile General Walker had left the garrison at Fort De Russy to its fate, as he considered it impossible, from the nature of the ground and the preponderance of the enemy's force, to cover or support the place.[25] It fell with its garrison on March 14, by a land attack. General Taylor estimated the strength of this column at 23,000 men.[26] Immediately after the fall of Fort De Russy the enemy occupied Alexandria. General Taylor was thrown off into the pine hills and took the road leading up Red River.[27] He halted a short time at McNutt's Hill, 12 miles above Alexandria, but soon moved 18 miles farther back to Carroll Jones' with his infantry.[28] Meanwhile Banks, with 25,000 men of all arms, drove Vincent up the Teche and joined Smith at Alexandria about March 18.[29] Every exertion was made to hurry up Green's cavalry from Texas, but it moved very slowly and did not all reach General Taylor till about April 5.[30] General Liddell was ordered down into the country north and east of Alexandria, between the Red and Ouachita Rivers, to annoy the enemy's transports passing.[31]

On March 21, the enemy came out from Alexandria and surprised the Second Louisiana Cavalry, capturing most of that regiment, together with Edgar's four-gun battery.[32] This force constituted our rear guard. General Taylor then fell rapidly back to the vicinity of Natchitoches. After remaining ten or twelve days in Alexandria Banks moved slowly up in pursuit. He met with no serious resistance till the battle of Mansfield.[33] In Arkansas General Price had his infantry near Spring Hill, 15 miles from Washington and 60 from Camden, while the cavalry under General

Marmaduke held the line of the Ouachita, scouring the country in front to within 25 miles of Little Rock, where Steele had for some time been preparing for an advance.[34] A brigade of cavalry under General Cabell was posted between Washington and Paraclifta in observation of the enemy, about 5,000 strong, at Fort Smith, and guarding the approaches east of the Arkansas line, while General Maxey, with two brigades of cavalry, watched those leading through the Indian Territory to North Texas.[35]

On March 23, Steele moved out from Little Rock with about 8,000 men. On the 21st, Thayer left Fort Smith with about 3,000.[36] They effected a junction at Arkadelphia about the 31st.[37] General Cabell was ordered to General Marmaduke.[38] The cavalry was in two divisions, one under Marmaduke and one under Fagan. General Maxey was ordered with all of his force, except such as was needed to prevent small raids, to hold himself at Laynesport, in the extreme southeast corner of the Indian Territory, so as to support General Price and operate on his left should he be forced back by Steele.[39] Steele's plan was to move by Washington to Red River, cross near Fulton, and destroy the stores and shops at Jefferson and Marshall, taking us in rear while we operated against Banks, or giving the latter an opportunity of getting our communications should we move against Steele.[40] Steele moved very slowly and cautiously, harassed by our cavalry, who impeded his march at every step. He was about sixteen days moving from Camden to Prairie D'Ane, a distance of about 100 miles. Our object was to delay a general engagement until the two columns of the enemy, or one of them, should approach sufficiently near Shreveport, our point of concentration, to enable us to strike with as much as possible of our force one of the two without abandoning our depots or communications to the other. Our important points were Shreveport, Jefferson, and Marshall—the last a vital point.[41] Accordingly, Price's old division, now divided into Parsons' (Missouri) and Churchill's (Arkansas) divisions, was ordered to Shreveport, where it arrived on the 24th.[42] At this time Banks was at Natchitoches and Steele near Little Rock, in view, both advancing, but Steele making slow progress, our cavalry disputing his advance stubbornly. Besides, he was obliged to haul all of his forage from Little Rock and to guard his trains closely. Thus Banks was 98 and Steele 200 miles from Shreveport. Banks continued to advance; General Taylor fell back before him.[43] On April 6, his advance was at Pleasant Hill; General Taylor was at Mansfield, where the roads fork to Marshall and Shreveport. Churchill's and Parsons' divisions were sent to him.[44] They reached Mansfield the night of the 8th.[45] Green's cavalry had also arrived, having been obliged to make a long detour to get in front of the enemy.[46] At 4 o'clock on

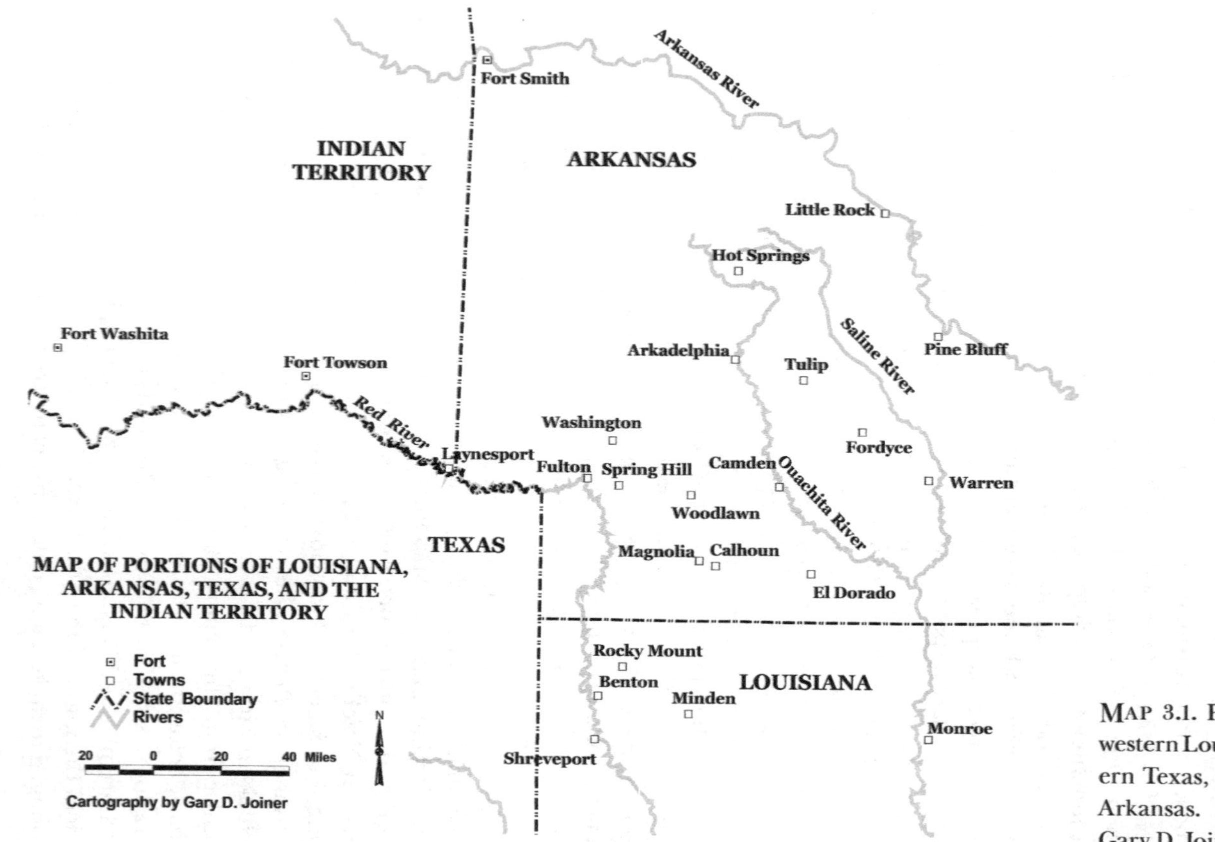

MAP 3.1. Portions of northwestern Louisiana, northeastern Texas, and southwestern Arkansas. Cartography by Gary D. Joiner.

the evening of the 8th, General Mouton, without the order or knowledge of General Taylor, attacked and repulsed the Thirteenth Army Corps and Cavalry Division, the advance of the enemy, from 8,000 to 10,000 strong, 3 miles south of Mansfield.[47] The first news brought to General Taylor of the fight was, as I am informed, that General Mouton had attacked the enemy and been killed. Walker's and Green's divisions were then put into action, when the engagement became a running fight for 4 or 5 miles, our men double-quicking a considerable portion of the way.[48]

The enemy got into a stampede and our men rushed after them pell-mell through the woods till dark. Four or five of their light batteries and the train of the Cavalry Division were in front. As soon as the fight commenced these vehicles blocked up the road, which was very narrow and ran through a thick pine woods. Most of the horses were carried off and the guns and wagons were left in our hands.[49] Only one of their batteries was brought into action.[50] About night, the Thirteenth Corps and the cavalry having been driven back about 4 miles, the Nineteenth Army Corps, General Franklin commanding, came up, and for awhile checked our advance, but it gave way also after a little, and was driven back some half a mile, when it became too dark for us to pursue farther.[51] The enemy continued his retreat during the night. Our loss was about 1,000 killed and wounded; that of the enemy greater. He also lost 150 wagons, 22 pieces of artillery, and 1,800 prisoners.[52] At this time General A. J. Smith, with one division of the Sixteenth and one of the Seventeenth Corps, was at Natchitoches. From Shreveport it is 42 miles to Mansfield, 65 miles to Pleasant Hill, and 98 to Natchitoches.[53] On the night of the 8th, Churchill and Parsons came up. The pursuit was resumed at daylight on the 9th. In the evening the enemy was found in line of battle at Pleasant Hill, A. J. Smith, who had come up from Natchitoches, on the left, Franklin (Nineteenth Corps) on the right, the whole about 24,000.[54] The Thirteenth Corps had gone on to Natchitoches.[55] The enemy's right was in woods, his left in open fields. Walker and Polignac (commanding Mouton's division) attacked on our left, Parsons and Churchill on our right. The charge of the Arkansas and Missouri troops was dashing.[56] On their left the enemy had five brigades and several batteries. Part of their infantry was in advance of the artillery and part in rear for a support. The Missouri division was to have been supported on the left by Scurry's brigade (Walker's extreme right), but instead of cooperating the two went into action separately, and were whipped in detail. The Missouri division drove back the enemy's line in its front, and came up within 50 yards of their batteries, but having no support on their left, were flanked by the enemy from that direction, and meeting a heavy fire from the supporting force, retreated in confusion. About the time they had gotten away from the enemy, who showed no disposition to follow, Scurry's brigade came up and was repulsed after having driven back the enemy's line in his front a quarter of a mile. The enemy followed him some distance, capturing several hundred prisoners. Night put a stop to the fight, Churchill's, Parsons', and most of Walker's command being in great confusion. On our left Walker and Polignac had rather the advantage of the enemy without gaining any material results.[57] Our troops were withdrawn.[58] Polignac remained about 2 miles from the field. Walker, Churchill, and Parsons, with all the cavalry except one brigade, moved back 6 miles, the nearest point at which there was sufficient water. Neither our cavalry nor that of the enemy did anything in this fight.[59]

The next morning, after sunrise, very much to our surprise, we learned that the enemy had retreated during the night. The cavalry was immediately sent in pursuit, while the infantry was taken back to Mansfield for organization, rest, and supplies. The enemy evidently considered himself whipped. He ought to know. Independently of the condition of the troops after the fight, the want of supplies below Mansfield and of transportation to haul them rendered immediate pursuit with our whole force impossible.[60] Below Mansfield all was a howling wilderness. The only way in which a large body of troops there could be supplied was by the river, which at this time was occupied by the gun-boats of the enemy up to within 30 miles of Shreveport.[61] Furthermore, the enemy's land force, even though it should be demoralized, had at all times the guns of their fleet, upward of one hundred in number, for a protection.[62] At best our chase, had we been able to advance, would have wound up at the Mississippi, with that barrier to our farther progress, and with nothing more accomplished than would be done by the enemy himself if let alone.[63] A campaign against New Orleans, had there been no enemy in the country besides Banks, would have been utter madness.[64] On the other hand, Steele, with 11,000 men, was moving on Camden, from the fortifications at which point he could, in perfect security from our cavalry, watch our operations, and if an opportunity offered, strike at Jefferson, Marshall, or Shreveport.[65] To leave him in this position, and transfer all our troops except our cavalry left in Arkansas to Lower Louisiana, would be to jeopardize our very salvation. Northward great results would follow Steele's signal defeat. The regaining of the Arkansas Valley and the breaking up of the Yankee State government, as well as having the route to Missouri open, were considerations of great importance. These results accomplished, the numerical strength of our armies might soon be doubled.[66] For these reasons General Smith determined to move against Steele, and accordingly Walker's, Parsons', and Churchill's divisions were put in motion.[67]

Here is the point: General Taylor and his friends assert with the most confident assurance that had he been allowed to "follow up his victory" the utter destruction of Banks and Porter would have been the result. Perhaps the exact force of this argument can be appreciated only by persons who saw General Taylor's victorious army just after it had attempted to destroy a part of General Banks' force without the fleet to support it; but still the idea of our annihilating in their intrenchments a force three-fourths of which we had failed to whip in open fight, and of transporting over a distance of 250 miles supplies we had been unable to haul 65 miles.[68] Such projects must appear in their true light to any sensible person who looks calmly and impartially into the matter. It was impossible for the enemy to maintain permanently at Natchitoches a force sufficient to hold the place. Red River must soon fall, and supplies would then have to be hauled from Simsport. The country would supply scarcely anything. General Taylor was left in command of the cavalry and Polignac's division to watch and pursue the enemy.

Parsons, Churchill, and Walker arrived at Shreveport on April 16, *en route* for Camden. Walker moved on the right via Minden, Parsons in the center via Benton, and Churchill on the left, following Red River 35 miles up and then turning to the right, passing near Magnolia. Walker's division was halted 20 miles beyond Minden on the reception of information from General Taylor that the enemy was intrenching at Natchitoches and had thrown two pontoon bridges across the Red River at Grand Ecore, the steam-boat landing for that place.[69] In this position (48 miles from Shreveport, 115 from Natchitoches, and 66 from Camden) General Walker was in a good attitude to meet any movement of Banks in the direction of the Ouachita or against Shreveport, or any movement of Steele in the direction of Red River. It was thought possible Banks and Steele might endeavor to effect a junction east of Shreveport, which accomplished, we could have but little hope of resisting their united strength.[70] Walker remained in this position till the enemy evacuated Grand Ecore and retreated south with his land and naval forces. The bridge had been thrown across Red River to enable the enemy's infantry to protect his transports and gun-boats from General Liddell's force, which had moved up opposite to them and inflicted considerable loss upon them, destroying one or two boats.[71] Five thousand or 6,000 men were thrown to the north side, but did not go far from the river. Parsons and Churchill had been held about 25 miles from

Camden, ready to move upon that place or in the direction of Minden, as occasion might require.[72]

Steele had gone into our works at Camden with his whole force on the 18th. General Price had been instructed to throw his cavalry into them before Steele's arrival if he felt sure of holding the position, but not to put a force there to be sacrificed. He was instructed at all events to send at least a brigade of cavalry to the north side of the Ouachita for the purpose of cutting off the enemy's supplies from Little Rock and Pine Bluff. Neither direction was followed.

On April 18, Generals Maxey and Marmaduke had fought the enemy (a foraging party about 2,500 strong) at Poison Springs,[73] 12 miles from Camden, dispersing the whole force and capturing a few prisoners, 212 wagons and teams, with 4 pieces of artillery. It was so close to the enemy's main body that we did not have time or opportunity to pick up the prisoners who dispersed in the woods, but contented ourselves with hauling off the artillery and train.[74]

When General Smith arrived at General Price's headquarters and ascertained that no cavalry had been thrown across the Ouachita he dispatched General Fagan with 3,500 men to go, if possible, into Little Rock and Pine Bluff and destroy the depots at those points. The garrisons at both places were understood to be small. General Fagan did not accomplish this great object. He could not get his artillery, of which he had four pieces, across the Saline River at the point where he attempted to cross. On the 23d or 24th,[75] he encountered a force of the enemy about 1,500 strong, in charge of a train at Marks' Mills, on the west side of the Ouachita.[76] He succeeded in capturing all the infantry (1,300); the cavalry (200) escaped. He also captured a four-gun battery and 200 wagons and teams, besides 100 which were burned during the fight. Meanwhile our forces were drawn close around Camden. The works, which had been constructed by us last year, were such as to make it very doubtful whether we could carry the place by assault. Every exertion was made to ascertain the exact amount of subsistence the enemy had, in the hope that he might be starved out and compelled to retreat. A pontoon train had started from Shreveport, but most unfortunately through some misconception of orders was turned back. On the night of the 26th, the enemy, having learned of the capture of his train, evacuated Camden.[77] His rear guard left the place at 4 A.M. on the 27th. Our advance entered at 7. It took us all day and all night to construct a bridge over which the infantry could pass. At sunrise on the morning of the 28th, the troops commenced crossing. The enemy had twenty-six hours' start of us. On the night of the 29th, the head of our infantry was at Tulip, 14 miles from the Saline, at Jenkins' Ferry, and 40 miles from Camden. A brigade of our cavalry was at the Bottom of the Saline, 3 miles from the river. Our rear was at Princeton, 22 miles from Jenkins' Ferry and 32 miles from Camden. The rear of the enemy's column had passed Tulip at 8 o'clock that morning. The Saline Bottom was, however, a quagmire 5 miles wide, and it was possible his trains had not been gotten over. We had but little expectation of getting a fight. Our pontoon train had not come up, and even with it we could not cross the river in face of the enemy. General Fagan had not been heard from for some days. It was hoped he would hear of Steele's retreat and throw himself in his front, thus giving us an opportunity of catching up and attacking him in rear. Here a dispatch was received stating that he (Fagan), after vainly endeavoring to cross the Saline at points lower down, had gone up near Arkadelphia for forage and would cross the Saline at Benton. He had not learned of Steele's retreat. In a vague hope of being able to overtake the enemy's rear guard next morning the troops were rested from dark till 1 o'clock, Churchill and Parsons at Tulip, Walker at Princeton. 8 miles to the rear. At 1 o'clock the column moved forward through deep mud, rain coming down in torrents. At daylight the two divisions were up with the cavalry advance, having marched 52 miles in forty-six hours. Skirmishing commenced and the enemy's pickets were driven in. We could hardly believe there was any large force of the enemy on our side of the river. The firing becoming more general, Churchill's division was thrown forward. I give you a rough sketch of the ground.[78] Dockery's brigade was thrown to the left of a bayou which ran parallel with and very close to the road by which we advanced. It was pushed down toward the Saline, while the other part of the division moved down on the right side. The enemy was soon found in force and Parsons' division was put into action on Churchill's right.[79]

Word was sent back to General Walker to hurry one brigade of his division forward on the road we had come, and to take the other two brigades by a road which turns off to the right 5 miles from the Saline, and was said by our scouts to lead to the enemy's left flank. The battle-field was a boggy marsh covered with timber and considerable undergrowth. The enemy were concealed by the undergrowth and fallen logs, so that our men could scarcely see them at all. Scurry's and Randal's brigades, of Walker's division, moved by the road leading toward the enemy's left. Waul's brigade was held in reserve in rear of Churchill and Parsons. The cavalry brigade was mostly thrown forward as skirmishers. Our troops, I regret to say, did not fight well. Before Walker reached the enemy Parsons'

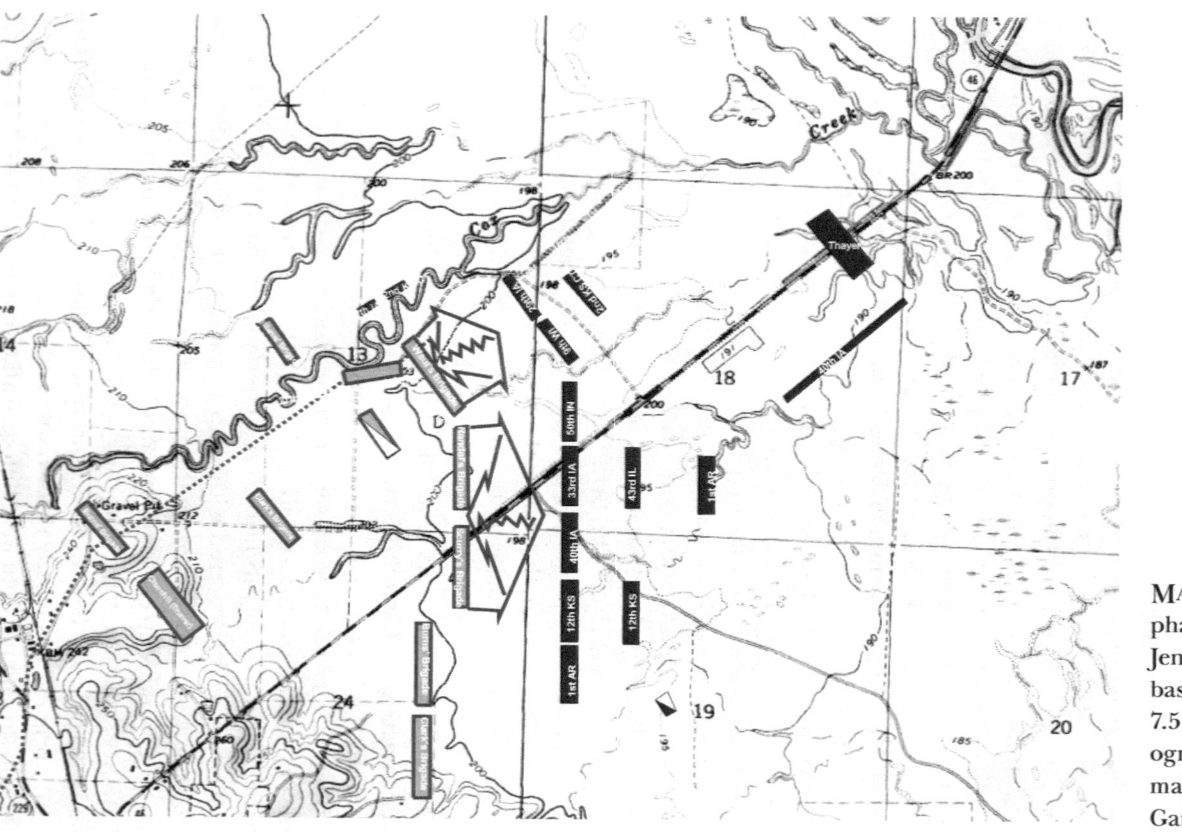

Map 3.2. The final phase of the Battle of Jenkins' Ferry. The base map is the USGS 7.5 minute Leola topographic quadrangle map. Cartography by Gary D. Joiner.

and Churchill's divisions were driven back.[80] They got in confusion and it was impossible for their officers, most of whom are of no earthly account, to do anything with them. The enemy showed little disposition to follow. As soon as Walker's guns were heard off to our right Waul's brigade was pushed forward to support his left, Parsons' division moving in its rear as a support. Waul soon became engaged. The firing was very heavy for about an hour. Our men fired very wildly. Waul's right was slightly overlapped by Walker's left. Waul's troops were repulsed. Randal, in the center, and Scurry, on the right, held their ground, though their troops were in great disorder. Parsons' division did not support Waul as it was intended, but moved somewhere to the right of our line and did no more fighting.

In about an hour from the time Waul's brigade went into action the enemy withdrew along their whole line.[81] Our troops did not follow immediately. They were in great disorder.[82] Churchill's men had been again collected and skirmishers were thrown forward. An hour and a half afterward, when our advance reached the river, about 2 miles from the battleground, the enemy had crossed. They did not take up their pontoon bridge, but punched holes in the boats and left the wagons on this side of the river. I cannot say to which side the victory, as far as the fighting goes, belongs. The forces engaged were about equal. Their severely wounded were left on the field and just on the other side of the river. They compare to our severely wounded as three to two. We lost about 800 killed and Wounded; I suppose that of the enemy to be about 1,200. We did not cross the Saline, for two reasons: First, our men had nothing to eat. The rations issued to them were out the night of the battle and our wagons had not come up, being delayed at Camden by the non-arrival of the pontoon train. Secondly, the incessant rains had so swelled the Saline that it was for four or five days after the next day (which was the earliest we could for the first reason cross) 2 or 3 miles wide, spreading over its bottom in all directions. To campaign permanently beyond the Saline without the establishment of depots of supplies was utterly impossible. When our cavalry got across they found a good many wagons stuck in the mud on the other side. General Fagan, hearing the true state of things while near Arkadelphia the evening before the fight, hurried up to join us. He reached Jenkins' Ferry just after the fight, which closed between 12 and 2 o'clock. He failed to accomplish his mission through circumstances perhaps over which he had no control. The destruction of the stores at Little Rock and Pine Bluff would have ruined the enemy.[83] During this time General Taylor had followed the enemy up very vigorously, capturing and destroying three gun-boats and six or eight transports.[84] He insisted that with Walker's,

Parsons', and Churchill's divisions he could overwhelm Banks, who was now at Alexandria assisting Porter, who was trying to get his gun-boats over the falls. The infantry in Arkansas was immediately put in motion to him, as it seemed possible the enemy might be compelled to abandon or destroy his fleet.[85] Unfortunately for us he built a dam across Red River, by the aid of which, together with a slight rise, he succeeded in getting all his boats off before our troops arrived in force.[86] General Taylor had thrown his forces all around the place and had entirely cut off communication with the river below. There was some severe skirmishing between the enemy and our cavalry, but the latter were always compelled to retire when the enemy came out in heavy force. It was on the river near Fort De Russy that our cavalry captured the two gun-boats above referred to. The Eastport, one of the finest iron-clads in the Western waters, was sunk by the enemy about 50 miles above Alexandria, where she had gotten fast aground.[87] While they were at Alexandria our boats went constantly down as far as Cotile, carrying subsistence and forage.[88] The enemy showed less enterprise than I have ever known them evince. Banks is clearly no commander. Once or twice while he was at Alexandria the posture of our force was such that by a short and comparatively safe movement of 10,000 men he might have insured beyond peradventure the capture of Polignac's division. He must have been in the main aware of the position and strength of our force.[89] Along with the hope of accomplishing his main purpose, he seems to have given up all desire to acquit himself with any credit.

The Yankees left Alexandria about May,[90] after burning two-thirds of the town. Whether it was their intention to burn the whole place, or only some of the public buildings, warehouses, &c., does not clearly appear.[91] My opinion is they did not intend total destruction. The wind was very high and the fire could not be managed. A considerable quantity of stores was destroyed. The gunboats took off some of their armor to lighten them, and ten or twelve heavy guns were burst on the river bank.[92] General Taylor fought them at Moreauville three or four hours and then drew off his force, which was between them and Simsport.[93] Following up their retreat he received a severe repulse at Yellow Bayou, 6 miles from Simsport, from some new troops brought from the Texas coast.[94] This fight occurred on [May 18], and virtually closed the campaign. Before being relieved from command General Taylor had given up his idea of a campaign toward New Orleans, and had ordered all of his infantry back to the vicinity of Alexandria, there to rest and prepare for future operations.[95]

I have given you as clearly as I am able the details of this campaign. I doubt if they will be interesting to you, in view of the great events now transpiring in Virginia and Georgia; but, as I have said, they are data from which you may judge the merits of a case which I am sure will not long fail to be discussed at Richmond. General Taylor has warm supporters there—men who will not be deterred from carrying their point by any scruples of honor or veracity. General Smith's policy and motives, as well as many facts connected with his operations, will be misrepresented. It will doubtless be asserted in the East, as it has already been here, that the movement of troops from Louisiana to Arkansas after the battle of Pleasant Hill was against General Taylor's views and protest. On this point I need only say that General Smith told me immediately after our return from Mansfield, where the decision was made, that General Taylor approved of his plan of moving immediately against Steele. He even selected the troops he wished to go. The plan at first was that he should accompany them.[96] Certainly I never heard a word of his disapproval of the movement until he arrived at Shreveport on his way to Arkansas, and it was determined that he should remain in Louisiana. I have not a shadow of doubt that all the subsequent criticisms and complaints of himself and friends are entirely the results of pique. There seems to be among them a settled determination to place to his credit all the favorable contingencies that might have happened had operations been differently conducted. People will not be content to let well enough alone. They cannot be made to understand that an enemy may sometimes be defeated, but that the most consummate skill cannot insure the capture of his whole force. Nowadays we rarely hear of a fight in which our men have conducted themselves respectably but that there comes along some account of our having the enemy hemmed, cut off, or already bagged.[97] Even sensible men will indulge and encourage this morbid appetite for the incredible. Hence it follows that frequently after a campaign in which the odds have been greatly against us, and during which the mass of the people exposed have been hopeless of the result and ready to take the oath of allegiance to the enemy, these very people, whose miserable cowardice and want of determination are a disgrace to a good cause, find it unaccountable—perfectly outrageous—that the Yankees were not all destroyed. Utter annihilation is generally the only, thing that will at all suffice for these pseudo-savage "stay-at-homes."

I do not think General Smith's late campaign admits a well-grounded criticism. All turns upon a comparison of the objects to be gained by operating against Banks or Steele after Pleasant Hill. That it was impossible for us to pursue Banks immediately—under four or five days—cannot be gainsaid.[98] It was impossible because we did not have transportation for supplies, and impossible because we had been beaten, demoralized, paralyzed in the fight of the 9th.[99] One week was the shortest time in which we could put ourselves before the enemy at Natchitoches.[100] By that time he had constructed strong works in a naturally strong position. Could we, weakened by the loss of 2,500 men and demoralized by defeat, beat the enemy here in a fortified position with a force superior to ours as seven to four?[101] It would seem that pursuit with a small force of men to harass the enemy constantly was more effective than would have been the clumsy and slow pursuit of a larger force destitute of supplies.[102] We were not strong enough to drive the enemy from his position, and if he retreated of his own accord we might as well be actively employed elsewhere—near enough all the time to meet any advance movement of his. A comparison can hardly be instituted between the results flowing from the defeat of Banks and that of Steele. The former rested on his gun-boats. His retreat was comparatively secure, and our pursuit beyond a certain point impossible. Steele was more than 200 miles from Helena, his permanent base of operations and supplies. His communications were through an open pine country, where his trains could be attacked at any point, and with nothing to protect him from being literally devoured by our cavalry could we once break his lines.[103]

The regaining of the capital of the State and the breaking up of the new State government would give us perhaps 8,000 or 10,000 men, while with Steele back upon the Mississippi or his force destroyed our cavalry might now be in Missouri.[104] Unfortunately in this department the immense tracts of desert country and the want of transportation sufficient to carry supplies over them places narrow limits to the possible achievements of our troops, and distance becomes one of the principal elements in a military problem. I contend that our failure to break up Steele's force, if not to capture or destroy it, resulted from an accident which could not be foreseen and had nothing to do with the conception of the plans—I mean General Fagan not putting himself in Steele's front between the Ouachita and the Saline. Even had our pontoon arrived in time we would most probably have fought him on fair ground and signally defeated him. On the other hand, had we become seriously involved with Banks on lower Red River Steele might have advanced and seized Shreveport and Marshall before we could extricate ourselves to meet him. The defeat of our army before Natchitoches would have lost the department. Some persons say the campaign was successful, but it might have been so much better had this or that been done differently. Very true, but it might have been so much worse. That any action will be taken in this matter by the President I have not the least idea, but I have a pride that matters should be understood correctly by the people, and particularly by General Smith's friends. As I should hate for the enemy to get this document I shall await a safe opportunity to send it.

Your affectionate nephew,
E. C[UNNINGHAM].
RICHARD H. CUNNINGHAM,
Lynchburg, Va.
JULY 11, [1864]

P. S.—Dr. Tom has just called and says he will take this for me. He will probably see you and tell you how I am getting on.
E.C. 1.

Notes

1. Joseph Edward Parks, *General Edmund Kirby Smith, C.S.A.* (Baton Rouge, 1954), 137–38.
2. Confederate Lieutenant General Edmund Kirby Smith to his wife, Nov. 30, 1861. Kirby Smith Papers, Southern Historical Collection, Wilson Library, University of North Carolina, Chapel Hill.
3. Parks, *General Edmund Kirby Smith,* 148.
4. General Orders No. 1, Mar. 7, 1863; General Orders No. 3, Mar. 10, 1863. Both were published in the *Shreveport South-Western,* a local newspaper.
5. *OR,* ser. 1, vol. 34 pt. 1:550–60. A footnote at the beginning of this section reads, "This document was captured *in transitu* and was forwarded to the War Department by General [E.R.S.] Canby." No notes or addresses were included in the *OR.*
6. Confederate Major General Richard Taylor, commander of the Department of Western Louisiana.
7. Taylor was removed from command on June 10, 1864, after a series of harsh communications with Lieutenant General Smith, commander of the Department of the Trans-Mississippi. See *OR,* ser. 1, vol. 34, pt. 1:538–48. Also on June 10, the Confederate Congress passed a joint resolution of thanks to Taylor citing his "brilliant successes" at the twin battles of Mansfield and Pleasant Hill. See *OR,* ser. 1, vol. 34, pt. 1:597. Shortly after Cunningham's letter on August 15, Taylor was promoted to the rank of lieutenant general and was ordered to take command of the Department of Alabama, Mississippi, and East Louisiana. See *OR,* ser. 1, vol. 39, pt. 2:777. The District of Western Louisiana included all of the state except that portion lying east of the Mississippi River and north of Lake Pontchartrain. That area, called the Florida Parishes, formed part of the Department of Alabama, Mississippi, and East Louisiana.

8. Lieutenant Cunningham served as aide-de-camp to Smith. He was, despite his protestations, decidedly pro-Smith in regards to his attitude toward General Taylor. The animosity between Smith and Taylor is extremely well documented. See Ludwell H. Johnson, *Red River Campaign: Politics and Cotton in the Civil War* (Kent, OH, 1993), 88–89.
9. General Smith. General Taylor had very close ties with the Confederate government in Richmond. He was the son of former President Zachary Taylor. His sister, Sarah, was Confederate President Jefferson Davis's first wife, who died of a fever three months after their 1835 marriage. The two men remained very close for the remainder of their lives. Taylor received his battlefield training under Major General Thomas J. "Stonewall" Jackson in the Shenandoah Campaign in Virginia prior to requesting a reassignment to Louisiana in 1863. He was very highly regarded within the Confederate High Command. See Dabney H. Maury, "Sketch of General Richard Taylor," *Southern Historical Society Papers* 7 (1879): 343–45; Douglas Southall Freeman, *Lee's Lieutenants: A Study in Command* (New York, 1942–44), 4, 263 n; Johnson, *Red River Campaign*, 88–89; T. Michael Parrish, *Richard Taylor: Soldier Prince of Dixie* (Chapel Hill, 1992), 12–13. The *Southern Historical Society Papers* article was written by Confederate Major General Dabney H. Maury, the commander of the District of Alabama, Mississippi, and East Louisiana immediately prior to Taylor's rise to that position.
10. The two generals had different command styles. Smith believed in the use of elaborate systems of fortifications and Taylor was an adherent of movement and free ranging forces. See Johnson, *Red River Campaign*, 88–89; Gary D. Joiner, *One Damn Blunder from Beginning to End: The Red River Campaign of 1864* (Wilmington, DE, 2003), 19–24, 33–34. The animosity between Smith and Taylor extended to staff officers within the department. Taylor believed Smith's was much too large for the numbers of troops under his command. In his autobiography published shortly before his death, Taylor wrote that Smith's staff was larger than Von Moltke's during the Franco-Prussian War and that "Hydrocephalus at Shreveport produced atrophy elsewhere." See Richard Taylor, *Destruction and Reconstruction: Personal Experiences in the Civil War* (New York, 1995), 153.
11. Smith was relatively certain of the planned invasion as early as January 4, 1864. See *OR*, ser. 1, vol. 34, pt. 2:819.
12. Ibid. Taylor had at least one spy relaying information from New Orleans in mid-January 1864.
13. The Mississippi expedition referred to was Major General William Tecumseh Sherman's Meridian Expedition, which acted as a dress rehearsal for the Atlanta Campaign. Cunningham is incorrect about Northern newspapers reporting on the campaign before it began.

Although several papers dispatched correspondents to accompany the Union column, the first published reports appeared in the *Saint Louis Daily Missouri Republican* on March 26, 1864, and *New York Daily Tribune* on March 28, 1864. The campaign began on March 12. See J. Cutler Andrews, *The North Reports the Civil War* (Pittsburgh, 1985), 497–99.

14. The Cavalry Corps under Brigadier General Tom Green. It was divided into two divisions, one under Green and the other commanded by Brigadier General James P. Major. Taylor ordered well-equipped supply depots established between the Sabine and Red rivers and between Alexandria and Shreveport. These depots contained enough food and supplies for several regiments. See *OR*, ser. 1, vol. 34, pt. 1:561; Joiner, *One Damn Blunder*, 53. See Appendix 1 for the Order of Battle for the Red River Campaign in Louisiana and Arkansas.
15. The Second and Third Brigades of the First Division and the First, Second, and Third Brigades of the Third Division of the 16th Corps and the First and Second Brigades of the Second (Provisional) Division of the 17th Corps. The troops embarked on steamboats at Vicksburg, Mississippi, on March 10 and joined Admiral David Dixon Porter's Mississippi Squadron flotilla at the mouth of the Red River on March 11. See *OR*, ser. 1, vol. 34, pt. 1:34; Joiner, *One Damn Blunder*, 45. One of the most important aspects of Cunningham's narrative is that he recounts the beliefs and rumors of the general staff in Shreveport. Sherman believed that he would lead the expedition until he attended a meeting with General Banks in New Orleans on March 2. See William T. Sherman, *Memoirs of General W. T. Sherman Written by Himself* (New York, 1875), 1:425–26.
16. Fort DeRussy located near the town of Marksville in Avoyelles Parish. The fort was a large antishipping emplacement that was almost complete. Taylor agreed with Smith that the fort should be strengthened in some manner to counter any naval invading force. The site was located on a hairpin turn in the Red River, and, if properly armed and manned, it could thwart gunboats. Confederate engineers designed the fort with forty-foot-thick walls of packed earth that stood twelve feet high, with the entire structure surrounded by a deep, wide ditch. This fort and its outlying works, including a potentially impressive, but hastily constructed, and ultimately fatally flawed wooden obstruction downstream, became the southern anchor of the Confederate defenses on the river. The fortification was to be augmented with a division of infantry, consisting of between 3,000 to 5,000 men, who were to operate in the vicinity, but not be garrisoned at the site. Taylor refused to garrison troops at the fort, believing, correctly, that they would be trapped if they were not mobile. He derogatorily referred to the fort as "Our Red River Gibraltar." See *OR*, ser. 1, vol. 34, pt. 1:574–76; Taylor, *Destruction and Reconstruction*,

148–49. The fort was taken on March 14 by troops under Brigadier General Joseph A. Mower, leading the Third Division (First and Second Brigades) of the 16th Corps. Although Sherman's men arrived with the fleet on March 15, Banks did not arrive by steamboat to Alexandria until March 24 and the main body of infantry arrived from an overland trek on March 25. See *OR*, ser. 1, vol. 34, pt. 1:426–27; Johnson, *Red River Campaign*, 94–99; Joiner, *One Damn Blunder*, 55–59. Cunningham displays a very limited knowledge of actions in Louisiana in this narrative. Writing a month after the conclusion of the campaign, he was apparently not privy to full field reports. He portrays a much greater knowledge of events in the Arkansas portion of the campaign, also known as the Camden Campaign.

17. Brigadier General Andrew Jackson Smith, commanding Sherman's forces of the 16th and 17th Corps.
18. Nine days.
19. Simmesport.
20. Walker is Major General John G. Walker commanding the First or Texas Infantry Division. Brigadier General Thomas N. Waul commanded the First Brigade, Brigadier General Horace Randal led the Second Brigade, and Brigadier General William R. Scurry led the Third Brigade. Brigadier General Jean Jacque Alexandre Alfred Mouton commanded the Second or Louisiana Division. Colonel Henry Gray led the First Brigade. Lieutenant Colonel Robert D. Stone initially led the Second Brigade; Brigadier General (and French prince) Camille Jules Armand Marie, the Prince de Polignac, replaced him. Trinity was the site of Fort Beauregard near Harrisonburg in Catahoula Parish. See Appendix 1.
21. The base was located at Brashear City, now Morgan City, in St. Mary Parish.
22. Brigadier General Saint John R. Liddell.
23. Green's regiments crossed into Louisiana at Logansport during the first week of April and joined Taylor at Pleasant Hill on April 6.
24. The first reports Walker received estimated fifteen thousand to seventeen thousand Union troops and thirty to forty guns. Brigadier General Andrew Jackson Smith actually landed about seventy-five thousand men. Walker had thirty-three hundred combat troops and twelve artillery pieces. See *OR*, ser. 1, vol. 34, pt. 1:34; Johnson, *Red River Campaign*, 91; Taylor, *Destruction and Reconstruction*, 156.
25. Walker evacuated the vicinity of the fort, leaving only a garrison of approximately three hundred men. He burned the Bayou Du Lac bridge to buy time and moved away from Bayou de Glaize, saving his division for the coming fight farther north. See *OR*, ser. 1, vol. 34, pt. 1:305, 338–39.

26. Cunningham is incorrect here. At this point in the campaign, Taylor only had Walker's initial estimates of fifteen thousand to seventeen thousand Union troops facing him. Actually, at the time of the fall of Fort DeRussy, the only Union troops facing Taylor were the ten thousand troops from Sherman's command, which was still greater than a factor of almost three to one over the number of men available to the Confederates below Alexandria.
27. Cunningham is distorting the actual situation. Taylor had no intention of being trapped in Alexandria, a town with no defenses and minimal military value to him. The term "thrown off into the pine hills" implies a rout or hasty retreat. Taylor gathered his force components and searched for a place to fight nearer his supply base at Shreveport.
28. McNutt's Hill is near Henderson's Hill near Bayou Cotile. They are the two higher promontories of the same ridge. Carroll Jones was a free, wealthy Mulatto who owned a grist mill near the village of Hinestown in western Rapides Parish, about twenty-eight miles from Alexandria. Taylor had located one of his large storage depots at Jones's mill. This was his destination, not Alexandria. See Gary B. Mills, *The Forgotten People: Cane River's Creoles of Color* (Baton Rouge, 1977), 215; Joiner, *One Damn Blunder*, 53.
29. Banks had approximately fifteen thousand infantry under Major General William B. Franklin, who commanded the 19th Corps, and five thousand cavalry and recently mounted infantry under Brigadier General Albert L. Lee, commander of the Cavalry Division of the 19th Corps. As stated above, Banks did not reach Alexandria until March 24, and the lead elements of the 19th Corps did arrive until March 25.
30. General Smith was ineffective in obtaining cavalry from the District of Texas, which was also under his command. Once released for deployment in Louisiana, General Green made remarkable time traveling from Hemphill, Texas, to Pleasant Hill, covering the distance in less than three days. The Cavalry Corps left Hemphill on April 5 and arrived in southern DeSoto Parish on April 7.
31. See Liddell's report of actions during the campaign in *OR*, ser. 1, vol. 34, pt. 1:633–37.
32. This action was known as the Skirmish or Battle at Henderson's Hill. Colonel William Vincent led 2nd Louisiana Cavalry. The battery was the 1st Field Battery, Texas Light Artillery (Edgar's Company). The battery lost its guns, four officers, and forty men when captured. Shortly after their arrival from shadowing the Union column heading for Alexandria, Taylor had sent the 2nd Louisiana Cavalry Regiment north to Bayou Rapides about twelve miles north of his location and some twenty-two miles north of Alexandria at the village of Cotile. Their mission was to keep Taylor informed, to skirmish with the lead elements of A. J. Smith's column,

and to try to slow the Union column's progress while Taylor and his two divisions proceeded north to Natchitoches. They arrived on the night of March 21 after riding hard or skirmishing for six straight days with little sleep. They encamped at Henderson's Hill, a toe-shaped ridge which rose above the confluence of Bayou Rapides and Bayou Cotile. The weather turned ugly and cold and they were pelted by rain and hail. Trying to keep dry, Vincent's pickets were not vigilant. A Union force led by General Mower of approximately one thousand men, including a light artillery battery sought to engage Vincent's cavalry, which had been harassing them. Rapidly marching twenty-five miles in seven and a half hours, Mower and his men ended their march in "knee-deep mud." The veteran 8th Wisconsin Volunteer Infantry Regiment led the regiments to the hill. Just before dawn, the exhausted cavalrymen were surprised to see a thousand rifles aimed at them. Mower captured 350 Confederate cavalrymen and 400 horses while suffering no losses. See Johnson, *Red River Campaign,* 96; Taylor, *Destruction and Reconstruction,* 157; Winters, *Civil War in Louisiana,* 330; Richard H. Zeitlin, *Old Abe the War Eagle: A True Story of the Civil War and Reconstruction* (Madison, WI, 1986), 53; Joseph P. Blessington, *The Campaigns of Walker's Texas Division* (New York, 1875), 178; James K. Ewer, *Third Massachusetts Cavalry in the War for the Union* (Maplewood, MA, 1903), 137–39.

33. This was Taylor's plan. The Texas district commander, Major General John Bankhead Magruder, did not release the cavalry corps for use in Louisiana until the first week in April. These regiments, under Brigadier General Thomas Jefferson Green, did not cross into Louisiana until April 6. They fought a delaying action at Wilson's Farm, three miles north of the village of Pleasant Hill on the seventh, giving Taylor the opportunity to prepare his trap three miles south of the Town of Mansfield on April 8.
34. Cunningham is referring to Major General Sterling Price, commander of the District of Arkansas, and Brigadier General John Marmaduke. Spring Hill is located in Hempstead County. Washington was the provisional capital of Confederate Arkansas.
35. Cunningham is referring to Brigadier General William L. Cabell and Brigadier General Samuel B. Maxey. Paraclifta was the county seat of Sevier County. Fort Smith was the headquarters of the Frontier Division of the Union Seventh Corps based in Little Rock.
36. Union Brigadier General John M. Thayer commanded the Frontier Division.
37. The two columns did not join at Arkadelphia. Thayer was late; apparently, he got lost south of Hot Springs and missed his rendezvous. The two columns joined on April 9 as the Battle of Pleasant Hill was being fought in Louisiana. Neither column, of course, knew about the events

in Louisiana. For a full treatment of the Camden Campaign, see Joiner, *One Damn Blunder,* 123–36; Edwin C. Bearss, *Steele's Retreat From Camden and the Battle of Jenkins Ferry* (Little Rock, 1990).

38. General Cabell, who commanded a brigade under Brigadier General James F. Fagan's cavalry division. General Marmaduke commanded a separate cavalry division. These two divisions were the primary operational units for the Confederates in southern Arkansas.

39. General Maxey, who commanded a third cavalry division. This unit operated in the Indian Territory (Oklahoma) based at Fort Towson on the Red River. It kept watch on Union Frontier Division based at Fort Smith, Arkansas. Maxey's cavalry division was divided into two brigades, Gano's Brigade and the Second Indian (Choctaw) Brigade under Colonel Tandy Walker. Cunningham was incorrect in his geography. Laynesport was the oldest town in Little River County, Arkansas, located on the Red River near the Oklahoma boundary. It was on the old immigrant road into Texas.

40. Washington, located in Hempstead County, was the provisional capital of Confederate Arkansas. Fulton, also located in Hempstead County, sits at the northeastern turn of the Great Bend of the Red River as it flows westerly out of Texas and turns southerly into Louisiana. Fulton was the site of the northernmost fortifications on the Red River as part of the outer defense perimeter of Shreveport. It was also the northernmost navigable point on the river for year-round steamboat traffic. Jefferson, located in Marion County, Texas, is located on Big Cypress Bayou, a western tributary of Caddo Lake. Marshall, located in Harrison County, is located about forty miles west of Shreveport. Both Jefferson and Marshall were the sites of Confederate military manufacturing and storage sites. Cunningham is describing a supposition about Steele's intent. There is no evidence in the record that asserts a movement into eastern Texas and bypassing Shreveport. Steele's initial plan was to move southwest from Little Rock and approach the Ouachita River somewhere between Hot Springs and El Dorado. From there, he would descend to Monroe, Louisiana. It was a straightforward line of travel devoid of Confederate units until he reached Louisiana. If he did not cross the Ouachita River earlier, he would do so at Monroe and follow the uncompleted bed of the Southern Pacific Railroad west in an almost straight line to the Red River. He would cross few streams until he reached the Red River opposite Shreveport. If he crossed north of Shreveport, he would be able to approach from the same side of the Red River. If he approached via the railroad bed, his artillery could harass the town while Banks attacked from the south. Probably to solve potential political problems, Steele changed his mind. He decided to veer more to the southwest to Arkadelphia and then

to Washington, about seventy miles north of Shreveport. He decided to gather forces from two locations and meet at Arkadelphia and then move south to Shreveport.

41. Cunningham is overemphasizing the important of the Texas facilities at the expense of Shreveport. He here lays the groundwork to support General Smith's later actions. Shreveport was the gateway to Texas, the headquarters of the Trans-Mississippi Department, and the location of foundries, sawmills, warehouse, and a navy yard. By 1864, the navy yard had built the ironclad CSS *Missouri,* repaired the high speed ram CSS *Webb* and the tinclad CSS *Grand Duke,* and, most important, it had produced five submarines, sisters of the CSS *Hunley.* All of the outlying factories, powder mills, and warehousing facilities served Shreveport. See Joiner, *One Damn Blunder,* 1–31.
42. Brigadier General Thomas James Churchill succeeded General Price as commander of the division. It was, peculiarly, subdivided into small divisions. Brigadier General James C. Tappan led the First Division, composed of Arkansas regiments. Brigadier General Mosby M. Parsons led the Second Division, composed by Missouri regiments.
43. See note 28.
44. Cunningham is continuing to make a case for General Smith's actions. Taylor had pleaded with Smith to release the Arkansas and Missouri troops to him to fight Banks and then go to Arkansas and fight Steele. Smith either could not or would not make up his mind. After a frustrating meeting with General Smith on April 6, Taylor seized the initiative to prepare for the coming battle. He was furious with the commanding general for not specifically allowing him to fight the battle at the time and place of his choosing and with all the forces available. During early April, as Smith vacillated, Taylor wrote his commander concerning the need to do *something,* "Action, prompt, vigorous action, is required. While we are deliberating the enemy is marching. King James lost three kingdoms for a mass. We may lose three States without a battle." See *OR,* ser. 1, vol. 34, pt. 1:522. Smith sent the two divisions, not to Mansfield but to the college town of Keachi, about a forty-five-mile march from the battlefield. When finally released, the two divisions rapidly marched to the battlefield but were too late to participate and would have been too exhausted if they had arrived in time. Cunningham's description of the road forking to Shreveport and Marshall is also somewhat incorrect. At Mansfield, the single road split into three segments, offering the enemy a choice of three roads to Shreveport. The eastern road would allow the Union column to link up with the navy. The other two roads also posed problems for the Confederates. The western road passed through the Wallace Bayou swamp, and the center road stopped at a ferry landing

with no place for the Confederates to maneuver. Taylor had no other clear choice for his stand. There was no direct road from Mansfield to Marshall, Texas. See Taylor, *Destruction and Reconstruction,* 159; U.S. War Department, *Atlas to Accompany the Official Records of the Union and Confederate Armies* (Washington, 1891–95), Plate LII.

45. Cunningham ignores the fact that the battle was fought on the afternoon of April 8.
46. The Cavalry Corps under General Green was released for service in Louisiana about April 5. It left Hemphill, Texas, and crossed into Louisiana near Logansport on April 6. After a brief rest in Keachi, the Texas cavalry found Taylor near Mansfield. Taylor sent them south along the Shreveport-Natchitoches stagecoach road to delay the Union column and buy time for the Rebel forces to gather. Green fought a delaying action at Wilson's Farm just north of the village of Pleasant Hill on April 7. For the remainder of that day and the morning of the eighth, Green slowed the Union column as it snaked north buying the needed time for Taylor to organize his forces three miles south of Mansfield. See Joiner, *One Damn Blunder,* 86–95.
47. This is incorrect. Richard Taylor was on the field and directed the placement of troops. Cunningham relayed the initial news the courier brought from Mansfield but did not correct that bad information by receipt of another courier just hours later. Taylor had asked for permission in the late evening of April 7 to attack on the eighth, and General Smith did not reply. As the fighting was winding down, Taylor received the reply to his letter to Smith from the previous night. Smith told Taylor to avoid a general engagement. Taylor sent the courier back to Shreveport with a message for the commanding general: "Too late, sir, the battle is won." Sarah H. Dorsey, *Recollections of Henry Watkins Allen* (New York, 1866), 263; William Henry King diary, Texas State Archives, Austin, copy in the collection of the editor; Joiner, *One Damn Blunder,* 103.
48. Brigadier General J. J. A. Alfred Mouton led the charge with the Louisiana troops. The Texas Division under General Walker followed. Green's Cavalry Corps was attached as outer portions of both wings and attacked concurrently with them. Cunningham's version suggests that a small contingent attacked and was then reinforced when it was overwhelmed. This was not the case. See chap. 1.
49. This is a correct account to this point.
50. Four batteries, all saw action. The batteries were Captain Ormand F. Nims's 2nd Massachusetts Battery with six guns, Captain H. H. Rottakan's 6th Missouri Horse Artillery Battery with two guns, the 1st Indiana Battery with six guns, and the Chicago Mercantile Battery with six guns.
51. Cunningham is describing the third phase of the battle, and he is reasonably accurate. See Joiner, *One Damn Blunder,* 93–104.

52. Taylor put the loss of Union wagons as high as 250. Union materiel losses in the battle were at least 156 wagons, possibly as many as 250, and approximately 1,000 horses and mules. See Richard Irwin, *History of the Nineteenth Army Corps* (New York, 1892), 306; *OR*, ser. 1, vol. 34, pt. 1:452; Taylor, *Destruction and Reconstruction*, 164; Johnson, *Red River Campaign*, 140–41.
53. Union General A. J. Smith and his two divisions were detached from Sherman's command for this expedition. The Provisional Division of the 17th Corps was aboard transports guarding the Mississippi River Squadron vessels under Rear Admiral David Dixon Porter. At the time of the Battle of Mansfield, they were with the lead elements of the flotilla between Grand Ecore and Loggy Bayou. A. J. Smith, with approximately seventy-five hundred troops, was encamped at Pleasant Hill because the Union column had bunched up due to the fighting and the entire force was using a single route of approach.
54. The Union forces were not in line of battle. General Banks did not believe that Taylor would or could pursue him. Most of Smith's men were kept south of the village of Pleasant Hill and were not told to form up. When the battle began, they formed up on their own accord. The 19th Corps held the road and village, but were placed piecemeal with no formal line; some actually faced away from the Confederate line of attack. As the battle unfolded, Banks was still debating whether or not to make another attempt on Shreveport.
55. The 13th Corps, which had taken the brunt of fighting the previous day, was ordered to Natchitoches, but some of its elements remained at Pleasant Hill.
56. The charge by the Missouri and Arkansas troops began in good order; however, as the battle plan dictated, the two divisions, advancing abreast, entered dense woods. They were to march approximately one mile and then wheel to the left, placing them behind the 19th Corps. The divisions became disoriented, wheeled too quickly, and came out into the open to the left of Smith's 16th Corps. They received heavy casualties in the engagement. The two sides wheeled in place, and after three to four hours of fighting, the battle ended in a draw.
57. These two sentences clearly illustrate Cunningham's lack of knowledge of events in Louisiana. His contradictory statements attempt to cover all possibilities. Walker's Division was not in great confusion at the end of the battle. The battle resulted in a tactical tie.
58. Both sides withdrew a short distance but remained on the far edges of the battlefield. The Confederates occupied part of the field the next day and tended to their wounded. For the second time in two days, Banks left his dead and many of his wounded on the field.

59. Polignac, commanding the Louisiana Division, encamped in a large field west of Pleasant Hill. This was the assembly area for the attack. The three divisions under Walker, Parsons, and Churchill encamped just north of Wilson's Farm, the scene of fighting two days before.
60. Cunningham is making excuses for General Smith's decision to take three divisions away from Taylor and operate against Steele in Arkansas. Although all three divisions received heavy casualties, their actions in Arkansas prove that Cunningham's assertion is baseless.
61. Cunningham is closer to the true location of the Union gunboats than any other period writer. He may have been guessing, but the advance units of the flotilla reached north of Loggy Bayou, perhaps as many as four or five miles.
62. Admiral Porter noted that the fleet carried a total of 210 heavy guns to support the army. See U.S. War Dept., *Official Records of the Union and Confederate Navies in the War of the Rebellion,* 31 vols. (Washington, DC, 1895–1929), vol. 26:747–48.
63. The three divisions diverted to Arkansas certainly would have been used to bottle up the Union force when it stupidly entered Cane River Island. All of Banks's force was, for a short time, stranded on a stretch of ground between Cane River and Red River, with steep banks and only two known points of entry and exit. The battle of Monett's Ferry proved how close this situation actually was.
64. Taylor never contemplated this.
65. Steele had to receive a direct order from Grant to even participate in the campaign. His desire was to offer limited cooperation. He certainly had no plans for a deep thrust invasion into eastern Texas. Bearss, *Steele's Retreat from Camden.*
66. This is Cunningham's rendition of the argument expressed by Smith to Taylor.
67. After the battle of Pleasant Hill, Smith met with Taylor to discuss what had transpired. Taylor offered to lead his infantry against Steele until that Union column was either destroyed or forced to retreat to Little Rock. He would then return to Louisiana to fight Banks with both his and Price's forces. Smith agreed to this arrangement, and on April 14 Taylor sent three divisions to Shreveport. These were the divisions of Walker, Churchill (commanded by Tappan), and Parsons. Polignac's small and hard-fought division was sent south to track Banks and make him think that Taylor was still in pursuit. See *OR*, ser. 1, vol. 34, pt. 1:571–72. Taylor rode to Shreveport the next day to lead his three divisions north and learned that Steele had turned his column toward Camden, about 110 miles from Shreveport. Smith told Taylor that he, not Taylor, would pursue Steele. Smith then dismissed Taylor from Arkansas action, telling

him that he could either remain in Shreveport or harass Banks at Grand Ecore. Taylor, livid, returned to his troops. In their discussion, Smith had promised Taylor that he would return his infantry through Minden to Campti when Steele posed no threat. Smith marched his men out of Shreveport on April 16. Walker was sent to Minden, thirty miles to the east, and then north on the Fort Towson Road to guard against Steele's effort to link up with Banks. Walker marched his men another thirty miles, making a rapid march of sixty miles. Smith marched north to Calhoun, Arkansas, only a few miles from Price's position. Smith planned to block any chance of Steele's combining with Banks or Porter and planned to destroy the northern column. This would leave Little Rock and even eastern Arkansas devoid of Union presence. He could then grandly march into Little Rock as the conquering hero. Steele reached Camden the same day Smith left Shreveport. Taylor, *Destruction and Reconstruction,* 180; *OR,* ser. 1, vol. 34, pt. 1:481, 486–87, 534, pt. 2, 766; and Blessington, *Campaigns of Walker's Texas Division,* 243–44.

68. If Taylor's plan had been followed, Banks's army would have been trapped on the completely flat Cane River Island, not within the defenses of Grand Ecore or the soon to be fortified area surrounding Alexandria. Cunningham's argument lacks validity.
69. Of the three routes and distances traversed in one day, Walker's "Greyhounds" of the First or Texas Division were the most remarkable. Minden is located thirty miles east of Shreveport. After fighting in both battles, the Texans performed a 109-mile march from April 10 to April 20, including a three-day rest from the seventeenth to the morning of the twentieth. Blessington, *Campaigns of Walker's Texas Division,* 241–44.
70. Banks wanted Steele to do this after the Battle of Pleasant Hill, but by then Steele was in no position to link up with Banks. *OR,* ser. 1, vol. 34, pt. 3:267–68.
71. This was General Liddell, who commanded the subdistrict of North Louisiana. This cavalry force operated between the Red and Mississippi rivers. The Union gunboats were the *Eastport, Champion No. 3,* and *Champion No. 5.* Rebel forces, particularly Cornay's battery and riflemen from Polignac's division, carried out this action on both sides of the river. A mine, laid by the CSS *Missouri,* sunk the *Eastport.* Also heavily damaged in these actions were the *Cricket* and *Juliet.* U.S. War Dept., *Official Records of the Union and Confederate Navies in the War of the Rebellion,* 31 vols. (Washington, DC, 1895–1929), vol. 26:26, 72–77 (hereinafter cited as *ORN,* followed by volume number and page reference); David D. Porter, *The Naval History of the Civil War* (New York, 1886), 523–24; and Joiner, *One Damn Blunder,* 147–50. See Appendix 2 for a list of Union vessels in the campaign.

72. Smith gathered his three divisions at Calhoun, Arkansas.
73. Battle of Poison Spring. There are numerous accounts of some Black Union soldiers being massacred in this battle. John M. Harrell, "Arkansas," in *Confederate Military History,* 12 vols. (Atlanta, 1899), 10:249–53.
74. Marmaduke captured 170 wagons, burned 28 others, and took 100 prisoners. Poison Spring was one of the greatest Rebel victories of the Camden Campaign, the other being the Battle of Marks' Mill. *OR,* ser. 1, vol. 34, pt. 1:744–45, 848–49; Harrell, "Arkansas," in *Confederate Military History,* 10:250.
75. April 25.
76. Fagan's Cavalry Division. Fagan, having insufficient numbers of troops to the attempt the capture of Little Rock or Bluff, was also given unclear orders. He moved from El Dorado, on the Ouachita River, north to Marks' Mill to attempt to cut off Steele's supply train. This action contributed to Steele's decision to abandon an attack on Shreveport and to return to Little Rock. *OR,* ser. 1, vol. 34, pt. 1:668, 712–13, 789, 794, 835–36; and John N. Edwards, *Shelby and His Men; or The War in the West* (Cincinnati, 1867), 279.
77. At the time of the Union evacuation of Camden, Smith had three divisions of infantry and two large cavalry forces to the west and south of Steele's column. The Rebel forces outnumbered the combined Union forces, who were extremely low on supplies. Steele did not exhibit any intention to either confront or circumvent Smith's positions. His evacuation of Camden was the beginning of a retreat via the shortest path to Little Rock. Smith knew this. The question therefore has often been asked, "Why did Smith pursue?" The threat to Shreveport from the north had ended, and Taylor was in desperate need of the men to trap Banks north of Alexandria. Most historians of the campaign believe that Smith was trying to attain a measure of glory while operating against a retreating, inferior force. Bearss, *Steele's Retreat from Camden;* Johnson, *Red River Campaign,* 170–205; and Joiner, *One Damn Blunder,* 123–36.
78. No sketch survived with the report in the *OR.*
79. See map 3.2.
80. Ibid.
81. Ibid.
82. In this needless attack against an enemy force that already sent its supply train, artillery, and cavalry across a swollen river, Smith and Price committed their forces piecemeal. The three brigade commanders of the Texas Division were wounded—Horace Randal and William Scurry, mortally. *OR,* ser. 1, vol. 34, pt. 1:801–2, 829–30; and Compte de Paris, *History of the Civil War in America,* 4 vols. (Philadelphia, 1875–88), 4: 557.

83. Fagan had too few men and inadequate orders to fulfill this mention. Cunningham's rendition is a justification for the argument put forth by General Smith to explain why the Arkansas portion of the campaign did not succeed in a strategic victory for the Confederates.
84. These were the gunboats *John Warner, Signal,* and *Covington,* and the transports *Emma* and *City Belle.* Prior to this, near the mouth of the Cane River, the Rebels sank the pump boats, *Champion No. 3* and *Champion No. 5,* and seriously damaged the tinclad gunboats *Juliet* and *Cricket.* See Taylor, *Destruction and Reconstruction,* 184–86; *ORN* 26:26, 102, 113–14, 117–19, 123, 134; *OR,* ser. 1, vol. 34, pt. 1:475; and Joiner, *One Damn Blunder,* 161–63.
85. Smith released the three divisions to Taylor after the fiasco at Jenkins' Ferry, but the three battle-weary units were unable to return to action south of Alexandria before the Union force exited the Red River. Taylor never forgave Smith for taking the three vital divisions. The animosity between the two men escalated into the events described earlier in this narrative. See note 3.
86. Bailey's Dam. Joiner, *One Damn Blunder,* 159–68.
87. The USS *Eastport* struck a mine less than two miles below Grand Ecore.
88. This is one of only two references to the Confederate navy replenishing supplies to Taylor's forces as far south as northern Rapides Parish. The other is the William Henry King diary. King states that as he marched south along the banks of Red River, he saw the wrecks of the *New Falls City* and the *Osceola.* Confederate engineers had cut the giant vessel in half and moved the two portions out of the main channel. The *Osceola* was a transport used by the Confederates on the Red River. Since no Union reports refer to the *Osceola,* the vessel must have met her fate after Porter and his small flotilla retreated from the wreck site of the *New Falls City.* Cotile was a steamboat landing in northern Rapides Parish. It was used by both sides during the campaign.
89. There is no evidence that Banks had any indication of the number of men Taylor had available against him.
90. May 13.
91. Historians are still not certain of the events leading to the burning of Alexandria. Banks certainly did not intend for this to happen because it would signal Taylor that his army was on the move. A. J. Smith's men had a penchant for incendiary activities. They had practiced "Total War" in the Meridian (Mississippi) Campaign immediately prior to the Red River Expedition. Banks ordered about five hundred cavalry to guard the town from burning by Smith's men, but reports at the time suggest that these guardians were in the middle of the torching and perhaps started it out of anger. See *Official Report to the Conduct of Federal Troops in Western Loui-*

siana, during the Invasions of 1863 and 1864, Compiled from Sworn Testimony under Direction of Governor Henry Watkins Allen (Shreveport, 1865), 72–73, 79; G. P. Whittington, "Rapides Parish, Louisiana—A History," *Louisiana Historical Quarterly* 18 (1935): 26–28, 31–32, 37; and *JCCW*, 335.

92. The action was done to lighten the vessels to get them over Bailey's Dam.
93. Battle of Mansura on May 16.
94. Skirmish at Moreauville and Yellow Bayou on May 17 and the Battle of Yellow Bayou on May 18. Cunningham is mistaken about the Union force. In all the actions from May 16 to May 18, the fighting was led by A. J. Smith's men of the 16th Corps. The new troops from the Texas Coast Cunningham refers to are the men of the Brigadier General Michael Lawler's Brigade of the First Division of the 19th Corps, summoned by Banks to join him at Alexandria when he thought he might make another attempt at Shreveport and to replenish his losses suffered to date. The First Division was led by Major General John A. McClernand, who upon arrival assumed command of the 13th Corps. These troops saw no action in the campaign.
95. See note 3.
96. See note 39.
97. Taylor had such a chance when Banks foolishly moved his army onto Cane River Island on the retreat from Natchitoches. The three missing divisions would have blocked the only exits on the south end of the island, the Confederate cavalry was pursuing the rear guard of the column, and Porter's gunboats, operating in increasingly low water, were hard pressed by Confederate artillery and trying to escape to Alexandria. This was the best opportunity during the campaign for Taylor to trap and capture Banks's army and capture or force the destruction of the bulk of the Mississippi River Squadron. He simply had too few men to complete the mission.
98. This is incorrect. Taylor made plans the night of April 8 for pursuit and included the plans to trap the fleet, which led to the Battle of Blair's Landing. Letter from Taylor to Major General John G. Walker, April 9, 1864, in Walker Papers, Wilson Library, Southern Historical Collection at University of North Carolina, Chapel Hill.
99. Belief at the time was that the Battle of Pleasant Hill was a tie. No Confederate source states that it was a defeat. Cunningham was not in Louisiana at the time and this indicates that he is reflecting the opinions of Smith.
100. This is incorrect. See note 89.
101. Taylor never planned to attack the strong Union fortifications at Grand Ecore and later at Alexandria. He wanted to starve them out, cut off their supply lines, and destroy their ability to retreat.

102. Taylor had prepositioned supply depots in several locations in central and western Louisiana. He was not destitute for supplies. In addition to these stores, he had at least 150 wagons from the cavalry train.
103. A similar comparison can be made of Banks's position, moving through a destitute land since the Mississippi Marine Brigade had torched every house and barn as they left the Red River Valley. Flanked by swamp and rivers, Banks had little choice in route. The distance to Baton Rouge was comparable to Steele and Helena.
104. This was attempted later in 1864 with abysmal results.

Private Julius L. Knapp, U.S.A.: A Union Soldier's Point of View

Edited by Gary D. Joiner and Jimmy H. Sandefur

THE DIARY OF PRIVATE JULIUS L. KNAPP[1] IS ONE OF THE FEW from a Union soldier who fought in the rearguard action following the Battle of Mansfield. Knapp was a senior musician with the 116th New York Volunteer Infantry Regiment. The portion of his diary included here covers March 1, 1864, through May 31, 1864. It provides an excellent account of life in the Union 19th Corps in the Trans-Mississippi during the period. This diary is the only reliable source for information concerning the aftermath of the Battle of Mansfield and the possible motives of Nathaniel P. Banks in ordering a retreat to Pleasant Hill while he still held the highest ground on the battlefield and had adequate reserves with which to fight the next day.

Julius L. Knapp Diary: March–May 1864

MARCH 1ST (in camp near the town of Franklin in St. Mary Parish, Louisiana)

The first day of this month passes a very disagreeable one it being very rainy and cold there is no drill and the men keep in their quarters the most of the time.

2ND

Weather fine but rather cool mail arrives from the north in the morning. I get two letters from home and one from Manilla. we raise a Splendid flag pole at night in the little grove where our camp is Situated.

3RD

we form line at 9 A.M. and march about two miles through the village of Franklin and have Brigade drill Col. Soane[2] in command of the Brigade.

4TH

We receive orders to turn in the knapsacks the boys busy the most of them in packing and turning them in weather fine

5TH

Company drill in the forenoon and no drill in the afternoon the men policing the camp and cleaning up for inspection.

6TH

inspection in the morning at ten A.M. 153rd N.Y.V.[3] arrive here from washington weather very warm[4]

7TH

Company drill in the forenoon and Battallion in the afternoon. Major Sizer goes to Division Headquarters.[5]

8TH

Brigade Drill in the forenoon at ten A.M. on the commons near town the band arrives from New Orleans in the afternoon.

9TH

Rainy and muddy all day no drill on account of the weather General Banks arrives from New Orleans and takes up his headquarters in Franklin[6]

10TH

Rainy in the morning mail arrives in the afternoon with letters from home Battallion Drill in the afternoon by Capt. Kinney.[7]

11TH

Weather dull in the morning three companies turn in their guns and get Springfield Muskets. Dress Parade at 5 P.M. with 8 companies.

12TH

Brigade drill in the forenoon Col. Love commanding the Brigade the afternoon is taken up in cleaning up the camp.[8]

13TH

Brigade Inspection at ten A.M. no Regimental inspection as usual. Col Seave[9] Inspector Leiut Clark inspected the arms of our company

14TH

Dolan and myself are busy all day in fixing drums and the Base drum of the 153rd Receive orders to march in the afternoon on the next day with two days rations in haversacks.

15TH

The morning of the 15 of March dawns upon us with a warm Sun and everything Seems prosperous on our first days march of the red river campaign[10] the men are in fine Spirits and every thing is in a lively mood as we pass through the village of franklin and Start out for a march of one hundred and fifty miles through the garden of Louisana called the teche country to the famous town of Alexanderia[11] Situatied on red river about one hundred miles from its mouth in a fine and flourishing country. the cavalry Start from franklin on the fourteenth and are hear they are at the village of New Iberia on the morning of our departure from camp. the first Brigade of the first division of the 19th Corps. takes the advance the Second Brigade Second in line and third Brigade in the rear this constitutes the troops that Start from this point and how they are Situated on the line of march. the first day we march 12 miles and bivouac for the night near a large plantation well Supplied with poultry and pork. and I will assure you the boys did not want for meat rations on the next days march.

16TH

Form lines at 7 A.M. and arrive at the village of New Iberia and halt for an hour in the town and then move on to camp Platt and biouvac for the night the distance being 17 miles this camp is noted as being an old rebel camp the barracs remaining on the ground yet the camp is Situated in the centre of a large plain and upon the border of a fine lake called Leak[12] Tech well known through the most of the State as hunting ground wild ducks geese and barrows kinds of fish always found here in large quantities and on the plain there is any quantity of wild cattle, hogs and horses. making Sport for men used to throwing the lasso the boys go out here and Shoot Some cattle and hogs Supplying them with meat rations for the next day the mail arrives to us late in the evening and the men rest more contented after hearing from home

17TH

We form line at 7 A.M. and renew the march our march to day is across a vast plain nothing visible to attract our attention except now and then a drove of cattle or horses flying across the plain appearing to be astonished at the Sight of so many blue bellyed yankees as the rebels term us. we march 16 miles and arrive at Vermillion biyou and encamp for the night the men being very tired Co. I is on picket and does not come off untill the next morning

18TH

On the 4th day of our march we form line at 5 A.M. and cross Vermillion biyou on a pontoon bridge pass through the village of Vermilionville[13] about 8 A.M. the Ladies of this town look upon us with contempt for the deed the yankee army did on their campaign in October 1863 in that vacinity robing hen roosts taking their eggs but the yankee boys only laugh at their attempts to ridicule them, we march four miles beyond carrion crow biyou[14] and bivouac for the night a distance of 17 miles

19TH

The Sun Shines out upon us on the morning of the 19th with more than usual Splender we form lines at 6 A.M. and Set out upon the march arrived at [?][15] this town is noted as a most notorious rebel place and all inhabitants closing their window blinds to prevent seeing the yankees but there was a little incident occured while passing through the town which I must not forget to mention. Upon a varanda of one of the houses where the whole army passed Stand a young lady well dressed and fine appearing with a Small union flag in her hand waving it at the troops as they passed with all the gentleness of the female for that for can describe and you can easily imagine to yourself the excitiment that prevailed in the ranks for as every regiment passed cheer after cheer are given for the loyal lady of [?] and the Stars and Stripes but whether this lady was truly a loyal lady or only doing this to See how the Soldiers would greet Such a lady I leave you to judge.[16] five miles from Oppalousas[17] is a little town called little washington[18] this is also a rebel nest and with its just deserts would be burned to the ground. we marched one mile beyond this town and bivouaced for the night on the catawbial biyou.[19] distance of days march 18 miles

20TH

a day of rest is approved of and the men do Some washing for themselves preparatory to another march. Some of the boys go out in the morning and get a plenty of poultry. Sugar, and Sweet potatoes to make them a number of good meals while we lay here about 8 or ten indians Seemingly wild come to our camp perfectly naked and nearly Starved the boys gave them clothes and Something to eat freely and with a thousand thanks for our kindness they returned to their home in the Swamp.

21ST

warm Weather rainy and dull in the morning but because the march is not postponed we form line at 7 A.M. and march 12 miles mud about four inches deep it commences to rain about three oclock in the afternoon and proves a very miserable night we go into bivouac just at night or rather lay down in the mud untill morning.

22ND

Very tired from the day befores march and no night rest we form line at 7 A.M. and march 16 miles in the mud and encamped for the night near the village of homesville[20] we bivouaced near a large swamp and before we had been in camp long the boys discovered about three hundred hogsheads of Sugar Secreted in this Swamp So that the yankees could not destroy it but it had not been discovered long before the boys had the camp pretty well Supplied with Sugar and after our Supper and a molasses pull we laid down for the night.

23RD

Weather fine form line at 7 A.M. and march 16 miles and encamp for the night within one half mile of Cheneyville[21] this village is Situated in as fine a country as ever was seen by *human* beings and is noted for its ancient buildings. during our day of march we passed by the plantation where the distinguised Solamon Northrop[22] was owned, and every thing looks about the Same as he States in the history of his life.

24TH

We have a very hard days march the roads being very muddy and the rain falling quite fast the most of the day but however under these disadvantages we march 15 miles and bivouac for the night within 14 miles of Alexandria.

25TH

Very mudy in the morning but we form line at 7 A.M. and after a march of Seven miles find our pickets out from Alexandria we continue our march and about 12 A.M. find our infantry pickets and after a parade through town we go into camp near the city the men being pretty well worn out from the long and rapid march

26TH

Company I comes off picket at noon we [?] the pay roll in the afternoon but do not untill the next day Col. have returned to the regiment mail arrives in the afternoon the boys improve the most of the day in washing and cleaning up their clothes

27TH

There is an inspection in the morning at 7 oclock the regiment is payed two months pay in the course of the day and the boys have until 5 P.M. to their own amusement they go down town and get tobacco and other necesaries for a long march the 16th and 17th Army Corps joins us here also the 13th corps. They leave Alexandria today for Shreveport and a detachment of gun boats goes up the river with them they have a hard Skirmish before night taking about three hundred prisoners and 2 pieces of artillery the cavalry getting in the rebel rear and the infantry on their front with red river on their flank the Johneys have to Surrender.[23]

28TH

Rainy and mudy in the morning prospects of no march but it clears away about 9 A.M. and we form line and at ten are follering up the 13th 16th and 17th Corps the roads are very muddy but our being behind the rest we march 18 miles before halting for night this is the hardest days march Since our Starting from camp at franklin.

29TH

1st Brigade in the rear the roads being So bad that the train can only move about Seven miles and we encamp for the night in the pine woods of old Louisana

30TH

Nothing Stiring in the morning we think perhaps we move but the order comes at 11 A.M. for to move 6 miles and go into camp arrive at camp at 2 P.M.

31ST

We break camp at 7 A.M. and march 5 miles wait an hour for the wagon train to cross the pontoon bridge over cane river and then continue on our Journey we pass through Clouterville[24] about 3 P.M. and march five miles beyond and encamp for the night on the bank of cane river getting into camp early the boys make a reconnaisence for poultry and find them plenty have a good Supper and breakfast and are in good Spirits for the next days march. End of 3rd Month

4th Month of Years diary, 1864

APRIL 1ST

We form line at 6 A.M. and renew to march and after crossing the river on pontoon we wait about two hours for the wagon train to pass and then continue our Journey to day we travel where the union army has never passed before and our line of march is lined with cotton gins filled with cotton and the darkies greet us along the way with unbounded joy, exclaiming lord bless de yankees dey come at last. We free now, and where am you all goan. these and Similar remarks we hear from them all as we pass the plantations we have the hardest days march we have yet had the weather being extremely warm and the roads very dusty.

2ND

we get up in the morning and cook our breakfast and form line at 8.20 A.M. and after a march of Six miles arrive at the village of Nachintoch[25] and go into bivouac about one mile beyond town on an old branch of red river[26] handy to water and wood and we hear we are to Stay in this camp for a few days.

3RD

There is no marching to day the men are ordered to wash their cloths and prepare for another march there is a forage train went out in the morning the boys get a good Supply of poultry Sweet potatoes ham, and Sugar and we live high for a few days I go down to the village in the afternoon this is a very nice little town the buildings being mostly brick, but built after ancient Style, the inhabitants exhibit a Stony desire for the union army to hold posession of the town being tired of being ruled by the powers of Jeff D. and Co. there is not an able bodied man to be seen in the town they all having been drafted into the rebel army we hear the rebel army at this time is laying at pleasant hill,[27]

4TH

There is nothing of importance going on in camp to day the wagon train goes to grand Ecure[28] and returns with ten days rations we hear the 16th and 17th Corps, are landing at grand Ecure to join us on Starting from this point,[29] we have a mail in the afternoon

5TH

All quiet in camp in the forenoon and in the afternoon we have inspection at three oclock, and at 5 we are reviewed by General Banks. we hear in the evening that we are to move in the morning. the cavalry Start from Nachintoch and advance twenty miles.

6TH

We form line at 6.50 and commence the advance the 19th and 13th Corps taking the direct road to pleasant hill.[30] the 16th and 17th Corps Starting from Grand Ecore to Join us at this place, we march 16 miles and bivouac for the night in what is turned the pine woods.

7TH

We form lines at 750 and continue the march. we march 27 miles and arrive at Pleasant Hill. about 4 P.M. the cavalry arriving here in the morning. they have a Skirmish about four miles from here in the afternoon with a loss of about forty in killed and wounded the rebels retreating towards Mansfield.[31]

8TH

The 16th and 17th Corps were at this time 20 miles behind us. and an advance was ordered by General Banks of the cavalry 13th and 19th Corps.[32] the cavalry in advance 13th Corps as their Support and the 19th Corps in the rear, the cavalry Skirmish with the Johneys from early in the morning untill 2 P.M. when they came to a halt, the 13th Corps halting 4 miles in their rear and the 19th Corps two miles in the rear of them. but the cavalry had not been at a halt long before the enemy were discovered in force when they were ordered to advance by General Lee in command[33] of our cavalry the rebel force numbered about 18 thousand men[34] under the commands of Generals Monton, Green, Mcgruder General Dick Tayler commander in Cheif.[35] The cavalry attacked them and after a desperate fight of nearly two hours were forced to fall back losing the most of their artillery and wagon train.[36] The 13th Corps were ordered to their Support. but the cavalry being perfectly demoralized gave them no assistance[37] and after fighting untill their men were nearly half killed wounded or taken prisoners, they began falling back the 19th corps were ordered up to the front at a double quick and arrived at Sabine Cross Roads, in time to Save the 13th corps the rebels had already gained about three miles and thought they had the yankees but a few volleys Such as the 19th corps dealt them appeared to Satisfy them and after a Short time they concluded to keep a little out of range.[38] They held them in check untill dark when firing ceased. the 16th and 17th corps were at this time 20 miles in our rear and could not come up to our assistance the General received information during the evening that Tayler had been reinforced with 15 thousand under the rebel General Price.[39] Accordingly a retreat was ordered by General Banks at midnight to Pleasant Hill leaving the dead and wounded behind. the loss of the Cavalry was very heavy. also the 13th corps General Ransom in command of the corps being mortally wounded dying from his wounds[40] Soon after we retreated 16 miles in the night arriving at Pleasant Hill. the next morning about 8 A.M. many of the men were asleep in the woods and did not wake up untill morning when they were awoke in the morning and asked to take a trip with them down to tyler Texas.[41] which of course was not Satisfactory to them but however they could not refuse

APRIL 9TH

This is one of the greatest days that the army of the gulf ever experienced.[42] the enemy after capturing about forty barrels of Whisky from us the day before are full of fight and are resolved to give us battle[43] before we can get away from them but we have got as far away from them by this time as we wish to be if they want to give battle, the 16th and 17th corps are upon the ground early in the morning[44] and are preparing all day with the rest of the forces to give the Johneys their fill if they make an attack, but the rebels follow us up and commence Skirmishing with our

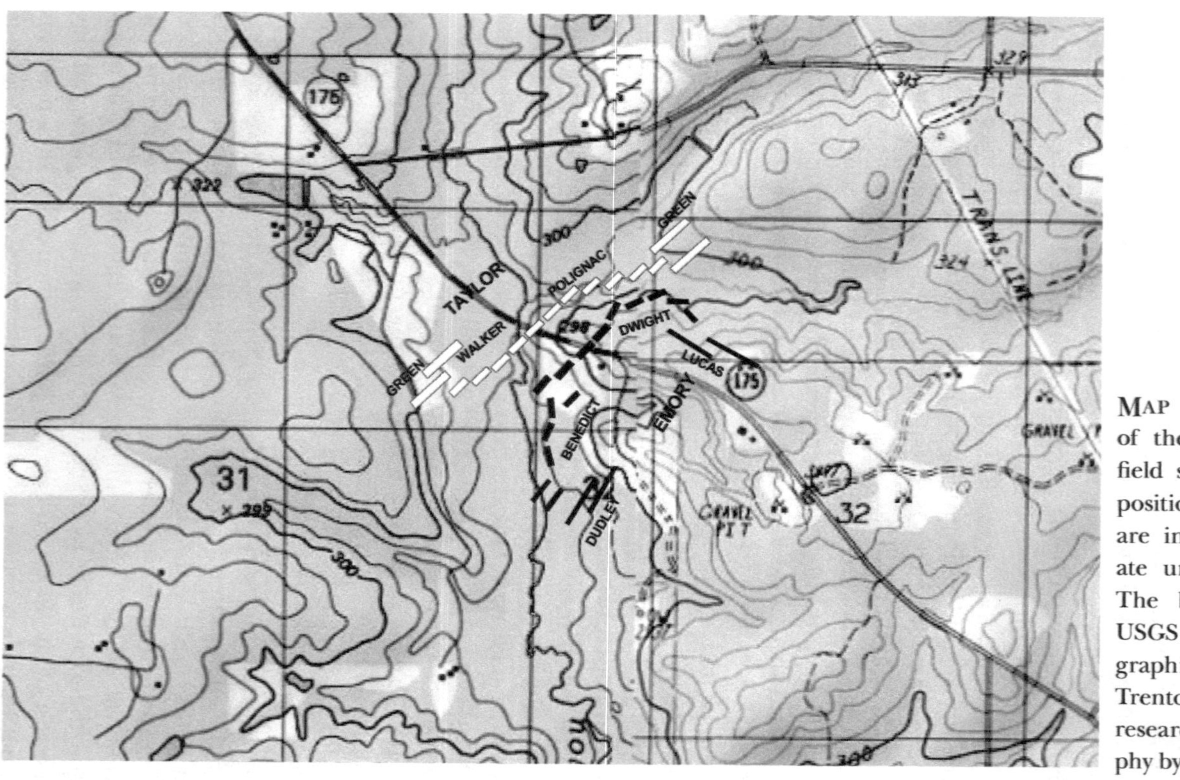

MAP 4.1. Third Phase of the Battle of Mansfield showing final unit positions. Union units are in black. Confederate units are in white. The base map is the USGS 7.5 minute topographic quadrangle map, Trenton, Louisiana. Unit research and cartography by Gary D. Joiner.

rear before we get in line in the morning lively Skirmishing is kept up all day untill 3. P.M.[45] when the rebels make a general attack from different points, perhaps it would be as well for me to give a description of the battle field here we had three lines of battle formed in an open field about one mile and a half in length and three quarters of a mile in breadth this opening was Surrounded by woods. having a gradual Slope from where our third line was formed to where the rebels made the attack. this is a low Swampy Country and there was but one road for the Rebels to move their artillery up to take part in the engagement. on both Sides of this opening our cavalry were formed in the woods as flankers and the infantry and Artillery in the field to resist their advance. at about three oclock the rebels threw out a Skirmish line which were driven back and after them came a Solid line of battle. and as Soon as they appeared our artillery opened on them doing great execution. but presently two more lines of battle were Seen coming out of the woods at a double quick to Support. the first line full of whiskey on they came never dreaming of the fate that awaited them we had at this time about thirty peices of artillery playing upon the rebels Still on they came not appearing to notice how their ranks were being thined by Shells grape and cannister. they were Soon in musket range and Such a volley of balls as they received from the yankees lying ready to receive has no rival with the Same number of men Since the commencement of the war, volley after volley was poured into their once full but now Scattered ranks untill they were forced to retire from the field leaving their dead and wounded behind them. the Shades of night now cover the battle field leaving it in possession of the union army. the loss of the rebels are terrible their dead and wounded lying in heaps upon the ground over which they charged upon our batteries. the loss of the union forces were large but nothing compared to that of the enemy, our forces held possession of the field untill two oclock the next morning when on account of rations and the Gun Boats failing to get up the river were ordered to retreat leaving our dead behind and many of the wounded.[46] the rebels at the Same time retreating towards Mansfield.[47] the dead and wounded lay upon the field two days before they were taken care of the rebels thinking we held possession of the ground and we thinking the Same of them.

10TH

We commence the retreat at 2 A.M. and march all night and the next day untill three P.M. when the men being perfectly worn out we came to a halt by the Side of a biyou and cook Something to eat the first time we have had a chance for nearly three days. we halt here for the night the wagon train going on to grand Ecere the men being very tired cook their Supper and lay down for to rest distance of days march 21 miles.[48]

11TH

We awake in the morning feeling much refreshed after a nights Sleep we cook Breakfast and form line at 7.50 to fall back to grand Ecore. we arrive at this place about 3 P.M. and go into bivouac about one half mile from the river.

12TH

Being where we can get Supplies and are not afraid of being driven out by the rebels it Seems to be the impression that we will remain here Some time. we have a mail in the afternoon and put up our tents in the course of the day. weather remarkably fine,

13TH

Every thing quiet in camp we hear very heavy firing up the river the gun boats are up the river and the rebels try to blockade the river below and destroy the boats but they fail in the attempt they are driven from their position with heavy loss and the boats all pass their battery with Small loss.[49] Colonel Seave[50] is placed under Arrest and General Dwight[51] makes a few remarks to each regiment in the Brigade in the afternoon.

14TH

Everything quiet along the river there is an immense amount of Supplies came up the river in the afternoon and every thing bids fair for us to remain here a number of days Colonel Seave is relieved from arrest and haves a line formed in the afternoon and makes a few remarks to the regiment. General Dwight is relieved from command of the Brigade and is placed upon General Banks Staff.[52]

15TH

The fleet of transports all arrive from up the river Some of them being pretty well Shattered from passing the rebel Battery but all of them in working condition. we hear the rebels are preparing to come down and Surround us cut off our Supplies and take us all prisoners. but dont feel much concerned about it weather fine,[53]

April 16th

We have a very large mail in the morning. Supplies continue to come up the river Sutlers Supplies begin to arrive and prices are more limited our regiment is on picket they go out at 2.30 P.M.

17th

every thing quiet in the forenoon and I busy myself in writing. the regiment comes off pickett in the afternoon at three oclock the band goes out to the reserve. to play the regiment into camp weather remarkable fine.

18th

Nothing of importance going on in camp all day transports continue to arrive from new orleans.

19th

Inspection of arms at ten A.M. and in the afternoon we arrange the camp forming company Streets and policing the whole camp thoroughly. the boys all remark this a Sure Sign that we are Soon to leave for some place

20th

Our old [?] proves true we hear we have orders to fall back to Alexandria in the afternoon the Sick and wounded are taken down the river on transports the 16th and 17th corps move out to Nachintoch[54] in the afternoon

21st

the 16th and 17th corps have a Skirmish near Nachintoch with the rebels they drive the enemy from their position with Small loss. the transports are all loaded with the comisary Stores and go down the river Just at night we form line at Sunset expecting to march all night but lay down and rest untill midnight.[55]

22nd

With little Sleep we commence the retreat at midnight and march all night and untill the next noon without rest when we halt for an hour and cook our dinner and then renew the march we march untill 11 oclock at night making a march of forty five miles with out a hours Sleep and only time enough given us to cook our dinner the longest march in one day ever done by the 19th Army Corps.

23RD

We form line at 5 A.M. and march Six miles and find the enemy in force on cane river[56] they have ten peices of artillery with ten thousand men and it is their intention to Stop our advance untill Dick Tayler may overtake our rear and thus have us Surrounded. the rebel force here is under the command of General Ree.[57] they have their position on a high Bluff and think it impassible for the yankees to dislodge them. the 16th and 17th corps are at this time in the rear and the 19th and 13th takes the front. our Second and third Brigades are thrown across the river with a part of the 13th corps to attack them on the flank[58] while the first Brigade and the rest of the 13th corps engages them on the front our regiment is thrown out as Skirmishing in the forenoon in a low Swamp Standing in water the most of the time up to their knees, and in the afternoon are ordered to go to the front to Support the 21st Indiana Battery. they no Sooner had the order than they Started the 2nd and 3rd Brigades at this time charged on the rebels left flank and after a desperate fight drove them from their position. the Battery opened on their front and there firing was So acurate that the Johneys could not Stand the presure and took to their heels leaving their dead and wounded behind and the river in the possession of the yankees to cross at their liesure General Emery was in command of our forces and after the fight he rode up to our regiment Saying bully boys. I never placed you in position yet but when you always Stood up to the rack. and I know you always will. we crossed the river marched four miles and went into bivouac for the night.

24TH

We form line at 6.A.M. and our march the most of the forenoon is marching and countermarching through the pine woods and at noon we Strike the red river about 30 miles above Alexandria. we halt here for dinner and then march 10 miles and go into bivouac for the night the boys visit Several plantations and get a good Supply of poultry to last them on the next days march.[59]

25TH

After a good nights rest we get up in the morning feeling much refreshed we form line at 7.A.M. and continue the march towards alexandria the band playing a national air as we Start from camp. after a march of 15 miles we arrive in town and go into bivouac across biyou Rapides about one mile from town. the men being very tired.

26TH

There is nothing going on in camp the boys washing and cleaning up their clothes mail arrives in the afternoon I receive a letter from home Supplies arrive from down the river.

27TH

All quiet in camp the men put up Shade over their tents and ocupy the rest of the day in laying in their tents and resting. weather extremely warm,

28TH

Heavy firing up the river by the gun boats[60] the first Division crosses the biyou and forms line of battle and remain in this position all night the Johneys thinking not best to venture to far

29TH

All quiet along the lines in the morning the first Division goes into bivouac about one half mile from town in the forenoon the weather extremely warm.

30TH

Regiment mustered for four months pay in the afternoon and Inspection afterwards. the men dig wells in camp for water during the day the water in the river getting warm and very dirty. and not water enough in the cisterns to Supply the army with drinking water.[61] end of fourth month

5th Month of 1864

MAY 1ST

Weather cooler than common we have Sunday Inspection at ten A.M. and the rest of the day I busy myself in answering letters. there is preaching in the 153rd N.Y.V in the afternoon at three oclock.

2ND

the Brigade goes on a foraging expedition the rebels make an effort to drive us in but do not Succeed in doing So. there is a light Skirmish with Small loss the Brigade returns to camp about 4 A.M.

3RD

All quiet in camp I am excused by the doctor from doing duty. General Franklin goes to New Orleans to recover from a wound Received at Sabine Cross Roads.[62] General Emmery takes command of the 19th Army Corps.

4TH

Col. Seve[63] received Orders in the morning for the four companies on the right to go across the river to work on the dam that is being constructed across the river below the Rapids to assist the gun boats in getting over.[64]

5TH

Weather Remarkble fine the rest of the regiment moves across the river and goes into camp by the Side of us we have a very cool camp in the woods.

6TH

Companies B.G.E.I. and D. works on the dam and the rest of the regiment does pickett and guard duty. weather continues fine 29th maine Sutler arrives.

7TH

The 29th Wisconsin comes across the river to work on the dam with us. the river is Blockaded below no boats coming up for two days there is two tin clads Sunk, by the rebel Battery.[65] Rations begin to get low.

8TH

The dam is nearly completed across the river the water raises enough to allow four of the light draft gun boats to run over the upper falls.[66]

9TH

Orders to turn in all the Officers tents Chests & and all the wagons but One[67] four of the Gun Boats go through the dam and over the Second Falls great excitement along the river

MAY 10TH

They commence building a Dam at the upper Falls in order to get the heavy draft Boats over the Falls. Some prospects of our moving across the river in the morning but prove not true.

11TH

I go across the river in the morning to get a horse for a pack animal there being Some prospects of a move. we practice in the afternoon. weather extremely warm

12TH

We practice two hours in the forenoon and two hours in the afternoon. four of the gun boats come over the upper Falls[68] and three over the Second Falls,[69] we move across the river in the afternoon and bivouac in town for the night Col. Seave[70] takes command of the third Brigade.

13TH

The Retreat is commenced from Alexandria at 7 A.M. we march thirteen miles and Bivouac for the night on General Price Plantation. weather very warm. the Gun Boats move down the river with us destroying the greater part of Alexandria before leaving in the morning.[71]

14TH

We form line at 7 A M. to continue the retreat find the enemy about 9 A.M. and there is lively Skirmishing the most of the day with the cavalry.

15TH

We renew the march at 7 A.M. and our march in the forenoon is through the woods. making comfortable marching. there is heavy artillery firing all day the rebels make a Stand about 4 P.M. near the village of Marksville but are driven from their Position before dark.

16TH

We renew the march at daylight and find the enemy in force the first thing in the morning form line of Battle and march in this way three miles across Manzura[72] Plains. the rebels make a Stand of about an hour but there is no fighting except an artillery Duel, the rebels retreating towards Simsport.[73] weather very warm,[74]

MAY 17TH

Hearing we were only going to Simsport we dont Start untill 7 A.M. and then Start the rebels try to break our wagon train but fail in doing it. we arrive at Simsport about 2 P.M. and go into camp the men being very tired we have a mail at night.

18TH

Remain in camp all day, the Chaffalia river[75] is Pontooned in the course of the day with transports.[76] Geneeral Smith haves a heavy Skirmish in the afternoon with considerable Loss. near Yellow Biyou.[77]

19TH

We form line at 3 A.M. and go down to the river to assist in putting the wagon train across. the train is all over and we cross the river and go into bivouac about two miles from the crossings for the night.

20TH

Remain in camp untill nearly Sunset the boys Ocupy the most of the day in washing their cloths we form line at Sunset and march fifteen miles in the night and lay down to rest about midnight

21ST

We form line at 7 A.M. to march to Morganza Bend the distance being 18 miles the weather the warmest we have yet had on the march. we Strike the Missippi river about Sunset. the men being very tired.

Notes

1. The portion of the diary presented here reflects the entries from March 1 through May 22, 1864. The diary, part of the collection of papers of James Sandefur of Shreveport, Louisiana, covers the entire year. All spelling and punctuation are identical to the original. The format as presented here has been altered from the original for the purpose of clarity. Brackets denote illegibility or show a word added to the original text. Knapp was a private in Company I of the 116th New York Infantry Regiment. He served as the drummer, the principal musician. See Record Group 94, Microscopy 551, Roll 78 National Archives and Records Administration. The 116th New York Volunteer Infantry Regiment was part of Brigadier General William Dwight's First Brigade, First Division, under Brigadier General William H. Emory, 19th Army Corps. Regiments in the brigade consisted of 29th Maine Infantry, 114th New York Infantry, 116th New York Infantry, 153rd New York Infantry, and 161st New York Infantry. Appendix 4 provides the diary entries for January and February in 1864. These entries do not directly correspond to the campaign and thus are not included in the main body of this chapter. They do, however, provide the best source of information from a 19th Corps soldier of the life immediately prior to the campaign.
2. A Colonel Soane does not appear on the roster of the 116th New York Infantry Regiment. There is no mention of an officer named Soane or Sloan or other variant in Richard Irwin, *History of the Nineteenth Army Corps* (New York, 1892).

3. The 153rd New York Volunteer Infantry Regiment was a sister regiment of the 116th New York, serving in the First Brigade, First Division (Emory's), of the 19th Army Corps.
4. The 153rd New York Infantry Regiment had been transferred from Washington, D.C.
5. Captain John Mappa Sizer, who commanded Company G of the 116th. He entered service with the rank of Captain and held that rank throughout the war. See Record Group 94, Microscopy 551, Roll 129, National Archives and Records Administration.
6. Major General Nathaniel Prentiss Banks, commander of the Department of the Gulf based in New Orleans.
7. Captain Richard C. Kinney, who commanded Company E of the 116th. He entered service as a captain and retained that rank throughout the war. See Record Group 04, Microscopy 551, Roll 77, National Archives and Records Administration.
8. Colonel George M. Love entered the service with the rank of major and was mustered out with the rank of Brevet Brigadier General. See Record Group 94, Microscopy 551, Roll 85, National Archives and Records Administration.
9. Captain John M. Sizer.
10. The 19th Corps began its march across southern Louisiana five days behind schedule. The column contained approximately nineteen thousand men. On March 12, the naval contingent, accompanied by ten thousand men of the 16th and 17th Corps, entered the mouth of the Red River. This force was to link up with the 13th and 19th Corps at the town of Alexandria on March 16.
11. The town of Alexandria in Rapides Parish.
12. This may be Spanish Lake located near Bayou Teche and just north of New Iberia.
13. Vermilionville is today the city of Lafayette in Lafayette Parish.
14. Carencro Bayou, originally "Carrion Crow" Bayou.
15. Illegible, but probably the town of Grand Coteau.
16. Other accounts list the woman as living in Opelousas, a few miles from Grand Coteau.
17. Opelousas in St. Landry Parish.
18. The town of Washington in St. Landry Parish. The town is located near Bayou Courtableau and Bayou Teche.
19. Bayou Courtableau.
20. Homesville is located just south of the town of Bunkie in Avoyelles Parish.

21. Cheneyville in Rapides Parish.
22. Prior to the war, Solomon Northrop wrote about his experiences in a widely read book entitled *Twelve Years a Slave: Narrative of Solomon Northup, a Citizen of New-York, Kidnapped in Washington City in 1841, and Rescued in 1853.* Derby and Miller of Auburn, New York, published it in 1853.
23. The skirmish at Henderson Hill, near Cotile Landing in Rapides Parish. Union forces under Brigadier General Joseph Mower captured almost all of the Confederate 2nd Louisiana Cavalry Regiment with very little fighting. One Union soldier lost his front teeth from being shot by a Confederate captain. Richard Lowe, *The Texas Overland Expedition of 1863* (Fort Worth, 1996), 180.
24. Cloutierville in Natchitoches Parish.
25. Natchitoches in Natchitoches Parish is the oldest town in the Louisiana Purchase, founded in 1714.
26. The regiment is probably on Cane River or one of its tributaries north of Natchitoches. The army camped along the old El Camino Real, the Spanish Royal Road between Natchitoches and its small port of Grand Ecore, located on the Red River about four miles to the northeast.
27. This is an interesting rumor. On April 3 and 4, Major General Banks and Rear Admiral David D. Porter discussed whether the navy should perform an armed reconnaissance upriver to find a good route or if the army should proceed on the known road to the west then head north to attack Shreveport. Banks did not believe the Rebels would offer battle before Shreveport. They did indeed mass north of Pleasant Hill near Mansfield. Against the advice of senior army commanders and the admiral, Banks decided to move his army inland, away from the protective guns of the fleet. This was the most crucial mistake made by Union commanders in the campaign. Banks's decision effectively allowed the Confederates to pick the time and place for a trap.
28. Grand Ecore, located about four miles from Natchitoches. The navy anchored under the bluffs, and the supply train gathered its stores from the U.S. Army Quartermaster Corps transport vessels operating with the navy.
29. The 16th and 17th Corps contingent traveled via steamboat from Cotile Landing to Grand Ecore. The Provisional Division of the 17th Corps remained with the navy to protect it, and the 16th Corps accompanied the 13th and 19th Corps on the inland march. Although they participated in the campaign in crucial roles, they were not under Banks's direct command and were sent to protect the fleet.
30. No road led directly to Pleasant Hill. The route the army took still exists today as roads and highways. Banks marched the force in a long column, sometimes stretching over twenty-five miles in length, using a single

road. Knapp's regiment would have been near the beginning of the 19th Corps, but still several miles behind the forward elements. The order of march called for the Cavalry Division of the 19th Corps to take the lead. Behind it were three hundred supply wagons. Troops of the Corps d'Afrique (U.S. Colored Troops) accompanied these wagons. The small 13th Corps and the six hundred wagons of the supply train of the 13th and 19th Corps followed them. The main body of the 19th Corps, followed by the 16th Corps, fell in behind them. The column followed the present-day Louisiana Highway 6 from Grand Ecore to Natchitoches then west along the same highway to White's Store (the present-day town of Robeline). From there, the column moved northwest on the present-day Louisiana Highway 120 to Crump's Corners (the present-day town of Belmont). The army then turned north onto the Shreveport-Natchitoches Stagecoach Road, which is the present-day Louisiana Highway 175. It followed this road through Pleasant Hill to just below the town of Mansfield, where it was met by the Confederates and turned back.

31. The skirmish at Wilson's Farm, located about three miles north of Pleasant Hill. The Confederate cavalry under Texas Brigadier General Tom Green were sent to slow the advance of the Union column. This skirmish was the first in a series of such engagements fought over the next seventeen miles. They extended from most of April 7 and the morning of April 8.
32. Knapp is describing the Battle of Mansfield (or Sabine Crossroads). This was the Cavalry Division of the 19th Corps under Brigadier General Albert Lindley Lee. Lee had under his command about five thousand troopers in ten regiments. Half of these were cavalry and half were recently mounted infantry.
33. Banks's staff spread this popular rumor within the 19th Corps. Lee asked for permission to retreat, and Banks denied it. After the campaign, Banks blamed Lee for the fiasco at the Battle of Mansfield, or Sabine Crossroads, as the Union called it.
34. The Confederates had no more than twelve thousand men on the field, and the Union had approximately seventy-five hundred.
35. On the field at Mansfield, Confederate Major General Richard Taylor had two divisions of infantry: the Louisiana Division, consisting of two brigades under Brigadier General Jean Jacques Alexandre Alfred Mouton, and the Texas Division, consisting of three brigades under Major General John George Walker. He also had the Cavalry Corps under General Green. Two other divisions could not reach the field in time. These were the Arkansas and Missouri divisions, which had been under Major General Sterling Price, but Brigadier General Thomas Churchill then commanded them. See chap. 1 in this volume.

36. The Confederates attacked the Cavalry Division and the 13th Corps contingent at 4 P.M., destroying their first position.
37. This was not true. The cavalrymen fought very well, but were completely outmanned and flanked. This line of narrative follows what Banks's staff spread, accusing the General Lee of incompetence and his men of near cowardice. See chaps. 1 and 2 in this volume.
38. The 19th Corps, specifically Emory's Division and 116th New York, were involved in the battle in its final stages at twilight. The division held the high ground above Chapman's Bayou. Night ended the fighting.
39. Knapp is the only source that verifies the rumor among the Federal troops that the Arkansas and Missouri divisions were thought to have arrived. They were, in fact, north of Mansfield near Keachi. Banks gave three reasons or excuses for the retreat in his report. This rumor is one. The others were lack of water, which Banks would use several times in the following days, and weakness of his position at the end of the battle. The Union forces, in fact, held the high ground and best position on the battlefield. Gary D. Joiner, *One Damn Blunder from Beginning to End: The Red River Campaign of 1864* (Wilmington, DE, 2003), 103–9; U.S. War Dept., *War of the Rebellion: The Official Records of the Union and Confederate Armies,* 128 vols. (Washington, 1880–1901), ser. 1, vol. 34, pt. 1:183.
40. Brigadier General T.E.G. Ransom suffered a severe wound to his knee and was removed from the field. He died during the Atlanta Campaign later that year.
41. Knapp is referring to Camp Ford prisoner of war facility at Tyler, Texas, located about ninety miles west of Shreveport. The passage is interesting for its suggestion (correctly) that the retreat was conducted very quietly so as to fool the Rebels into believing the Union army still commanded the high ground above the battlefield. The Joint Committee on the Conduct of the War criticized Banks later that year for abandoning such a strong position.
42. Knapp is describing the Battle of Pleasant Hill.
43. Several Union accounts during the campaign, including one from Admiral Porter after the Battle of Blair's Landing, attribute Confederate courage under fire as being only strong after the soldiers were drunk on captured or stolen whiskey. Knapp is apparently repeating what he heard officers or other soldiers saying. It is improbable that the Confederates could keep up fire discipline if they were intoxicated. The Confederates were fighting to save their homes from invasion, their property from ruination, and for their pride. These were enough reasons to fight fearlessly.
44. The Provisional Division of the 17th Corps was aboard transports guarding the fleet. The 16th Corps contingent, under Brigadier General

Andrew Jackson Smith, consisted of the Second and Third brigades of the First Division and the First, Second, and Third Brigades of the Third Division.

45. For a more complete account of the battle, see Joiner, *One Damn Blunder,* 107–22; Ludwell H Johnson, *Red River Campaign: Politics and Cotton in the Civil War* (Kent, OH, 1993), 146–69.
46. There was great dissention in the ranks of Union officers. General A. J. Smith wanted Banks arrested and for General Franklin to assume command. Banks seems to have been totally unprepared for this battle. The three lines of battle referred to in the narrative were simply the three areas in which the Union column was bivouacked with the exception of the forward position of Shaw's Brigade. Banks did not listen to the counsel of his senior commanders and retreated from the field, turning a tactical tie into a strategic victory for the Confederates.
47. The Confederates pulled back a short distance—not more than a mile or two—from the final positions of fighting. After the battle Lieutenant General Edmund Kirby Smith, commander of the Confederate Department of the Trans-Mississippi, ordered the Texas, Arkansas, and Missouri Divisions to march to Shreveport in preparation for an advance on Arkansas. The Louisiana Division and the Texas Cavalry Corps remained in the vicinity of Pleasant Hill and shadowed the Union column back to Grand Ecore.
48. Banks ordered the column to retreat to Grand Ecore using the same route it took on the advance.
49. Knapp is referring to the Battle of Blair's Landing, in which the monitor USS *Osage,* the timberclad USS *Lexington,* and the transport *Black Hawk* fought an unusual battle with approximately twenty-five hundred Texas cavalry under General Green. The battle lasted for about two hours and resulted in few casualties. A shot from the *Osage* killed Green. Blair's Landing saw the first use of the periscope in battle. The action took place on April 12. Joiner, *One Damn Blunder,* 144–46.
50. Captain John M. Sizer.
51. Brigadier General William H. Dwight, commander of the First Brigade of the First Division of the 19th Corps.
52. Dwight, a close confidant of Banks, replaced Brigadier Charles P. Stone as chief of staff. This was part of the fallout after the Battle of Pleasant Hill, as Banks sought scapegoats for the ill-conceived battles of Mansfield and Pleasant Hill. Banks also fired his cavalry chief, General Albert Lindley Lee.
53. Banks was certainly concerned. He ordered extensive entrenchments built around Grand Ecore to the extent of six square miles.

54. Natchitoches.
55. Banks decided once more to use a single column on the retreat. Confusion about the route delayed the middle and rear portions of the column in their departure. The route took the column onto Cane River Island and set up a near disaster.
56. Battle of Monett's Ferry. The Confederates tried to cut off the retreat at the only known ferry landing at the south end of Cane River Island. They held high ground to the south of the ferry landing and placed artillery there.
57. Brigadier General Hamilton Bee commanded the Confederate troops. Only a single brigade of soldiers was there, making the rebel force less than 1,500 men.
58. The Union force sought help from a runaway slave who informed them of a ford to the rear of the Union position. Emory sent Benedict's Brigade, then under the command of Colonel Francis Fessenden, to flank the Confederate position. Bee became timid against the new threat and ordered his men to retreat. This action offered the best possibility for the Confederates to capture Banks's command.
59. This encampment was apparently near Bayou Cotile and Bayou Rapides. This was the staging area for the 16th and 17th Corps troops on the advance.
60. This refers to a serious engagement between Rebel artillery and the vessels that had been guarding the USS *Eastport* prior to its scuttling. In this action, the USS *Champion No.3* and the USS *Champion No. 5* were both sunk. The USS *Cricket*, with Admiral Porter aboard, and the USS *Juliet* were heavily damaged. Joiner, *One Damn Blunder*, 148–50.
61. On March 18 the Confederates destroyed a dam they built just south of Shreveport. The water was diverted into a parallel stream called Bayou Pierre. This action starved the Red River of water and was the source of the navy's problems with rapidly decreasing water levels. Knapp experienced the lowering water table, as the army was forced to dig wells to supply potable water. For an examination of the Confederates' plan, see Joiner, *One Damn Blunder*, 22–26.
62. Franklin broke his elbow when he fell from his horse during the rout at Mansfield.
63. Captain John M. Sizer.
64. This is Bailey's Dam, widely considered to be one of the great engineering feats of the Civil War. For a more thorough examination of the dam in context of the Red River Campaign, see Joiner, *One Damn Blunder*, 159–68; Johnson, *Red River Campaign*, 249–50.
65. These were the USS *Covington* and USS *Signal*. Also lost were the USS *John Warner*, and on May 1, the transports *Emma* and *City Belle*.

66. USS *Osage,* USS *Neosho,* USS *Fort Hindman,* and the USS *Lexington,*
67. About 1 P.M.
68. Probably six vessels: USS *Louisville,* USS *Mound City,* USS *Pittsburg,* USS *Carondelet,* USS *Chillicothe,* and the USS *Ozark.*
69. USS *Osage,* USS *Neosho,* USS *Fort Hindman,* and probably the USS *Lexington.*
70. Captain John M. Sizer.
71. Portions of the army destroyed all of downtown Alexandria. Banks did not want the town torched since it would alert the Rebels of the Union army's departure. The fire was intentionally set using camphor and turpentine. The 16th Corps contingent was blamed for the damage.
72. Mansura.
73. Simmesport.
74. The two previous entries refer to the positioning and Battle of Mansura, which was actually an artillery duel.
75. Atchafalaya River.
76. Colonel Joseph Bailey, the builder of the dams at Alexandria, again saved the army, creating a sophisticated pontoon bridge by lashing the army's transport vessels side-by-side and allowing the army to pass over the then-raging Atchafalaya River.
77. Battle of Yellow Bayou was the last action of the Red River Campaign. The Confederates did not have pontoon boats and could not chase the Union force across the river.

CONFEDERATE LETTERS

Edited by Gary D. Joiner, Jimmy H. Sandefur, Thomas A. Pressly, Nancy B. Wilson, Molly Wiggins, Monica R. Pels, Dyson Nickles, Ann Turk, Steven Mayeux, Bryan James Maedgen, and Allan Richard

THIS CHAPTER CONSISTS OF SOURCES FROM AND ABOUT WELL-known Confederate leaders and from little-known soldiers. The individual documents range from the general order issued by Major General Richard Taylor to his troops immediately following the Red River Campaign to pleading letters from a Texan concerned with his health and interest in his family's well-being.

Richard Taylor's unnumbered general order has been printed in various versions, most of them sanitized. This version was printed in the *Washington (Arkansas) Telegraph* and is considered to be the full, correct version. The Prince de Polignac wrote the letter concerning his difficulties with some Southern officers in 1863, just as he was becoming tremendously popular with his troops. The Texans could not pronounce his flowery French name and dubbed their commander "General Polecat."

The next portion of the chapter consists of letters of participants. The last letters of Confederate Colonel James Beard, commander of the Louisiana Consolidated Crescent Regiment, were penned shortly before his death at the Battle of Mansfield. The letter of Captain Joshua L. Halbert of 15th Texas Infantry Regiment is a rare example of a Confederate description of the fighting at Mansfield and subsequent actions. The letter from W. T. Shaw, written in 1918, is perhaps the only eye-witness account of the death of Confederate Brigadier General Tom Green. In the third week of April, Private R. A. Knox of the 2nd Texas Infantry Regiment wrote his letter describing the actions in the campaign up to that time and indicating how much information the common Confederate soldier may have known. Private Zack Howell's letter to his wife describes the army news he gathered while serving in Shreveport. The letter from B. E. Ballard to his sister is a poignant account of the death of their brother, George, in the final battle of the campaign.

A series of letters from Private Jefferson Morgan of the 35th Texas Cavalry Regiment is also included in this chapter. The letters reflect the urgency of gathering the widely separated Texas cavalry units, in this case from near the Gulf Coast, for assembly in Hempstead County, and the final mad dash to join Confederate forces in repelling the Union Invasion. Morgan began his trek to the Red River Valley from Matagorda, Texas. Shortly thereafter, he contracted measles, which created severe health problems. Morgan missed the battles of Mansfield and Pleasant Hill but arrived for the Battle of Blair's Landing, where his commander, Brigadier General Tom Green, was killed. Morgan's correspondence is added to this collection because his rustic eloquence describes some of the hardships of the Confederate soldier and brings to bear the knowledge that glory on the battlefield was not the only manner in which the brave fell. Also included is a letter W. E. Fields wrote to Morgan's wife telling her of her husband's death.

F. B. Harris of the 4th Texas Cavalry wrote a friend about his unit's participation in the battles of Mansura and Yellow Bayou. Harris's descriptions are vivid and forthright. Another member of the 4th Texas Cavalry was Moritz Maedgen. This German immigrant described the same period of time as Harris but includes other insightful information as well. Maedgen is humorous in recounting events. D. E. Causland was a member of Company H, 4th Confederate Engineers, based in Shreveport. The letter included here describes preparations for perhaps the final mission of the engineers west of the Mississippi River in 1865.

This chapter concludes with excerpts from the 1915 journal of Elizabeth Jane Samford Fullilove, the wife of Private

Thomas Pope Fullilove of Company D of the 6th Louisiana Cavalry. The author describes the work done on their farm before her husband's enlistment, the excitement brought on by furloughs, and her memories of the Battles of Mansfield and Pleasant Hill.

General Orders of Lieutenant-General Richard Taylor to the Soldiers of the Army of Western Louisiana, May 23, 1864

[Edited by Gary D. Joiner]

Headquarters District Western Louisiana[1]
In the Field, May 23, 1864.

General Orders Number—
Soldiers of the Army of Western Louisiana!

On March 12 the enemy, with an army of 30,000 men, accompanied by a fleet of ironclads, mourning 150 guns, moved forward for the conquest of Texas and Louisiana. Alter seventy days continued fighting, you stand a band of conquering heroes, on the banks of the Mississippi. Fifty pieces of cannon, 7,000 stand of small arms, three gunboats and eight transports captured or destroyed, sixty stands or colors, over 10,000 of the enemy killed, wounded or captured—these are the trophies which adorn your victorious banners. Along 300 miles of river you have fought his fleet, and over 200 miles of road you have driven his army. You have matched your bare breasts against his ironclads and proved victorious in the contest. You have driven his routed columns beyond the Mississippi, although fed by reinforcements of fresh troops, while many of your gallant comrades were withdrawn to other fields. The boasted fleet which lately sailed triumphant over our waters, has fled in dismay, after destroying guns and stripping off armor in its eagerness to escape you. Like recreant knights the ironclads have fled the field, leaving shield and sword behind.

The devotion and constancy you have displayed in this pursuit have never been surpassed in the annals of war, and you have removed from the Confederate soldier the reproach that he could win battles but could not improve victories.

Along 100 miles of his path the flying foe, with more than savage barbarity, burned every house and village within his reach. You extinguished the burning ruins in his base blood, and were nerved afresh to vengeance by the cries of woman and children, left without shelter or food.

Long will the accursed race remember the great river of Texas and Louisiana. The characteristic hue of his turbid waters has a darker tinge from the liberal admixture of Yankee blood.

The cruel alligator and ravenous garfish wax fat on rich food, and our native vulture holds high revelry over many a festering corpse.

If the stern valor of our well trained infantry was illustrated on the bloody fields of Mansfield and Pleasant Hill, this long pursuit has covered the cavalry of this army with undying renown.

Like generous hounds with the game in full view, you have known neither hunger nor fatigue, and the hoarse cannon and the ringing rifle have replaced in this stern chase the sonorous horn and joyous halloo. Whether charging on foot, shoulder to shoulder, with our noble infantry, or hurling your squadrons on the masses of the foe, or hanging on his flying columns with more than the tenacity of the Cossack, you have been admirable in all. Conquer your own vices and you can conquer the world.

Our artillery has been the admiration of the army. Boldly advancing, without cover, against the heavy metal of the hostile fleet, unlimbering often without support within range of musketry, or remaining last on the field to pour grape and canister into the advancing columns, our batteries have been distinguished in exact proportion as opportunity was afforded.

Soldiers! These are great and noble deeds, and they will live in chronicle and in song as long as the Southern race exists to honor the earth. But much remains yet to do. The fairest city of the South languishes in the invader's grasp. Her exiled sons mourn her fate in every land. The cheeks of her fair daughters yet mantle with the blush raised by the brutal tyrant's insult—not a Confederate soldier returns to his colors from this sad Venice of the South, but recounts with throbbing heart and tearful eyes, how, amidst danger and insult, these noble women—angels upon earth—cheered his confinement and relieved his wants. To view the approving smiles of these fair dames, will he a soldier's proudest boast, the brightest leaf in his chaplet of laurels.

Soldiers! This army marches towards New Orleans, and though it does not reach the goal, the hearts of her patriotic women shall bound high with joy, responsive to the echoes of your guns.

[RICHARD] TAYLOR, Major General.
Official. A.J. Walt, Assistant Adjutant General.

[*Washington (Arkansas) Telegraph,*
June 8, 1864]

FIG. 5.1. Heavily altered image of Major General Richard Taylor. Archives of the Mansfield State Historic Site, Mansfield, Louisiana.

Letter from the Prince de Polignac to General Sterling B. Hendricks

[Edited by Thomas A. Pressly and Gary D. Joiner]

The following letter[2] was written while Polignac was still struggling to gain the trust of his Texans.[3]

Camp in the Field[4]
October 28, 1863

My dear Colonel[5]

I was very sorry that you left without bidding a final farewell as I wanted to thank you again for the warm assistance you gave me on all occasions & renew the assurences of my heartfelt gratitude & lasting friendship but since I couldn't do so verbally I will state to you in writing that my well wishes go with you & that I will follow you up in the new position which you have selected & will always be gratified to hear from you whenever you shall be able to draw off your attention from your more important occupation to fix it on an absent friend—the report which you handed me on leaving upon the condition of your regt contrasts very much with that of Col. Stevens[6] who took that method of venting his own feelings & prejudice against me—not those of his regt as I have had occasion to ascertain & poured out a long string of reflections on my foreign birth & went even the length of casting a slur on my southern feelings which he asserts *cannot be genuine* & to those causes he ascribes the insubordination, want of discipline & even the desertions of his regiment.[7] You who have been associated with him for a longer period than myself know what reliance can he placed on him & his statement but as such slanders can leak out & have done so perhaps to a certain extent, I wish you would bring your personal influence to bear upon your personal friends & the the [*sic*] high officials who have called you to the position which you now occupy in order to oppose truth to those wanton aspersions for indeed it is hard for a man who has asserted himself abroad as I did for the success of the southern cause who volunteered to fight its battles & lend its citizen soldiers the assistance of whatever experience he may have gathered on other battlefields to see himself looked upon as an interloper. It is however due to justice to say that none of the other commanders of this brigade have shown the feelings of their men in that light; some on the contrary paid me very high & flattering compliments which made amends for the injustice of one & only one man but it was reserved to your regt to compensate me for those troubles & gave me the best reward for the assiduous performance of my—sometimes very arduous task; your regt was mainely on picket—or outpost—duty a few days ago & I went to see how the outpost had been located & as I rode up to the regt the men spontaneuously raised a loud & hearty cheer & upon my enquiring into the causes of it they answered that they were glad to see me.[8] Now my dear Col. I wish you had been there to share in that cheer for half of it is certainly due to you. Let me add that the petty spirit of opposition lately exhibited has only served to establish me firmly in the brigade without excepting Stevens regt.[9] I am afraid my dear Col. that I have already written more than you will find pleasure in deciphering & I find that I have made *myself* the topic of this letter, but not without entreating you to let me hear from you soon & often & to do as I have done & write a great deal about yourself. I wish when you write you would state what are the chances of getting clothing for this brigade from the penitentiary; also shoes if any can be obtained.

With the expression of
my highest regards I remain

Very sincerely
your friend
C.T. Polignac
To Genl
S.B. Hendricks
X X

Last Letter of Col. James H. Beard (Inscribed on the Envelope)

[Edited by Nancy B. Wilson and Gary D. Joiner]

Pleasant Hill April 2nd 1864

My Dear Wife,[10]
I reached here to-day about 12 o'clock and am in camp with my Regiment about 1 mile below here.[11] I write this by Fred, whom I permit to go down to see his parents for a few days. I came up to take dinner with Mrs. Childers.[12] The old lady is in a peck of trouble. The soldiers are camped all around her & are coming in every five minutes in the day to get something

FIG. 5.2. The Prince de Polignac. Carte de visite in the collection of Gary D. Joiner.

eat either for themselves or make a pretext of getting it for a Sick Soldier. Gen. Walker's Division[13] is a few miles below here on the Old Natchitoches Road[14] and Genl Mouton's Division[15] in which you know I am is on the other Natchitoches Road[16] one mile from here; We expect reinforcements to arrive in time to make a successful stand here. These are to come from Price's force[17] at Shreveport and Green's[18] from Texas; 2 Regiments & a Battery of Artillery have already reached here. I do not have any fear of our being able to whip the scoundrels here, having the advantage of a good position & the army wants a fight. If we have to fall back towards Shreveport from here tell your Pa that it is my advice for him to send off all of his negro men and such women as Lucy. The safest thing in my opinion would be for him to have them as cooks & teamsters in Regiments of the Army. I am so glad that there is a prospect of our going no higher than this. It would disturb me so much to be forced to retreat and leave you behind.[19] I am quite well and hope for the best. The best of spirits pervades the entire army and no demoralization is produced by our falling back. The good people of Pleasant Hill are opening their astonished vision to sights they never saw before. Geo. Childers and Gooch have both been run out by the Yankees from the Swamp and are moving up the most of the negroes inside our lines, and in the direction of Texas. They left this place with everything and a few negro women in charge. Fred will give you such particulars as I cannot think of to write. Our old friend Frank Armon is married to a Widow Jones in Bossier Point.[20] I have not seen Dolph yet his Regt has not arrived. Kiss the children for me and give love to all the family. Goodbye Darling and may God bless and protect you and my little ones.[21]

Your Devoted Husband,
[James H. Beard]

The Last Known Written Communication from Colonel James H. Beard

(Addressed to)
Major L. F. Tompkies[22]
Headquarters
Consolidated Crescent Regiment
in the field

6 April 1864

Dear Major:
It is impossible to say yet what will be done by Gen. Taylor as his movements will depend on those of the enemy. I think with the majority of

FIG. 5.3. Colonel James H. Beard. Archives of Mansfield State Historic Site, Mansfield, Louisiana.

the officers that when we march which will be in a few days, we will go down the country. In the meantime make yourself busy for if anything transpires which would involve your safety I will inform you at once. Let me know whether your property has been troubled by the soldiers. If you are annoyed by there killing your hogs, theft etc. I will send you a guard. Tom Lester has just been here and tells me he has been robbed of all his hogs except three, mostly all his chickens, some of his sheep and potatoes. to add to his misfortune. Some scum will stole his horse the night before our troops arrived. A member of the Sixth Louisiana Regiment has just arrived from Virginia and reports that Lee had gained another signal victory through happens of all that [?]Virginia that Longstreet had gone a little way into Kentucky and captured more supplies than he could carry off and that Johnson had [?] of Chattanooga. He says that he found everybody east of the Mississippi in jubilant spirits and that he did not see a whipt man until he reached Louisiana.

Yours fondly
J. H. Beard

Field Office
Consolidated
Crescent Regiment
in the field

Feb. 2, 1864

I certify that I have this day paid Col. J.H. Beard CON. Crescent Regt—re-three hundred ninety dollars monthly pay from Dec. —63 to Jan —64 inclusive of this office

S. P. DuBois
Captain and [?]
CON Crescent Regt

Confederate Letter Written by Captain Joshua L. Halbert 15th Texas Infantry, 2nd Company E

[Edited by Jimmy H. Sandefur and Gary D. Joiner]

Camp near Mansfield, LA April 13, 1864[23]

My Darling Wife,

On the day after our bloody encounter with the enemy closed at Pleasant Hill I pencilled you a hurried note concerning my safety to relieve the any anxiety I knew you would feel about me on hearing of the battles of the 8th and the 9th[24] with the hope it has reached you and that you have slept soundly since finding I am still in the land the living with no bones broken.

I will try now to give you some more connected account of these fights which have resulted so gloriously for us—in routing Gen. Banks grand army of invasion—and ended in securing the Trans Mississippi Department from being overrun. For had this army been defeated there is none other to oppose the enemy's progress.

On the morning of the 8th of April at this very camp[25] our men were [?] around at 2 O'clock & ordered to prepare two days cooked rations, put in the haversacks and be ready to move at a moments notice. This was promptly obeyed and at sunrise we marched in the direction of Mansfield to the tune of "Bonnie Blue Flag" to our regimental band. Mouton's division was in front and our brigade in front of the Division—Walker's division next—we marched through Mansfield and three miles below to a *very large* plantation through the center of which the road ran.[26] We took position on the side of this next to town along the fence, Walker on the right and Mouton's division on the left of the road expecting to receive the attack of the enemy.[27] Infantry skirmishers were thrown out a few hundred yards to our front in the fields but our cavalry was a mile or more to our front skirmishing with the enemy and leading them in to us.

Presently the cavalry could be seen falling back through the field to our extreme left hotly pursued by a number of Banks mounted men.[28] On sight gallantly they swept over the field all unconscious of the infantry ambush awaiting them till they were within range of the trusty Enfields. Then there burst forth a sheet of flame from behind the fence and the very heavens [?] with the rattle of musketry. The rising smoke revealed the enemy retreating in disorder from the field many dead weltering and countless wounded lying on the ground. This was the first blood shed, and it would have done your soul good to have seen Gen. Mouton ride down our line and exultingly inform us that ours was the first division under fire. We then waited some hours for the enemy to attack us, but as he would not Gen. Taylor determined to attack him.

So *forward* was the order, and onward we moved across the field under a heavy fire from the enemy artillery posted in the timber in front of us. Polignac's Brigade moved to the right to [?] on the attack then the whole of Walker's division [?] be with [?] as reserves. We then pursued through a stand of timber with thick underbrush—the bullets whizzing by most uncomfortably—to another plantation and [?] we [?] the hill [?] the valley beneath us and on the opposite [?] were the host of the enemy infantry, cavalry and artillery.

We opened fire on them with our Enfields and for twenty minutes there was a solid blaze of flashing [?]. Then the Federals began in confusion to fall back to the rear of this field and cover themselves behind some houses[29] and the adjoining timber. In the meantime Mouton's Brigade on our right having less distance to march had become engaged before we did and being numerically weaker were suffering terribly under the enemy's fire, and being badly cut up to pieces.

Gen. Mouton, Col. Armant of the 18th LA, Col. Beard, Lt. Col. Clack & Major Canfield of the Crescent Regt. And Lt. Col. Walker of the 28th LA had fallen and yet the gallant Louisianians continued to fall in scores and in turn kill scores of the enemy. Our Brigade moved [?] to dislodge the enemy from their strong position in front [?] when Gen. Polignac ordered this regiment to move to the left flank [?] This was promptly [?] the opposite side of the [?] on the Kentucky regiment[30] which was fighting the Louisiana Brigade. In a few minutes it surrendered it's other [?] in front of the rest of Polignac's Brigade. Then was there a pause on the left which was used in reforming ourselves and restoring order out of the confusion that had occurred.

In the meantime, Polignac's Brigade on the right (except our regiment which was being transferred to the left as before stated) charged the enemy. [?] the houses, fences & in the timber in the strong position already spoken of. Our men were in this open field, and as they advance through this murderous fire numbers of them fell. Routed from here they fell back in disorder on their reserves and our lines rested for a short time.

Then it was that Walker's division came up.[31] Oh it was a gallant sight to see their solid lines more than a mile long come sweeping down the hill over the field from which the enemy had been driven, their banner flying, their step firm, their looks defiant and determined, as if victory or death were their motto. Forward they went past us and right on to the enemy. There again could be heard the thunder of artillery and the rattle of small arms without intermission, our whole army pressing on, the enemy falling back but stubbornly contesting every inch of ground, as the numbers of slain on both sides attest. Back they were driven for nearly four miles from their first position, then night intervened.

[?] after night some heavy vollies were given and returned [?] the heaviest fire was a [?] in my life was just after dark—we were moving up to attack [?] his last [?] as we [?] a hill they opened heavily on us from ambuscade.[32] [?] was a [?] and I would not have give two cents for my life. Happily the enemy were excited and shot too high or scores of our boys would have been killed. [?] I passed over this place after the fight and have never in my life seen trees so shot to pieces with small arms. Man of the [?] were ten or fifteen bullets and in some trees [?]. Our army then bivouacked on the battlefield.

During this time the Confederates been capturing wagons, artillery, ambulances, prisoners of war and leaving them miles behind when he was at night fall the [?] to Pleasant Hill where having been reinforced by a fresh army corps[33] he made a stand and we fought and whipped him again. I will give you a history of this at some time as this [?] is already covered with the account of our four days fight. Some of the fruits of this victory are 21 pieces of artillery, 2500 prisoners, 230 wagons, besides wagon loads of small arms, commissary & quartermaster stores, etc. I cannot give you the number of killed though it is heavy on both sides. The Federal loss though is about three to our one, judging from the best information I can get. It is said that a few hundred of Scurry's Brigade were taken prisoner by the enemy but I do not know as to the truth of this [?].

I have taken a fresh piece of paper to finish my letter but will not undertake to give you any account of the battle of Pleasant Hill. We fought it with reinforcements of six thousand of Price's men.[34] I think they did the heaviest part of that fight. It did not begin till about two hours before night and lasted about four hours. Next morning [?]

Now has just come the news confirming the death of General Greene.[35] The top of his head was taken off by a cannon ball from one of the gunboats. This news is sad. Oh! so sad. Our bravest and best thus fall with their harness on. Their glorious name and rich heritage for their families, ages and their states too. We have just heard that Kirby Smith is made a full general.[36] Col. Randall of the Texas Brigade[37] and Col. Grey of this state,[38] Brig. Gen. also. Commodore Porter's[39] fleet (of which I spoke on the former page) is retreating down the river harassed on both sides by our cavalry and artillery. The enemy are collecting at Grand Ecore to cover the retreat of their gun boats. If they stay there, I expect the army will move down and attack them, though I do not think they will do that.

I [?] learn that [?] of this regiment starts home in the morning early, so I must end as it is growing dark and have my letter ready for him to carry. Now my darling love, my hearts own in all these [?] through which have gone by best thoughts and aspirations and [?] for you and our darling little [?]. Take care of yourself and them for my sake and good care too. Write to me often—to Shreveport. Love and kisses to all whom we love. Your Budd looks tolerably well though his is not entirely recovered. I expect to be with you before many weeks—after Lt. McElevea returns, and shall be sorely disappointed if I do not Goodbye.

Your devoted husband.
J. L. Halbert

The Death of General Tom Green

[Edited by Gary D. Joiner and Molly Wiggins]

Headquarters of the Trans Mississippi Department[40]
United Confederate Veterans

Ft. Worth, Tx
April 13, 1918

Dr. Milton Dunce
Colefacts La[41]
Dear Comrade

I have your communication via Dr. Van Zant of date inst. 10 1918[42] is received and contents noted. I am unable to give you the names of the vessels that were captured at Ft. DeRussy as I was not present and have never seen a statement of them.[43] I was present at Blair's Landing charging the inemies Gunboats near where Gen. Tom Green was killed.[44] One half of his skull was taken off by a shell. As our Brigade retreated from that Engagement generally known as the Gunboat fight, Gen Green's body was carried out on horse back held on by two comrades. I noticed the erroneous statement of his having being killed at or near Pleasant Hill you refer to.[45] I have also read a statement locating his death at Yellow Bayo,[46] the closing battle of that campaign. Such errors frequently get into print through the carelessness of hurried writers depending upon their miewsses.[47] I have for some years been honored with a position as a member of our national Historic Committee of Comrades. These errors are very annoying to one interested in the preservation of Confederate history, but I presume we will have to wait for some impartial historian at a later date to produce a complete history of the causes and details of the conduct of the war between the states. The true mission of the UCV-US of CV and D of the C[48] is to compile all possible data for supplement that [is] contained in our official journal, Confederate Veteran. In this way some honest and capable historian will be well equipped to do justice to the great subject.

Sincerely, your Comrade
W.T. Shaw

FIG. 5.4. Brigadier General Tom Green. Collection of Molly Wiggins, General Green's great-granddaughter, Covington, Louisiana.

Letter from Lucien Flournoy to Dr. Alfred Flournoy, His Uncle

[Edited by Gary D. Joiner and Allan C. Richard Jr.]

Camp in the Field, April 26th 1864[49]

Dear Uncle:

I have been waiting for several days for a good opportunity of writing & at the same time sending a letter to you. I did not catch up with my command until they were near Natchitoches, April 22d.[50] We learned the enemy were evacuating Grand Ecore.[51] Gen. Taylor immediately ordered Gen. Bee with about five thousand cavalry and fifteen pieces of artillery to Monett's ferry which is directly on the Alexandria road.[52] This placed Bee in the *rear* of the enemy. His, Bee's position at Monett's was very strong if he had of properly guarded his flanks. Gen. Bee had twelve hours to post his army. The enemy were followed or pressed in *rear* by Parsons Regt. of Cavalry, some eight hundred or a thousand strong.[53] On the 24th near Cloutierville the enemy made a stand, our Cavalry charged them & we (Cavalry) were driven back a mile or so.[54] It was at this time that for an hour or so Gen. Bee checked his advance. Then and their we should of had our Infantry. If Gen. Smith had of remained in Shreveport & left Gen. Taylor with his army he would of had *all* of his Infantry at Monetts Ferry. It turned out as usual. The Cavalry became frightened & fled in utter confusion—Bee's entire command. You see we had him cut off from Alexandria. Monetts Ferry is very strong. The pine hills running right to the river. Our small Division of Infantry was in a few miles in rear of Parsons Regt. following up the enemy. All accounts that have reached us go to prove that Gen. Bee was flanked on his left by a *very* *small* force of the enemy.[55] Of *course* the Cavalry gave way as soon as they were pressed. Then the whole Cavalry force fled in utter confusion. (I mean Gen, Bee's command.) We maed our camp just in front of Monetts Ferry. I have just returned from the Hills where Gen. Bee had his force. I feel satisfied that Moutons old Division could have held the position against the entire Yankee Army.[56] The cavalry are in pursuit of the enemy. Report from the front this afternoon states our Cavalry at James Store, twenty-five miles from Alexandria.

April 27th.

I was sent by Gen. Gray yesterday to Red River where we have Batteries planted & protected by Infantry for the purpose of firing on transports

& Gun boats. Whilst there I heard heavy firing both above & below me. Remained with the Battery nearly four hours hoping to see a boat appear. About five o'clock P.M. I gave up all hopes of a boat passing. Started back to camp & had gone about four miles when a heavy fireing commenced on the River. The fireing was very rapid for fifteen or twenty minutes. The result of the engagement we received last Night. We had one battery of four guns.[57] Three Gun Boats with *two* trans ports came down.[58] Capt. Cornay commanding the Battery reserved his fire until they were in two hundred yards. Then opened on them. He had no protection whatever for his pieces or men. The largest Gun Boat after *receiving Considerable* damage run by.[59] (It was Commodore Porter's *flag* Boat & he was aboard) The next boat was a trans port. Capt. Cornay had to depress his pieces to fire into her.[60] One shot striking the boiler caused instant *Explosion*. The boat surrendered immediately. The Capt. then turned his attention to the two remaining Gun Boats & trans port. His fire was so accurate that one Gun Boat was badly disabled.[61] The other droped ahead & succeeded in saveing her. But all three were forced to ascend the river again.[62] We feel confident of Capturing all three. Alas, as in all of our fights, We are called upon to deplore the loss of the gallant & Brave. When the Gun Boats drew off one of them fired a *shell* which killed Capt. Cornay.[63] He being the only Man Killed. One Lieut. with the Infantry, Lieut. Bourge of the 18th La. Was badly, if not Mortally, wounded.[64] A company has just past to escort the remains of Capt. Cornay to his last resting place. A brave, gallant & worthy gentlemen. All who knew him honored & respected him. Fireing on the river just commenced, I will not close this letter until I hear the result. The trans port captured had a hundred & fifty negroes aboard, only twenty-five or thirty were taken out alive.[65] The rest were killed & scalded to death. The distruction of property from Natchitoches to Monetts Ferry is indescribable. With the exception of Madame Blanchards residence, every thing was burned. Her corn, fodder, smoke house, gin house was burned. They did not burn Cloutierville but plantations were destroyed. This whole Country is an utter waste. Desolation prevails. I suppose Gen. Taylor is waiting for Walkers Division, which is expected down in a day or so.[66] We will move on Alexandria as soon as it arrives. I cannot see how Gen. Taylor is to subsist his army in this country. Every thing must come from above unless we can get into the Lafourche country. Well I must tell you the unexpected position offered to me by Gen Gray. I am now A A.& Insp. Gen. on his staff with the rank of 1st Lieut., I would not of excepted the position if there had of been any chance of getting a promotion in my Regt. Not being a member of any company in the Regt. of course I was out of the line of promotion in the Regt. My position is a very pleasant one.

FIG. 5.5 Lucien Flournoy. Flournoy Papers, Louisiana State University in Shreveport Archives, Noel Memorial Library, Shreveport, Louisiana.

I have just returned from the burial of Capt. Cornay. The fireing heard this morning on the river was from Cornays battery & the two Gun boats driven back last night. The Gun boats run by.[67] But we captured the trans port.[68] So we have captured two trans ports & caused the enemy to *blow* up one Gun Boat.[69] Orders have just been received to march in the direction of Alexandria tomorrow morning. Have you heard from Charley & Sibley[70] —Gen. Lidell's men have been fireing on the enemies trans ports from the other side of the river.[71] I will write again soon. Tell Lizzie[72] I wrote to her three or four days ago—Love to all—As ever I remain your afft. Nephew

Lucien Flournoy

Letter from Private R. A. Knox

[Edited by Gary D. Joiner and Jimmy H. Sandefur]

On Old Cany River Forty miles below Natchitoches[73]

April 21, 1864

Dear Father

Wil reached me near Grand Ecore with the gray horse & I like him very well. We have come down in here with two divisions of Cavalry and five Batteries of artillery to annoy the Gunboats and Transports as they go up with company stores to the yanks at Grand Ecore. They have a large force there yet; but report says they are crossing the river there and are going to reinforce Steel.[74] We are in Natchitoches and our picketts and Moutons Division is near also.[75] I think we can hold our ground with them down here. Our loss in the first day['s] fighting[76] was Forty of our regt. out of 240 & there wasn't no troops ingaged only our brigade. But I tell you it was the hardest fighting that was done the whole three days. With only 600 men we charged & routed 5000 yanks. They had their position behind houses and fences and we got up to fifty yards of them before they run. We killed & wounded about 150 of them; but then they reinforced and we had to give back & when we got in three miles of Mansfield we met the infantry.[77] We captured all of the train of the 13th & 19th Army Corps amounting to 250 wagons loaded with medicine, Substance, Clothing and everything we mostly needed. We got all their artillery, amtg. to 21 pieces. There is no doubt in my mind but that Randalls Brigade saved the last days fight.[78] They held the position that Polignacs' Brigade was driven out of against four times their numbers and would not give back. He[79] is a dashing officer and deserves promotion. They [*sic*] yanks didn't get off without the loss of at least 10,000 men in killed, wounded, and captured. Our loss was great; but his loss the last day was greater than all of ours. The Missourians fought like Tigers and they bore near to the hardest part of the battle. We have to mourn the loss of a great many officers. I must close very abruptly for want of room. Me & Nat Turner arrived here on the 17, but he left. Lt. Grant [?] sick. He advised him to go back home. If so tell him Capt. Perry says tell him to stay until he gets well but send Lt. Heull word to hurry back.

Nothing more.
I am you yours,
R.A. Knox

Letter to Isabella Jane Whitworth Howell from Zack Howell, Shreveport, Louisiana, May 11, 1864

[Edited by Gary D. Joiner and Monica R. Pels]

Shreveport La May 11th 1864[80]

My dear Bella[81]

I write you a few lines to tell you that I am well and when I will come home,_ Col Zacharie[82] does not like for the officers to leave camps and I do not exspect that I can come out before the 20th inst,_ However I want you to send for me if you get sick and if I should not get out home at the time I write, you must send for me when ever you want me to come home + I will be sure to come,_ The Army news is very good we have captured says Gen Smith[83] in the last month Six Thousand prisoners, twelve hundred wagons, four thousand mules, thirty-six pieces of artillery, + wounded + killed Eight thousand of the enemy, _Gen Majors[84] Captured below Alexandria a transport with an Ohio Regt on board, The crew arrived here yesterday The Capt of the boat + the [clerks?] are good looking men_ We have captured two Gun Boates near Saline Pass[85] with 16 Guns + Eighty Prisoners We have also captured + discharged two Yankee Gunboates at Plymouth N. C._ took the city with 2500 prisoners_ The Yankees have called out their militia to serve for 100 days, The object is to take Richmond Va. There is a rumor in town that we have captured the Vicksburg Garrison but I do not believe this,_ Gen Banks[86] army is in Alexandria, They are trying to get away but I am in hopes we will [bag?] some more of them before they do_ I will close_ write to me soon_ Yours as Ever

Zack

The Death of George Ballard

[Edited by Gary D. Joiner and Dyson Nickles]

The following letter is from a Confederate soldier to his sister after the Battle of Yellow Bayou.

May the 20th. 1864[87]

On the Battlefield near Simmesport, Louisiana.[88]
Beloved Sister Araminta[89]

O what a joy it would be to me if I could write to you as I have always had the happy privelige of doing before But in the providence of God's goodness He has seen fit to deprive me of the privelige.

It is with a broken heart that I attempt to address you but it becomes my painfull duty to write you the solumn facts But how can I write my eyes are full of tears But I cannot withhold the truth from you though it is painfull Let us try and be resigned to the will of God while I am yet unhurt. Brother Georges[90] body lies in the ground while his deathless and immortal soul is at rest in heaven Our loss is his eternal gain then why should we mourn a departed friend or shake at deaths alarms It is but the voice that Jesus sends to call us to his arms. Are we not tending upward too as fast as time can move nor should we wish the hour more slow to keep us from our happy home above. Brother George was killed on Wednesday eavnig the

18th. We had a hard fight he was killed dead shot right through the heart he did not speak but died instantly. He had been dead about 15 minutes when I got to him. Mr. D.W. Dudley was with him when he was killed. We were all charging on the enemy when he was shot He had just shot and loaded his gun again. He did not fall when he was shot he lay down on his hands and knees and looked back at Mr. Dudley He run to him and layed behind a large tree but he was dead. Mr. Dudley helped carry him off the battlefield and stayed with me until he was Burried never can I forget his kindness there were 4 others went with me the Burry him. I thank God for such friends. We Burried him in a nice garden at Howards Plantation on Bayou DeGlaze we dressed him and Burried him decent . . . Dear Sister the object of your happiness is gone from your embrace forever in this life but I bless God for the assurance that we have of meeting our friends in heaven it is true we can go to him if we will put our trust in God and be faithfull Christians until Death the Lord will fullfill all his promises to us then. My Dear Sister the trial is great but we all have to die. O do not weep for the loss of your Dear husband but put your trust in God and look forward with bright hope to the day when you shall meet him in heaven. We are bound to part with our friends on earth but not forever—No tis not the whole of life to live in this troublesome world nor all Death to Die. Well we can say with the Pace Time is winging us away to our eternal life is but a winters day journey to the tomb. Youth and vigor soon will flee, blooming beauty loose its charms, all that's mortal soon will be Enclosed in deaths cold arms. But the Christian shall enjoy heath and beauty in a home for beyond this worlds allure Secure in Jesus Love. George left many friends who morn his loss, He was loved by all the company and while I morn his loss I thank God that he died bravely in defense of his country surrounded by his friends who will never forget him. Well Dear Sister try and take the death of your Dear husband as easy as possible, ask the Lord to bless you in your troubles— The fight is over at last the Yankees are gone badly whipped I dont think they will ever come back to Louisiana again.[91] We have been fighting them nearly every day since we got to Louisiana.[92] Our loss has been but little compaired to theirs. Col. Woods was slightly wounded the same day as George was killed and four other men wounded. Capt. Stemens was mortally wounded wounded [*sic*] . . . I have got George's horse and everything he had and I will send them home the first opportunity I have. I will try to go home as soon as the excitement is over here. the Enemies loss has been very heavy we have killed a great many of them and taken a great many prisoners. Well I do not field like writing about that now and I know you will not feel like reading about it. Charlie[93] is sick though not much. Well Sister try to be as well contented as you can and remember that your Brother will shair a part of your troubles . . . You nor your children shall never suffer while I live.

Well I suppose you have heard of Sister Josephines Death. Our sorrow is great but Gods grace will be sufficient for our trials— O that the Lord may comfort my Dear Sister in her troubles. If we never meet again on eart O may we meet in heaven let us live right and then we will be shure to die right nothing more. I remain your affectionate Brother until Death—

B. E. Ballard

Direct your letter to Mansfield, Louisiana.

P.S. I am well this morning the fight is over we left the Battleground last night and fell back to rest. The Yankees are clear gone. We drove them over 200 miles they have lost about 20 thousand men since they came to Louisiana.

Jefferson Morgan's Letters to His Wife

[Edited by Gary D. Joiner and Ann Turk]

Malugarady Co March 2 1864[94]

Dear wife I once more try to rite a few lines to let you know how I am. I have binn down with the meascles but I am about a gain. I was very sick with them but I will be able to start to the command in a few dayes. I am about sixty miles behind the ridgement[95] with about 39 others. D. M. Fields, Jentry Haindes are left here. ther well. the rest are with the ridgement. I received 2 letters from you cence I have binn sick which [I] red with plashure,[96] the from you and delisa. Lerne from them that you was a doing well which was grate satisfaction to me for I have bin very uneasy a bout a name. you can name it your self. I think that I will get come home some time this summer. they is a talk about peace. you must excuse me for this short letter for I can not rite. I am so nervous. I will rite when I get to the redgment again. I remain yours.

Jeff Morgan
To A A Morgan

adress Jeff Morgan Houston Hares[97] County Co (E) likens redgement 35 Texas calvery

Undated letter[98]

Dear wife I once more try to rite you a few lines which will inform you that I am on my feet. hoping that it will find you in good helth and a doing well and will find you in good spirits. I have not done eny dewety[99] cence I had the messeles but I am a geting stout againe. I would like to be at home at this time for I hered that bufordes[100] men was at home and I mite get to see bill. besides I mite git to see the rest of you which wood be agrate satisfaction to me. I can not tell when I will get to come but I think now all will git come hom by Chrismas for I do not beleave that the army will be held to gether much longer.

I will come hom the first chance that I can get. I am giting tired of a camp life and I think that all the boyes are in the same fix. the Ellis boyes are all well. D. W. Fieldes will come home before long and I send a letter by him. I have not no letter from home cence Lee Cooper come in and want to here from home very bad. I gave my best respect all of my friends and to the children for me. my hand is so trimley I will have to quit for will. but remain your untill dath Jeff Morgan

To A A Morgan

March 23, 1864

Dear wife I will try to rite you a few more lines which will in form you that I am on foot at this time. hoping when this get to you that it will find you in good helth and a doing will. I have not bin right well cence I had the measles. I rote a few lines a few dayes ago to send and was disapoinet. D. W. Fieldes is a going to start home in the morning. I thought that I would rite a few more and send it by him. I woul like to see you well very well but I can not git to come up there. I am out of clos. I would like to have a shirt and a pare of draers.[101] J. Morgan

Lousana May 13 1864

Dear wife I will try to rite you a few lines which will inform you that I am well. hope that thay find you all well and a doing well. I have no news to rite but the time. we have no rest day nor nite. Som times the fedes run and some times we will run. we have seen some the letters was capturde. thay say that yankes is badly whiped and thay say that thay tired of the wore and sum of theme sese that they will not fite eney more.[102] I seene bill. he got his hors shot from him. the ellis boyes is all on foot. our third lientend[103] got shout in the arm that is all the one of our company that was shout. I will rite soon a gaine for I am slepy. we are know nere mockvill[104] on red river be low alexandera.[105] I want you to rite soon as you git this leter and let me know how you are giting long. I will quit for now. you will

Jeff Morgan
To A A Morgan
adress Jeff Morgan
35 Calvey J. B. likens redgemt wes port lousarana Generel Baggery Breggade[106]

Camp near Washington La May 26th 1864[107]

Dear wife I write to let you know how I am. my health is as good as usual at this Season of the year. I hope this may reach you all well. the Federals have all left this part of the Country.[108] we are now resting up a little after a long siege of battling with the enamy and various are the consedering about wheare we will go next. Sum say to Brazere City,[109] som to Bowmont.[110] non can tell the health of the Reg. only tolerable good. not much fatal sicknes most: diare.[111] the water in these bioes[112] geting bad at this season. there has been and continues to be a great drouth in this Country. So much so the roads are awful dusty. we are geting plenty of rough corn bread and poor beef to eat but little forage. Consequently our horses look badle. My old horse looks bad and has quite a sore back. William expects to start home in a few days. I have not seen him. My eyes are very sore in the dust. direct your letters to Boumont Texas. we have the news in camp that the yankees are a cuting us in Ellis. I am happy to here that James Turvey brout the news that crops lookes well. I have not yet but one letter cence left. we have bin run too. I have not hade the chance for to rite. J. R. Bearnes but in a petition to have us fellers pardean fo going home without leaf and it was granted. William Morgan will start home in a few dayes. I would like to see him before he goze. I do not know wether come over for wer about twenty miles a foot. Grene Heckey had me that mony. Seen bill once cence I arived in la. I herd from Evins boys thay was will out there. Lieutenant got shot in the arm. we lost one man in a retreat. we have not hered from from him sence. my eyes hurt me so bad. I must quit. I want you to rite ofton.

To A A Morgan Yours untill deth
Jeff Morgan

May 29 1864
Camp nere washington la

Dear wife I one time try to rite you a few lines which will in form you that I am still on foot yet. hoping that thes will find you and the childrean a doing and in good spirites. we are a restting a few days after a bout 6 weeks marching and fiting but we will not stay here long. I can not tell where well go to from here. I hope that well go to Texas for I do not want to summer in la for it is to sickly. I would like to see you all. I hope how quick the time will come when well all can return to our wifes and little ones and injoy the short remment of our dayes. for our day are but few and ful of sorrow. I want you to do the best that you can for your self if I never return to you and the children. I want you to rese them up to work and to be honest and in good credite. I may git to come home after while. I hav the sore eye yet very bad so I will have to quit. I want you to rite as often you can for I am ancious to here home.

adress Jeff Morgan
Beaumont Texas
likins redge Texas Calvary
bagery brgade

Letter Written by D. W. Fields to Amanda Ann Sportsman Morgan in Ellis County, Texas, Concerning the Death of Her Husband, Jefferson

Camp at Sparta Louisiana,[113] July 17th 1864 Mrs. Morgan

Dear Madam

It becomes my painful duty to write to you stating the death of your husband and my friend. He breathes his last on the 7th day of this month at or near Lock Dam at the General Hospital near Alexandria.[114] I [?] this reaches you will get a letter I wrote to you stating he was sick at that time. He was not considered dangerous but on the morning of his death he taken a congestive chill which lasted him until he drew his last breath. We were not allowed to leave a man of his acquaintance with him. Still I am satisfied he never wanted for anything after he went to the hospital. One of his acquaintances saw him every day after he went there until the day he died. That day I started a man to see him but the pontoon bridge was broke and he could not cross the river.

I saw him the day before he died and as soon as I heard he was dead I went over directly to see and learn all I could about him. He was buried before I reached the place and was decently buried and his headboard is marked with his name, company and regiment. I know this looks hard to think you will see the face of your dear husband no more until you meet him at the Judgement seat of Jesus Christ but let me say one thing for your consolation that he maintained his integrity to the last. Never did I hear him speak one immoral word during a campaign of 12 months. If you ever expect to see him to live with him in eternity prepare to meet your God in peace. I am satisfied he has gone home to die no more. I [?] with him. I rested closely by him every night and could he speak to you today he would tell you I was ever kind to him in the last world. He was ever heard to speak he said I am going home. I must close. May heaven's blessings attend you in your lonely house. I am your friend.

D.W. Fields
To A. A. Morgan

A Letter from the End of the Red Campaign Describing the Battle of Mansura

[Edited by Steven Mayeux and Gary D. Joiner]

Camp on Bayou De Glaze
May 23d /63[115]

Friend Dick

Three years in Confederate States service this day, and very tired, I might say I am surfieted, in point of fact I am all most ready to "holler 'nuff'" been fighting for 46 days, Yanks gone at last, thank the Lord! I have come very near being "sent up the spout" several times, but "nary went", Dick, you know enough about cavalry skirmishing to understand what we have passed through since the Mansfield and Pleasant Hill fights,[116] when I tell you that it has been one continued skirmish in the daytime and sometimes in the night. Nothing to eat our selves and nothing for our horses, I think I am safe in saying that our horses have not been unsaddled 8 days in the last 45, while the yankees were retreating we would throw our cavalry in their front, they would come along whip us like hell, kill and wound a good many and we would step aside, and let them pass, fall in their rear again, and with the help of that immortal band of heroes, Mouton's Division would injure them somewhat, but pretty soon in front again, whipped again, step aside again, that has been the programme for the last three weeks, once in an open prarie near Marksville[117] all of our cavlry, and the Infantry threw themselves in the front to *"make the enemy mass his forces" and he_"massed"*, you hear if you call four heavy columns of infantry 3 miles long, massing, I say that yankee army *"massed"*, and as soon as it had massed, we *"assed"*, I will leave it to any sane reasonable, unprejudiced, *prudent* individual if it was not time to *"ass"*, I will give you the particulars, our brigade and Major's composed the right wing, the infantry and one regiment of cavalry composed the center, the balance of the cavalry on the left, we had an artillery duel for about an hour they threw their whole force on our left and center, we were in a ditch dismounted, all right when hell broke loose, on our left, & here comes a courier for us to reinforce, we mounted and rode three miles, under the fire of 6 heavy batteries, and strange to say, lost only 4 killed and 6 wounded, Lieut. Coffee of company C and Capt Clint Henry of Co F among the wounded, one of our co a Mr. Poole from near Linn was slightly wounded, our company was marching single file through a gap of a fence, just as I got opposite a 32 pound ball struck the ground, and lifted the rails right over my head, never touched me nor my horse, the boys thought I was killed, and I thought every body was killed but me and that I was mortally wounded, or seriously frightened, or struck with and earth quake, or Vesuvius had opened, or hell had broke loose or *"sumthin"* else, well Dick, we were not through yet we had 10 heavy field pieces, they got awful hot, our regiment right at the old Valverde,[118] rip! rip! Bam! Bam! put me in mind of two big men pouring the fist into each others ribs, King, Roberts and Tho. Rusk for instance "fiten", they got too hot for us, and now the most beautiful sight I ever saw in my life, though I did not enjoy it at the time, in an open prairie, nothing to obstruct the view, our batteries *"retired" (run like Hell)* the infantry were ordered to fall back, and they did not like to go a bit, but retired slowly and in good order, now cavalry check those yanks until the infantry and artillery gets to the timber, about 6 hundred yards. Oh, how I did wish I belonged to the infantry then, well, the smoke blew off, and we were left alone in our glory, doubts and fears, and then came that pretty (ugly) sight, when everybody had left we looked, here came a line of skirmishers 6 or 8 feet apart, 2 miles long, about 200 yards in their rear about 6 brigades of infantry and right and left cavalry, and so on back as far as we could see pretty shortly zip! zip! spat! spat! that hell roaring hateful music we got too hot for their skirmishers they reinforced them, too heavy for them, their advance column opened! and shrine of the Mighty! if they had not shot too high, they would have killed every one of us *very* dead, but as I mentioned, only 4 killed and 6 wounded in our regiment. I do not know our loss in the whole brigade, and it is impossible to find out our [loss] I expect you know more about our loss down here than I do. Well, Polignac says we saved his infantry we then fell back to timber slowly and in good order we then fell in their rear, they took down Bayou De Glaize we followed, run them to Yellow Bayou,[119] in getting there we killed 26 that we got, wounded I do not know how many captured 96 cavalry, and stopped at sundown, and would have done well to have let them cross the Atchafalaya in peace, but next morning pitched into their whole army and got most beautifully cut up, our Brigade lost 96 killed and wounded 3 in our wounded Haney Jacob Pennington and another Poole none of them seriously hurt, I do not know the loss of the infantry, but none in [Bruton's?] nor Hancock's companies, the yankees think they were whipped, and I know we were, and so she goes, the yankees have gone up the Miss River, Major's men fired on the last transport yesterday, and we are this far on our way somewhere, some says the Miss, some says the Lafourche, some New Orleans, some on the way to starvation, Bully for us!

F. B Harris

The 4th Texas Cavalry at the Battles of Monett's Ferry and Mansura

[Edited by Bryan James Maedgen and Gary Joiner]

Rapides Parish La. Camp of the 4th T. C.[120]
at Thompsons plantation 5 miles above LeCount[121]
June the 23rd 64

Capt. H. G. Carter
Dear Sir, hoping
that you have succeeded in getting home and as I have an opportunity to send you a letter by Marion Zellner I seat myself to write it. I have no news to tell you, but will try to recount to you our ups and downs after the (so fatal to you) 9th day of April.

Our Brig.[122] left Mansfield the 11th for Bayou Pier[123] where they encamped. I got to them on the 12th.[124] We ranged about but done nothing but fight gnats, until after the Fed. fleet had got safely to Natchitoches. We were then ordered there commanded by Gen. Bee.[125] He kept us in hot water all the time whenever the Feds felt like running in our pickets, which by the by was a very easy thing to do as the old Brig. could not be on picket all the time. When we were on picket the rest of the troops rested but when it was our time to rest we had to do that in line of battle to prevent a surprise and perhaps capture of the pickets on duty at such a time. About the 18th or 19th we were ordered Gen Bee comdg. to Monets ferry[126] on Cane or old river. We got there on the 20th. Early next morning we were ordered to saddle. we did so, then came an order to fall in on foot. we did that too and then moved down to the bank of the old or Cane river having crossed it the evening before. here we formed line of battle and entrenched ourselves on the hill expecting that the yankees would come every minute, we waited and waited on until next morning, our horses saddled, ourselves without bread. The next morning April 22nd the feds drove our skirmishers across the river.[127] As soon as the yankee skirmishers came in sight some 2 miles off Bee ordered the artillery to open on them, all our artillery some 15 or 20 pieces opened and ran them back, of course there was nobody hurt. He fought them with artillery at long range all day and although he knew that the enemy was flanking our left yet there was no preparation made to meet them not even after they had succeded in crossing the river.[128] about Sundown we were ordered to our horses. we had not seen a yankee except the smoke of a battery that they used on us pretty lively as we fell back but without doing any harm. As soon as we were mounted we began a retreat the like of which I never have seen. We ran about 30 miles, nobody knew what for and everybody cursing because we did not stop and camp.

The next morning found us at Beans station on the road from Carroll Jones to Barrs ferry.[129] Here all the footmen were ordered to Pleasant hill, and I was ordered to report to Capt J. C Roberts to assist him in the discharge of his *ardous duty*. Since then I have not been with the Company in battle. Our run left a gap for the feds and they made their way down Red river to Alexandria. After the Feds had passed we followed them up, and the first evening we were send to skirmish with them old Gotch in Command of Brig. drove them within three miles of their breastworks at Alexandra. We skirmished with them that day and the next we were send round by Pauls store down Bayou Bouef to Changville.[130] From here we were send to the river where Majors Brig.[131] and ours captured some boats 2 gun boats and three transports we saved the best guns from the gun boats and burned them all.[132] Then the yankees made a faint down this bayou and we are now camped and grass our horses on the very ground where our Brig. had a little fight on. The boys can pick up shells in abundance. The yankees finally succeded in getting the most of their fleet over the falls, all they did not get over they destroyed. I think some five.[133] After they had got their fleet over and all ready the Feds proceded to move down Red river by the way of Simsport across the Atchafalaya.[134] Our Brig. skirmished with them by day and picketed by night. And as they came out on the Marksville prairie[135] our forces consisting of Majors Division and the Division that Gen Bee had commanded and Polignacs Division of Infantry. We had about fifty peaces of artillery in line and among them the Bull Battery two rifled 30 pound Parrott guns. The whole affair was out on the open prairy.[136] Our brigade was on the extreme right and there was some Cavalry, I dont [know] whose command it was neither do I want to know it. on the extreme left to support Polignacs infantry as soon as the yankees brought up a battery and shelled them a little they concluded that our train was threatened by the Bouef road and they reported in the shortest possible time at Pittsmill two miles above Evergreen some 18 miles from Marksville prairie.[137] Then our Regt.

was ordered to the left and they passed in good range of the Fed batteries along our whole line some mile and a half. They remained exposed to the Fed batteries some two hours. The boys describe it as the most terrific bombardment they had ever been in and if you can imagine, skirmishing with fifty guns on a side firing all as fast as they could load and fire you can form an idea. I was some three miles in the rear and I never heard the like. The Bull battery dismounted five Fed. guns in about 10 minutes. They then massed their force against our left and Gen Wharton who was in Command[138] withdrew from the field just far enough for the yankees to go down the Simsport road, which they took and traveled, with all possible speed. Wharton again followed them and attacked them on Yellow bayou.[139] There we sustained a considerable loss without effecting a thing but to kill a few yankees perhaps more than we lost. This was the last of our active operations. We moved out to the Bouef for Washington,[140] and have been moving round like the Arabs to find grass for our horses ever since Now about our Brig. it has undergone almost entirely a new organization Col. Hardiman Comdg. Col. Bagby has some other Brig. as the boys did not like him at all. Capt. Crossam is Brig. Qr. Master.[141] Capt. Dennis Corwin Commissary of Subsistence W. S. Moore a d a general.[142] Frank Stars a de Camp,[143] J. Colins act. adjt. of Regt.[144] and Elam Sergt. Maj.[145]

All the boys that went home from Hempstead who have come back have been send to Polignac,[146] but they have been send for and I think they will all be back in a few days. All the dismounted men who can mount themselves have gone home for that purpose. The health of the Regt. is very good but I fear for them the latter part of the Summer as it has not missed but two or three days rainy weather since the first of June. We are now in quarters [*sic*] negroe quarters but will have to leave them. Joe Pike is poorly yet but he is well enough to anoy me smartly while I am writing. Thos Carter was thrown from his horse and nearly broke his leg. Kolb is puny and Charly had a chill day before yesterday. Hugh Partin was thrown off his horse on Bayou Cotilie[147] and he has not got well yet, he has been furloughed and gone Somewhere I dont know where. J. Wood is not well but he keeps up and about. The rest are all well.

Day before yesterday we were ordered to make out a report of all the horses turned over in N. Mexico[148] and all the horses lost in battle. I assure you it is a devil of a job, I have been at work all day and am not through yet with one copy. If you have any papers that are of interest to the Company I wish you would send them by some of the boys who have been furloughed. Whaley lost his horse on his way here and instead of coming to the company he reported to Compy[149] B of the 15th Tex. Inf and applied for a transfer and it has been ordered. I cant find a good many of the descriptive lists of the boys who have been transferred to our Company. Write to Some of us about the amount of pay the transferred boys: T. S. Jones. Elza Carter, J. Callow, and others if there are any, drew at Vermilion Bayou in Nov. when the Regiment was passed off the 31, of October 1863.

We have no news at all on the other side of Miss that is reliable. I had almost forgot to tell you that after the yankees had crossed the Atchafalaya, Polignac took position at the junction of the Bayou and Red River and the Bull Battery we send there (two peaces) so one fine morning after the river got up the yankees came up with some iron clads and drove the gunners from the Bull Battery after they had bursted one of the peaces. the other they took on board and carried it off

The boys all send their their best wishes and so do "I". As there is no one particular in your neighbourhood with whom I am aquainted, you may give my respect to Capt Haskel, Lutner and if you are a mind to, to the ladies if you can manage to introduce me to them at a distance.

Write soon to Charly, Kolb, or

Yours
truly
Moritz. Maedgen

N. B. We are quite military now we do everything by the sound of the bugle. I expect that old Charly is gone he is no doubt in some of this Cavalry and we shall keep a sharp lookout for him, and if we ever see him he is ours or rather yours.

The Final Trans-Mississippi Engineering Mission

[Edited by Thomas A. Pressly and Gary D. Joiner]

Head Quarters Engineer Department

TRANS-MISSISSIPPI DEPARTMENT

Shreveport March 4th[150]

Capt. Kirby[151]

D[ea]r S[i]r

I send by Furr & Grubb a lot of letters for the Commander, have been waiting the completion of orders to go to Ark for the train. A week in the meantime in charge of the bridge which two nights since was swept away almost entirely. 16 boats yet not found given up in storms and still missing. As soon as I get them [I will go on] the trip to Ark. I suppose will join you. Please take care of my box of clothing. It is intended that the men here shall go with me to Ark. I believe but heavens how will I ever get the train when the whole country [is] under water. Bad news from Charleston[152] & Bentonville.[153] It looks a little like we've given up but hope for the best.[154]

Regards to Wiggs
Yours,
D.E. Causland

Journal of Elizabeth Jane Samford, Wife of Thomas Pope Fullilove, Written 1915

[Edited by Gary D. Joiner and Monica R. Pels]

The troops were in camps in Ala.—raw volunteers for military instruction. War had always been such a far away reality that none of us realized its significance.[155]

The daily review of the soldiers was daily scene of attraction & drew large crowds of pleasure seekers to the Encampment. I had no dream of the drill import—my brothers & cousins were enlisted & were only gay cavaliers in my young imagination, rather on a gay escapade than with any serious intent. A sixty or ninety day frolic when the storm would blow over & all return to their firesides for the winter. [. . .]

The war increased & it was not many months before the spirit of the conflict entended to the "Trans. Miss Department" & many companies were formed and held in reserve. My husband felt that he could aid the cause more by contributing supplies than by inactivity in camp & public opinion was that the war would soon end. He said when the enemy crossed the Miss. River he would fly to arms—until then he bent every energy to his farm sending all he made to he front in supplies except just enough to feed his family. He equipped a man with the best horse he had—the best gun he could find and $1,000.00 as his substitute—as he said to rest on his arms in camp while he—my husband—worked indefatigably on the farm making & giving supplies to feed the army. I have known him to kill 150 fat hogs and send 100 of them to the commissary—besides corn, wheat, cotton, and everything else in proportion.

It was not long however before the Fall of Vicksburg & the surrender of N. O.[156] & then the appearance of the Federal troops near the Miss. in Ark.

Then my husband bade us good bye, shouldered his gun and jointed the army, Com. D. [6th] La. Cavalry.

His scene of action was mostly in Ark. where Gen. Marmaduke's Bragade was stationed to protect the Border lands on the Miss. River.

His letters to me during his service tell of his engagements & hardships—too numerous to repeat here—the trials of a private's life—which embalm the service of many "unsung heroes".

Our Second child—Preston Greer was born Feb. 23, 1862.[157] My husband left me in our country home with this little son & my sister to do the best I could. He asked a neighbor—Mr. Christian to hold himself in readiness to come to my relief if necessary & he got a boy 14 yrs. old Tom Scott, to spend the nights in the home as often as possible. Father Fullilove lived 8 miles away on his own farm with mother and two children under his care—Jimmy and Ella—& he promised to keep a general oversight of our home.

But practically I had to run the farm—through the seasons. There were but about 50 negroes on the place & I must say—they behaved well—were obedient, respectful & helped me as far as possible.

There was an old man—Uncle Edgar—who came to my door every night & reported the day's work—asking directions & making suggestions for the next day's work.

I had the stock pen—the hogs killed & meat cured—lard and sausage etc. all stored—the corn & wheat stored—ground and distributed.

Uncle Edgar's wife—Minerva—cooked dinner for the plantation. Old Aunt Violet took care of the negro babies & children & fed the chickens.

There was nothing to buy & we literally lived from the place. These negroes had to be clothed—the women spun the thread from the cotton and wool—we raised sheep—All our supplies on hand at the beginning of the war were soon exhausted & all our ports were blockaded so we were thrown on our own resources from the farm for the supply of all our needs. [. . .]

During the first half of 1864—our soldiers were kept in Ark. fighting now and then driving in the federal pickets etc.

There arose great dissatisfaction in the command however at Head Quarters & charges of incompetency were found against some of the officers of the Brigade. As a consequence, there was a reconstruction of the command & my husband's Co. D was dismounted indeed many other companies met the same fate. In the fall the Federals held N. O. and all points along the Miss. River & there was a threatened advance of the Gun Boats up Red River to attack Shreveport where Gen. Kirby Smith held headquarters for the Trans. Miss. Department.

As a barricade against the Yankee Gun Boats it was decided to obstruct the Falls or Rapids in the Red River near Alexandria. My husband was appointed to this work with several hundred negro men under his management. How well I remember—when he came to this work and in transit from Ark. passed our home.

He was allowed to ride his horse & spent two days with us—happy days! How we baked and brewed & made ready for his short visit! Among other things we made a cake—actually a cake—as follows—We had no flour—Sister Fanny took a coarse soft, clean towel & pushed it down & around in a bowl of meal—home ground—then the towel was taken out & carefully shaken on a large piece of paper. This process in time, yielded quite a pile of very fine meal which was sifted through thin old muslin until we had probably two pounds of what looked like wheat flour. This with our home made sugar, eggs etc. was evolved into a delicious cake & when iced (icing rather brown) was a crowning for the dinner which was to honor our expected guest.

I will remark here that the yeast we used in this cake as well as in all our cooking was made by burning corncobs or hickory. The ashes, when washed in water & settled & drained off make a strong alkaly which was bottled & when used with buttermilk in the right proportion made a tolerable yeast.

During the winter months at F. DeRussy,[158] & Camp Galaher on R. River,[159] Mr. F.[160] contracted rheumatism. The winter was unusually severe & was very hard on the negroes. Constant rains & freezing weather made the exposure fearful—for the work necessitated exposure all the time & frequent change of camp required more precaution than was possible.

Mr. F. wrote me once of his serious regret at a move of camp which took him to a jungle & leaving a domicile which he said was comparatively comfortable—viz. a platform of rough boards, 7 ft. x 4 ft. on 2 ft blocks which kept him off the wet ground—over this floor a roof was made of 3 poles on each side stuck in the mud, & meeting on top. A blanket on either side made the sides of the tent & into this hut he & another overseer, Capt. Lacy[161]—crawled side by side thankful for shelter.

The negroes were half clothed & poorly fed as they felled immense trees & drove piling in the river against which the logs were floated down & thus an immense raft was the forlorn hope for obstructing Gun Boats. My husband was very sick at last & Genl. Harrison took him into his quarters & made him his clerk, after which he fared well & was more comfortable. In the spring of 1865 all soldiers were recalled to Shreveport and there my husband was remounted.

The Fed. forces made their way up & came on up to Grand Ecore & the Fed. soldiers rushed on to Pleasant Hill on their way to Shreveport. I think the Gun Boats were left below the Raft. At this distance of time I can't remember distinctly At any rate Shreveport was their objective Point & they abandoned their gun boats & were led by Genl. Banks through the country. The Confederates were ordered to concentrate at Pleasant Hill to meet Banks. The troops had to pass my home & it took them nearly all day. My sister Fanny & I sat on the front steps & could do nothing but watch the procession—thousands & thousands of men—tramp, tramp, tramping by, hour after hour followed by a train of wagons a mile long.

I did not know where my husband was—hadn't heard from him in weeks. On and on these soldiers went—to Mansfield & on to Pleasant Hill.

After three days, one morning Ed Pope—who had followed my husband through the war, came up the road from Shreveport & handed me a note from my husband saying his command was ordered to Mansfield & he had sought and obtained permission to ride on from Shreveport ahead of his command & thus might gain an hour or two to stay at home & join the ranks as the command passed later in the day.

Oh! the ecstasy of that expected visit & the "hurrying to & fro" to make ready for the honored guest! About 10 A.M. three horsemen galloped up— Mr. F. was accompanied by two other men who lived in the neighborhood & although they hadn't time to seek their own homes, they wanted to hear all they could and leave messages. It was a sweet, sad visit for the parting (& such a parting leading to the very scene of action) cast its black shadow backward over our joy at meeting.

At 1 P.M. we heard the south of the coming cavalry loud & louder came the hoof beats— until a roar as of thunder filled the air. We waited at the gate with our arms encircling each other until Co. D. came in view and then one embrace & a long kiss & my darling mounted & rode away. The battle of Pleasant Hill was fought that same day & the result was disastrous to both sides. Our forces retreated to Mansfield pressed by the Fed. & the next day the battle was renewed at Mansfield & Banks was driven back to Grand Ecore & sought refuge in his Gun Boats leaving hundreds on the field wounded & slain.

We could hear the cannonading all day at our house at Preston.[162] I spent almost the entire day in my garden under a large oak tree not knowing but that each boom of the cannon meant death to my Love. The couriers passed every hour on their way to Shreveport Head Quarters with dispatches & I would go to the roadside to ask the news of them as they passed in a gallop. They each without stopping would call back "Feds are giving way", "Battle raging" etc. I will never forget the day & its agony & suspense.

Next day Tom[163] sent his man Ed[164] to me with a letter- the battle had been fought and won— Banks was in retreat with the Confederates in hot pursuit.

Tom's company was met as they approached the battle field near Mansfield by a messenger from our Head Quarters detailing the entire Co. to escort 200 Yankee prisoners to the stockage at Tyler, Tex. He wrote me that they would camp on their first night on their march at the spring one mile from his father's home & for me to go to Pa F.'s the next day & if possible he would get a permit to spend the night with me. I took Sister Fanny in the buggy with little John as outrider, we drove the two next days to Pa's.

About sundown the cavalry came in sight & sure enough Tom had a furlough for the night. His Capt. Lacy also spent the night at Pa's. Next morning at breakfast Capt. Lacy told me he had a present for me— viz— an extension of my husband's furlough for the two weeks during which time the march to Tyler and return would be made— saying Tom could join the Company on his[165] return. Happy hardly expressed my joy— Two whole weeks at home with my long absent husband! This was April 10th. News traveled slowly but before the two weeks expired the news of Lee's surrender had reached the Department & the war was over.

The years which followed— during the reconstruction period were years of terror & loneliness. The soldiers, let loose on the country, stole & pillaged until we never knew what a day might bring forth.

After the battles of Pleasant Hill and Mansfield the wounded soldiers from both armies were brought in our midst to be cared for. In the village of Keachie the Female College & the churches were turned into hospitals and those soldiers who were not helplessly wounded were scattered through the country into every house which was opened. About 12 were sent to our home & for weeks & weeks we nursed & cared for them to our utmost ability. It was three months before the last one left us. They were grateful— poor, maimed, wounded, sick fellows & gave them our best. We were bereft of the luxuries & many of the comforts of living but such as we had was freely given.

Notes

1. This General Order appears in at least two versions. The one printed here was intended as an open letter to the troops and contains language not found in the other. As noted at the end of the letter, this version was printed in the *Washington (Arkansas) Telegraph* on June 8, 1864. One hand-transcribed version, not in Taylor's hand, is found in the Historic New

Orleans Collection. This version was previously recorded in *Civil War Regiments* 4, no. 2 (1994): 129–30.

2. Letter in the personal collection of Thomas Pressly, Shreveport, Louisiana.
3. For an excellent biography of the prince, see Jeff Kinard, *Lafayette of the South: Prince Camille de Polignac and the American Civil War* (College Station, TX, 2001).
4. Polignac's Brigade was encamped at Moundville, near the town of Washington in St. Landry Parish, Louisiana. This letter is found in the personal collection of Thomas Pressly, Shreveport, Louisiana. All spelling and punctuation are the author's.
5. Brigadier General Sterling B. Hendricks, former commander of the 17th Texas Consolidated Cavalry Regiment, Dismounted.
6. Colonel James G. Stevens, commander of the 22nd Texas Cavalry Regiment, Dismounted.
7. At this point in the war, Polignac commanded the Second Texas Brigade, composed of the 22nd Texas Cavalry Regiment, Dismounted; the 34th Texas Cavalry Regiment, Dismounted; and the 17th Texas Consolidated Cavalry Regiment, Dismounted. Stevens had caused problems for Polignac since July, fomenting discontent within his regiment against the French nobleman. Kinard, *Lafayette of the South,* 97–101.
8. Camille Armand Jules Marie, Prince de Polignac diary, October 27, 1863. Microfilm located at Russell Library, Northwestern Louisiana State University, Natchitoches, Louisiana, and at Archives and Special Collections, Noel Memorial Library, Louisiana State University in Shreveport, Louisiana. The original diary, letters, and attached papers are in the Polignac family archives, Paris, France. Kinard, *Lafayette of the South,* 114.
9. Prince de Polignac led his troops valiantly during the Red River Campaign and achieved great fame during and after the Civil War. His troops, having trouble pronouncing his French name, referred to their commander as "General Polecat."
10. Letter in the personal collection of Nancy Beard Wilson, Kentfield, California. Wilson is Colonel Beard's great-grand niece. Colonel Beard was the regimental commander of the Louisiana Consolidated Crescent Regiment.
11. The camp would have been located on or near the Natchitoches-Shreveport Stagecoach Road, which is present-day Louisiana Highway 175. In 1864, the village of Pleasant Hill was located in DeSoto Parish, three miles north of its current location. The town moved to take advantage of the railroad, constructed in about 1900. The current location of the town is in Sabine Parish. The location of the Consolidated Crescent Regiment's camp would have been on or near the parish boundary line between DeSoto and Sabine parishes.

12. Mrs. Childers's home, no longer in existence, was located on the eastern edge of the village, near the intersection of the Natchitoches-Shreveport Stagecoach Road and the Blair's Landing Road.
13. Major General John George Walker's Division of Texas infantry.
14. Blair's Landing Road.
15. Brigadier General Jean Jacques Alexandre Alfred Mouton's Division of Louisiana Infantry.
16. Natchitoches-Shreveport Stagecoach Road.
17. Major General Sterling Price, District Commander of Arkansas. The forces were Brigadier General Thomas Churchill's Division of Arkansans and Brigadier General Mosby Parsons's Division of Missourians.
18. Brigadier General Tom Green's Texas Cavalry Corp.
19. Colonel Beard had homes in Keachi in DeSoto Parish and in Shreveport in Caddo Parish. His concern was that either the department commander, Lieutenant General Edmund Kirby Smith, or the district commander, Major General Richard Taylor, would retrograde the army farther north, either to Shreveport or perhaps to eastern Texas. Taylor would decide to fight the Union invaders three miles south of Mansfield, about eighteen miles north of Beard's position.
20. Bossier Point was the southernmost tip of Bossier Parish, Louisiana, located at the junction of the Red River and Loggy Bayou. The position was east and somewhat north of Beard's location.
21. Colonel Beard's infant son, Charlie Edward Beard, age four months, had died on March 28, but it appears that he had not heard the sad news.
22. Colonel James H. Beard, commander of the Louisiana Consolidated Crescent Regiment, wrote this letter, his last formal communication, two days before his death at the Battle of Mansfield. It is evident from the timing of the letter that General Taylor had not decided to fight at Mansfield but still believed that the engagement to save Shreveport would be fought farther south. The letter was written to the brother of his wife, Catherine E. Hoyle Tomkies, of Kingston, Louisiana.
23. This letter is one of only a few personal accounts from the Confederate side in the Red River Campaign. Water damage and foxing have destroyed much of the contents. Illegible areas are indicated. This letter is part of the collection of Jimmy Sandefur, Shreveport, Louisiana.
    The 15th Texas Infantry Regiment was part of the Second Brigade of the Second (Louisiana) Infantry Division of the Army of Western Louisiana. General Mouton commanded the division. Lieutenant Colonel Robert D. Stone led the Second Brigade and also led the 15th Texas. The other regiments in the brigade were the 17th Texas Consolidated Cavalry, Dismounted; 22nd Texas Cavalry, Dismounted; 31st Texas Cavalry, Dismounted; and the 34th Texas Cavalry, Dismounted.

24. The Battle of Mansfield was fought on April 8, and the Battle of Pleasant Hill was fought on April 9, 1864.
25. Five miles above Mansfield.
26. Moss Plantation.
27. See chap. 1.
28. Troopers of General Green's cavalry corps, who had been skirmishing with the Union column to slow their progress since the previous day. The arrival of the cavalry on the field places the action at noon.
29. Buildings in the Fincher homestead. See chap. 1.
30. 19th Kentucky Infantry Regiment.
31. Major General John George Walker led the First (Texas) Division of the Army of Western Louisiana.
32. The act of concealment and lying in wait to attack by surprise.
33. The Union 16th Corps.
34. Major General Sterling Price's division formerly had been divided into two small divisions of Missourians, commanded by Brigadier Mosby M. Parsons, and Arkansans, commanded by Brigadier James C. Tappan. See Appendix 1.
35. General Green at the Battle of Blair's Landing.
36. General Edmund Kirby Smith, commander of the Confederate Department of the Trans-Mississippi.
37. Brigadier General Horace Randal of the Second Brigade of the Texas Division.
38. Brigadier General Henry Gray of the First Brigade of the Louisiana Division.
39. Union Rear Admiral David Dixon Porter.
40. Letter in the personal collection of Molly Wiggins, Covington, Louisiana. Wiggins is Tom Green's great-granddaughter.
41. Colfax, the parish seat of Grant Parish, Louisiana.
42. April 10, 1918.
43. This refers to an engagement in 1863 prior to the Red River Campaign.
44. The Battle of Blair's Landing was fought on April 12, 1864. The Confederates, under General Green, attempted to capture or destroy all or part of the Union Admiral Porter's fleet. The fleet was retreating after a failed rendezvous with the land forces under Major General Nathaniel P. Banks. Blair's Landing, located today in extreme southern Red River Parish, was the eastern terminus of a road that lead from Pleasant Hill. In one of the strangest battles of the Civil War, Green and his cavalrymen fought a battle with the ironclad monitor USS *Osage,* the timberclad gunboat USS *Lexington,* and the transport *Black Hawk* for about two hours. Few casualties resulted, the most grievous being the loss of Tom Green,

the commander of the Texas Cavalry Corps. Green was arguably the best cavalry leader west of the Mississippi River on either side during the war. The USS *Osage* fired a shot that killed Green from a very short distance. Green was mounted on his horse, exhorting his men to attack the gunboats. The vessel's canister round was aimed with the use of a periscope rigged just days before. This is apparently the first use of a periscope in battle. Green appears to be the only casualty of that round.

45. Battle of Pleasant Hill fought on April 9, 1864.
46. Battle of Yellow Bayou fought on May 18, 1864.
47. Muses.
48. United Confederates Veterans, United Sons of Confederate Veterans, and the [United] Daughters of the Confederacy.
49. Letter in the Alfred Flournoy Papers, Louisiana State University in Shreveport Archives, Noel Memorial Library, Shreveport, LA. Lucien was born in Pulaski, Giles County, Tennessee in 1837. The family moved to Caddo Parish, Louisiana, shortly thereafter. Lucien was the second oldest of five children. His siblings were Silas III, Mary, Camp, and Elizabeth (Lizzie). The last three were born in Caddo Parish. Lucien's father, Silas, was killed in a hunting accident in southern Caddo Parish in 1844, and thereafter his paternal uncle Alfred acted as a father figure for the youngsters. He was a graduate of Kentucky Military Institute at Frankfort. See U.S. Department of Commerce, Sixth Decennial Census (1840), Giles County, Tennessee, unpublished tabulations in the National Archives and Records Administration (NARA), Washington, D.C.; *Virginia Magazine of History and Biography* 2 (1894): 443–44.
50. Lucien Flournoy served the Confederacy in two capacities. He enlisted in New Orleans on May 9, 1861, and was appointed second lieutenant in Company H, 2nd Louisiana Infantry Regiment. He served in the Army of Northern Virginia in 1861 and early 1862, at which time his enlistment was complete. He then served in the Louisiana Consolidated Crescent Regiment as adjutant, Field and Staff, to Colonel Henry Gray (who was later promoted to brigadier general). Andrew B. Booth's *Records of Louisiana Confederate Soldiers and Louisiana Confederate Commands* (Spartanburg, SC, 1984), vol. 1:873.
51. The forward elements of the Union column were sixteen miles south of Natchitoches by 2:30 A.M. that morning on Cane River Island, also known as the *Isle Brevelle*. U.S. War Dept., *War of the Rebellion: The Official Records of the Union and Confederate Armies*, 128 vols. (Washington, DC, 1880–1901), ser. 1, vol. 34, pt. 1:439 (hereinafter cited as *OR*, followed by series number, volume number, part number, and page reference).
52. Confederate forces consisted of one thousand, six hundred cavalry and four batteries of artillery, usually with four guns each. Monett's Ferry

lies at the southern end of the *Isle Brevelle* on the modern Louisiana Highway I.

53. The cavalry was commanded by Major General John A. Wharton. He took command of the Texas Cavalry Corps following the death of Major General (Brevet) Tom Green at Blair's Landing on April 12. The number of cavalry mentioned may be accurate. Flournoy was an infantry officer and may not have known who was in command of the cavalry contingent. Brigadier Mosby Parsons' division was ordered to Arkansas along with the Arkansas and Texas divisions on April 14. They would not participate in the Louisiana portion of the campaign after that date.
54. This engagement saved the town of Cloutierville from the torch. Francis Richard Lubbock, Six Decades in Texas; or Memoirs of Francis Richard Lubbock, Governor of Texas in War Time, ed. C. W. Raines (Austin, TX, 1900), 540; *OR*, ser. 1, vol. 34, pt. 1:581.
55. These forces were the Third Brigade of the First Division, 19th Corps, and remnants of the 13th Corps that had survived the Battle of Mansfield. *OR*, ser. 1, vol. 34, pt. 1:262.
56. This was the Louisiana Division, commanded by Brigadier General and French prince Camille Armand Jules Marie, the Prince de Polignac after the death of Brigadier General J. J. A. Alfred Mouton at Mansfield on April 8.
57. Captain Florian Cornay's Battery with four cannon consisting of two brass 12-pounders and two howitzers. Accompanying them were two hundred infantry from Polignac's Division. Ludwell H. Johnson, *Red River Campaign: Politics and Cotton in the Civil War* (Kent, OH, 1993), 238, 239n; Gary D. Joiner, *One Damn Blunder from Beginning to End* (Wilmington, DE, 2003), 149–50.
58. These were the tinclads *Cricket, Fort Hindman,* and *Juliet* and the pump boat transports *Champion No. 3* and *Champion No. 5.*
59. *Cricket.* See U.S. War Dept., *Official Records of the Union and Confederate Navies in the War of the Rebellion,* 31 vols. (Washington, DC, 1895–1929), vol. 26:26, 74, 167, 169, 176, 781–82, 786 (hereinafter cited as *ORN,* followed by volume number and page reference).
60. *Champion No. 3.*
61. *Juliet. ORN* 26:75, 81, 83.
62. Ibid.
63. Richard Taylor, *Destruction and Reconstruction: Personal Experiences in the Civil War* (New York, 1995), 184.
64. There is no entry for an officer of this name or common variations in this unit. This may be a misspelling or records may be incomplete.
65. This was the Champion No. 3. There were 175 contrabands (freed black slaves) aboard. About one hundred died very quickly from being scalded.

All but three of the remaining blacks died within twenty-four hours. Taylor, *Destruction and Reconstruction,* 183-84. Porter made no mention of this in his official reports. See *ORN* 26:75, 81, 176.

66. Major General John George Walker's First or Texas Division.
67. The *Juliet* and *Fort Hindman* were badly damaged. *ORN* 26:82–84, 169, 176.
68. *Champion No. 5.* Ibid.
69. This is not correct. All three gunboats made it back to Grand Ecore. Flournoy may be referring to the *Eastport,* blown up by Porter at Montgomery, Louisiana on April 26. For a more complete account of this action, see Joiner, *One Damn Blunder,* 149–50; Johnson, *Red River Campaign,* 238–241.
70. Charley was Lucien's cousin. Sibley was Samuel H. Sibley, the husband of Charles' sister, Mary Camp.
71. Brigadier General St. John R. Lidell operated on the eastern bank of the Red River. At that time his artillery was harassing the Union vessels near the mouth of Cane River.
72. This was Lucien's sister Elizabeth, born in Greenwood, Louisiana in 1843. See U.S. Department of Commerce, Seventh Decennial Census (1850), Caddo Parish, Louisiana, unpublished tabulations in the NARA.
73. Letter in the collection of Jimmy H. Sandefur, Shreveport, Louisiana. Private R. A. Knox's muster card lists him as being a member of Company H, 2nd Texas Infantry Regiment. This regiment was not involved in the Red River Campaign. From his writing, it is evident that he belonged to a mounted regiment and fought at Wilson's Farm on April 7, 1864. Janet B. Hewitt, *Texas Confederate Soldiers 1861–1865* (Wilmington, NC, 1997), 295. Confederate forces engaged at the Battle of Wilson's Farm were attached to the Texas Cavalry Corps commanded by General Green. These units were Brigadier General James Patrick Major's two brigades. They were Bagby's Cavalry Brigade, under Brigadier General Arthur Pendleton Bagby, consisting of the 4th, 5th, 7th, and 13th Texas cavalry regiments, and Lane's Cavalry Brigade, under Colonel Walter P. Lane, which included the 1st and 2nd Texas Partisan Ranger regiments and the Second and Third Arizona Brigade cavalry regiments. Opposing them were units of the Cavalry Division of the 19th Corps, commanded by General Albert Lindley Lee. The first of the two brigades involved was the First Cavalry Brigade, under Colonel Thomas J. Lucas, including the 17th Indiana Mounted Infantry Regiment, the 2nd Louisiana Mounted Infantry Regiment, and the 14th New York Cavalry Regiment. The other brigade involved was the Third Cavalry Brigade, led by Colonel Harai Robinson, with the 87th Illinois Mounted Infantry Regiment and the 1st Louisiana Cavalry Regiment. One section of artillery of the 6th Missouri and one section of Battery G, 5th U.S. Light Artillery assisted these brigades.

Knox wrote this letter while Union forces were entrenched at Grand Ecore and Alexandria. The author's description of his location places him near the southern end of the Isle de Brevelle, or Cane River Island, near Monett's Ferry. The day after Knox penned this, the Confederates lost a battle at Monett's Ferry in an effort to trap the Union army between the Cane and Red rivers.

74. Knox is referring to a possible attempt by the Union commander, General Banks, to link up with another Federal column commanded by Major General Frederick Steele that was approaching Shreveport from Little Rock. In fact, the opposite was true. Banks ordered Steele to come to his assistance, but Steele was unable to comply.
75. Following the Battle of Pleasant Hill, Lieutenant General Edmund Kirby Smith removed three divisions from Louisiana to oppose Steele's thrust into southwestern Arkansas. These three divisions consisted of Arkansas, Missouri, and Texas troops, leaving only the Texas Cavalry Corps and the Louisiana Division in Louisiana to oppose the Union forces. At the time this letter was written, the Louisiana Division had lost its commander, General Mouton, at the Battle of Mansfield. Brigadier General Camille Armand Jules Marie, the Prince de Polignac, then led the division.
76. The Battle of Wilson's Farm on April 7, 1864, was followed by the much larger Battle of Mansfield (Sabine Cross Roads) on April 8 and the Battle of Pleasant Hill on April 9.
77. Battle of Mansfield.
78. Battle of Pleasant Hill.
79. Prince de Polignac.
80. This letter is contained in Archives and Special Collections, Noel Memorial Library, Louisiana State University in Shreveport, Louisiana. Collection 256, Samford C. Fullilove Collection, Box 1, Folder 17.
81. Zack Howell's wife, Isabella Jane Whitworth Howell.
82. Colonel Frank C. Zacharie of the 25th Louisiana Infantry.
83. Confederate Lieutenant General Edmund Kirby Smith, Commander of the Department of the Trans-Mississippi.
84. Brigadier General James P. Major.
85. Sabine Pass.
86. Union Major General Nathaniel Prentiss Banks.
87. Orval Beaty, the great-grandson of the recipient of the letter, transcribed this letter from the original. Beaty is a resident of Port Neches, Texas. Dyson Nickles, a graduate student at Stephen F. Austin University, annotated this letter.
88. Also known as the Battle of Yellow Bayou.
89. Araminta Ballard McGuire of Atacosa County, Texas, was the sister of Barclay E. Ballard, the letter's author.

90. George McGuire of Atacosa County, Texas, was the husband of Araminta Ballard McGuire. He enlisted in the 36th Regiment of Texas Cavalry on April 26, 1862, for three years or the war. He was mustered with his horse and equipment into Woods's Regiment, Company D.
91. The battle fought near Simmesport, Louisiana, was the Battle of Yellow Bayou. This was the last battle of the Red River Campaign and compelled Federal forces to retreat to New Orleans.
92. Woods's Regiment was engaged at the Battle of Mansfield on April 8 and again on the ninth at Pleasant Hill. Woods's Cavalry followed the Federal fleet down the Red River, engaging whenever practical.
93. Charles B. Ballard, also of Wood's Regiment.
94. Jefferson Morgan served with Company E, 35th Texas Calvary Regiment, J. B. Likens's Regiment in Bee's Brigade, commanded by Brigadier General Hamilton Bee, and in Major's Cavalry Division, commanded by Brigadier General James P. Major. Although there is no reference in the *Official Records*, Morgan's letters direct his wife to send her letters to Bagby's Brigade, commanded by Colonel Arthur P. Bagby. The letters are to his wife, Amanda Ann Sportsman Morgan, living at their home in Ellis County, Texas. All of Morgan's original spelling and grammar have been retained. Explanatory notes define places or terms not readily identifiable. Brackets are used to insert missing words. The letters are in the collection of Ann Turk, Arlington, Texas.

    Morgan is referring to Matagorda County, Texas. From January to March 1864 the 35th Texas Cavalry operated near the Gulf Coast between Caney Creek and Matagorda Bay on picket duty. With it were the 23rd Texas Cavalry Regiment, commanded by Colonel N. C. Gould, and the 32nd (36th) Texas Cavalry Regiment, under Colonel P. C. Woods. *OR*, ser. 1, vol. 34, pt. 2:837, 854. On March 16, 1864, Special Order No. 76, designated six cavalry regiments to be sent to Louisiana to assist in halting the Union invasion. Bee's Brigade comprised the 1st Texas Cavalry Regiment, commanded by Colonel Augustus C. Buchel. Colonel Xavier B. Debray's 26th Texas Cavalry Regiment and Gould's 23rd Texas Cavalry Regiment were to be formed into Hawes's Brigade, under Brigadier General Hawes. Wood's 32nd (36th) Texas Cavalry Regiment; Likens's 35th Texas Cavalry Regiment; and Terrell's Texas Cavalry, under Colonel Alexander W. Terrell; and the commanding officers would report to Brigadier General Hamilton P. Bee. *OR*, ser. 1, vol. 34, pt. 2:1048. The movement of these six regiments to the interior of Louisiana forced a reorganization. Likens, Wood, and Gould were delayed and did not join the body of the Cavalry Corps until after the Battle of Pleasant Hill on April 9. *OR*, ser. 1, vol. 34, pt. 2:606.
95. Regiment.
96. Pleasure.

97. Harris County, Texas.
98. This letter was apparently written a short time before March 23, 1864. It appears on the same page as the following letter of that date.
99. Duty.
100. Colonel Nathaniel M. Burford's 19th Texas Cavalry Regiment.
101. Drawers, underwear.
102. The letters Morgan references were probably captured on May 4 on the Union transport packet *City Belle* at David's Ferry about thirty miles south of Alexandria on the Red River. *OR*, ser. 1, vol. 34, pt. 1:475; Taylor, *Destruction and Reconstruction*, 186; Joiner, *One Damn Blunder*, 161. The 35th Texas Cavalry was detailed to work with artillery operating against the U.S. Navy gunboats on the Red River. On April 26, the regiment participated in attacks on the fleet that ensured the scuttling of the USS *Eastport*. *OR*, ser. 1, vol. 34, pt. 1:583–84.
103. Lieutenant.
104. Marksville in Avoyelles Parish, Louisiana.
105. Alexandria in Rapides Parish, Louisiana.
106. This should be read as 35th Cavalry, J. B. Likens's Regiment in the west part of Louisiana, General Bagby's Brigade.
107. Washington in northern St. Landry Parish, below Alexandria.
108. Federal forces completed their evacuation of the Red River Valley on May 20. *OR*, ser. 1, vol. 34, pt. 3:644; S. C. Jones, *Reminiscences of the Twenty-second Iowa Volunteer Infantry* (Iowa City, 1907), 69; Joiner, *One Damn Blunder*, 172.
109. Brashear City, modern Morgan City, in St. Mary Parish, Louisiana.
110. Beaumont, Texas.
111. Diarrhea.
112. Bayous.
113. Sparta was located in Bienville Parish, Louisiana, between Shreveport and Monroe.
114. The hospital referred to was apparently near Bailey's upper dam site on the Red River, just upstream from Alexandria. It was located on the eastern side of the river in what is today Pineville, on the grounds of the Louisiana Seminary of Learning of Military Institute, the forerunner of Louisiana State University.
115. F. B. Harris of the 4th Texas Cavalry Regiment wrote this letter on the day following the close of the Red River Campaign. The unit, with most of the Confederate forces in the area, remained at Bayou DeGlaize near the mouth of the Red River for several days to make certain Union forces did not reenter the river. The 4th Texas Cavalry was part of Colonel

Bagby's Brigade, part of General Major's cavalry division. See Appendix 1. Although the author wrote "May 23rd 63," this was a mistake. The events are positively identified as occurring during the Red River Campaign of 1864. This letter is found in folio 6 of the Aimer Collection, Cammie Henry Research Center, Northwestern State University in Natchitoches, Louisiana.

116. The Battle of Mansfield was fought on April 8, 1864, and the Battle of Pleasant Hill was fought the following day.

117. Battle of Mansura, fought on May 16, 1864. See Joiner, *One Damn Blunder*, 170–72.

118. This was the ValVerde Battery, part of the artillery attached to Major's Division. See Appendix 1.

119. The Battle of Yellow Bayou was fought May 18, 1864. This was the final action of the Red River Campaign.

120. The letter is from Sergeant Moritz Maedgen to Captain H. G. Carter, who served with Maedgen in Company D of the 4th Texas Cavalry. Carter was wounded at the Battle of Pleasant Hill and was sent home to convalesce. Maedgen also had two brothers, Gustavus Adolphus Maedgen and Franz Maedgen, who served with him. Both were privates. The letter is in the personal collection of Bryan James Maedgen, Houston, Texas. Maedgen is the great-nephew of Moritz Maedgen and the great-grandson of Gustavus Adolphus Maedgen's great-grandson.

121. Letter written at the camp of the 4th Texas Cavalry on Thompson's Plantation, between the towns of Alexandria and Lecompte in Rapides Parish, Louisiana. The 4th Texas Cavalry, under Colonel William P. Hardeman, was part of Colonel Arthur P. Bagby's Brigade. The other regiments in the brigade were the 5th, 7th, and 35th Texas cavalry regiments and the 13th Texas Cavalry Battalion.

122. Brigade.

123. Bayou Pierre, an ancient channel of the Red River. Following the battle of Pleasant Hill, several cavalry units were sent to the bayou and to the Red River in an attempt to capture or destroy the Union fleet under Admiral Porter.

124. The Texas Cavalry found the rear of Porter's fleet on April 12 at Blair's Landing, near the village of Lake End in Red River Parish. In a sharp engagement, Confederate General Green was killed and the fleet escaped to Grand Ecore in Natchitoches Parish. See the W. T. Shaw letter in this chapter.

125. Confederate General Bee.

126. Monett's Ferry, located at the southern end of the Isle de Brevelle in Natchitoches Parish. This was the only place in which the Confederates

could trap the Union force fleeing south toward Natchitoches. Bee commanded the Confederate forces and held both the ferry and the heights above it.

127. Maedgen is describing the crossing of the Cane River by Union troops in an attempt to flank Bee's position. Joiner, *One Damn Blunder,* 151–57.
128. This account agrees with Confederate General Taylor's accusations against Bee. *OR,* ser. 1, vol. 34, pt. 1:580, 611–15; Taylor, *Destruction and Reconstruction,* 152.
129. Bean's Station was a stagecoach stop located west of Alexandria between Carroll Jones's supply depot at Hinestown and Burr's Ferry, the central crossing point on the Sabine River. It is located on Louisiana Highway 8.
130. Bayou Beouf at the town of Cheneyville.
131. General Major's Division of the Texas Cavalry Corps.
132. This refers to artillery and cavalry actions against Union vessels at Egg Bend and David's Ferry, below Alexandria. The Union vessels destroyed were the gunboats *Signal* and *Covington,* the armed dispatch gunboat *John Warner,* and the transports *Emma* and *City Belle* on May 1 and May 4.
133. No Union vessels were lost in the passage through the dam.
134. Simmesport.
135. Avoyelles Prairie.
136. Maedgen is describing the Battle of Mansura, fought on May 16. Joiner, *One Damn Blunder,* 170–72.
137. Pitt's Mill was located on Bayou Huffpower (or Houghpower) at the junction of the Bayou du Lac Road and the Evergreen-Holmesville Road, about five miles south of Bayou du Lac and two miles west of Evergreen. On October 16, 1863, Lieutenant E. H. Wells of the Engineer Troops sent a scouting report to Major General John G. Walker. Wells reconnoitered all of Avoyelles Parish. The report included a map of the area. The original material is found in the John G. Walker Papers, Southern Historical Collection, Manuscripts Department, Wilson Library, UNC Chapel Hill. The applicable portion of the report reads: "The road from Marksville to Bayou Du Lac is like the other prairie roads obnoxious to no objections whatever: distance 9 miles. The long bridge across the Bayou was destroyed last spring, and the old ferry-boat is at this time broken. The bayou is 50 yds. wide at this place. From the bayou to Pitt's mill on Houghpower Bayou is about 5 miles and the road good."
138. Confederate Major General John Wharton, who assumed command of the Confederate cavalry following the death of General Green. Many of his officers and men disliked him. See chap. 1.
139. Battle of Yellow Bayou, fought on May 18, 1864.
140. Washington in St. Landry Parish.

141. Brigade quartermaster.
142. This is either acting adjutant general or assistant adjutant general.
143. Aide-de-camp.
144. Acting adjutant general.
145. Sergeant major.
146. Confederate Major General Camille Jules Armand Marie, the Prince de Polignac, at that time the commander of the Louisiana Division in the Army of Western Louisiana. See the Polignac letter in this chapter.
147. Bayou Cotile in Rapides Parish.
148. The 4th Texas Cavalry served in Sibley's Brigade during the 1862 ill-fated invasion of New Mexico.
149. Company.
150. Letter written on March 4, 1865, perhaps the last Confederate letter to be written to an engineer field commander serving in the Trans-Mississippi Theatre. The operations discussed concern the removal of the engineering unit and its pontoon train and supply trains from the Ouachita River at Camden, Arkansas. This was the last outpost to be withdrawn before the end of hostilities. It is included in this volume for continuity and importance as a Trans-Mississippi document. For a more complete account of Company H, 4th Confederate Engineers, in 1864–65, see Gary D. Joiner, Marilyn S. Joiner, and Clifton D. Cardin, *No Pardons to Ask, nor Apologies to Make* (Knoxville, 2006).
151. The recipient is Captain Smith Kirby, commander of Company H, 4th Confederate Engineers based in Shreveport. Captain Kirby was Lieutenant General Kirby Smith's first cousin, his maternal uncle's son.
152. Charleston, South Carolina fell to General William T. Sherman on February 18, 1865.
153. The Battle of Bentonville, North Carolina, would be fought March 19–21, 1865. This is a reference to events leading up to the engagement.
154. This letter proves that even near the end of the war, communication within the Confederate lines was fairly rapid.
155. Samford C. Fullilove Collection, Archives and Special Collections, Noel Memorial Library, Louisiana State University in Shreveport.
156. The author reports these two events out of chronological order. New Orleans fell to Union forces on April 25, 1862. On May 22, 1863, Union Major General Ulysses S. Grant began a siege of Vicksburg, and after six weeks, Confederate Lieutenant General John Pemberton surrendered the city on July 4, 1863.
157. Their first child, Susan Tabitha, was born on March 23, 1861, and died on March 30, 1861. Their second child, Preston Greer, died on October 21, 1863, while his father was in Arkansas.

158. Fort DeRussy.

159. Red River.

160. "Mr. Fullilove," her husband.

161. This is probably junior Second Lieutenant and Acting Adjutant William A. Lacy, the only Lacy in the 6th, according to the National Archives and Record Administration's Civil War Soldiers and Sailors list.

162. North of Keachi on Louisiana Highway 3.

163. Her husband.

164. Ed Polk was likely a slave. When Tom Fullilove was injured in Arkansas, Lizzie mentioned Ed finding his master.

165. Lacy's.

Union Letters

Edited by Gary D. Joiner, Jimmy H. Sandefur, Tara Z. Laver, and Monica R. Pels

Men from a variety of backgrounds, educational attainment, and regions of the United States wrote the letters included in this chapter. They are presented in chronological order and reflect the attitudes of the soldiers and mark significant events of the Union force at specific points during the campaign.

William H. Scarborough of the 96th Ohio Infantry, 13th Corps, wrote his letter toward the end of March 1864, prior to the battles of Mansfield and Pleasant Hill. He vividly describes the journey overland toward Alexandria. The letter by Thomas, an otherwise unidentified soldier, was written while the author was under fire and pinned down at Pleasant Hill. Writing with difficulty, the author believes this may be his last communication. Wilson Novyus, an immigrant serving with the 161st New York Infantry of the 19th Corps, penned his letter on April 15 at Grand Ecore. Frank Pearce describes what he knew of the action as of April 21; he served with the 2nd Maine Cavalry Regiment, which was assigned to support duties. Jim, an otherwise unidentified soldier, served with the 30th Maine Infantry. Writing in May 1864 from Simmesport, he mentions that he worked on Bailey's Dam. A Westerner, Hugo Voigt was a member of the 29th Wisconsin Infantry in the 13th Corps. In his letter of May 4, Voigt describes the decimation of the 13th Corps at the Battle of Mansfield. Thomas Hayden of the 38th Massachusetts

Infantry of the 19th Corps writes a very witty and cynical letter about what he had observed and is very forthcoming about his opinions. The letter was written on May 4 while at Alexandria. Another perspective is offered by a soldier named Delamaster. Writing at the end of the campaign from Morganza, Delamaster defends General Banks's actions. Rufus C. Kemp, a New York Zouave, wrote a series of letters describing his experiences before, during, and immediately after the campaign. D. R. Wallace wrote a letter to the wife of an attaché in his regiment, describing her husband's wounds and his medical care.

Also included is a series of communications and background of another soldier of the 38th Massachusetts, William Whitney. The reader learns much about this soldier through his writings. His letters prove he was educated and thoughtful, and they provide excellent insight, particularly about the closing days of the campaign and his unit's duties through June 1864.

These men reflect the regional and cultural differences and attitudes of the Union soldiers in the Department of the Gulf during 1864. Their writing tends to be less emotional than that of their Confederate opponents.

William H. Scarborough on the Ascent to Alexandria

[Edited by Gary D. Joiner and Jimmy H. Sandefur]

Camp 96th Regiment Near Alexandria, La[1]
March 27, 1864

My Dear Parents

After a long and fatiguing march of 12 days seat [*sic*] to inform you that I am still on the land of the living and enjoying good health I am sorry that I cant write you a long letter but truly will be impossible at this time for tomorrow we march and today is given for to Wash our cloths and clean up Consequently I cannot give you a full a history of our march as I would like to, to begin with we left Berwick City[2] on the morning of the 6 and marched to Franklin on the 8th Remained their 8 days and then Proceeded for Some place at that time unknown. marched five days and then stoped to rest one day near Washington[3] passing through a great many little Towns. Viz New lberia. Vermillionvill Opelousus[4] &tc on the morning of the 21 left Washington and marched to this place[5] in five days. Passed through Montsville Cheinyville[6] & Alexandria

I think the distance from Berwick City to this place is 190 miles marched in 12 days. I think I never saw more Beautiful Country than what we have come through the Buildings wer truly Magnificent But most of these fine Buildings we deserted I Suppose the owners are most if not all in the Rebel Army. when we reached this place the Confederates had Skedaddled and tis Supposed by them that Pretends to Know that they are now fortifying at Shreveport the Sixteenth Army Corps have already gone that Direction and is Supposed that that place is our Destination if we have to march it will he 140 miles Some Conjecture that we go on transports up Red River when I came here the Mail was immeaditly Opened and Reced[7] five letter from the mail and two from Lieutenant Mitchell[8] which Returned to the Regiment the 26. I reced one from Mearia date the 23 of last mouth one from Amos date the 2 of this month one from Thom 28th of last month and the last from you this day one month ago John Recd one from Wm Phillips 20 Ohio at Vicksburg in all. I thank Thom. Kindly for writing Such a lengthy Epistol and for working the Example I gave him Sometime ago I Shall answer Soon. I also am indebted to Father for his Kind letter I think it was read with greater Interest than any other one you give just what I wanted to hear Exactly I am glad you Sent what you did Just what I needed Lieutenant. Says that he Brought them as far as New Orleans and thought he had best leave them their not Knowing when the Regiment was or when he would find it he Says when we get Settled down in camp some where will send for the trunk your letters contents gave true Satisfaction the amount of money is correct and Everything else you Requested me to tell you the No[9] of postage stamps I had recd since the Battle this I cant Say Exactly for I have Rced no perticular account of them but will go as far as to say that I have sold the full No you sent me the 50 you sent by Lieut. Mitchell an all night I am glad to think I have Such Kind Parent to send me anything I want and am always ready to Redeam the want of those that are in neede the Paymaster Came last Evening and this morning we was paid two months they Owe us three months more the last if this month Some Say that we get two month more to day if we do I shall send 34.00 home if not I shall send none this time.

Excuse this poorly written letter and answer now I Shall write Soon again I am your Son William H. Scarborugh. James & Elis our Regt has been transfered to the Seckond Brigade

Direct Co. B 96 th Regt (Ohio)
13th Army Corps
Write Soon Write
Will H. Scarborugh

Letter from "Thomas" Describing the Fierce Fighting at Pleasant Hill

[Edited by Gary D. Joiner and Jimmy H. Sandefur]

April 9th /64[10]

My Dear Wife and children,

In the line of battle on Pleasant Hill or God Knows Where

As the musketry has ceased for a few minutes at least, I wish to write you a few words lest they be my last words to you. We have got ourselves in a terrible spot here. We are terribly outnumbered and the rebs have been pounding us with blistering volleys which has had a telling effect upon our ranks. As I look around me I see eight or nine dead bodies some literally blown to bits. Can not tell whether they are friend or foe. We have held the rebs fast but for how long I cannot say. We are outnumbered and our tactical position is unfavorable. Our cartridges are running low and I don't know how long we can hold this position. Just now the reb sharpshooters are poppin at us. I have found pretty good cover here and I have not suffered a scratch. I apologize for my poor writing but I am forced to write on the top of my cap. The Lieutenant is yelling something down the line about reinforcements. I don't know why they call this place Pleasant Hill. Seems darned unpleasant to me right now. The rebs are fighting like dogs but we will whip them. You can bet on that. It is only a matter of time. I must close as there is movement along the line. I love you my dearest. Kiss the children for me. In Haste.

Your Affect[ionate] Husband.
Thomas

Wilson Novyus Describes the Fighting and Retreat to Grand Ecore

[Edited by Gary D. Joiner and Jimmy H. Sandefur]

Grand E Core, La[11]
April 15th, 1864

Dear Niece

I received your kind letter on the 12 and also one from Petter & one from Hester and was very glad to hear that you wer all well at Home.

I am well as useule & so is all the boys that are here. I answered Petes letter right away for I exepected the mail was going out right away but I will tell you something about what has bin going on in this country. On the 8th of this month we marched 8 miles and stopped a couple of hours and at 5 oclock we started again & marched 8 miles in about 1 and 1/2 hour and commensed fighting & fought untill after dark[12] Co A, F, D & I was Sent out as Scirmishers in the woods & each one got behind a tree then we Saw the rebs a comming in line & we commensed fireing. Some of the boys thought they was some of our men at first but soon saw the difference we fired & the rebs fired untill the rebs got up within 10 or 15 rods and some nearer & there more of them than there was of us about 6 or 8 to one & we thought it was time to begetting out So the Captain told us to fall back and we started the bullets flew like hail and the rebs after us holering Surrender you yankee Sons of biches but that was no place for us to stop. We run back about 8 or 10 rods to a high fence & I was so tired I throwed my knapsack & then went over the fence like a deer Stoped & fired the rebs close behind then fell back again to another fence. Wm Egleston[13] & E Spreg[14] was wounded while in the woods but boath went back with us. We staid by the last fence and fired several times then we had to leave and went back to the regt. Geo S Prentiss[15] was with the regt cairing the flag & corperel Wheeten[16] was with him they were boath wounded. Geo was shot throw the right shoulder Wheaten was shot in the shoulder & came out near the midle of his back so he died. at dark we stoped fireing had pickets out and we got together & staid untill about 11 ockock then we started back and marched 16 miles that night & morning & the rebels followed us as quick as they found we had left & came down where we was[17] but we was ready for them we had help of some 6000 or more, and about noon the rebes commensed fireing again & throwing shells rather careless. Some of them went over our heads & cut off the topes of the trees but they did not hurt eney of us that after noon our regt was kept back in the rear as reserve to act in case that we was flanked we was out on a plain and could see the rest work there was one regt of rebels that charged on a batery of ours that was hid behind some bushes and they mowed them most all down with grape & cannister we took over 2000 prisiners besides several thousand that we kiled, the bullets would come whisling over us every once in awhile then would lay down or move to some other part. Wm H. Garvy[18] was hit in his left shin he was the onely one that was wounded in our regt that day the 9th. but to come down to the point I think that they was two as short battles as has been fought lateley. We was calculating to get supplys a little above where the first battle was from the boats on the river[19] but as we did not get up there we was short of hard tacks so we had fall back to Natachitoches[20] where we could get some or retret to this plaice and as the rebes bother us so we could not have time to cook eney meet we fared rather slim & the rebes under took to take the boats that was up the river with our supplys but they could not come it they charged on a gun boat and they gave them a broad side and kiled a rebel General Green[21] besides quite a no of privates but the boats have all come back and we have plenty of hard tacks now. the rebels say that they are coming down here soon but I think they will have to leave of thear straps and guns before they come in our lines the darkeys are fortufying all around here[22] in front and we have severel gun boats laying in the river ready for them but I can not tell wether we will stay here long or not the boys that was wounded have bin sent away to New Orleans or some other plaise and likeley you will hear from them as often as I will your uncle Jimey was with us in the battle and is here all right So is Wm Hess[23] Gus Prentiss[24] Geo Clark[25] and all of the boys onely them I have mentioned that is all this time let your Pa & Ma read this and you must take good care of Joseph Wilson

Direct as before

From Wilson Novyus (Nevens)[26]

To his Niece Mary Novyus

F. W. Pearce Describes Cavalry Action during the Campaign

[Edited by Gary D. Joiner and Jimmy H. Sandefur]

Alexandria La. April 21st, 1864.[27]

Brother Varney,

I have written a number of letters home since leaving, Portland, but have received none. Also one to Charles and one to [?]. I must tell you now of my voiage up the Mississippi Rivert Capt J F Twitchell[28] and Lieut Mansur[29] left New Orleans last Monday with (55) fifty five men. On the next day (Tuesday) I started after them with (16) sixteen men. Lieut Barker,[30] remaines at New Orleans with the rest of the Company. We should have taken the whole Company if horses could have been furnished us. While going up the Mississippi we enjoyed ourselves by looking at the beautiful plantations [?] the Red River for it. Lest we passed through a gloomy looking country made more so by the thoughts of being fired into by the Rebels. But it so happened that we were into fired into. A boat loaded with Cavalry came up a little behind us and were fired into by the Rebs killing three an wounding sixteen. We arrived at this place[31] at about twelve oclock last night. In the morning we came ashore and found that the Cavalry had gone out about fifteen miles on Picket duty. They will be back here again tomorrow. Four of their men they left here sick thought not very bad. William Reed[32] is in my squad. He wishes me to tell you that he is gay and happy. David Betts[33] is also with me and is smart. Eugene Shaw[34] we left at New Orleans.

Gen Banks has been having a big fight. gess he didnt get much the better of it. He is now falling back with his army. The water is so very low that supplies cannot be taken up.[35] He will probably make this his headquarters. another battle is expected soon. It is late in the evening and I must go to my rest as I am very tired so good night.

Write soon

From your Brother
F.W. Pearce
2nd Maine Cavalry
Co H

"Jim" Describes His Work on Bailey's Dam

[Edited by Gary D. Joiner and Jimmy H. Sandefur]

Simsport, La. May 1864[36]

Dear Folks,

Your last is rec'd with the greatest of pleasure and I am glad that you are all well. I have not written because our communications have been closed while our gunboats were above the rapids at Alexandria waiting on the dam of the Red River in effort to raise the water level.[37] I was detailed to work on the dam 2 nights and days. We have had no great engagement yet but constant skirmishing. On the 13th inst. the enemy made a stand at *Marksville* in strong force about 8000[38] Our lines advanced in line of battle for 2 or 3 hours supported by our artillery which blazed away at the rebs. Sharp fighting occurred with our infantry of skirmishers and the balls did fly around us like hail during a Nor'easter. We gave them a severe [?]. That day we also heard the news that Grant had won a 3 day battle at [?] Hurrah! I surmise that our regiment will be sent for a time to hold some point in the [?]. We also got news that old Fessenden has lost a leg. Too bad for now he is a peg leg. I felt that this river expedition will not close soon and much blood is to be shed before it closes. I must close with much love for all.

Jim

Hugo Voigt Recounts the Destruction of the 13th Corps

[Edited by Gary D. Joiner and Jimmy H. Sandefur]

Alexandria La, May 4th/64[39]
Absent but not foregoten

Friend Charls

It is with pleasure that I set down to inform you that I recieved your kind letter March 16th but I could not answer eny sooner I am sorry myself because I could not write before now but sircumstance would not allow me and I will tell you why. in the first place wee ware on a March when I recieved your letter, the next was I had no Papier and that was not to be got fore May but I spose if I had tride hard I might have roat before this time but I am to careless about riting, that is sure. but I hope that you will be kind enough to foregive me fore my carlesness.

well Charls I think you woold like to know how the things loock in this part of the Contry and sumting about our Marches, in the first place wee Marched about 400 Miles and then wee runn on the rebs about 3 Oclock P.M. at Sibean Cros Road[40] our Army Corps was in the front. Genl. Banks commanded oure forces wee fought the rebs till sundown and then wee ware for to fall back but as luck woold have it the 19th Army Corps com to oure suport but to late oure Corps was cut up so bad that they coold not be stopt from runing the 19th Corps went on the field and held it till wee was in good order and then wee fal back wee Marched the holl Night till 8 Oclock A.M.[41] then Genrl Smith[42] com to reinforce us, wee was ordert to retreat as fast as posibil but Genrl Smith and his force remains thare at Pleasant Hill and he fought them thare and he whipt them bad but he was oblight to fall back on account of Provisions. I have no dout what the rebs lost more then wee did fore the rebs don all the charging and another thing they ware all drunk and that is why they had good courage.[43]

well Charls the rebs have followed us clear down to Alexandria wee have bin after them twice but they will not stand. Day before yester day wee ware ordert to go out and meet the rebs wee went about 2 miles and then wee met the rebs wee skirmished with them till sundown then evry thing was still wee stackt oure arms and lade down to rest wee had not lade thare more than 5 minits till ashall com right in our flank but with out harm the rebs fiered 5 shots but they ware of now aftects and that ended the day

well Charls I dont know of eny more news this time so you must excuse this short letter. I am yet well and healthy and I hope that this letter may find you the same give my best respects to all of my aquaintens and with this I remain your afectionated friend excuse all mistakes and poor writing

Hugo Voigt
To Charles Darrah
Co. C 29th Regt Wis Vols
3rd Divs 13th Army Corps
Dept of the Gulf

remember me when this you se
though thousent miles apart.
I do not know how soon may com
the time that wee shal meet

Thomas Hayden Pens a Witty and Cynical Account of the Expedition

[Edited by Gary D. Joiner and Jimmy H. Sandefur]

38th Mass. Vols.,
3rd Brigade. 2nd Div. 19th Corps.[44]
Dept of Gulf. Alexandria, La
May 4th 1864

Dear Jim,

How are you, old fellow? I believe I received a letter from you before we went on our expedition up to Grand Ecore, of which you may have heard from the newspapers. This is the first opportunity I have had to reply to your note. We have been on a great tramp through this lovely (?) State of Louisiana. The last letter you received from me was doubtless written from Baton Rouge. There we were getting along finely. We left that interesting city Mar. 23,[45] and came up to this place, passing Fort De Russey[46] where the rebs prisoners were taken. Apr. 12th we started up towards Shreveport (though by the way we didn't get up quite as far as that) While going up the river, we were fired into by guerrillas April 13. We were on board the transport "Mittie Stevens",[47] and there was some confusion there for a moment or two. We lost 1 killed and 5 wounded. After the first shock, we returned the fire and cleaned the woods out and went on. Arrived at *Grand Ecore* April 13 in the evening, landed, and next day commenced throwing up intrenchments.[48] Before our Regiment got up to Grand Ecore, there had been a fight at Pleasant Hill,[49] which was *not exactly a victory for us.* Our army had fallen back. Gen. Banks, it seems, thought he had seen enough of that part of the country, so, April 21, we began the grand retreat to Alexandria, marching down by land. We had to destroy considerable property at Grand Ecore for want of transportation. We marched day and night, with the rebs all round us, fighting all the time. We drove them at all fronts and made good our retreat. It was an awful hard march, Jim. Little to eat and *thin mud* to drink. Our regt. lost 2 killed and 6 wounded on the march at the battle of Cane River Ford.[50] Capt. Lathrop of my Co. was mortally wounded. He died three days after the battle. He was not as popular as some, but all acknowledged his bravery on the field of battle. We arrived at Alexandria Apr. 26, all tired out. Soldiering out here is no joke. Fifteen months more of it for us, Jim! Shall we re-enlist? Don't you or Henry want to come out? Now's the time! Going—Going—!!!— Delightful prospect! Excellent opportunities for study, travel, and promotion! Pay & Rations commence from Enlistment! Could anything be more charming. Not to mention the delightful companionship of the poor, oppressed, down-trodden niggers!!!!! But my tears are falling. I must stop, Jim.

Write often. My regards to all. How are you getting along in these times? How is everything? Goodbye.

Yours truly,
Tom.[51]
[Thomas Hayden]

A Soldier Defends Banks

[Edited by Gary D. Joiner]

Morganzia Landing[52]
May 27th/64

Dear Cousin.

Once more I am permitted to sit down, even upon the bank of the great Mississippi river and pen a few lines to my far distant Cousin. Your kind letter of April 24th was rec'd in due season and found myself and company in good health and fine Spirits which experience has learned me to be two great comforts to a soldier. We are now camped along the bank of the Mississippi at a place called Morganzia[53] Landing which is about 25 miles below the mouth of Red river and about 15 miles above Port Hudson. Our Corps[,] the 19th[,] has command of the river this summer, we are under orders to be ready to move up or down at any time. our men captured a Rebel the other day bearing dispatches from Gen Lee to Gen Maggruder,[54] ordering him to abandon this country immediately and come to his aid. For him to accomplish this movement he has got to cross the Mississippi and how is he going to cross without something cross upon.[55] This movement is easier ordered than performed, as yet we have not heard of his crossing. some of Mr. Linklum's[56] Gun Boats may be there to aid him should he attempt to cross. I suppose you have read all about the Red river Expedition er'e this also about our Battles you to have doubtless heard Gen Banks abused and that shamefully, but Gen Banks is not to blame, for I am told that he was strongly opposed to this movement but acted according to orders. for my part I lay all the blame to the low water in the river which prevented our getting supplies for our army. as for the Rebels driving us out of the country is false, for three hotley contested Battles of three days dealt death and destruction to the Rebels and their Army.[57] the Battle of Pleasant Hill was probably a hot a contested Battle as there has been according to the numbers since the war began. the Rebels greatly outnumbered us and came on certain of Victory. they made charge after charge upon us but were as often repulsed and beaten back with terrible slaughter. Just as the sun was going down the 2d Brigade of our Corps charged upon their left—broke two of their lines and took between six and seven hundred Prisoners.[58] this soon ended the strife and the Rebels badly whipped and all in utter confusion Skedaddled leaveing their dead and wounded in heaps upon the field.[59] our men being out of rations were obliged to fall back to Grand Ecore Landing 35 miles. here we stopped some eight or ten days and as the river continued to fall we were obliged to fall back to the Mississippi where we now are. we had to build a dam across Red river at Alexandria to get our Gun Boats over the Rapids.[60] we have marched something over 600 miles this Spring and had five Battles[61] and of course are glad of a little rest. the weather now is so warm that the men can hardly stand it to march. we are getting all sorts of news from Gen Grant and his army. every body is anxious to hear of his success. I hope victory will be his with Richmond throwed in. this done I can see no hope for the Rebels. I received a letter from Bule the other day. he was well and I should judge by his letter the same old Bule of old. how I would like to see him if you see Jennie Brigham tell her I am going to write to her. give my love, and Respects to Uncle, Aunt, Cousins, Grandfather, GrandMother, and all, never forgetting your own dear self. write and let me know of Edward and Spet. This was sent to New Orleans with the sick so I could not do your errand. I hear that he is well, hoping soon to see you all.

remain as ever Your affectionate
Cousin
—-oke Delamaster.
To Darah A. Brigham Esq.

Rufus C. Kemp: 165th New York Zouaves

[Edited by Jimmy H. Sandefur, Gary D. Joiner, and Monica R. Pels]

Franklin La. Jan 11th 1864[62]

Dear Mother

I have just received your welcome letter of the 25th and I hasten to answer it. I was very glad to hear you got my money. The same night I sent it the mail was robbed so I was anxious to hear wheather mine escaped. I have not received the box yet but will in a few days. Our Quartermaster is going to N.O.[63] and he will fetch it with him along with the rest of them. We left New Iberia or Newtown[64] as some call it on the 7th and marched to this place in to days a distance of 26 miles. Talk about the mud on the Army of the Potomac. About two days before we started it commenced raining hailing and storming altogether. It kept on for about 12 hours and then commenced to freeze hard. Just before we started it grew warm and commenced raining and of all the mud for sticking to your shoes. One cant walk two steps before he has a whole plantation on his shoes. The roads were so soft that the wagons could hardly get along. A great many men had to throw away their knapsacks and there were about 50 wagons broke down. I am still on Benedicts guard.[65] I now been with him four months on the 16th. We are away from the regiment and have nothing to do with it. We have our luggage all carried on the march and do not have to march with the regiment. Our regiment does the provost duty[66] in every town we go to. There is always a great comparison between ours and the other regiments camps. Some camps have old bones rags bottles tins &c laying around on the ground. You never see least speck of dirt or rubbish around our camps. Col Benedict has his quarters in a large plantation house. He lives in the large house and we (his guards) live in the Overseers house so we have it very comfortable. Gen Franklin[67] and staff have gone to N. O. Gen Emory[68] takes command. There is no news of any interest here just now. I suppose we will stay here a little while. I am now in first rate health and I hope this will find you the same. I wrote you a letter on the 25th. I wish you would tell me the date of the letters you receive from [me] as I do not know wheather you get all of my letters or not. I cannot think of any more at present. I must close With love to all I am as ever

Your Affectionate Son
Crosly
Direct
R. C. Kemp

Co. D 165 Regt. NYZ
New Orleans
LA
Or Elsewhere

Write soon

Camp in the Field on Red River, La.
April 1864

Dear Mother

I write you these few lines to let you know that I have come out of the two late battles up here which I suppose you have hard of long before this. I was in the hottest of them both and came out without a scratch. The first was April 8th I think they call it Pine Woods.[69] The other was Pleasant Hill April 9th. I have not time to tell You the details here as the mail is going in a half an hour and I must get this in in time. Our loss in killed wounded and prisoners is about 100. Col Carr[70] is wounded in the arm Shreveport is taken and Gen. Stelle[71] is driving the rebels towards us. We expect another fight soon. We are prepared for them. I will write you full particulars in a few day or as soon as the next mail leaves. I did not know this mail was going so soon or I would write more. Send my best love to all in haste

Your Affectionate Son
Crosly

P. S. We are now at a place called Grand De Core[72] on the Red River about 90 miles above Alexandria.
Write Soon Send me the paper with the account of the fight in.

Morganza, LA.[73] June 3rd 1864

Dear Mother

I have just received your very welcome letter of May 10th. I was very glad to hear from you again. I also received 3 packages of paper. I was glad that you sent the papers as we had scarcely any news out here at all. It gives me a good deal of pleasure to look over them. Have you made up your mind where you are going to move to this fall. We are still here with no prospects of leaving at present. I understand that this army corps is to be stationed along the river from Vicksburg to N. O. to keep the river free from the rebels. They are continually planting batteries at different places to stop the boats. It is about time that we done something to stop it. The regiment is very small at present notwithstanding we have had about 250 recruits sent us. There is now a Co. G in our regiment. It was formed from the last lot of recruits. We have about 170 men away from the regiment sick &c. Our camp is situated right on the banks of the river so it is rather cool to what it would be otherwise. We are expecting the paymaster any day. I will send as much home as I can out of it. When I get it I am going to get you to get me a pair of pants mad[e] out of some heavy stuff that will last some time. The pants we get out here do not last no time at all. I have drawn seven dollars over my clothing account last year all on account of so many pants being charged against me. They are made of poor flannel and are very short. The[y] get thread bare in no time. We cannot always get them either. I have just now heard the paymaster has come up on the boat. The express man[74] is here and the sutlers[75] are flocking around a sure sign that he will be here soon. I will get my picture taken as soon as we get to some town where there is a picture gallery. This is no town although it has a name. It is just a landing where boats stop to take on wood. There is only a few nigger shanties around here. It is now commencing to rain pretty lively so I will have to leave this off for the present an fix up the tent for a rainy day. Give my love to all the folks. I will write soon again and I want you to do the same. So good bye for the present.

From
Your ever Affectionate Son
Crosly

P. S. I wrote a letter to may the other day and directed it to your care as I did not know her direction. Is Col Carr recruiting in the city now. Crosly

D. R. Wallace's Letter to the Wife of a Wounded Attaché

[Edited by Gary D. Joiner and Steve Mayeux]

Hospital, Coco's Quarters De Afrique[76]
Mrs. Carter.

Dear Madam:

In an engagement between the Confederate & Federal forces near Yellow Bayou on the 18th inst.[77] your husband was very severely wounded in right thigh, the bone being broken, spiculated for about three inches.[78] A large spiculum of bone was removed a few hours after wound was received, the ball and a number of smaller spicula the next day. It was, at first, determined to amputate, subsequently it was thought best to make an effort to save the limb. It is unnecessary, I trust, for me to assure you that he will receive the best attention possible. His wound has been attended to up to present time chiefly by Dr. Martin, Div. Surgeon, than whom Dr. Stone excepted, there is no one of more reputation or skill in the South. Up to yesterday evening, I was to see him every few hours when I was ordered in charge Div. Hospital with the care of near a hundred wounded five miles distant from him so that I have not been able to see him today, but hear he is doing well.[79] He seems to desire me with him but I have every confidence in Dr. Martin, & while I exceedingly regret not being able to be with him all the time, it is not that I think I could make any suggestion to the Dr. that would add anything to the chance of the recovery of one in regard to whom we are all so anxious. For it is not improper in this connection, I trust, to state that of the great number of wounded of this command, no one has ever been so generally regretted. His general popularity, his going voluntarily into the fight when other attaches in the same department never do it, his coolness in the face of danger on a former occasion & his bravery on the one when wounded, all tend to cause the accident to be so much regretted & lamented.

It was an exceedingly unfortunate place to be in under such circumstances, as being immediately behind the Federal army that was burning & devastating the whole country as it retired before us, it was almost impossible to find a place where he could be properly cared for. We succeeded, however, in getting him in at a M. Coco's, brother to the gentleman whose negro quarters I am now occupying for a hospital, where he has & will receive every possible attention.

Be assured I will do all in my power to contribute to his comfort, mitigate his sufferings & forward the event, his restoration to health & loved ones for which we all so fervently pray.

Will you please to accept of my poor sympathy, my dear sister, & believe me,

Very respectfully
Your humble friend
D. R. Wallace[80]

William H. Whitney in the Red River Campaign

[Edited by Tara Z. Laver]

William H. Whitney of Cambridge, Massachusetts, was nineteen years old when he joined the 38th Massachusetts Infantry Regiment in July 1862 as a private.[81] Like many New England soldiers, he was sent to Louisiana, where he participated in the Teche Campaign, the assault and siege of Port Hudson, the occupation of Baton Rouge, and finally the Red River Campaign. His letters, preserved in the Louisiana and Lower Mississippi Valley Collections at Louisiana State University, detail his experiences in Louisiana during the war.

Prior to enlisting, Whitney lived in the area of Cambridge known as Cambridgeport with his mother, Caroline Stimson Whitney Russell; his stepfather, Nathan Russell, a shoe dealer; his stepbrothers William F. and Nathan Russell Jr.; and his siblings Ella Constance and Frank Erving Whitney. His father, Charles Whitney, had died in 1850. After graduating from Cambridge High School around 1860, he took a course at the Lawrence Scientific School at Harvard. He then studied and worked for a year in the Boston civil engineering office of Stephen P. and J. Franklin Fuller. Immediately after enlisting, he was made first sergeant. In March 1863 he was promoted to second lieutenant, first lieutenant in October 1863, and captain in August 1864.[82]

Whitney departed Baton Rouge on March 23, 1864, to participate in the recently launched Red River Campaign. His regiment reached Alexandria on March 24.

Alexandria La. March 25th 1864[83]

Dear Mother:

Again I am writing you from this place after the lapse of nearly twelve months.[84] We arrived here last night by steam boat from Baton Rouge. To-day we have been very busy landing and making camp. The mail leaves here this afternoon. On Wednesday the 23rd we left our nice quarters (we have just begun to appreciate them). My flower garden looked nicely and many of the plants were full of blooms.[85] I have with me pressed two or three flowers from the geranium which I send in this. Now I am and this letter is written in a shelter-tent in the midst of a large ploughed field. We are not near where we were before, which you may recollect was at the Railroad Depot. You will read in the paper of the capture of Fort DeRussey and this place by Gen. Smith from the west.[86] We found them and the cavalry brigade of the 19th Corps here.[87] They have come up by the route we passed over last year. To-day the infantry begin to come in. Soon there will be accumulated here a large army under Gen. Banks for offensive purposes. Shreveport will probably be our first capture. I say probably for we expect success. The rebs can't stand and fight in this region, at least they have not as yet. We generally carry with us overwhelming numbers besides superior guns.[88] We will have a larger and better army than that with which we left Algiers. Better because there is little here that is new, and experience is a great thing. The theory is advanced that the infantry will take transports here and proceed up river while the cavalry go by land with the train, keeping abreast with the fleet. There are rapids a few miles above here;[89] beyond which the river is clear to Shreveport. We are expecting a mail by the boat which brings up the rest of our brigade today or to-morrow. Letters will be doubly valuable now as they days of their arrival become less frequent. Though I cannot answer so [?] now as when at Baton Rouge I shall certainly improve every opportunity to keep you posted on our movement, wherever we may be. Papers will be scarce. Give love to all and answer soon.

Truly your affectionate
Son William

> Whitney and the 38th Massachusetts remained in Alexandria on garrison duty until April 12, when they moved to Grand Ecore, below Natchitoches, to support the units depleted by the losses at Mansfield and Pleasant Hill. At Grand Ecore, Banks awaited reinforcements from Major General Frederick Steele, but when Steele failed to materialize, and with the Red River too low to receive supplies from Alexandria or assistance from the navy, Banks decided to retreat to Alexandria. They reached the town on April 30 and encamped there until May 10, when the regiment moved on to Morganza, as he describes below.[90]

Morganza La. May 23rd 1864

Dear Brother:

I have two letters from you "on hand" unanswered. The first April 14th I have had for a number of days and perhaps I might say weeks. It is lucky I did not answer it when I received it, for several letters I wrote then fell into the hands of the rebs, and they had the bother of destroying them. I wrote Mother and Ella two long letters about the battle of Cane River Ford, etc by that mail.[91] Ever since our communication with N. O.[92] has been stopped or else we have been marching. You know that when the army left Alexandria we remained for two weeks, when we took transports and land[ed] at Grand Ecore. The army was then recovering itself from the great battle they had fought at Mansfield and Pleasant Hill—a battle in which some splendid fighting was displayed and all of a great victory was achieved by our forces, with all the results of a great defeat.[93] Our time there was occupied in building fortification, not knowing whether we were to continue the expedition or not. But it soon became evident that we were to fall back and soon too, if we desired to save our fleet, for the river was very low and falling every day. When we left we destroyed a large quantity of stores which we were unable to transport. It was about eighty-miles to Alexandria and we reached it in the afternoon of the fifth day including one day's fighting. The first twenty four hours we marched forty two miles. In the fight our regiment took quite a prominent part in skirmishing up to them (the enemies) position.[94] They were on a high hill, and two brigades of the 19th Corps made a charge and drove them off double quick with a loss of about three hundred. It was the most exciting work I ever participated in and rather more unpleasant than any of our fighting hitherto. But I must not occupy time and space writing about that now. At Alexandria we remained nearly two weeks trying to get the gunboats over the falls. The river was dammed and thus with few exceptions the boats saved.[95] In marching from that place to this the rebs troubled us a good deal, and at Marksville we had quite an artillery duel in which we were engaged.[96] Now we expect to spend most of our time on boats patrolling the river as a sort of a Marine Guard headquarters at Vicksburg. I don't like the prospect very well. Will write soon in answer to your other letter. What a surprise your picture gave me; I was much pleased with it, but more anon.

Brother Will

Morgansa La.[97] June 12th 1864

Dear Brother:

Having promised in my last to answer your letter of the 14th of May at the first convenient opportunity I commence to fulfill my promise. Letters from home are rather scarce now, Owing I presume to the impossibility of our writing for a short period last month. We are still encamped where I first wrote you. For four days only we have been absent from it. Then we went out towards the Atchafaylia[98] on a scout. We had no fight though expected one. While marching in the dark one night a band of guerillas fired on us from across the bayou, twice killing an officer of another regiment and wounding several.[99]

We have very queer weather here of late. For thirteen days we have had from two to three showers every day. The rain comes down heavy for a few minutes and then is over and a hot Sun succeeds.

We are not under Gen. Banks now, but under Gen. Canby[,] headquarters at Vicksburg.[100] I cannot tell how soon we may leave this place nor where we will go. The river between Vicksburg and Baton Rouge will be our cruising ground. Nothing unusual is taking place here now. We were paid off a week ago for four months and the troops buy out every sutler who opens here. A busy time it is for them, hurrying up goods from New Orleans. You must know that there is no town here. But two dwelling houses with the attendant negro quarters are in sight.[101] We encamped between the levee and the river. The former is twelve feet high and very strongly built. We are about thirty miles from Port Hudson and fifty from Baton Rouge. I have received since we have been here quite a number of papers Watchman and Chronicles and Journals.[102] I forgot in the first letter from this place to acknowledge the receipt of box with pants, cap etc. The letters taken by the rebs contained the acknowledgement. It came into my hands the day of our arrival in Alexandria from Grand Ecore and supplied me with a number of necessary things. Pants fit well also cap. I was especially pleased with the knife, fork and spoon in case and the pocket knife, which has proved exceedingly useful to me. Your picture took me by surprise. I hardly thought Punk had grown so.

Will

Morganza La.
June 12th 1864

Dear Mother:

I received your letter of May 2nd on the 1st of this month. I wrote you the 22nd of May. Ella the 26th and Frank the 22nd also with Frank to-day. I have received no letter from home since. Last week we were paid off for four months. I am enabled to send home four hundred by Adams Express to Mr. Thayer. I write him to-day concerning it and direct him to give you fifty dollars for your own use—no objection is allowed—Prices are high and not likely to fall. Winter is coming. Provide for your present wants. I forgot to acknowledge a second time the arrival of box. It came safely while at Alexandria. The trunk is what I want. I sold my other one to a cavalry officer on leaving A[lexandria]. News of the death of Levi and so soon after that of Aunt Eliza took us by surprise. It is a sad blow to both families, and one of those dispensations which human wisdom cannot understand. We look at the families suddenly deprived of their head and wonder at the plans of the Almighty. I cannot help thinking how it must affect Elbridge when he hears of the death of his mother. If he survives the terrible battles in which his corps is engaged the news will reach him when he little expects it, in the rush of letters following interrupted communications.[?]

One of our frequent heavy showers has just interrupted my writing. We have four or five daily.

Nate has just been to Baton Rouge.[103] I sent those two sheets to be placed on store there as I cant expect to use them much as the army is so liable to move at any moment. We are all of course very anxious to hear from Gen. Grant['s] army before Richmond. He certainly has achieved more than any General as yet who has faced Lee. We have received full particulars of the battles in the Wilderness and rumors now come to us of Lee and his army besieged in Richmond—if true he ought to hold him till he is starved out. God grant him success in defeating and capturing that army and then we will come home again in a few months. Almost a year since our bloody assault on P.H. the second time.[104]

Your affectionate
Son Will

Morganza La June 26th [1864]

Dear Mother:

Your letter of June 9th received yesterday. Letters from home are scarce in camp now, and of course more highly welcomed. Warm weather is upon us and we lose one half of our energy and feel more inclined to keep in the shade and do nothing. Still we have sometimes to go on a little expedition. I certainly hope we will not have to march any this summer. It is impossible for men to stand fatigue under a broiling Sun without injury. Day before yesterday I had occasion to walk about two miles in the middle of the day and felt the heat considerably. I find that I am able to endure the heat far better than many. Indeed I have cause to, and do thank God that I ^am^ sufficiently endowed with physical strength to endure all the hardships, we have encountered, so well.

One year ago about this time I was suffering in the woods before Port Hudson with the Dysentery. The time nearly approaches when I can say that I have been away from home and in the service two years. We are looking with considerable anxiety for news from Gen. Grant and hoping that he may be crowned with success in his efforts before R[ichmond].

We have just got the reported news of the capture of Petersburg and the line of rail-road south from the town.[105] If the place is invested we may make up our minds with patience for a number of months before we have the great success for which we look. I hope the government will be able to keep up the supply of reinforcements to him that his army may not fail for want of numbers, as did the army of the Peninsula.

I wrote Ella this morning or rather finished letter commenced a few days ago. You have the right idea about my course in telling you if any thing happens to Nate. I should not think myself justified in withholding the truth. Our health is good. He saw fit to be released from the duty on which he was detailed as Act. Asst.[106] Quarter Master on account of the expense attendant. As I sit I can see both up and down the river for a number of miles; when we have a breeze here the weather is tolerable. The soil, a light sand, is so hot that the bare foot cannot be placed on it in the day time. Our bathing facilities are excellent.

Son Will

Morganza La July 2nd 1864

Dear Brother:

Your letter of June 16th has arrived. My letter in answer must be short for we have just received orders to cork two days rations and prepare for transportation to New Orleans at an hour's notice. Our destination after we get there is not know[n] to such as I. I will not [fail?] to inform mother if opportunity offers there. Nearly all our army will leave this place and I am not sorry to go. I wish you would acknowledge the arrival of two Journals, a Watchman, and Era from mother. I have received a Chronicle also of late. I find my shirts rather ragged and need some more. I have bought two here which will last a few weeks. I can't get flannel shirts large enough to allow for the shrinkage here ready made. Will you tell mother to buy flannel and shrink it if possible and make ^two^ shirts that will retain their usefulness until they are worn out. I shall need stockings in two months and handkerchiefs also. I think mother had better not send a box unless I write differently soon. There is a way provided by which small bundles may be sent to soldiers by mail. They will be more likely to reach me speedily than there than any other way.

In haste

Goodby
Will

Whitney and his regiment left Morganza on the following day, July 3, 1864, landing across the Mississippi from New Orleans at Algiers. Thereafter, the 38th embarked for Washington, D.C., leaving the Department of the Gulf. The unit was then transferred with the Third Brigade, Second Division, 19th Corps, to the Army of the Shenandoah, where it participated in Sheridan's

Valley Campaign. Whitney was commissioned captain of Company G in August 1864 and wounded at the Battle of Opequan Creek near Winchester, Virginia, on September 19. He was discharged in December as a result of his injuries. In 1868 he was brevetted a major, to date from March 1865.[107]

William Whitney's wartime experiences stood him in good stead for the social and professional position he would attain in his hometown Cambridge. Whitney returned to Cambridge after his discharge and recovered slowly, but his steady rise in rank during the war proved to be an indicator of his abilities. In 1865 he again took up civil engineering in the Fullers' firm, where he worked until 1871. In 1868 he married his longtime sweetheart, Emma Sargent Barbour. They had two children, Clara Mabel and Charles Fuller, who survived to adulthood. After a short time in the Boston city engineer's office and a brief partnership with J. Franklin Fuller, he opened his own civil engineering firm, which he operated until his retirement in 1904; at that time his son took over.

Whitney was an accomplished engineer and surveyor. He published several scientific papers and pamphlets, and in 1881 the Massachusetts Charitable Mechanics' Association awarded him a bronze medal for his improvements and development of a French process for making blueprints. His interests, however, were not limited to science and engineering. Whitney was a member of the New England Historic Genealogical Society, the Watertown Historical Society, the Massachusetts Society of the Sons of American Revolution, and the Grand Army of the Republic. He authored a history of the Whitney family, *A Watertown Farm in Eight Generations* (1898), and of Sheridan's campaigns, *Union and Confederate Campaigns in the Lower Shenandoah Valley Illustrated* (1883). A Republican, he served on the Cambridge board of aldermen in 1879 and ran for the Massachusetts Legislature in 1881, but was defeated because he was a so-called mugwump. He also served on the Board of Health from 1886 until 1893 and as its chairman in 1896. Additionally, he chaired the Boston Baptist Social Union's committee on Christian work. His social memberships included the Colonial Club and the Cambridge Club. He died on May 4, 1909, of a cerebral hemorrhage after a long illness and is buried at Mount Auburn Cemetery in Cambridge.[108]

FIG. 6.1. Captain William H. Whitney. *Cambridge Chronicle*, May 8, 1909.

Notes

1. The author of this letter was William H. Scarborough, who entered service as a private and was mustered out as a sergeant in Company B of the 96th Ohio Infantry Regiment. He also served in Company C of the same regiment. Record Group 94, Microscopy 552, Roll 94, National Archives and Records Administration. The original letter is in the collection of Jimmy Sandefur, Shreveport, Louisiana.
2. The town of Berwick in St. Mary Parish. The area of Berwick, Franklin, and Brashear City (modern Morgan City) was the staging ground for the 13th and 19th Corps in the Red River Campaign.
3. Washington in St. Landry Parish.
4. New Iberia in Iberia Parish; Vermilionville is the current Lafayette in Lafayette Parish; and Opelousas is in St. Landry Parish.
5. Alexandria in Rapides Parish.
6. Montsville is in Avoyelles Parish; Cheneyville is located in Rapides Parish.
7. Received.
8. Probably Lewis H. Mitchell, who entered service as a sergeant and reached the position of adjutant in the 96th Ohio Infantry Regiment. He served in companies F and S. Record Group 94, Microscopy 552, Roll 75, National Archives and Records Administration.

9. Number.
10. This letter, penned by an unknown Union soldier during the height of the Battle of Pleasant Hill, gives perhaps the best sense of the desperate fighting during April 9. The description of his unit being pinned down and unable to move indicates that he was a member of the First, Second, or Third Brigade of the First Division of the 19th Corps or, less likely, a member of the Second Brigade of the Third Division of the 16th Corps. The original letter is in the collection of Jimmy Sandefur, Shreveport, Louisiana.
11. Grand Ecore on the Red River was and is the port for the town of Natchitoches. The author, Wilson Novyus, was a private in Company A, 161st New York Infantry, under Lieutenant Colonel William B. Kinsey. The regiment was part of Brigadier General William Dwight's First Brigade of Brigadier General William Emory's First Division of the 19th Army Corps. The original letter is in the collection of Jimmy Sandefur, Shreveport, Louisiana.
12. Emory's Division of the 19th Army Corp was brought forward late in the Battle of Mansfield to stem the route of Union forces after the virtual destruction of the 13th Corps and a large portion of the cavalry division of the 19th Corps. Dwight's Brigade, of which the 161st New York Infantry Regiment was a part, held the high ground above the only water source on the battlefield. Night halted the fighting, and this brigade saw action for an hour or less.
13. William Egleston (or Eggleston) entered service as a sergeant and was demoted to private in Company A, 161st New York Infantry Regiment. Record Group 94, Microscopy 551, Roll 42, National Archives and Records Administration.
14. Elijah Sprague served as a private in Company A, 161st New York Infantry Regiment. Record Group 94, Microscopy 551, Roll 133, National Archives and Records Administration.
15. George S. Prentiss entered service as a corporal and was mustered out as a sergeant in Company A, 161st New York Infantry Regiment. Record Group 94, Microscopy 551, Roll 113, National Archives and Records Administration.
16. Charles L. Wheaton served as a corporal in Company A, 161st New York Infantry Regiment. Record Group 94, Microscopy 551, Roll 150, National Archives and Records Administration.
17. This was at the village of Pleasant Hill, where fighting resumed on April 9 and resulted in a stalemate.
18. William H. Garvey served as a private in Company A, 161st New York Infantry Regiment. Record Group 94, Microscopy 551, Roll 51, National Archives and Records Administration.

19. The planned meeting place at or near Springfield Landing northeast of Mansfield. The land was located four miles west of the Red River at the narrow junction of Bayou Pierre Lake and Lake Cannisnia, and it is not clear how the navy and army could rendezvous. It illustrated that the army and navy were using two different maps with divergent features. Gary D. Joiner, *One Damn Blunder from Beginning to End: The Red River Campaign of 1864* (Wilmington, DE, 2003), 75–79.
20. Natchitoches.
21. Battle of Blair's Landing.
22. Novyus is referring to the 97th and 99th Engineering regiments of the U.S. Colored Troops, who would also be instrumental in building Bailey's Dam at Alexandria. This is the only known nonofficial source that states who augmented the fortifications at Grand Ecore before the Union retreat to Alexandria.
23. William A. Hess served as a private in Company A, 116th New York Infantry. Record Group 94, Microscopy 551, Roll 64, National Archives and Records Administration.
24. Gus Prentiss is likely George S. Prentiss, although four men named Prentiss served in Company A. The others were Angelo Prentiss, John Prentiss, and William A. Prentiss. Record Group 94, Microscopy 551, Roll 113, National Archives and Records Administration.
25. George F. Clark was a private in Company A, 116th New York Infantry. Record Group 94, Microscopy 551, Roll 25, National Archives and Records Administration.
26. Novyus tried to Americanize his name and is listed also by the alternate name of Wilson Nevins. Record Group 94, Microscopy 551, Rolls 104 and 105, National Archives and Records Administration.
27. The author of this letter was Ordinance Sergeant Frank W. Pearce, who served in Company A, 2nd Maine Cavalry Regiment. See Record Group 94, Microscopy 543, Roll 16, National Archives and Records Administration. The original is in the collection of Jimmy Sandefur, Shreveport, Louisiana.
28. Captain Joseph F. Twitchell served in Company A, 2nd Maine Cavalry Regiment. Record Group 94, Microscopy 543, Roll 21, National Archives and Records Administration.
29. Lieutenant Warren Mansur served in Company A, 2nd Maine Cavalry Regiment. Record Group 94, Microscopy 543, Roll 13, National Archives and Records Administration.
30. Lieutenant Silas C. Barker served in Company A, 2nd Maine Cavalry Regiment. Record Group 94, Microscopy 543, Roll 1, National Archives and Records Administration.
31. Alexandria

32. William Reed was a private in Company A, 2nd Maine Cavalry Regiment. Record Group 94, Microscopy 543, Roll 21, National Archives and Records Administration.
33. David Betts was a private in Company A, 2nd Maine Cavalry Regiment. Record Group 94, Microscopy 543, Roll 17, National Archives and Records Administration.
34. Eugene Shaw was a private in Company A, 2nd Maine Cavalry Regiment. Record Group 94, Microscopy 543, Roll 19, National Archives and Records Administration.
35. This letter was written prior to the construction of Bailey's Dam. The navy was in dire straits for lack of adequate water to float their vessels, and Union Major General Nathaniel P. Banks was considered abandoning the fleet to save his army from capture or siege.
36. This letter by an unknown soldier was apparently written by a member of the 30th Maine Infantry, commanded Colonel Francis Fessenden. The regiment was part of the Third Brigade, under Lewis Benedict of the First Division, commanded by Brigadier General William H. Emory, of the 19th Army Corps. The unit saw heavy action at Pleasant Hill, where Benedict was killed, and at Monett's Ferry where Fessenden led an attack on Rebel positions and dislodged them. Fessenden was seriously wounded in the action. The letter was written after May 16 and prior to May 22, 1864. Illegibility is noted. The original letter is in the collection of Jimmy Sandefur, Shreveport, Louisiana.
37. Bailey's Dam.
38. This was preliminary action to the Battle of Mansura.
39. The author of this letter was Hugo Voigt, a private in Company C of the 29th Wisconsin Volunteer Infantry Regiment, under Major Bradford Hancock. The regiment was part of the Colonel William H. Raynor's Second Brigade, Brigadier General Robert A. Cameron's Third Division, Brigadier General T. E. G. Ransom's 13th Army Corps. During the battle of Mansfield on April 8, 1864, this brigade formed the second line of defense at Sabine Crossroads, from which the Union named the battle. Voigt was very fortunate not to have been killed or taken prisoner in the battle. Record Group 94, Microscopy 559, Roll 31, National Archives and Records Administration. The original is in the collection of Jimmy Sandefur, Shreveport, Louisiana.
40. Sabine Crossroads or Mansfield.
41. To Pleasant Hill.
42. Brigadier General Andrew Jackson Smith, commanding the 16th Army Corps.

43. This was a common rumor among the Union troops. They could not believe the Confederates would make a stand to protect their territory. General Banks started the rumors, which his command staff spread.
44. This letter was written by Thomas Hayden, a member of the 38th Massachusetts Volunteer Infantry Regiment, which was part of the Second Division commanded by Brigadier General Cuvier Grover and the Third Brigade under Colonel Jacob Sharpe. Lieutenant Colonel James P. Richardson commanded the regiment. The other regiments in the brigade were the 128th New York Infantry, the156th New York Infantry, and three companies of the 175th New York. The Second Division of the 19th Army Corps was relegated to garrison duty at Alexandria during the Red River Campaign. It did not participate in the large battles or skirmishes north of this central Louisiana town. After the battles of Mansfield and Pleasant Hill, the division was ordered north to Grand Ecore as reinforcements to replaced depleted units. The original is in the collection of Jimmy Sandefur, Shreveport, Louisiana.
45. This was one day before the forward elements of the main Union column marched into Alexandria and eight days after the naval flotilla arrived in the town. The major self-imposed problems the Federal forces encountered were the timetables for rendezvous, the manner in which they were ordered to advance, and the methods by which the advance were undertaken. The seeds of the campaign's failure were sown before it began.
46. The Union forces' first encounter with a large Confederate defensive work on the Red River Campaign was at the incomplete Fort DeRussy. Manned by a skeleton force, it was taken by Union forces with relative ease on March 14.
47. The *Mittie Stevens* was a U.S. Army Quartermaster Corps transport vessel.
48. See chap. 4.
49. April 9.
50. Battle of Monett's Ferry.
51. Two soldiers named Thomas Hayden enlisted in the 38th Massachusetts Volunteer Infantry Regiment. The author was either Thomas O. Hayden of Company D, who entered service as a private and was mustered out as corporal (Record Group 94, Microscopy 544, Roll 18, National Archives and Records Administration) or Thomas W. Hayden of Company I, who entered service as a private and remained in that rank for the duration of the war (Record Group 94, Microscopy 544, Roll 18, National Archives and Records Administration).

52. This letter, written by an unknown Union soldier of the 19th Corps, is found in the collection of Gary D. Joiner, Shreveport, Louisiana. The author's first name is scrawled, making positive identification impossible.
53. Morganza was the site of the cantonment of the Federal Forces following the Red River Campaign. The 19th Corps was stationed there until orders were given for deployment to Virginia. Morganza is located approximately halfway between the towns of New Roads and Melville. It sits at the mouth of Bayou Fordoche.
54. Confederate General John Bankhead Magruder, commander of the District of Arkansas at the time.
55. When the author wrote this letter the Confederates were seriously considering sending the Texas Division east of the Mississippi River for operations in Alabama and Georgia. The division would have been under Lieutenant General Richard Taylor's command. Some boats were assembled but the plan was never enacted. The Union navy was aware of the plan, and armed vessels heavily patrolled the stretch of river from the Arkansas line down to Port Hudson.
56. Lincoln.
57. Wilson's Farm on April 7, Mansfield on April 8, and Pleasant Hill on April 9.
58. The author is referring to Second Brigade, under Brigadier General James W. McMillan, of the First Division of the 19th Corps, commanded by Brigadier General William H. Emory. Ludwell H. Johnson, *Red River Campaign: Politics and Cotton in the Civil War* (Kent, OH, 1993), 160–62.
59. Both the Confederate and Union forces almost simultaneously withdrew about one mile apart to end the fighting, which was a tactical tie.
60. Bailey's Dam. Joiner, *One Damn Blunder*, chap. 10.
61. Additionally, Mansura on May 16 and Yellow Bayou on May 18.
62. Rufus Cosly Kemp enlisted at the age of eighteen on September 17, 1862, in New York City. He was mustered into Company D of the 165th New York Infantry Regiment, "Duryee's 2nd." Kemp was wounded in his regiment's charge at the Siege of Port Hudson, Louisiana, on May 27, 1863. He was promoted to the rank of corporal on March 6, 1864, and to the rank of sergeant on January 21, 1865. He was mustered out of service on September 1, 1865, at Charleston, South Carolina. Report of the Adjutant-General for New York, http://www.civilwardata.com. Franklin, Louisiana, from which this letter was written, is the parish seat of St. Mary Parish.
63. New Orleans.
64. New Iberia is the parish seat of Iberia Parish, Louisiana. The town was transitioning during this period from New Town. See chap. 7.

65. Colonel Lewis Benedict, commander of the Third Brigade, First Division, 19th Army Corps. See Appendix 1.
66. Military police or guard.
67. Major General William Buel Franklin, commander of the 19th Corps. See Appendix 1.
68. Brigadier General William H. Emory, commander of the First Division, 19th Corps.
69. Battle of Mansfield or Sabine Crossroads.
70. Lieutenant Colonel Gouverneur Carr, regimental commander of the 165th New York Infantry Regiment.
71. Major General Frederick Steele, commander of the Union Forces in the northern pincer of the Red River Campaign. Kemp's information is incorrect. Steele never reached Shreveport but was turned around while still in Arkansas.
72. This is Grand Ecore on the Red River in Natchitoches Parish. Union forces retreated to Grand Ecore following their defeat at Mansfield and withdrawal from Pleasant Hill.
73. Following the Red River Campaign, the 19th Corps troops remained on the Mississippi River downstream from the mouth of Red River for several weeks awaiting orders.
74. The pay agent bringing mail and money to the regiment.
75. Traveling shopkeepers selling items to the soldiers.
76. Original letter found in Mrs. Claude B. Tate Papers, Barker History Center, University of Texas, Austin. Copy in the personal collection of Steve Mayeux, Cottonport, Louisiana.
77. May 18, 1864.
78. In this context a spiculated bone is one that has been shattered and splintered.
79. This letter was likely written near the steamboat wooding station of Morganza on the Mississippi River. Most of the 19th Corps languished there, awaiting orders in the weeks following the close of the Red River campaign.
80. Although not stated in the letter, Wallace was likely a medical doctor. The wording of the letter is obtuse. Mrs. Carter may have been a family friend, the author's sister (although this is unlikely since he signed the letter "Your humble friend"), or perhaps a sister-in-law. There is not adequate information to determine the identity of the people mentioned. No "D. R. Wallace" appears in the National Archives and Records Administration's Civil War Soldier and Sailor's database. Since the field hospital is located in "negro quarters" and the author's location is listed as "Hospital, Coco's Quarters De Afrique," it can be assumed that the

wounded man's unit is one of the regiments of the First Division of the Corps d'Afrique.

81. The 38th Massachusetts Infantry, under Lieutenant Colonel James P. Richardson, was assigned to the Third Brigade of Colonel Jacob Sharpe, of the Second Division, commanded by Brigadier Cuvier Grover, of Major General William B. Franklin's 19th Corps.
82. 1860 U.S. Census, Series M653, Roll 508, p. 510, in *HeritageQuest Online* (database online), ProQuest Information and Learning Co., Ann Arbor, MI. "Death Follows Long Illness" (obituary of William H. Whitney), *Cambridge Chronicle,* May 8, 1909, 1, 4; William H. Whitney, *A Watertown Farm in Eight Generations: A Memorial of the Whitney Family* (Cambridge, MA, 1898), 100; George W. Powers, *The Story of the Thirty Eighth Regiment Volunteers* (Cambridge, MA, 1866), 284.
83. Whitney did not consistently use terminal punctuation, so periods and question marks are provided; commas are not. His use of colons, semicolons, and dashes is retained. In-line and marginal insertions are indicated by carets (^), and superscript letters and interlineations have been brought down to the line. His capitalization (or lack thereof) is retained, except when provided by the editor for first words of sentences. Missing letters or words supplied by the editor are enclosed in brackets; a word with a question mark within the brackets indicates the transcription is uncertain. Whitney's misspellings are retained. Paragraph indentation and the placement of dateline and salutation have been standardized. Line breaks within the closing are retained, but indentation is also standardized.
84. During Banks's operations in western Louisiana (April 9–May 14, 1863), Whitney and the 38th Massachusetts reached Alexandria on May 8, after the Battle of Bisland or Bethel Place. They stayed in Alexandria until May 16, ultimately taking up positions at Port Hudson. Richard B. Irwin, *History of the Nineteenth Army Corps* (Baton Rouge, 1985), 453–54; Frederick Dyer, *A Compendium of the War of the Rebellion* (New York, 1959), 3:1262.
85. The 38th Massachusetts had been garrisoned at Baton Rouge since August 1, 1863. During that time Whitney and his fellow officers planted garden plots outside their tents. Letter to "Dear Mother," March 14, 1864, William H. Whitney Letters, MSS 1043, 1046, Louisiana and Lower Mississippi Valley Collections, Louisiana State University Libraries, Baton Rouge.
86. Brigadier General Andrew Jackson Smith, commanding detachments of the 16th and 17th Corps from Vicksburg, had captured Fort DeRussy on the Red River on March 14. The Federals occupied Alexandria two days later. Ezra J. Warner, *Generals in Blue* (Baton Rouge, 1964), 454; Winters, *Civil War in Louisiana,* 327–30; National Park Service, Civil War

Soldiers and Sailors System (CWSS), at http://www.itd.nps.gov/cwss/, "Battle of Fort DeRussey."

87. Brigadier General Albert Lindley Lee, commanding the Cavalry Division, Department of the Gulf, had left winter quarters at Franklin, Louisiana, on March 10, in advance of the rest of the 19th Corps. He arrived at Alexandria on March 19 with approximately thirty-nine hundred men. His command included five cavalry brigades and two batteries and was comprised of the following regiments: 16th Indiana Mounted Infantry Regiment, 2nd Louisiana (U.S.) Mounted Infantry, 6th Missouri, 14th New York, 87th Illinois Mounted Infantry, 1st Louisiana, 2nd Illinois, 3rd Massachusetts, 31st Massachusetts Mounted Infantry, 8th New Hampshire Mounted Infantry, 2nd New York Veterans, 18th New York, Detachment from 3rd Rhode Island, Battery "B" of 2nd Massachusetts Light Artillery (Nims' Battery), and Battery "G" of 5th U.S. Light Artillery. Johnson, *Red River Campaign,* 100; Irwin, *History of the Nineteenth Army Corps,* 279–80, 289; http://members.fortunecity.com/thegunnyl/red_river_campaign_la_10mar64.htm
88. At the start of the expedition, Banks had approximately twenty-eight thousand men under his command compared to Confederate General Richard Taylor's six thousand. By April 2 reinforcements from Texas increased Taylor's numbers to about eighty-eight hundred, and the addition of four thousand infantrymen from Arkansas on April 8 brought his force to almost thirteen thousand. Bergeron, "A Colonel Gains His Wreath," 1–2.
89. The rapids proved an impediment for advancing the troop transports up the river toward Shreveport. From March 23 to April 3, large groups of soldiers worked to heave the vessels over the rapids and succeeded in getting thirty transports and twelve tinclads across. The remainder was left at Alexandria or returned to the Mississippi. Grover's Division, of which Whitney's regiment was a part, was left at Alexandria. Winters, *Civil War in Louisiana,* 333–34.
90. CWSS, "Regimental History of 38th Massachusetts Volunteers"; Power, 129–51; John D. Winters, *The Civil War in Louisiana* (Baton Rouge, 1963), 356–65.
91. During the retreat from Grand Ecore to Alexandria on April 23, Whitney and the 38th Massachusetts participated in the Battle of Monett's Ferry, also called the Battle of Cane River or Cane Crossing. Powers, *The Story of the Thirty Eighth Regiment Volunteers,* 138–40; CWSS, "Monett's Ferry."
92. New Orleans.
93. The Battles of Mansfield (April 8) and Pleasant Hill (April 9) sealed the fate of the Red River Campaign and the military career of Banks. Mansfield was a Confederate victory and effectively stopped the Union's

advance to Shreveport. Though troops fought to a bloody tie the following day at Pleasant Hill, shortages of supplies and water led Banks to retreat toward Alexandria. Winters, *Civil War in Louisiana,* 346, 356.

94. Again, Whitney is referring to the Battle of Monett's Ferry.
95. Porter's fleet was stuck in low water at the falls above Alexandria. Lieutenant Colonel Joseph Bailey, an engineer on Major General William Buel Franklin's staff, proposed damming the river to raise the water level enough to allow the gunboats to pass. More than three thousand men worked on the dam, including the 38th Massachusetts. Winters, *Civil War in Louisiana,* 367–69; CWSS, "38th Regiment, Massachusetts Infantry."
96. Also known as the Battle of Mansura, May 16, 1864. As the Federals followed the Red River in retreat, Taylor massed his forces in an open prairie from which he could control roads the Federals were traveling as they retreated. Taylor opened up an artillery barrage as they approached. After four hours of skirmishing, the Union forces formed up to flank the Confederates, who soon fell back, and the Federals proceeded to Simmesport. CWSS, "Mansura." They reached Morganza around May 20. A small skirmish also occurred at Marksville on May 14, but the artillery duel Whitney describes occurred at Mansura. Winters, *Civil War in Louisiana,* 374.
97. Morganza.
98. Atchafalaya River.
99. From May 30 to June 6, the 38th Massachusetts was with Brigadier General Michael K. Lawler on reconnaissance to the Atchafalaya River from Morganza. During the night of May 30, as they proceeded to Livonia, guerillas fired upon them from across Bayou Fordoche. One officer of the 22nd Iowa Infantry was killed and several were wounded from the 156th and 175th New York Infantry. CWSS, "Regimental History of 38th Massachusetts Volunteers"; Powers, *The Story of the Thirty Eighth Regiment Volunteers,* 152–53; Report of Lawler, June 3, 1864, in U.S. War Dept., *War of the Rebellion: The Official Records of the Union and Confederate Armies,* 128 vols. (Washington, 1880–1901), ser. 1, vol. 34, pt. 1:961.
100. Due to Banks's failure in the Red River Campaign, Major General Edward Richard Sprigg Canby assumed command of the Military Division of West Mississippi, which included the Department of the Gulf and of Arkansas, and replaced Banks as military commander. Though Banks retained command of the department in name, with Canby's appointment, Banks's duties became limited to civil matters. Warner, *Generals in Blue,* 68; Winters, *Civil War in Louisiana,* 378.
101. In 1860 the village of Morganza had a hotel, large store, and post office. Judy Riffel, ed., *A History of Pointe Coupeé Parish and Its Families* (Baton

Rouge, 1983), 29. In retaliation for their defeat at the Battle of Fordoche Bridge, also called the Battle of Stirling Plantation, Federals had set fire to Morganza in early October 1863. Brian J. Costello, *A History of Pointe Coupeé Parish Louisiana* ([New Roads, La.], 1999), 115.

102. *Cambridge Chronicle;* probably *Boston Daily Journal* or some edition thereof; *(Boston) Christian Watchman and Reflector,* a Baptist newspaper. Newspapers identified using the online union catalog WorldCat.

103. Lieutenant Nathan "Nate" Russell Jr. (b. 1836), 38th Massachusetts, Co. F. Whitney's stepbrother, Nate, was promoted to first sergeant March 3, 1863, to second lieutenant April 19, 1863, to first lieutenant and transferred to Company I, January 9, 1864, and finally to quartermaster, July 1, 1864. He was listed as a clerk in the 1860 census. 1860 U.S. Census, Series M653, Roll 508, p. 510; Powers, *The Story of the Thirty Eighth Regiment Volunteers,* 243, 277.

104. The 38th Massachusetts participated in the unsuccessful assaults on Port Hudson on May 27 and June 14, 1863.

105. Grant had reached the outskirts of Petersburg in mid-June, and he lay siege to the city. It would not fall to Federal forces until April 1865. Whitney had heard correctly that they had cut the Weldon Railroad, one of the major supply lines into Petersburg, in the Battle of Jerusalem Plank Road, June 21–22. CWSS, "Jerusalem Plank Road."

106. Acting assistant.

107. CWSS, "Regimental History of 38th Massachusetts Volunteers"; Powers, *The Story of the Thirty Eighth Regiment Volunteers,* 154, 284; Massachusetts Adjutant General's Office, *Massachusetts Soldiers, Sailors, and Marines in the Civil War* 4 (1932): 7; Winters, *Civil War in Louisiana,* 356–65.

108. "Death Follows Long Illness," 1, 4.

Miss Sidney Harding: A Daughter of Privilege Flees Northward

Edited by Gary D. Joiner and Cheryl H. White

Sidney Harding was the daughter of prominent sugar cane planter Winthrop S. Harding and his wife, Frances Elizabeth Conrad Harding, in St. Mary Parish, Louisiana. The couple, married in May 1828, had eight children. Sidney, the sixth child, was born in 1845. A records search reveals that Sidney first appeared on the U.S. Census in 1850, living in St. Mary Parish with her parents and siblings, although her age on that census was incorrectly listed as ten years.[1] The details of her life as well as that of her family members are, unfortunately, relatively obscure, although sketchy records exist.

The Harding family home in St. Mary Parish, Old Brier, was destroyed by the Union army in 1864; however, the Harding family also apparently owned fifty-nine acres of land in Opelousas, Louisiana, purchased by a Winthrop Harding in October 1852.[2] Since Sidney had an older brother named Winthrop who predeceased their father, it is unclear whether it was the father or son who purchased this property.

Sidney's elder sister Anne married her first cousin, William Taylor Palfrey Jr. in 1855. Anne's mother, Frances Elizabeth Conrad, was the sister of William's mother, Sidney Ann Conrad, for whom Sidney Harding was apparently named. A third sister was Mary Clara Conrad Weeks, of the Shadows-on-the-Teche

Plantation in New Iberia.[3] There is little known of the remainder of the family.

At eighteen Sidney began keeping her diary during her travels to north Louisiana. She apparently never married. The next time she appeared on the U.S. Census in 1880 she was listed as living with her sister, Frannie (Frances), again in St. Mary Parish. Sidney's age in 1880 was listed as thirty-five; her sister was forty-five and also unmarried. A twenty-four-year-old cousin, Orleans Brown, also was listed as living with the women.[4] It is unclear exactly where in the parish Sidney and Frances were living at this time. A records search revealed no death information for either Sidney or Frances, although the cousin, Orleans Brown, apparently died in New Orleans in 1919.[5] Neither Sidney nor Frances appears on any future available census records.

Although vague references are given for a "Harding Plantation" in St. Mary Parish in subsequent records, it is unclear the exact nature of the familial relationship involved. Coroner records indicate that one Casmire Moore died on January 31, 1881, when hit by a train on the railroad tracks on Morgan Railroad at Harding Plantation, Louisiana.[6] Another reference to the same plantation appears in lynching records of Louisiana, indicating a black man named Daniel Pleasants was hanged for murder on August 11, 1887, at the Harding Plantation in St. Mary Parish.[7]

Harding's personal story lacks detail, but her diary nevertheless provides a fascinating glimpse of Civil War Louisiana. Through her passages readers are able to see what she saw—the buildup to the historic battles that took place at Mansfield and Pleasant Hill, colorfully peppered with her own observations about personal contacts with soldiers and citizens. Her diary concludes with an entry at the end of 1864 on a note of despair; she could not know, of course, that the war's end was only months away.

Harding, whoever she might have been and whatever fortunes might have befallen her in later years, left a fascinating legacy in her words. It is unlikely that a woman like Harding, pampered by her aristocratic plantation lifestyle and still immature at her young age, would have imagined that her diary would be read generations later and preserved as a historical document.[8] In many ways, this makes her entries all the more compelling, for she provides the unique and honest, unedited and unpretentious, insight of a young woman displaced from her home and her family by the tragedy of war.

The editors have chosen to place Harding's entries from July 21, 1863, through December 1863 and scattered entries from June through December 1864 as Appendix 5.

The Diary of Miss Sidney Harding

I will commence my journal once more after so many sad catastrophies.[9] The journal of all my retreats from the enemy has been burned up in our Keachie house.[10] I found my dear old home looking outside last as usual and so lovely. I have seen nothing like our grand old live oaks since we left here in April. The negroes were, perfectly delighted to see us. I found the house so dirty we could not stay there. Went to Mrs. Murphy's. Oh, the sufferings of the people while the parish was in the hands of the enemy. The enemy destroyed a great deal for us. I will not attempt to tell of the people's sufferings. It would take pages. The house has been full of sick soldiers ever since our arrival.[11] Sent to Mrs. Parkersons for Willie Furman. Promised his sister to take care of him. Has been quite sick. Brought young Peters with him. I hope to attend a great del[12] to them. Both their heads and so forth. Alas, Vicks[burg] and Port Hudson have fallen and we will have to retreat again.[13] Our army retreated. Young Marshall been staying here. Very agreeable. all gone now. Col. Vinar[14] ate breakfast here with many others. All the furniture sent off. Ready to start. W. F.[15] and J. P.[16] will go to W. with us, I will try to keep a faithful account of my trip this time. Oh who can tell how I dislike for the third time to leave the dear old homestead[.] Lut.[17] Corrier here sick. Ned not going south with us.[18] Had my hair cut short. Look like an ugly bug.

Jan 1st, 1864

Another year opened on our national troubles. It saddens me to think of it. But I thank God that we have all been spared to see the dawn of another year and pray that before the end we will all be in our dear old home in St. Mary's. Here I am at Col. Watson's. Been spending some time with my dear friend and schoolmate Mollie. We all dressed about ten, for the callers. Waited in the parlor some time, began to think no one would come, but let me here say something of the terrible weather we are having. Two days ago we had a snow storm. Then sleet and oh how bitter

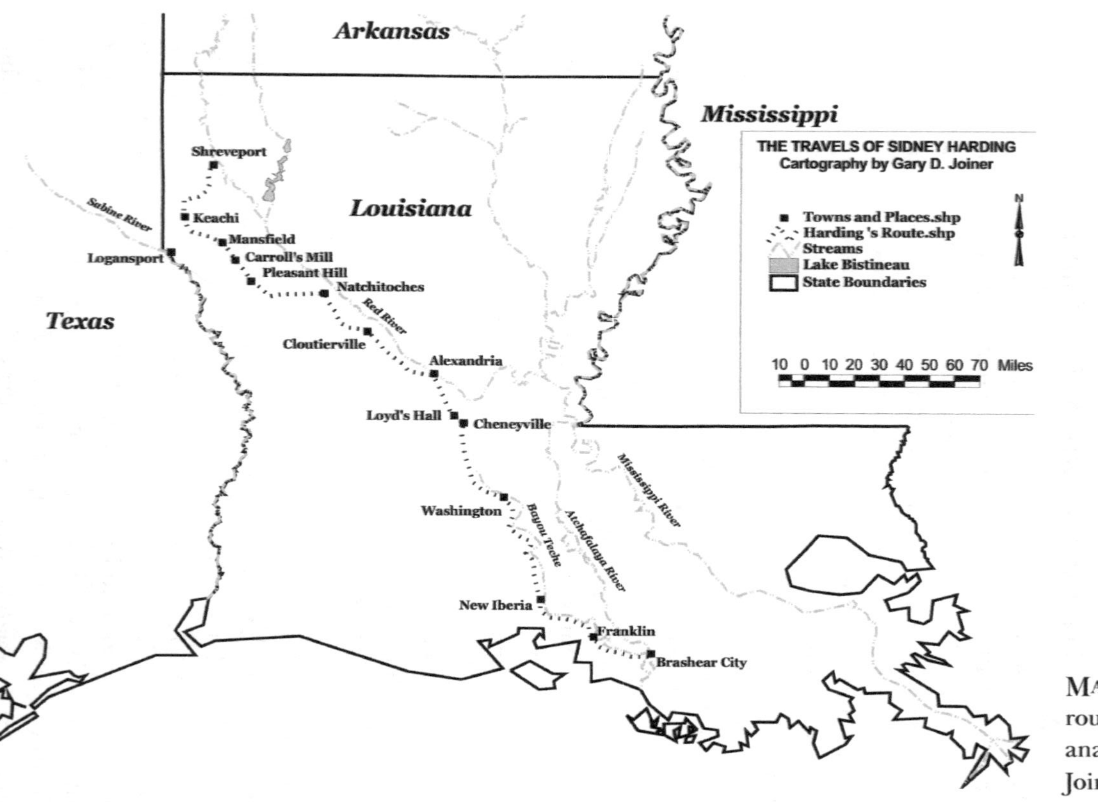

MAP 7.1. Sidney Harding's route to northern Louisiana. Cartography by Gary D. Joiner.

cold. We dressed very warmly and sat over the fire. Then was not warm. Much colder than I have ever felt it in my sunny home farther south. Well, about twelve, there was an arrival. Mr. Selden Gen. Smith's brother in law.[19] Quite handsome. Not smart. Then Mr. Duncan, but he is almost home folks. Then Capt. Marston, fair hair, eyes, whiskers. Then old Col. Landry.[20] Capt. Carter.[21] We all went into a nice lunch. Hot gumbo. Other things. Mrs. W. made a bet that all the young people at the table would be married before next new year. We soon went back to the fire. Then came Maj. Ken Williamson,[22] Col. Anderson,[23] Dr. Hadin, Mr. Mirely, together. Staid a few moments. Took lunch and left. The staff sent word they would be out in the evening. Saved supper for them. Mr. S and D. staid. Mr. S. Bet me a pair of gloves against a cravat that Capt. F. would not come. After dark, Capt. Jones[24] came. Said others were not coming. Played synonimous, blind man's bluff. Capt. J. caught me around the waist, I, of course, did not like it. Said so, They all laughed very much. So ended the first day of the year. Had a pleasant day but could not help thinking of the last which I passed at home and of the dear boys out, perhaps, in this dreadful weather.

March Thursday 10th

I commence my journal today again after neglecting it for several months—on my 23rd birthday. Is it possible, yes I am really getting old—and sometimes, now I feel old—but not generally—Who wants to think that we would have a wedding in this old log house—As Alice was married to Mr. Weightman at three o'clock this afternoon by Mr. Londeto—only Judge Moore and Ben Prescott here—not another it was so private we had some fun—young W. and his [illegible] from—S.[25] was expected but did not come.

Unknown date

A week or two has lapsed since I wrote, as usual the more there is to write, the less I write. There was a great alarm about the gun boats expect up to Shreveport immediately.[26] Land for [us?] at Mansfield. Sister F's[27] house was in Shreveport. We started up—it rained all day—we got to Mrs. Watson's late in evening—they packed up to go in country. Next morning just as Ella, Sis F. and self were getting in carriage to go to town Capt. Williams[28] rode up in great hurry—the gunboats certainly coming up and troops at Mansfield.[29] We hastened off in great hurry. Had not gotten far when down we stuck in mud hole. Two nice gallants rode up—to help us—had to get out.

Some soldiers coming along pushed the carriage along in the midst of it, Price's army passed.[30] There we were, walking one way, they another—Well we got to town at last—and found panic all over—not boats but falls no troops [above?][31] but we came home that day—got stuck in woods—night came on—had to stay at Mrs. Allen's stage stand—came home next morning found B. Witherspoon.[32] Col. A. Oh— Dr. Howe and Mr. Bert dined with us.

All went to church. Judge Moore came to go saw Capt. Freeman[33] —helped us in carriage—great many of the 2nd La. captured—felt very anxious about the boys.[34]

Several days later

We started to Pleasant hill to see about the boys, but heard they were not there. Went to Mansfield, saw Benny Marshall B. P. came to see us after dinner. So glad to see an old friend—one we had known below—I like him so much.

Julia, M. G. and Miss Eliza and self—thinking all quiet started to church—what was our surprise to see the road strewn with wagons—the army retreating but we went on not knowing the extent of it when Aaron Prescott met us and asked us to return. Our army was really retreating.[35] Oh how handsome he looked. We returned—had difficulty in passing train. We got ready to come home immediately. Julia to come with us. I hated to leave poor Mrs. G.. We started hard to pass all the trains—gave up—here safely—saw Lt. Winchester[36] said he wanted to send his servant up to give us warning in time to leave. It does me so good to see the soldiers from below.[37] Everything so quiet and peaceful here, not like the same place.

Just as quiet as can be, everything begins to look so pretty and green but oh, not like the springs in our old St. Mary's. Ma told us that Major Cosby,[38] a nice gentlemen who was camping near here, had been to call. A lady staid all night on way to see sick brother. Spent a quiet day. Heard the enemy had not advanced. Our troops at Mansfield. Sorry we came up.

We all wanted to go below again to see the troops and our friends. Sis A. proposed that Julia and myself should ask Lt. Edwards[39] for a pair of mules—so in the evening we went over, The old gentlemen was very kind, had a nice pair selected. He is gallant. He promised to let Julia have her shoes before Mr. W. We were quite triumphant—I believe Mr. W. tried to get his carriage done before our waggon.

We got ready and started early. They were all very much surprised to see us at Mrs. Glassell's. Went to Taylor['s] headquarters and saw Lt. Vincent—very white—said he knew Lyman was not taken prisoner.[40] Cus.

May and Maj. A. had gone—the house full of soldiers we passed Capt. Blair[41] and Mr. Whitney said they would come up in evening which they did. The soldiers from Buchell's reg.[42] seemed delighted I played for them said they wanted to bring band up next evening to play for us.

Wednesday April 6th

We went down to Carrol's mill to see the 2nd La.—Passed through Texas Camps[43] Just got there as reg. was mounting. Saw Lt. Kelly[44] Mr. Lyne Labarre and Richardson, They all seemed delighted to see us. Cannot stay long. Oh how I hated to see this. Saw John Murphy. Had not been at Mrs. G's two hours when a wounded came up—fighting near Plea Hill,[45] we all ran out to the war to look saw another went right back and started home. Saw hundreds of men retreating.[46] Staid all night. Mrs. Gibs met Capt. Bradford[47] and some other men. They did not seem to mind it.

Thursday April 7th

Next morning we were waked up early by shouts, our reinforcements. We dressed in a hurry to see them. Nearly all of our army passed down. We staid in most all morning. We saw nearly every one we knew. All Walker's division, Moutin and Polignac's brigade[48] and a great deal of artillery. The Lt. and gallant Col. Arman,[49] at the head how handsome he looked. All of our brave soldiers. How sad it made me feel to see them all marching down to meet their fate. Poor fellows, many of them will never return.[50]

Friday April 8th

Major H. came in and told us we had a general engagement—Whipped the Yankees all to pieces—they retreating. Poor Gen. Mouton killed. Poor fellow did not live to enjoy his laurels. We decided to go down immediately to see about Frank and other friends. The crescents terribly cut up.[51] Ma, Cus. Ally and self started down—rest to come in morning. The staff passd us. Feseret Jones, Walworth staid all night at Mrs. Pitts, this side B. very kind indeed.

Saturday April 9th

We saw the crescent go by but did not see Frank so we got in carreiage and rode around to meet them. Lt. Horton[52] called him and Mr. Melville. Poor boys I hated so see them go—they caught up in carriage. Saw Major Simmes,[53] Gen. Wick,[54] Capt. Fusiller,[55] [illegible] and many others. The bands played as they marched through town. Fought all enemy before and this morning the wounded coming in—not a great many. We started home about twelve. Met Capt. Fussern[56] and Capt. West,[57] the most excited man I ever saw. Fighting three miles below Mansfield. In evening we got home. Five of wests men came to get supper. Major Cosby spent evening with us is very fine looking and a great talker and laugher. Everyone says we are sure to whip the Yanks. I never saw more confidence than is displayed by all. God grant that we will not be disappointed.

Saw all the captured waggons, artilery, two thousand prisoners and everything. A glorious victory, but dearly bought. Saw A. West, told us Frank was well. Col. Armand killed, poor fellow. Nearly all the officers in Crescent killed or wounded.

Sunday April 10th

Cos. Ally proposed going over the battlefield. I had rather gone to the hospital as it was Sunday, but would not say anything as the rest wished to go. Mrs. Pitts went. As we passed the hospital the gallery was full of our dead.

Oh how sick it made me. It was a draedful ride to me, very sad. Hot and thirsty, we saw nothing but an open field. Came back to Mrs. Gibbs. All busy picking lint. Mrs. Prescott, Cus. A., Mrs. King and other there. Ma and Mrs. Pitts went to hospital. I went after dinner. Oh what a dreadful site. Our poor men just lying on the floor in cotton. And such an odor. And they bore it so bravely. Not a groan was heard, all so cheerful. I only went to one church. There are more than a thousand wounded. Every house in town like a public building and every private house full. Lt. Horton very ill at Mrs. Crosby's. Sister A. and myself went to see Lt. Legery[58] and young Lewis, friends of Franks. At Mrs. H.'s, Sis. A., F., and Julia went to Mrs. Gibbs—We went back, to Mrs. P's. Cus. A's carriage broken. They are very kind. Asked us to stay as long as we wished to. Plain but good patriotic people.

Monday April 11th

Went the next morning to hospital. As we were coming out a Missourian asked me to please go see the Missouri boys.[59] They like to see ladies. So of course we went. Poor fellows they did seem glad. Asked us to come again. One poor boy had an eye shot and seemed to suffer, so we went over to another one— Someone said Ladies our boys feel neglected, no one has been to see them. Went to two back rooms, no one knew of. Then one asked us to go see his brother. They like so for the ladies to visit them. Oh the sickening sights. Some shot in face, both eyes out, head bent arms, legs everywhere.

TUESDAY APRIL 12TH

We had nowhere to go to in town. Had promised to send for Mrs. Pitts. Did not like to go to Mrs. G.'s so many have staid so long. Got Mrs. Prescott's carriage to go out to Mrs. P's. When in, the old lady drove. We told her we were not in a hurry. Went out to see about Cos. A's carriage. Saw Lt. Billy, Willie and Capt. Furman, Mr. Lyne. They were going to camp on Keachie Road. I was so glad they said they wanted to come see me at Mrs. P's in evening. Met Capt. F. and Prescott ordered back, could not see me. I am so sorry they have gone below. Dear old 2nd La. saw Frank and Mr. Melville. Got some Yankee letters, going up in morning. Sent Sis A's carriage back for some wounded. Such a very handsome Capt. wounded at Mrs. Pitts, so interesting.

Came home this evening without any adventures. Had not been home long when Mr. Tourmillion came slightly wounded. A handsome Missourian staid all night. Went down in carriage. Sent five pillows to hospital.

WEDNESDAY APRIL 13TH

Got a funny epistle this morning. A joke of Major Cosby's. I answered it. In the midst of the excitement a poor wounded soldier was brought in from the waggons. Sixty going up to L.[60] This one so ill could not go. Thought he would die. Sent for Doctor Lee. Got him warm. A little better but very ill.

Major C. came up. We thought poor little fellow would not live half an hour. Major Cosby came up this evening—staid till late—very pleasant—we will sit up all night.

THURSDAY APRIL 14TH

Mallow better this morning. Walker's staff stopped here. All the divisions passed.[61] Brothers of Mallow stopped—one staid. Many stopped for dinner. Oh how I hate to refuse them—but we have to, Two wounded came up—ugly common, not much wounded. People coming in and out all the time. The room was in great confusion. One just been laid on top of bed when Major came. Such a commotion. putting things to rights. I went and dressed. Ma did not come in, they all laughed so much.

FRIDAY APRIL 15TH

Nothing unusual—Soldiers coming all the time. Poor little Mallow no better, two of wounded left. Tourmillion still here. I like him, so much—will be sorry when he leaves. Took a little walk in evening.

SATURDAY APRIL 16TH

Mr. M worse, last wounded left this morn. They do not know how to behave. One undressed before Ma. It would be much more pleasant to have officers or gentlemen I would not be partial for the work. They have all fought and bled in our defense.

SUNDAY APRIL 17TH

Poor little Mallow died this morning. I sat up till two this morning. He gradually got worse. Died at six. His poor brother so distressed. They made the coffin at Maj. Cosby's camp and attended to everything. We all went to see him buried. The Farrer's and Feranans there. Poor soldier, the warfare is over. We felt such an interest in him a handsome boy. Maj. C. did not come back from Shreveport. The house has been very sad, of course all day.

WEDNESDAY MAY 11TH

I busied myself knitting today, I want to finish those gloves for Col. Edwards. Maj.C. Has not been to see us yet. Something is certainly the matter, but I do not care enough for him to mind it tho I like him very much. The rest are always wondering and speculating on the subject. It was pleasant to have him come up of evenings. I am overcome sometimes with homesickness. The news now is all so cheering. Grand victories in Va.[62]

Notes

1. U.S. Dept. of Commerce, Seventh Decennial Census (1850), St. Mary Parish, LA, unpublished tabulations in the National Archives and Records Administration (NARA), Washington, DC.
2. Bureau of Land Management's General Land Office (GLO), Washington, DC; Louisiana Dept. of Natural Resources, Bureau of State Lands, Louisiana Land Records, 1852.
3. Records of the Grevemberg House, Franklin, LA.
4. U.S. Dept. of Commerce, Tenth Decennial Census (1880), St. Mary Parish, Louisiana, unpublished tabulations in the NARA.
5. State of Louisiana, Secretary of State, Division of Archives, Records Management, and History, *Vital Records Indices,* Baton Rouge, Death records for Orleans Parish, 1919.
6. Records of the St. Mary Parish Coroner's Office.
7. See a list of lynchings in Louisiana from 1878 to 1946 at http://academic.evergreen.edu/p/pfeiferm/Louisiana.html. The list was prepared by Professor Michael J. Pfeifer, American Social History,

Evergreen State College, Olympia, WA. The entry reads "August 11, 1887, Daniel Pleasants (alias Hoskins), Harding Plantation, St. Mary Parish, Murder, Black, Posse (Mixed)."

8. Harding (Miss Sidney) Diaries, 1863–64, 1865, Manuscript Group #721, Louisiana and Lower Mississippi Valley Collections, Hill Memorial Library, Louisiana State University, Baton Rouge. This chapter includes only those portions of the diary relevant to the time period of the Red River Campaign. Appendix 5 contains entries prior to and following the campaign. The material prior to the campaign is particularly important because it is the only existing account of the route taken by refugees from extreme southern Louisiana to the northwestern area of the state.
9. Sidney frequently spelled individuals' names differently and at other times abbreviated names, often using only a single letter. The first time an identified individual is named in an alternate manner a citation is given. It is not noted separately thereafter. All mentions of military personnel were checked in Andrew B. Booth's *Records of Louisiana Confederate Soldiers and Louisiana Confederate Commands*, 3 vols. (Spartanburg, SC, 1984). Any who are identified are listed in the citation. If a person is one of several possibilities, all are listed. Only personnel from Louisiana were searched. Although not specified by the author in these entries, it is apparent that the Harding family had close connections with DeSoto and Caddo parishes and that they owned the log cabin to which they fled. It also appears that they knew the route they took and places in which they planned to stay.
10. The Harding family plantation in St. Mary Parish was named Old Brier. A confusing item in this diary is that the family apparently named their house "Keachie," although Sidney consistently spelled it "Beachie." Once the family moved north out of the reach of the Union army, they went to Keachi in DeSoto Parish. Keachie is an often-used variant for Keachi. Federal soldiers occupied Old Brier in spring 1863 during operations along Bayou Teche. Union soldiers burned the main house in 1864.
11. Apparently Confederate soldiers serving under Brigadier Jean Jacques Alexandre Alfred Mouton.
12. Deal.
13. Vicksburg fell to Union forces on July 4, 1863. Port Hudson fell on July 9, 1863. These actions opened the entire length of the Mississippi River to Union forces.
14. No record of an officer by this name is found in Booth's *Records*.
15. Willie Furman.
16. Johnny Peters.
17. Lieutenant.

18. Ned was Sidney's brother.
19. There is no record of Kirby Smith having a brother-in-law by this name.
20. This was possibly Colonel J. Landry of the 28th Louisiana Infantry Regiment. Booth's *Records* states that he was listed on the "Official Rolls of Paroled Officers, Paroled at Washington, La., June 24, 1865."
21. 2nd Lieutenant A. V. Carter Jr. of Company E, 2nd Louisiana Cavalry Regiment. According to Booth's *Records* he was captured at Henderson Hill on March 21, 1864, and sent to New Orleans on March 26. He was exchanged at Red River Landing on July 22, 1864.
22. No record of an officer by this name is found in Booth's *Records*.
23. Ibid.
24. Ibid.
25. Shreveport.
26. This was written at least one week after the Union navy entered the Red River on March 12. The entire region knew that Shreveport was the target of the expedition.
27. Sidney's sister Fannie.
28. 2nd Lieutenant E. B. Williams of Company B of the 2nd Louisiana Cavalry Regiment. Booth's *Records* state that he was paroled in Houston, Texas, June 23, 1865.
29. Sidney incorrectly believes that there are Union troops in Mansfield.
30. Sidney is mistaken. She believes these to be the soldiers of the Arkansas and Missouri divisions. This information would place the date of the passage at April 8, 1864. They would not reach Taylor in time to fight at Mansfield but would be heavily engaged the following day at Pleasant Hill. The troops she refers to are possibly units of the Louisiana or Texas divisions passing through to their camps just north of Mansfield. The divisions were often routed on back roads to alleviate slow travel times.
31. The falls or rapids at Alexandria.
32. Boykin Witherspoon of Buena Vista Plantation near Stonewall.
33. No record of an officer by this name is found in Booth's *Records*.
34. The 2nd Louisiana Cavalry Regiment was captured almost intact at Henderson Hill in Rapides Parish on the night of March 21, 1864.
35. Sidney is describing not the aftermath of a battle but the troops of Major General Richard Taylor moving north along the Shreveport-Natchitoches stagecoach road, which ran through Pleasant Hill and Mansfield. Taylor was preparing to meet the Union column just south of Mansfield. She is only seeing a portion of the Confederate units.
36. No record of an officer by this name is found in Booth's *Records*.
37. She is referring to Mouton's Division.

38. No record of an officer by this name is found in Booth's *Records.*
39. 2nd Lieutenant William J. Edwards Jr. of Company K, 28th (Gray's) Louisiana Infantry Regiment.
40. At Henderson Hill.
41. Lieutenant Colonel James D. Blair. He received his promotion to Lieutenant Colonel on January 13, 1864.
42. 1st Texas Cavalry Regiment led by Colonel Augustus Buchel. Buchel would be mortally wounded at the Battle of Pleasant Hill on April 9.
43. This was an unwise move. Carroll's Mill was approximately halfway between Pleasant Hill and Mansfield. Confederate forces knew that Banks's column had moved out of Natchitoches toward Pleasant Hill beginning on April 6. Confederate units were still gathering at Mansfield. Less than a day from the time she penned this passage, the head of the Union cavalry division encamped at Carroll's Mill on their way to Mansfield.
44. This officer cannot be verified in Booth's *Records* due to a large number of candidates.
45. Cavalry skirmish by General Tom Green's regiments slowing the Union column to buy Taylor time to ready his trap at Mansfield.
46. General Green's troops preparing for the next trap.
47. Possibly Captain Robert Hector Bradford of Company F, 28th Louisiana Infantry (Gray's) Regiment.
48. Possibilities include men from Major General John George Walker's First or Texas Division, General Mouton's Second or Louisiana Division, and Brigadier General Camille Jules Armand Marie, the Prince de Polignac's Brigade of Mouton's Division, of which the Consolidated Crescent Regiment was a part. The 2nd Louisiana Cavalry Regiment would have marched with this group as well. See Appendix 1.
49. Colonel Leopold L. Armant commanded the 18th Louisiana Consolidated Infantry Regiment, part of Gray's Brigade. This was a sister regiment of the Consolidated Crescent Regiment.
50. Sidney was apparently viewing the troops from a position within the town of Mansfield.
51. General Mouton was killed as he led the Louisiana troops in the charge that opened the battle. The Consolidated Crescent Regiment lost over 49 percent casualties in this action. See chap. 1.
52. 2nd Lieutenant C. M. Horton of Company A, Consolidated Crescent Infantry Regiment.
53. 1st Lieutenant and Adjutant R. N. Sims of the 2nd Louisiana Cavalry Regiment. He was captured at Henderson Hill on March 21, 1864, and

according to Booth's *Records* was "Paroled New Orleans, La., Jan. 4, 1864. Exchanged Red River Landing, July 22, 1864."

54. No record of an officer by this name is found in Booth's *Records.*
55. This is possibly 1st Lieutenant and Adjutant Ferjus Fuselier, of the Confederate Guards Response Battalion, Louisiana Volunteers.
56. No record of an officer by this name is found in Booth's *Records.*
57. Ibid.
58. No record of an officer by this name is found in Booth's *Records.*
59. Soldiers of Parsons's Division.
60. Probably Logansport, Louisiana.
61. This was the passage of the Arkansas, Missouri, and Texas division on their way to Arkansas to fight in the Camden Campaign. See chaps. 3 and 5.
62. Probably the Battle of the Wilderness. The battle was fought on May 5 and 6, and it is likely that information reached northwest Louisiana by May 11. Richmond papers reported the Confederate victory at Mansfield on April 12, only four days after the action.

JOSEPH PITTY COUTHOUY: THE DEATH OF A SAILOR-SCIENTIST

Edited by Gary D. Joiner and Jimmy H. Sandefur

JOSEPH P. COUTHOUY WAS AN AMERICAN RENAISSANCE MAN. Born on January 6, 1808, in Boston, he entered the Boston Latin School in 1820. Couthouy was a merchant vessel captain, treasure hunter, author, and a Civil War U.S. naval officer. He is most remembered in the scientific community as a pioneering conchologist, a collector and student of mollusk shells, and as a malacologist, a scientist who studies the structure and habits of mollusks.[1] Couthouy was a member of the Boston Society of Natural History. He married Mary Greenwood Wild on March 9, 1832, but little is known of their married life.

In 1838 Couthouy asked the president to be assigned to the Scientific Corps of the U.S. Exploring Expedition. He was selected as one of the naturalists.[2] The expedition consisted of six naval vessels, 500 officers and crew, scientists, and artists. During a four-year voyage the expedition achieved spectacular success, created maps and charts of over two hundred islands in the Pacific, and mapped much of the Antarctic coastline. The specimens gathered and the information digested from this first great American overseas expedition created the core of the collections of the U.S. Botanic Garden, the National Herbarium, the Naval Observatory, and the National Museum of Natural History.[3]

After some time, Couthouy ran afoul of the Admiral Wilkes, the expedition commander, and he was sent home from Honolulu for "disobedience of orders." Couthouy apparently separated specimens from the field tags to better organize them. Some of the other scientists objected to this and complained to Wilkes, who fired the conchologist.[4]

Wilkes and the other scientists may have believed that Couthouy was an amateur, and, perhaps, even dangerous in his techniques. Others did not. He returned to his profession as a sea captain and continued his studies. He published prodigiously and maintained a correspondence with Charles Darwin and Augustus Addison Gould, among others.[5] In late 1838, upon returning to his native Boston, Couthouy authored an article, "Descriptions of New Species of Mollusca and Shells, and Remarks on Several Polypi Found in Massachusetts Bay."[6] In this work he described twenty-one species of mollusks, previously unknown, that inhabited the bay. In 1844 Couthouy wrote another article, "Remarks upon Coral Formations in the Pacific, with Suggestions as to the Causes of Their Absence in the Same Parallels of Latitude on the Coast of South America."[7] His sea travels took him to several locales in South America and the Pacific. He became proficient in Spanish, French, Italian, Portuguese, and several dialects spoken in the Pacific Islands.

From 1854 to 1857, he led an expedition in the Bay of Cumaná in Ecuador, seeking the wreck of a Spanish treasure ship, the *San Pedro*. Although unsuccessful in this venture, he used part of his time to study the vascular plants of Equador.[8] His rather cynical account of his treasure hunt was published posthumously.[9]

After the Civil War began, Couthouy volunteered for service and was given command on October 3, 1861, as an acting volunteer lieutenant of the Bark USS *Kingfisher*.[10] His duty station was with the Gulf Blockading Squadron based at Key West, Florida. In early January, Couthouy and *Kingfisher* were operating at the mouth of the Mississippi, near the Head of Passes in an effort to halt commerce from the great river.[11] On March 4, 1862, after a three-day, 420-mile chase, the *Kingfisher* captured the blockade runner *Lion*.[12] This was prior to the Union invasion that led to the capture of New Orleans in April. The Kingfisher operated along the coast of the Gulf of

FIG. 8.1. USS *Osage.* Library of Congress, Prints and Photographs Division, LC-B816-3126.

FIG. 8.2. Acting Lieutenant Joseph Pitty Couthouy. Museum of Comparative Zoology at Harvard University.

Mexico from Louisiana to Florida. In June 1862 Couthouy was reprimanded for allowing two of his boats and their crews to be captured while procuring water near the Florida coast.[13]

The U.S. Navy acquired the USS *Columbia* from the Naval Prize Court in November 1862 and Couthouy was given command. The vessel was outfitted as a cruiser and began operations off the South Carolina coast.[14] The vessel was wrecked during a severe gale on January 14, 1863, off Masonboro Inlet, North Carolina, and Couthouy and the crew was captured. Couthouy was separated from his crew and taken to a prisoner-of-war camp near Salisbury, North Carolina.[15] By May 1863 he was exchanged and back in Boston, where wrote a report concerning his knowledge of trade at Brownsville, Texas.[16]

Shortly thereafter, Couthouy was assigned to a position with the Mississippi Squadron based in Cairo, Illinois. Upon his arrival he was assigned command as the first captain of the newly built Eads monitor USS *Osage*.[17] From Cairo, the *Osage* began patrolling the Ohio River to counter the threat of Confederate raiders under the command of John Hunt Morgan.[18] In August the *Osage* was ordered south to participate in Admiral Porter's first raid up the Red River.[19] Following this with nothing great accomplished, the *Osage* was ordered to patrol the Mississippi River near Ellis Cliffs, in Adams County, Mississippi.[20]

In late December 1863 or early January 1864, Couthouy was transferred to and given command of the ironclad steamer USS *Chillicothe*.[21] Less formidable than the *Osage,* the *Chillicothe* was more of a lightly armored tinclad than an ironclad. This was to be Couthouy's last assignment. The *Chillicothe*'s patrol assignment was from the mouth of the Red River to Fort Adams, Mississippi.[22]

In March, the Union was involved in the largest combined arms expedition west of the Mississippi River during the Civil War. The Navy and the U.S. Army Quartermaster Corps operated 104 vessels in the Red River Campaign. The inland fleet was all but stripped of fighting hulls in an effort to capture Shreveport, Louisiana. The flotilla operated deep within hostile territory, often with no assistance from the army.[23]

The logbook of the *Chillicothe* tells, in typical terse language, the events of late March and early April during the campaign.[24]

Abstract Log of USS Chillicothe, Acting Volunteer Lieutenant Joseph P. Couthouy, Commanding, March 7 through April 5, 1864

March 7, 1864.—Off Red River. At 1:30 P.M. the flagship made general signals. The several vessels of the fleet landed armed boats' crews near the flagship. At 4 P.M. they returned to their respective vessels.

March 13.—Off Simmesport, La. From 4 to 8 A.M.: Troops disembarking from transports. At 4:15 P.M. got underway and the fleet stood up the river in the following order: *Pittsburg, Chillicothe, Carondelet, Mound City, Benton,* and *Louisville;* the flagship and the *Ouachita* remaining in the rear with the transports. At 5:25 P.M. entered Old River. At 7:45 tied up to the left bank in company with the fleet.

March 14.—Meridian to 4 P.M.: underway, steaming up Red River. At 6:10 P.M. tied up to the left bank.

March 15.—At 1:45 A.M. tug came alongside with an order from the admiral to the commanding officer. At 2:20 A.M. got underway and steamed up river in company with some other vessels of the fleet. At 3:30 A.M. came up with the first division of the fleet tied up to the right bank of the river. Exchanged distinguishing pennants. At 4 A.M. tied up to the left bank of the river astern of the *Price.* At 4:15 A.M. cast loose from the bank and steamed up river to the blockade[25] and tied up to the right bank. At 5:20 cast loose and steamed up river, the *Price* towing us past the blockade. At 6:45 tug came up and gave us an order from the admiral to tie up and let the transports pass. At 9:40 A.M. received orders from the admiral to proceed up to Alexandria without delay. Stood up river. At 10 passed Fort De Russy, which was occupied by our army.

March 16.—Off Alexandria, La. At 8:30 A.M. *Eastport* showed general signal. Sent 20 armed men in charge of Acting Ensign H. A. Hannon on board of the *Eastport.* The commander went ashore in charge of armed party. At 4:30 P.M. expedition in charge of Acting Ensign H. A. Hannon returned to vessel and commander returned on board.

March 21.—At 9:35 A.M. flagship signaled us. Called away 40 armed men in charge of Acting Ensign C. A. Calvert and Acting Master's Mate C. S. Welles, with orders to land abreast of the *East-port.* At 10 the commander left the vessel to take command of the armed party. At 5:15 P.M. cutter came alongside with armed expedition.

March 23.—At 7:15 P.M. tug *Dahlia* came alongside with orders, and Acting Ensign C. A. Calvert, with 6 men armed with cutlasses and rifles, were mustered and left the ship on tug *Dahlia* to do picket duty up the river.[26]

March 29.—From 8 to meridian: Vessel underway, ascending the Falls.[27] After two hours' endeavor, succeeded in getting over and stood up river. At 8:15 A.M. made 6 horsemen at a small house on the left bank of the river. We lay to and sent 16 armed men in charge of Acting Ensign C. A. Calvert to ascertain who they were. At 9:35 the boat returned, bringing the 6 men, and also 1 musket, which was found in the house. The men were searched, and failing to find anything suspicious about their persons, permitted them to return on shore in charge of armed boat. Examined house and destroyed small flat. At 11 boat returned and vessel again stood up river.

April 3.—Off Grand Ecore, La. At 2:15 P.M. the flagship spoke us and requested the commanding officer to come on board. At 2:20 the commanding officer went on board the flagship. At 2:30 returned on board and ordered steam to be raised.[28] At 2:45 cast loose and stood up river and made fast to the right bank of the river, astern of the *Lexington.* At 5:30 we got underway and followed the *Lexington.* At 6:40 a large quantity of cotton was burned on the left bank of the river. The *Lexington* fired two shots in order to drive away the cotton burners. At 7 P.M., while passing the burning cotton, Acting Volunteer Lieutenant Joseph P. Couthouy was shot and mortally wounded by a guerrilla concealed behind the bank. We immediately beat to quarters. At 7:40 signaled the *Neosho* to communicate and requested her surgeon to come on board and see our commander.

April 4.—Underway, Red River, La. At 6:30 A.M. laid to, alongside the left bank, and sent a small boat to fish up torpedoes.[29] At 8:10 Acting Volunteer Lieutenant Joseph P. Couthouy, who was mortally wounded on the evening of the 3d, expired. At 9:20 beat to quarters in consequence of our cavalry being attacked by the enemy at Campti, La. At 9:30 the *Fort Hindman* opened fire upon them, firing three shell; we instantly followed by firing a 5-second shell from our howitzer. Cast loose and stood up river. At 11 beat the retreat. At 3:30 P.M. sent cutter with 6 armed men to destroy a flatboat. At 6:45 tied up to the right bank of the river.

April 5.—Underway, Red River, La. At 8:45 got underway and ran alongside the *Fort Hindman* and put the remains of Acting Volunteer Lieutenant Couthouy on board in an air-tight coffin and then proceeded on up the river in rear of the fleet.

At 9 we took on board two men, who said they belonged to the USS *Sachem* and were taken prisoners at Berwick Bay, September 7, 1863, and were taken to Shreveport, from which place they escaped. Sent them on board the *Louisville.*

More information on the death of Joseph Couthouy, and how his fellow officers and others felt about him survive in a number of letters.[30] Together, they tell a much more personal story and are presented here in chronological order.

U.S.S. Chilicothe Red River

150 miles above Alexandria La
April 5th 1864

Fred E. Stimpson Esq
Dear Sir

It becomes my painful duty to inform you that A.V. Lieut. Jos. E. [*sic*] Couthouy late Commanding the "Chilicothe" received a mortal wound from a guerilla on the evening of the 3rd inst resulting in death early the next morning.

His body leaves the ship this Aft. and is to be sent to Boston his clothing &c will be sent by the next despatch boat. The mail is to go immediately and would give you more particulars. Shall write again.

Very Respectfully, &Cc
J.H. Hathaway
A.A. Paymaster
U.S. Navy

U.S. Stmr "Chillicothe"

Off Alexandria La
April 23rd, 1864

Miss Rebecca L. Duncan

It is my painful duty to have to return to you two letters addressed to Capt. Couthouy, and suppose you know ere this, the reason for my doing so.

The "Chillicothe" was about 100 miles above Alexandria on the evening of April 3d—when Capt. Couthouy's attention was called to a man on the shore. he went upon the pilot house, and just as he raised his glass to look, a ball passed completely through the center of his body, from the effects of which, he died the next morning. Captain Couthouy suffered severely but was sensible to the last and bore his pain with a great deal of fortitude. He gave me your address before his death, explained to me how your letters were addressed to him and requested me to write you and return your letters, speaking of you as his most particular friend, and sending his love and wishes that you would never forget him.

His body we put in a leaden coffin, and it is now on the Stmr "Benefit" and is to be sent to Boston by the next despatch boat, that is—Lt. Com'r Watson Smith, now commanding this vessel informs me he will do all he can to have his body sent to his friends.

If you should wish to know anything more in relation to Capt. Couthouy's affairs, address me at any time.

Very Respectfully &
J.H. Hathaway
A.A. Paymaster
U.S. Navy.

Senate Chamber

27th April '64

My dear Sir,

I was pained by your letter, which gave me the first information of the fate of Capt. Couthouy.

Have lost no time in making proper inquiry at the Navy Department, now enclose to you a copy of the despatch of Admiral Porter, announcing the death of this brave officer & good man.

Hope you will do me the favor to express to his family my sincerest sympathy in their great sorrow. From the beginning of this war he has seen with perfect clearness its true character & how it was to be conducted.

His life is another offering to slavery.

Believe me, my dear Sir,
very faithfully yours,
Charles Sumner

U.S.S. Choctaw

Off Mouth of Red River
May 4, 1864

My dear Sir,

Your letter of the 23d ult. has this moment reached me and I regret exceedingly that I am not in possession of all the circumstances of the death of my esteemed friend Capt. Couthouy. I have heard that Mr. Hathaway, the Paymaster of the "Chillicothe," has possession of all of Capt. Couthouy's papers, and that the Captain gave him directions in regard to them. I have written to Mr. Hathaway asking him to give me all the particulars of his death. As soon as I receive his letter I will again write you.

A few days before the Captain's death I was ordered up the Ouachita river and it was nearly a week after it happened before I heard of it. I learn that one of the vessels ahead of the "Chillicothe" was fired into and Captain Couthouy hearing the firing went up on the upper deck of his vessel to see what it was. While he was standing on deck, two men were seen riding down towards the bank but no one noticed that they were armed. When they got near the bank, they dismounted and walked to the levee, when one of them suddenly raised a gun and shot Capt. Couthouy through the body near the waist. He lived, I believe, a little more than seven hours.

An effort was made to keep his body but as the proper means for doing so could not be had, they were obliged to bury it.[31]

It was near Grand Ecore on the Red River that he was killed but I do not know where he was buried.

His death was much lamented by all who knew him.

Captain Couthouy and myself have been together a great deal since August last and altho' entire strangers to each other when we met, soon became great friends and passed many pleasant hours together. He often spoke to me of his family and I almost feel that I [have] known his daughters.

I regret exceedingly that I cannot get to the "Chillicothe" in order to make all inquiries and to see that everything belonging to Capt. Couthouy is taken care of and sent to his family. I am confident however that every thing has been properly attended to and that all directions the Captain may have left will be fully carried out. Should it ever be in my power to be of any service, I hope you will not hesitate to call on me.

Your ob't servant
Frank M. Ramsey
Lt. Comdr—U.S. Navy

Notes

1. W. H. Dall, "Some American Conchologists," *Proceedings of the Biological Society of Washington* (1888), 4:95–134. R. I. Johnson, "Occasional Papers on Mollusks, Museum of Comparative Zoology," *Harvard University* 1, no. 5 (1946): 33–40.
2. Dall, "Some American Conchologists."
3. The best short history of this expedition and those who participated in it is found at http://www.amphilsoc.org/library/guides/stanton/3644.htm.
4. Dall, "Some American Conchologists."
5. See the Darwin Correspondence Project at Cambridge University, United Kingdom, and the Augustus Addison Gould Papers, Houghton Library, Harvard College Library.

6. J. P. Couthouy, "Descriptions of New Species of Mollusca and Shells, and Remarks on Several Polypi Found in Massachusetts Bay," *Boston Journal of Natural History* 2 (1838): 53–111.
7. J. P. Couthouy, "Remarks upon Coral Formations in the Pacific; with Suggestions as to the Causes of Their Absence in the Same Parallels of Latitude on the Coast of South America." *Boston Journal of Natural History* 4:66–105, 137–62.
8. See http://www.mobot.org/MOBOT/research/ecuador/history.shtml.
9. J. P. Couthouy. *San Pedro's Treasure: Exploring Scheme to Visit Cumana Habor: Believed to Be a Waste of Time and Money, as Captain Joseph B.* [sic] *Couthouy of Boston Went There in 1856 and Found the Spanish Ship's Hulk, but Only a Few Scattered Coins* (Boston, n.d.). Copy in the Boston Athenaeum.
10. U.S. War Dept., *Official Records of the Union and Confederate Navies in the War of the Rebellion,* 31 vols. (Washington, DC, 1895–1929), vol. 16: 696 (hereinafter cited as *ORN,* followed by volume number and page reference).
11. *ORN* 17:33.
12. Ibid., 181–82.
13. Ibid., 154–57.
14. *ORN,* Index 1: 62.
15. *ORN* 8:424–25, 454–55.
16. *ORN* 17:441–42.
17. *ORN* 25:272.
18. Ibid., 315.
19. Ibid., 379–80.
20. Ibid., 427–28.
21. Ibid., 691–92.
22. Ibid., 692, 754.
23. For a full treatment of the Red River Campaign, see Gary D. Joiner, *One Damn Blunder from Beginning to End: The Red River Campaign of 1864* (Wilmington, DE, 2003) and Ludwell H. Johnson, *Red River Campaign: Politics and Cotton in the Civil War* (Kent, OH, 1993).
24. *ORN* 26:776–77.
25. The Confederates created this obstruction about six miles downstream from Fort DeRussy. The fort was located just north of the town of Marksville, in Avoyelles Parish, Louisiana.
26. From this entry until March 29 the fleet was at Alexandria gathering cotton and waiting for Major General Nathaniel P. Banks and his land forces to rendezvous with the naval units and their attached army units.
27. These boulders, lying under the Red River just above the town of Alexandria, formed rapids that gave the parish its French name, "Rapides." In periods of low water, they made navigation difficult or impossible.

28. This armed reconnaissance was undertaken in preparation of six gunboats and twenty transports proceeding upstream in attempt to link up with the army at or near Springfield Landing.
29. Torpedoes were mines that had been planted by the Confederate ironclad CSS *Missouri* about March 18.
30. Letters in the collection of Jimmy Sandefur, Shreveport, Louisiana.
31. This is incorrect. See previous letters.

J. E. HEWITT: COMMEMORATING MANSFIELD

Edited by Gary D. Joiner

JOHN E. HEWITT WAS BORN ON THE HEWITT PLANTATION near Mansfield, Louisiana, on March 4, 1851, to Alfred M. and Antoinette (Garrett) Hewitt. The couple had been married in 1848 at the Garrett House near the site of the Battle of Mansfield. Alfred Hewitt had served in the Mexican War with the 5th Louisiana Infantry, and in 1860 became a member of the 1st Texas Cavalry. In 1861, this command was called into service of the Confederacy. Hewitt served under Brigadier General Jean Jacques Alexandre Alfred Mouton at Mansfield with the Texans. He remained in the army until he became ill in January 1865. He returned home and died shortly before General Robert E. Lee's surrender.

John Hewitt was thirteen years old at the time of the Battle of Mansfield. His maternal uncle was Captain J. H. Garrett, commander of Company K, 27th Louisiana Infantry Regiment. It was through Garrett's surprising friendship with Colonel John Reid of the 130th Illinois Infantry Regiment that Hewitt gained his knowledge of the Battle of Mansfield. The two opponents struck up their friendship after Garrett saved Reid's life in a fire following the battle. John Hewitt was educated in Mansfield and entered the publishing field with the *Mansfield Times* in 1866. He was involved in several newspaper ventures in DeSoto Parish during the postwar period. In 1887, he established the private banking firm of J. E. Hewitt & Company that eventually merged with Traders' Bank, for which he served as president.[1] Hewitt founded the *DeSoto Democrat*, first published on July 8, 1890.[2] John Hewitt died March 8, 1936, and is buried in the Mansfield Cemetery.

1864 Battle of Mansfield

Mansfield, Louisiana
Fought April Eighth, 1864

Gen. Richard Taylor
Commander, Confederate Forces

Gen. N. P. Banks
Commander, Federal Forces
Published on the 61st Anniversary of the Battle, on
The occasion of the Unveiling of the Monuments to
Gen. Richard Taylor and Gen. Polignac
1925
Price 50¢
For Sale By
ENTERPRISE PUBLISHING COMPANY[3]
TO CAMP MOUTON, U.C.V.[4]
and
TO KATE BEARD CHAPTER, DAUGHTERS OF THE SOUTHERN CONFEDERACY[5]

In presenting this little pamphlet to the public, I desire to dedicate it to the Marquise de. Courtivron, the only daughter of Prince Camile de Polignac whose enthusiasm for the Southern cause, stimulated the erection of the Polignac monument on the battle field at Mansfield, where her father won his commission as Major General in the Confederate army.[6]

May her patriotic zeal inspire all Southrons[7] to a like effort, until all historic places on that glorious field are so marked, that future generations may realize that the Southrons are proud of the cause, for which so much of its best blood was shed. Not that we love the United States less, but because we loved the Southern Confederacy more at that time. May La Belle France ever prosper, and the United States continue its titantic strides to make the world safe for Democracy.

With the highest considerations,
I subscribe myself,
J. E. Hewitt,
Mansfield, La.

In the horoscope of memory, there is always some event that shines resplendently within the minds of men, that eclipses as it were, all other recollections and with the writer the 8th day of April A. D. 1864 was that occasion, for on that day he witnessed in part, the bloody battle fought on the hills around the little town of Mansfield, La., which was the last decisive victory won by the Confederate army, in the bloody struggle from 1861 to 1865, that drenched our Southland with the blood of the land and spread desolation and ruin over its fields and valleys, from the Potomac to the Rio Grande, and from the Ohio to the Gulf.

The Federal government with the view of wiping out the last vestage of the rebellion as they termed the action of the Southern States, in setting up a separate government. The Confederates held only that part of Louisiana west of the Atchafalaya, the Black and Ouachita rivers, about one-third[,] the southwest part of Arkansas, and all of Texas, with its military headquarters, under Gen. E. Kirby Smith at Shreveport.

There was a force of 21,000 men west of the Mississippi river under Gen. Kirby Smith, a considerable part of which had to be kept on the gulf coast to prevent invasion from that direction, a part had to protect the Mexican border which was our only outlet to the world leaving only about 16,000 men with which to repel invasion from Missouri and Mississippi river. To overcome this small force did seem to be an easy matter and to accomplish that purpose, the Federal government in the spring of 1864, sent an expedition out from New Orleans under Gen. Banks, to capture Shreveport. This army was supported by a fleet of 150 gunboats and transports, manned by 10,000 men, who were to steam up Red River with munitions and supplies for Gen. Banks' army.[8] Gen. Dick Taylor, one of the most successful and resourceful officers in the Confederate service, was second in command to Gen. Smith and was the actual commander in the field.

Gen. Kirby Smith had planned to fight behind fortification[s] at Shreveport, but Dick Taylor had other plans. He believed that by pretending to retreat ignominiously, Gen. Banks would divide his forces to facilitate a more rapid pursuit, and Gen. Banks fell into this trap. When the Confederates marched through Mansfield on April 7th, the fact was made known to Gen. Banks and he threw forward the 13th corps, with the 19th ten miles behind it, and Smith's[9] division ten miles in its rear. However,

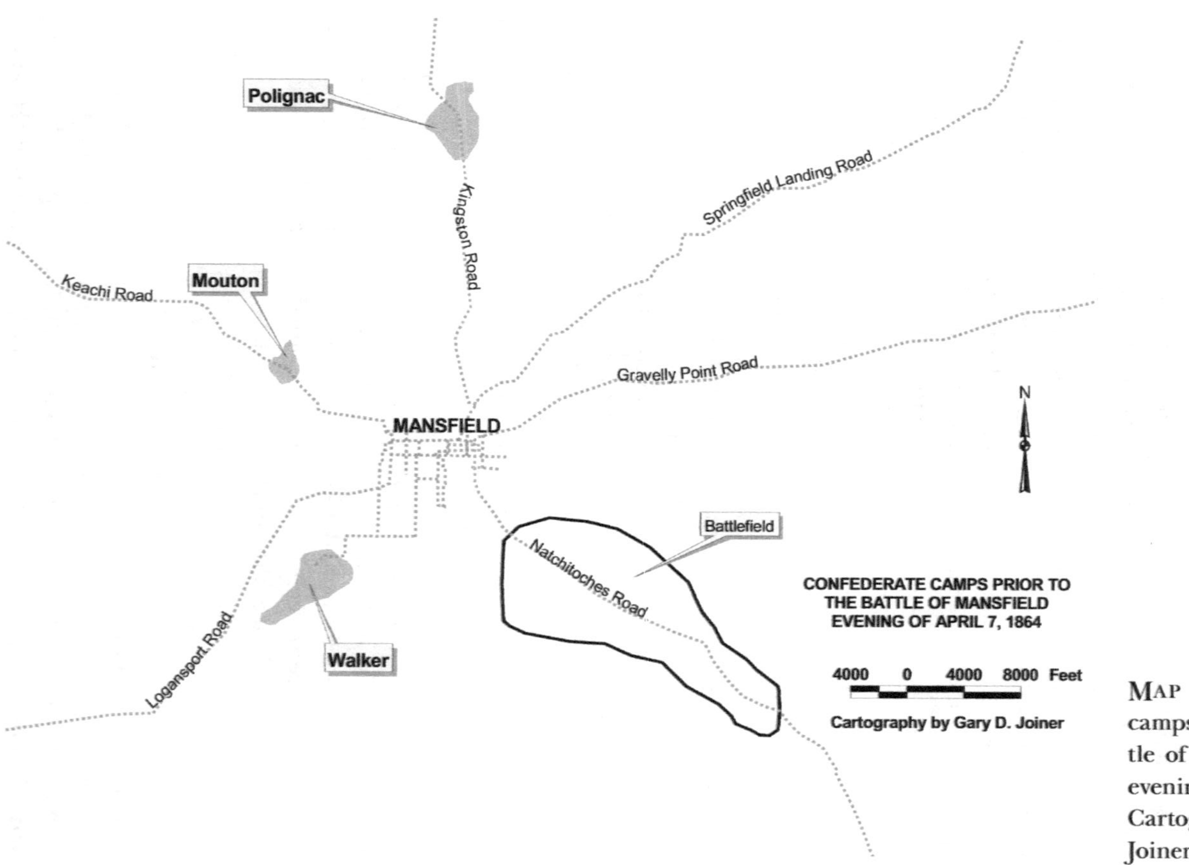

MAP 9.1. Confederate camps prior to the Battle of Mansfield on the evening of April 7, 1864. Cartography by Gary D. Joiner.

the Confederate infantry had not gone far, for Polignac's brigade had camped at the six miles bayou on the Kingston road, Mouton's brigade at the three mile bayou on the Grand Cane road, and Walker's division on the branch at the old Texas and Pacific depot, 2 1-2 miles south of Mansfield.[10] Next morning, April 8th they rushed back through.

Mansfield with Polignac's brigade in the lead, followed by Mouton's Louisiana brigade, and then by Walker's division and at a point 2 1-2 miles east of Mansfield they formed a line of battle on the west side of the Moss plantation, and the advancing federals took position on the east side of that big open field and the stage was set for one of the hardest battles ever fought on American soil.[11]

Dick Taylor's strategy had been a complete success for he found himself with as many men at the point of contact as his opponent had, but you will read of the battle further on, and we will tell about

The Dick Taylor Monument

On the 61st anniversary of this great victory, when the Southern cross was sustained by the unprecedented valor of the South's devoted sons, a monument will be dedicated to that hero of heroes, General Richard Taylor, who was like his father, Ex-President Zachary Taylor, a soldier, not by training but by his native genius. As the father was the hero of the Mexican war without a rival, the son was an outstanding hero in the Confederate army, wherein heroism seemed to spring from the very soil, for no army in history ever made a brighter record than did the men that fought and died for what they thought was right. The monument is not worthy of the man, but in the hearts of the gallant sons of Louisiana, it stands for all that is honorable, upright and true. The monument was erected by his daughters, whose heritage is without a stain and beyond reproach. These daughters are Mrs. Bettie Taylor Stauffer and Mrs. Marthe Taylor Stauffer both of New Orleans.

This little pamphlet is issued on the occasion of the celebration of the 61st anniversary of the battle fought at Mansfield, on the 8th of April, 1864. The celebration is held in honor of the old Confederate Veterans who fought on that occassion and is given under the auspices of Kate Beard Chapter of the Daughters of the Confederacy, the domicile of which is at Mansfield. The chapter is named after Mrs. Kate Beard, widow of Col. Beard, who commanded and led the Consolidated Crescent Regiment on that occassion in one of the most gallant charges recorded in the history

FIG. 9.1. General Richard Taylor monument (foreground) at the Mansfield State Historic Site. Photography by Gary D. Joiner.

of our civil war.[12] He lost his life as did every other field officer of his regiment, and it was at its head that the gallant Gen. Alfred Mouton fell.[13]

It is the purpose of the writer to review casually that part of the great military activities of the Southern Confederacy that occurred on Louisiana soil, but the principal object is to describe the battle of Mansfield, or the events actually occurred.

For many years the Daughters of the Confederacy have celebrated the day by doing honor to the surviving Confederate Veterans, but their labors will soon be over, for the youngest Veteran of record is 79 years of age.[14] There are now only 38 in DeSoto parish and the extent to which their ranks have been thinned can be seen when you are reminded that DeSoto parish sent 1,355 men to the Confederate army when there was less than 400 voters that took part in the secession election that brought on the war. Although the average age of these 38 old heroes is well above 80 years, and while some few of them are yet active, the vast majority are tottering on the verge of eternity.

This anniversary has been designated as "Polignac Day" in commemoration of the heroic deeds of that valiant Frenchman, on that occasion. Gen. Polignac has been dead for quite a number of years, but his widow,

FIG. 9.2. Surviving members of the Mouton Camp, United Confederate Veterans. Photograph taken on the sixty-sixth anniversary of the battle of Mansfield on April 8, 1930. The photo was taken on the front steps of the Mansfield Parish Courthouse. Photograph in the collection of Gary D. Joiner.

Princess Polignac and his son Victor Mansfield Polignac will have traveled nearly half around the world to be present at this celebration, when a grand monument in memory of their dead hero will be unvailed.

THE POLIGNAC MONUMENT

is the first to he erected on the battle field at Mansfield, and it will be dedicated on the 61st anniversary of that historic event. It is erected in memory of Prince Carmile[15] de Polignac, a Prince of the Royal house of France, who is known as

"The Lafayette of the South"[16]

Although he with other members of the Royal House, were expelled from France at the time of the revolution of 1847–48, the family made their home in Austria where they had large estates, and in accordance to the traditions of the family, young Polignac was educated as a soldier, and

FIG. 9.3. Monument to the Prince de Polignac and General Alfred Mouton at the Mansfield State Historic Site. The monument was placed by the United Daughters of the Confederacy on battlefield land they purchased. It is not located at the spot where General Mouton fell. Photography by Gary D. Joiner.

Fig. 9.4. Detail of the Polignac/Mouton monument at the Mansfield State Historic Site. Photography by Gary D. Joiner.

Fig. 9.5. Undated photograph of members of the Mouton Camp, United Confederate Veterans, which appeared in the Mansfield Enterprise, circa 1900. The photograph was taken on the front steps of the DeSoto Parish Courthouse (listed as "Old Courthouse" on a family note). The women are believed to be widows or daughters of veterans. Photograph in the collection of Gary D. Joiner.

won his spurs in the Crimean war as a volunteer with the French army and fought against Russia. When the American Civil War began, and when it was thought France would aid the Confederacy, he came South and was given a commission as Major, and by his ability and valour, rose to rank of Major General.

At the time of the battle of Mansfield he was only a Brigadier General and commanded a brigade of Texans who were with Mouton's division and holding the center of the Confederate line, he did valient service and won a commission as Major General.

The monument stands near the center of the Mansfield Battle Park, which was established by the Mansfield Chapter of the Daughters of the Confederacy. It stands 80 feet on the north side of the Jefferson Highway,[17] and will be seen by thousands of tourists.

The monument was erected by the Daughters of the Confederacy of Paris, France, at a cost of about $5000.00. The shaft is of Georgia granit[e], from Stone Mountain and is 14 feet high, being 5 1-2 feet at the base, weighs 19,000 pounds. It stands on a five foot concrete foundation and its top towers 19 feet above the ground. It was constructed by the Weibler Marble and Granite Co., of New Orleans and was erected under the supervision of Mr. Henry G. Gandolfo, their agent.

At the dedication on April 8th, next, the Princess Polignac widow of the Confederate General, and her son, Victor Mansfield Polignac, will be present, as will be Miss Mary Poppenheimer, of Charlston, S. C., a friend of the family who is traveling with the Polignacs.

The annual meeting of the state chapter of the Daughters of the Southern Confederacy, will be in session at Mansfield on the 6th, 7th and 8th of April next. They usually meet in May, but the date was advanced this year that the members might be present at the dedication of the monument on the Mansfield battle field to be erected to the memory of Prince Carmile Polignac, who commanded a Texas brigade of Confederate infantry in that historic battle and to him is due no little share of the Credit of the victory gained by the Confederates on that occassion.

At the outbreak of our civil war, he was 35 years old, an educated and highly trained soldier, and was evidently anxious to up-hold the traditions of his family and gain some experience in his profession, that of arms. At the beginning of our civil war, Napoleon III, then Emperor of France, proposed to recognize the Southern Confederacy and proposed that England and France open the ports of the South to the commerce of the world, which of course meant the freedom of the South, but England after much hesitation and the fear, if not direct threats by Russia to join the United States and invade India, refused to join France and the project fell through.

In reference to the above incident that caused the South to lose the war, but little is to be found in our one-sided histories with reference to this incident, but it is a fact that Russia bluffed England and the Southern Confederacy was left to its fate, but France feeling that the Monroe Doctrine was dead, invaded Mexico and established an Empire in that country under the ill-fated Maximillion.[18]

At that time Prince Polignac ran the blockade and offered his services to the South. He was given a commission as Major and assigned to duty on the staff of Gen. Braxton Brag, who then commanded the army of Tennessee. He soon distinguished himself as a brave and able soldier and was made brigadier general and sent west of the Mississippi, where he was placed in command of a brigade of infantry, composed of three regiments of dismounted Texas cavalry and it was in command of that brigade that he fought at the battle of Mansfield and next to Gen. Alfred Mouton, was the outstanding hero on that occasion. When Gen. Dick Taylor formed his line of battle at a point 2 1-2 miles east of Mansfield on April 8th, 1864, to resist the march of the Federal Army under Gen. Banks,[19] Polignac's brigade held the center of his line and formed across the old Natchitoches road known now as the Jefferson Highway: his left was held by Mouton's Louisiana brigade, composed of the Consolidated Crescent Regiment, and the 19th[20] and 28th Louisiana Regiments, and the left flank was protected by the 4th Texas cavalry and the 2nd and 8th Louisiana cavalry under Gen. Majors.[21] To the right of Polignac's brigade was Walker's brigade[22] of Texas infantry and his right flank was protected by 4 regiments of Texas cavalry commanded by Gen. Tom Green.[23] The Confederate line, thus formed, held the west and north side of the Moss plantation and the Federals held the east side. At noon on April 8th, two armies faced each other, each expecting the other to attack. At 2 P.M., Gen. Taylor, with the view of provoking an attack ordered up the Val Verde Texas battery, that took a position on the high ground on the left of the road just in front of Polignac's brigade, and they opened fire on the Federal line, which

FIG. 9.6. Union Colonel John B. Reid in a postwar photograph wearing his GAR medal. Image from Hewitt's 1925 pamphlet. Copy in the Collection of Gary D. Joiner.

must have been effective, for the Federals who had posted their artillery on Honey Cut Hill,[24] ordered forward a battery of nine rifle guns, that took position on the hill on the right of the road, where the negro church now stands, and a fierce artillery duel ensued, in which three of the five Confederate guns were put out of action, but the other two stood firm and returned shot for shot.

At 3:30 Gen. Taylor realizing that the Federals would not attack, ordered a general attack and one of the fiercest battles of the war was on. We can't relate all the incidents as our purpose is to simply show the part that Prince Polignac took in the fight. When the charge across the open field was ordered, he and his staff officers led his brigade in person and routed the strong line of infantry, drove nine pieces of artillery at the church from their position and captured the guns at Honey Cut Hill. This was a desperate charge and the losses were great and it is to commemorate the gallantry of this brave Frenchman that the monument is to be dedicated on April 8th next, the 61st anniversary of the brilliant charge.

The money to pay for this monument was raised by a daughter of Prince Polignac, who organized a chapter of the Daughters of the Confederacy in Paris, France, among the Southern women who live in that city, and it is a graceful tribute to the hero who fought for Dixie.

That our readers may the more understand the record of Prince Polignac as a Confederate Solder, we reproduce the following account of his services to our Southland, from his own diary, which is absolutely authentic although at variance statements from other inaccurate narratives of our civil war:

In the latter part of March 1864, Gen. Banks, in command of a federal force of 31,000 men, marched out of New Orleans with a view of capturing the city of Shreveport. He had the aid of a fleet under Admiral Porter that at the same time ascended Red river. This expedition was acting in conjunction with a force of 15,000 men under Gen. Steele, who was to march from Camden, Ark., join Gen. Banks at Shreveport, and occupy Texas.

To oppose the advance of Gen Banks, Gen. Dick Taylor could command about 11,000. On the morning of April 8 the advancing Federals found a Confederate cavalry force drawn up on Honeycut hill, three and a half miles east of Mansfield. The Federals pushed forward a strong detachment of mounted troops, but Gen. Green with his Texas cavalry made bold demonstration on their right, and the Federal cavalry fell back. Green had simply played a successful bluff to give Dick Taylor time to form his line of battle on the opposite or western side of the Moss Plantation.

Had the Federal advance been resolutely pushed they could have occupied Mansfield that morning without scarcely firing a gun. A brigade

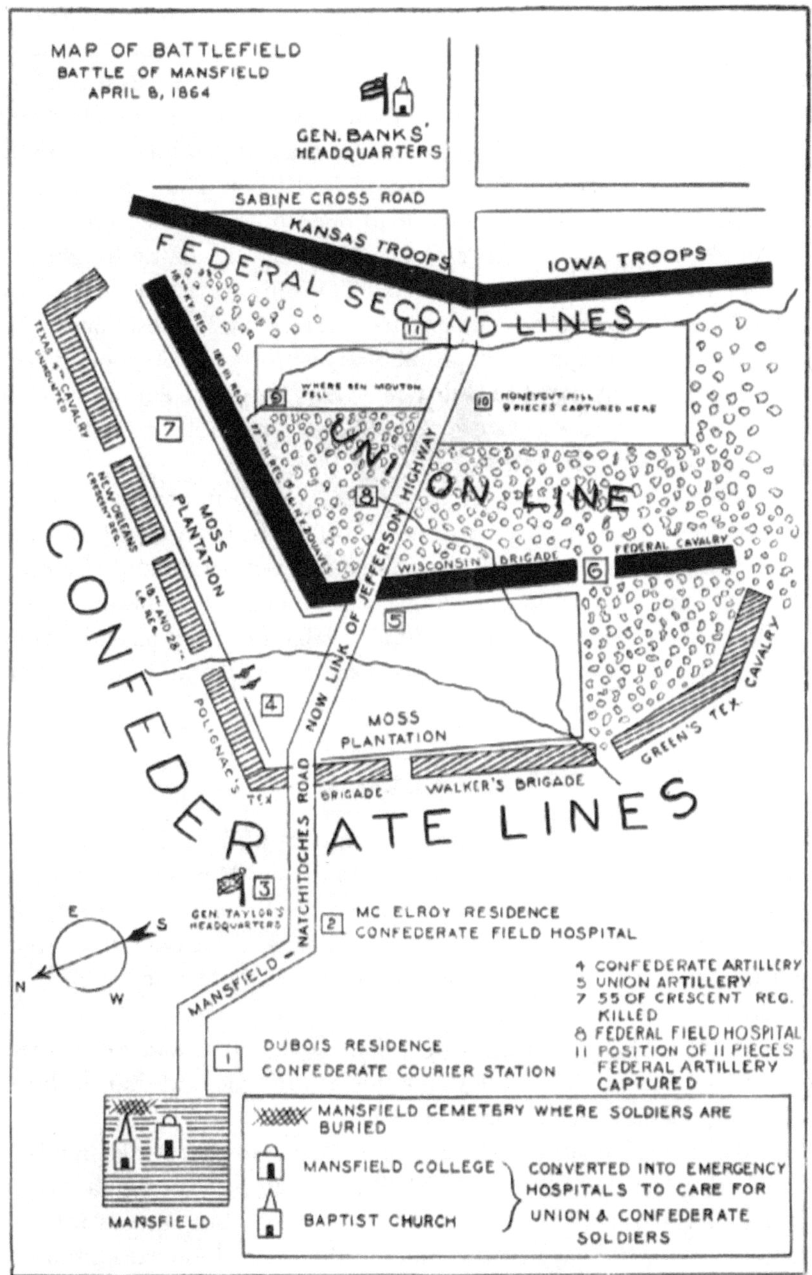

MAP 9.2. Sketch map by J. E. Hewitt of the battlefield at Mansfield as part of his pamphlet "Published on the 61st Anniversary of the Battle, on the Occasion of the Unveiling of the Monuments to Gen. Richard Taylor and Gen. Polignac," April 1925. Copy in the collection of Gary D. Joiner.

of Iowa infantry was then brought forward and a line of battle formed just west of the old Sabine crossroads in the edge of the Birdwell field, now owned by Mr. R. L. Taylor.[25] This point was then known as the Sabine Cross Road from the fact that a road then crossed the Natchitoches road at that place that was used in early days in hauling cotton from points to the west to various shipping points on Red River. The cross road led out via the old John Glassell homestead or so it was marked on the old military field maps, and all federal historians call the battle fought that day, "The Battle of Sabine Cross Roads."[26] This line of battle, on the map printed herewith is marked "the 2nd federal line" and is designated (**11**) on said map, although in fact it was the first line formed.[27] As soon as Gen. Taylor had posted his forces on the west side of the Moss plantation, Gen. Green retired to the south of the road and took position on the extreme right of the Confederate line.

The federals evidently apprehended something unusual and before advancing they posted eleven pieces of artillery in front of the Birdwell residence at the point marked **11** on the map, so as command Honeycut hill.[28] This artillery was supported by the Iowa brigade, in battle array at that point. With this support the federal cavalry advanced passed Honeycut hill and reached the eastern edge of the Moss plantation without encountering a foe.

Charged a Regiment

After reconnoitering they discovered a company of the Eighth Louisiana cavalry under Col. Favrot off to their left in the old Moss field and immediately charged them with a whole regiment. But much to their surprise the Confederates fled through a gap in the fence and the federals charged point blank against a regiment of Confederate infantry in ambush for their special edification.

Gen. Dick Taylor tells us in his book "Destruction and Reconstruction" that he was on the Confederate line at the time and that his horse was struck by a ball fired by the federal cavalry.[29]

This occurred at 10:30 A.M., and made known to Gen Banks that Dick Taylor had at last made a stand. Gen. Banks holding his original line of infantry and artillery intact, ordered forward two brigades of infantry that were at Six-Mile bayou,[30] two miles in the rear. These troops hurried forward, passed the original line of Iowa infantry, already in position near Sabine cross roads, at point marked **11** on [the] map, and pushed forward a brigade composed of the 18th Kentucky,[31] the 130th Illinois, the 77th

Illinois, 161st New York Zouaves[32] and two Wisconsin regiments, forming a new line in front of the Iowa troops and facing the Louisiana brigade as shown on the map.

The other brigade, of Wisconsin troops took their position on the federal left. The 2nd brigades constituting the 13th army corps.[33] Nine pieces of artillery took position at the point marked **5**[34] while eleven pieces were posted at the point marked **11**. These movements were completed by 1 o'clock and Gen. Banks having packed all his baggage and supply trains in the rear of his line at Sabine cross roads, located his headquarters at Antioch church and waited an attack, or the arrival of the remainder of his army.[35]

On the part of the Confederates, Gen. Taylor had thrown forward three brigades of infantry from Mansfield, and while Gen. Green had detained Banks at Honeycut hill, the Confederates had taken position shown on the map and posted six pieces of artillery at a point marked **4**. As the line was first formed only the three Louisiana infantry regiments and a part of the Second and the Eighth Louisiana and Fourth Texas cavalry regiments formed the Confederate line on the left of the road, and the two Texas brigades and Green's cavalry were on the right of the road. The Louisiana regiments were the Crescent, the 18th and 28th regiments, constituting Mouton's brigade. The Texas infantry regiments present were Polignac's and Waterhouse's brigades,[36] composing Walker's division, and they formed the right wing of the Confederate line of battle.

This was the condition of affairs at 1 p. m., when it was seen that the federal right was about to outflank the confederate left, to prevent which the Louisiana brigade was pushed further to the left and part of Polignac's Texas brigade was moved from the right to fill the gap. Thus the two armies faced each other both evidently expecting the other to attack. At 2 P.M. the nine pieces of federal artillery posted at a point marked **5** seeing the shifting of positions, opened fire on the Confederates line, which attack was promptly responded to by the six confederate pieces posted at the point marked **4**. A sharp artillery duel was the result, and two confederate guns were soon disabled. On the left, Capt. Thigpen's company from the Crescent Regiment had been thrown out as skirmishers, and concealed in a branch in the center of the intervening field, were annoying the federals considerably.[37] It was at that point that Major Dickey[,] a son of Judge Dickey, then Chief Justice of the Supreme Court of Illinois was killed.[38] He was a staff officer, and rode out into the field to make observations, and as he approached the skirmish line, he was shot dead by a soldier by the name of Laffite, who was concealed in a ditch beside Capt. Thigpen. It was now 3:30 P.M. and neither seemed to want to attack, but after the death of Major Dickey who was the first man killed in the battle of Mansfield, the federals made a demonstration against this skirmish line, and General Dick Taylor ordered Mouton to support the sharp-shooters, as the federals were about to capture Capt. Thigpen's company.

This order was carried by Major Moncure of Shreveport, then serving on Gen. Polignac's staff. Gen. Mouton immediately ordered the Louisiana brigade forward, which movement at once developed into a general charge by the whole Confederate line.

The federals were strongly posted and reserved their fire for closer range. The Crescent struck the enemy first and at close range received a volley from the 130th Illinois regiment, that killed fifty-five men, including every field officer of the regiment, and wounded 150.[39]

Staggered the Regiment

This dreadful shock staggered this gallant regiment, man after man grabbed the fallen colors and tried to bear them inward, only to fall as fast as they took it. Six had fallen, including the gallant Capt. Robert Seth Fields of New Orleans, when that peerless regiment without colors and with few officers rushed forward, forced the lines of federals, barricaded behind piles of rails, overwhelmed and captured the 130th Illinois regiment and threw into confusion the whole federal line. The cost was terrible, for the 130th Illinois was a typical regiment of American farmers who did not shoot and run away, but stood up manfully, realizing that they held the key to the situation and that victory or defeat depended upon their being able to hold their position.

It looked like the immovable had been struck by the irresistible and that something had to happen. The Illinois regiment had suffered almost as much as had the Crescent, and Col. Reed[40] lay wounded on the field. In this moment of furious fighting and utter confusion Gen. Mouton and staff rushed forward and placed himself at the head of the leaderless but furiously fighting Crescent. One of his staff had brought forward the blood-stained regimental flag, when it was again greeted with a volley from the stubbornly resisting federals, and again fell to the ground, this time stained with the life-blood of Gen. Alfred Mouton, as game a man as ever laid down his life as a willing sacrifice upon the altar of his country.[41] Three balls had pierced his manly breast. The conflict was almost a hand to hand affair but the Illinois regiment were soon all killed, wounded or prisoners. It was a soldiers fight, for neither regiment had [a] field officer to make or accept a surrender.

While the Crescent regiment and the 130th Illinois were struggling, the one to take and the other to hold the key to the station, the 18th Louisiana had struck the 77th Illinois regiment, and the 28th Louisiana had come in contack with the 18th Kentucky regiment, and the fight was fast and furious.[42] Polignac's Texa[n]s then struck the 161 N. Y. Zouaves and the 77th Illinois regiment and promptly forced them to retire.

While these stirring events were transpiring on the Confederate left, let us see what was going on over to the right. You will observe from the map that the two lines of battle were much nearer to each other on the left than on the right, and hence the opposing forces came in contact on the left before they did on the right, when the Confederate charge was made. However, Gen. Green, with three regiments of Texas cavalry on the right,[43] was a fighter from the word go, and as soon as the Confederates began to advance he threw his whole force forward, scattered the Kansas cavalry in his front[44] and seeing the end of the federal line of infantry exposed, with a spark of military genius that might only have been expected of Gen. Forest, he dismounted one of his regiments and furiously attacked the federal infantry line on the end, doubling it up and throwing the whole line into confusion.

To relieve this distressing situation a strong force of federal cavalry made a vigorous charge, but were readily driven back by Green's two mounted regiments, while he drove the charge home against the end of the infantry line with his dismounted regiment. One feature of this cavalry fight is said to be picturesque indeed, in which two regiments met at full speed, the Confederates using the revolver and the federals the sabre. But few were killed, but the Texans repulsed their opponents and left their dismounted comrades to continue to demoralize the federal infantry by repeated rear and flank attacks. About the time the Crescent regiment severed the federal line the 18th and 28th Louisiana regiments came in contack with the 77th Illinois and 18th Kentucky regiment in their immediate front.

Short and Sharp

The contest was short and sharp, and while these two Louisiana regiments lost very heavily, they struck just as hard blows as they received, for more dead yankees were observed in front of the 18th than anywhere else. As to Polignac's brigade, scarcely stronger than a good regiment, facing nine pieces of artillery and a strong line of infantry, it bore down all opposition, drove the nine pieces of artillery from position (No. **5**) and finally captured the guns at Honeycut hill.

The other Texas brigade to the right of Polignac[45] did not come in contact with the federals as they crossed the Moss plantation. because the federals, seeing their line broken by the Louisiana brigade on their right, their line doubled up and demoralized by Green's attack on their left, their artillery driven back by Polignac in the center and their own front threatened did not wait upon the order of their going, but went at once. This happy culmination must be attributed largely to Gen. Green, for he promptly assaulted every force he met, whether horse, foot or dragoon and demoralized the whole federal left.

Thus the whole federal line was driven pell mell from their original position and panic-stricken, were rushing back upon their second line near the Sabine crossroads. The fleeing federals were so closely followed by the pursuing Confederates that this second line could not fire a shot—but again Gen. Green, with the genius and daring of a Murat, threw his whole force of calvary on the flank of the second federal line. and the whole line joined the stampede. As before stated, Gen. Banks had packed his whole supply train immediately behind this second line of battle, and as he now had no organized force between it and the victorious Confederates, and as there was but one narrow wagon road through the forest by which it could retreat the whole train fell an easy victim to the Confederate cavalry. Most of these wagons were picked up by Col. Favrot of the Eighth Louisiana cavalry and the 4th Texas cavalry and none would have escaped but for a tendency to loot on the part of the boys.

True to that instinct that so marked him as a leader, Gen. Green was at once in pursuit of the fugitives and came very near capturing Gen. Banks and his staff, who had barely left Antioch church when he reached it. Onward he went, but upon passing Six-mile bayou and ascending Chapman hill he found the whole 19th army corps in battle array.[46] Not knowing what force confronted him, he made a resolute attack, but was repulsed. The Texas infantry brigade that had seen but little fighting, was then thrown forward and engaged the 19th corps at Chapman's peach orchard.[47] The federal position was strong, and they had 9000 fresh troops on the ground, but the Texans pressed them steadily until darkness put an end to the fight. Under cover of night the 19th corps retreated leaving many supplies on the field. The battle of Mansfield had been fought and won.

Although the Texas brigade on the confederate right suffered but little in the charge. it would be out of place not to mention the fact that Col. Raines of the 8th Texas infantry[48] was the first officer, and perhaps the first man on the confederate side killed in the battle as he was struck by a shell from a federal gun just after the charge began, and that Col. Kinc of the 18th Texas infantry[49] did gallant service at the Chapman peach orchard, when with his own regiment and the 8th Texas they furiously assaulted the whole of the 19th corps, and was specially commended by Gen. Dick Taylor in general orders.[50]

The Philadelphia Press had a correspondent watching the fight and he gave the following description of the condition of affairs inside the federal line, at the time that the Louisiana brigade crushed the Federal right.

Worse Than Bull Run

"I was slowly riding along the edge of a wood, conversing with a friend, about the events of the day when suddenly there was a rush, a shout, the crashing of trees, the breaking down of rails, the rush and scamper of men. It was as sudden as though a thunderbolt had fallen among us and set the pines on fire. What caused it, or when it commenced, no one knew. I turned to my companion to inquire the reason for this extraordinary proceeding; but before he had a chance to reply, we found ourselves swallowed up, as it were in a hissing, seething, bubbling whirlpool of agitated men. We could not avoid the current; we could not stem it, and if we hoped to live in that mad company, we must ride with the rest of them. Our line of battle had given away.["][51] Gen. Banks took off his hat and implored his men to remain, his staff officers did the same, but it was of no avail.—Then the General drew his sabre and endeavored to rally his men, but they would not listen. Behind him the rebels were shouting and advancing. The musket balls filled the air with that strange file-rasping sound that war has made familiar to our fighting men. The teams were abandoned by the drivers, the traces cut, and the animals ridden off by the frightened men. Bare headed riders rode with agony in their faces; and for at least ten minutes, it seemed as if we were going to destruction together. It was my fortune to see the first battle of Bull Run, and to be among those who made that celebrated midnight retreat. The retreat of the 4th division was as much a rout as that of the first Federal army, with the exception that fewer men were engaged.

Horace Greeley in his book, The American Conflict, quotes a grumbling private of the 83rd Ohio, who thus sums up the situation:

"The battle was shockingly managed. It was, no doubt, a surprise to the General commanding. He endeavored to charge the enemy with a baggage train but it didn't work."[52]

Two Hero Colonels

To write a story of the battle of Mansfield and not make [it] special would be to write Hamlet with Hamlet left out. We allude to Col. J. H. Beard, who commanded the Consolidated Crescent regiment at the battle of Mansfield and Colonel Jno. B. Reid, who commanded the 130th Illinois on that occasion. Not necessarily that these two officers were better than many others in both armies, but because an emergency presented itself and both proved equal to the occasion for they led the fight at a part of the line of battle that men victory or defeat, in case either failed.

On that fateful April day, just 61 years since, when Gen. Dick Taylor threw the Confederate line of battle against the Federal forces it so happened that Col. Beard with his Crescent regiment faced Col. Reid, with his Illinois troops, and they were the first to come in contact to grapple in a death struggle. As the Crescent charged forward and when it had reached a point about fifty yards from the Federal line, the location of which was not exactly known, the 130th Illinois from a barricade of fence rails, delivered a volley that shocked the Crescent, for 55 men fell dead at that spot, and about 150 wounded, the dead including Col. Beard, Lt. Colonel Clark,[53] Major Canfield[54] and seven of the ten Captains. However, the men rushed on, scaled the barricade and quickly overwhelmed the gallant 130th Illinois, that fought desperately, when they might have ran away if they had so desired. This was a splendid charge and a great defense but it was costly to both sides, for Major Reid lay with a musket ball through his body, and a third of his men lay dead or wounded around him, while Gen. Alfred Mouton, the gallant Confederate Chieftain who had placed himself at the head of the Crescent, when Col. Beard fell, lay dead on the field. This was a dearly bought victory, but when the Crescent broke the Federal line, the other Confederate units swept everything before them, and the Federals abandoned the field, leaving all their artillery and everything else to the victors. Besides all their artillery, several thousand prisoners.

Incidentally, Col. Reid figured conspicuously in one of the real tragedies of the whole war, the [sentence continues with subheading]

Burning of the Federal Hospital

at Mansfield two days after the battle. The old Baptist church, an immense frame building that stood where the Baptist Tabernacle now stands, was converted into a hospital for the Federal wounded.[55] There were no cots, beds or other provisions for their care and comfort, and the floor had been covered with cotton, and blankets spread upon it as improvised beds. About 250 wounded soldiers were in this make-shift hospital. The weather was hot, there was no ice and but little medicine, and the conditions were horrible in that crowded hospital and nothing like sanitation as now understood was to be had.

At about 7:00 P.M., on the night of April 10th, two days after the battle, the writer, a thirteen year old boy, was standing on the corner, just across the street from the hospital, talking to his uncle, Capt. J. H. Garrett,[56] who was at home from the army, as a paroled prisoner who had been captured at Vicksburg. When the cry of fire was heard, we looking across the street beheld a most horrifying scene, for the whole interior of the hospital was a raging flame. A delerious wounded solider had knocked a tallow candle, the only lights out of an attendant[']s hand and the loose cotton was in a blaze immediately. The old church was built on the slant of a hill and while the front door was only about a foot above the ground, the rear of the structure was about twelve feet high. and the window sills through which the wounded had to be removed was perhaps 15 feet high. The nurses were heroic in their efforts and many were brought out the front door, but many of the wounded, as well as some of the nurses were badly burned. Capt. Garrett rushed to the rescue and got out several helpless men. The writer being too small to do much, helped to remove the wounded to a place of safety after they had been rescued. The nurses worked manfully and this bravery exceeded anything that could be imagined on a field of battle, but they got most of the wounded out, but a few were burned to death, and a number died from the shock of their removal through the high back windows.

As Capt. Garrett rushed in for the last time, he saw a wounded man helpless and unable to move who appealed to him for help, and Capt. Garrett took him up in his arms and carried him to safety. This wounded man was Col. Jno. B. Reid, of the 130th Illinois infantry and his rescuer took him to his own home, secured medical aid, and the family nursed him back to life and strength. Col. Reid remained in the Garrett home for five or six months when Capt. Garrett arranged a parol[e] under which Col. Reid returned to the Federal lines and Capt. Garrett went to his own command. A strange friendship grew up between the two and Col. Reid visited Mansfield after the war and spent some time at the home of the writer and it was from him that much of the data in this write-up of the battle was obtained. In the way of verifying the map and the positions of the forces in the Federal line.

Col. Reid was a prominent figure in the G. A. R., circles and was Commander of one of the camps. He died only a few years since greatly to the regret of his "rebel" friends. Col. Reid was born in Ireland, but came to

America as a boy, and was educated at the public schools of Massachusetts. Like all good Irishmen, he was a good democrat and served as Postmaster at Greenville. Ill., under President Pierce, Buchannon, and Lincoln but resigned and entered the army after Lincoln was inaugurated.

Col. Beard was a valiant soldier. At the beginning of the war he organized the Shreveport Grays, which company was with the first troops that left Louisiana for the Confederate service. He was in the campaign against Pensacola, Fla., then went to Virginia where he quickly distinguished himself and was made a Colonel and sent west of the Mississippi river and placed in command of the Consolidated Crescent regiment[,] which he made according to Col. Read's opinion, the best fighting regiment in either army or else it could not have overwhelmed the 130th Illinois that had never met with a repulse before it met the Consolidated Crescent at Mansfield, La.

The article which appeared in the *Confederate Veteran* magazine of May 25, 1925, also included the following:

The Confederate Congress added its tribute in the following:

"*Resolved by the Confederate States of America,* That the thanks of Congress are eminently due, and are hereby most cordially tendered to Maj. Gen. Richard Taylor and the officers and men of his command for the brilliant successes obtained by them over the enemy in Louisiana during the past year, and particularly for the victories at Mansfield and Pleasant Hill on the 8th and 9th of April last, and their subsequent operations against the retreating army of the Federal General Banks in the valley of the Red River.

"*Resolved,* That the President communicate this resolution to Maj. General Taylor and the officers and men of his command."

"Approved June 10, 1864."

It is interesting to recall that during the winter of 1861–65, "when the South was so desperate for lack of supplies of all kinds, General Polignac was dispatched by President Davis as a special envoy to the court of Emperor Napoleon III to intercede for material aid.

"General Polignac was chosen because of his friendship with the Duke de Morny, then powerful at the French court, but on arrival in France he found that the duke had died a few days previously, and he himself was arrested on order of the new premier. He succeeded, however, in gaining an audience with the emperor, who received him affably and ordered his release, but failed to provide any vital aid to the Confederacy.

"General Polignac then attempted to help the Confederacy with his pen and wrote many articles upon it, the best known being, 'The War of Secession and Its True Causes.' He died in Paris, November 15, 1917."

Notes

1. *Biographical and Historical Memoirs of Northwest Louisiana* (Chicago & Nashville, 1890), 263–64.
2. W. T. Block, "Southwest Louisiana Found in Beaumont Enterprise," http://www.wtblock.com/wtblockjr/southwes.htm.
3. J. E. Hewitt wrote the core of this document to commemorate the dedication of the monuments to Richard Taylor and the Prince de Polignac on April 8, 1925. The account was published in the *Confederate Veteran Magazine* 33 (May 1925): 172–73, 198. The additional information contained in this chapter consists of the sections concentrating on the monuments, the Polignac family, the fire of April 10, 1864, and the relationship between his family and Colonel John Reid of the 130th Illinois Infantry Regiment. The monument dedication pamphlet was reissued on April 8, 1949, on the 85th anniversary of the battle. It is from that version that the text of this chapter is derived. Missing letters or words have been inserted in brackets when the error appears in the 1949 version. These errors do not appear in the *Confederate Veteran* article and are not attributed to J. E. Hewitt.
4. United Confederate Veterans.
5. Later became the United Daughters of the Confederacy. The Kate Beard Chapter still exists and is the home chapter for Mansfield, Louisiana.
6. Camille Armand Jules Marie, the Prince de Polignac.
7. Southerners.
8. There were actually 104 naval and army transport vessels. See Appendix 2.
9. Brigadier General Andrew Jackson Smith.
10. This is the only source for this crucial information. Since it comes from a knowledgeable source, it must be taken as correct. Other sources allude to the location of Polignac's Brigade, which adds credence to Hewitt's account. Blessington states that Walker's Division encamped four miles north of Mansfield on the Kingston Road on April 7. Hewitt's account specifically states that all three groups encamped near water sources and, in his narrative, he places Polignac with the Texas command. It is possible, if not probable, that both authors are correct. A portion of Walker's Division may have encamped with Polignac. All of Walker's men encamped at the stream near the later Texas and Pacific depot would have depleted the stream of potable water. The stream Hewitt calls "six mile bayou" is Bayou

Bon Chasse, and "three mile bayou" is Elam Creek. J. P. Blessington, *The Campaigns of Walker's Texas Division* (Austin, 1994), 180.

11. See chap. 1. James A. Jarratt's account closely follows Hewitt's version. Jarratt was a sergeant in Company B of the Consolidated Crescent Regiment.
12. Colonel James Beard.
13. Brigadier General Jean Jacques Alexandre Alfred Mouton.
14. This pamphlet was written in 1925.
15. A consistent typographical error. The proper name is Camille.
16. For a thorough biography of the prince, see Jeff Kinard, *Lafayette of the South: Prince Camille de Polignac and the American Civil War* (College Station, TX, 2001).
17. Louisiana Highway 175.
18. Ferdinand Maximilian Joseph, the archduke of Austria, became emperor of Mexico when Napoleon III sought to extend French imperial power.
19. Union Major General Nathaniel Prentiss Banks.
20. This should be the 18th Regiment under the command of Colonel Henry Gray.
21. This should be Brigadier General James Major.
22. This should be Major General John George Walker's Texas Division.
23. Brigadier General Tom Green.
24. Honeycutt Hill, named for the family that farmed it.
25. See chap. 1, maps 1.1, 1.2, 1.3.
26. Ibid.; see chap. 1 n. 44.
27. See fig. 9.1. These units were the Third Division of the 13th Corps, commanded by Brigadier General Robert A. Cameron. They were the First Brigade under Lieutenant Colonel Aaron M. Flory, which included the 46th Indiana Infantry, under Captain William M. DeHart, and the 29th Wisconsin Infantry commanded by Major Bradford Hancock and Second Brigade led by Colonel William H. Raynor. Units in this brigade were the 24th Iowa Infantry commanded by Major Edward Wright, the 28th Iowa Infantry under Colonel John Connell, and Captain Maschil Manring's 56th Ohio Infantry. See Appendix 1.
28. This artillery was the Chicago Mercantile Battery and the 1st Indiana Battery. Both had six guns.
29. Richard Taylor, *Destruction and Reconstruction: Personal Experiences in the Civil War* (New York, 1995), 162.
30. Chapman's Bayou, or, as it is incorrectly named, "Chatman's Bayou," on the USGS 7.5 minute topographic quadrangle maps of Mansfield and Trenton.

31. The 19th Kentucky Infantry Regiment.
32. The 161st New York Infantry was part of Emerson's Brigade of the 19th Corps. They were present on the battlefield and fought in the third phase of the battle, but Hewitt is incorrect here. This unit was not in the initial phase fighting. See Appendix 1.
33. This is a reasonably accurate, though simplified, unit position description. On the north side of the road, facing the Louisianians, were the 13th Corps's Second Brigade, commanded by Colonel Joseph W. Vance, consisting of the 130th Illinois Infantry led by Major John B. Reid, the 48th Ohio Infantry under Lieutenant Colonel Joseph W. Lindsey, the 83rd Ohio Infantry under Lieutenant Colonel William H. Baldwin, and Lieutenant Colonel Albert H. Brown's 96th Ohio Infantry. Positioned on their right was the First Brigade of the Cavalry Division of the 19th Corps, under Colonel Thomas J. Lucas. This brigade consisted of the 14th New York Cavalry, led by Major Abraham Bassford; the Lieutenant Colonel James H. Redfield's 16th Indiana Mounted Infantry; and the 2nd Louisiana Mounted Infantry, commanded by Major Alfred Hodsdon. Straddling the road was the 13th Corps's First Brigade, commanded by Colonel Frank Emerson. This brigade consisted of the 77th Illinois Infantry, commanded by Lieutenant Colonel Lysander R. Webb; the 67th Indiana Infantry, led by Major Francis A. Sears; the 19th Kentucky Infantry, commanded by Lieutenant Colonel John Cowan; and the 23rd Wisconsin Infantry, under Major Joseph E. Greene. On the south side of the road, facing the bulk of the Texans and protecting the Union left flank, was the Cavalry division's Fourth Brigade under Colonel Nathan A. M. "Goldlace" Dudley. This brigade consisted of the 2nd Illinois Cavalry under Major Benjamin F. Marsh Jr., the 3rd Massachusetts Cavalry (31st Massachusetts Mounted Infantry) of Lieutenant Colonel Lorenzo D. Sargent, and the 2nd New Hampshire Cavalry (8th New Hampshire Mounted Infantry) under Lieutenant Colonel George A. Flanders. At this point in the battle the senior officers on the field were the commander of the 19th Corps Cavalry Division, Brigadier General Albert Lindley Lee, and the commander of the 13th Corps, Brigadier General Thomas E. G. Ransom. See chap. 2, map 2.1. See Appendix 1.
34. 2nd Massachusetts Light or Nims's Battery.
35. The site of the church has a modern church in the same location today. It is also called Antioch Baptist Church.
36. Hewitt is mistaken. He is referring to the 19th Texas Infantry commanded by Colonel Richard Waterhouse Jr. This was part of the Third Brigade of Major General John G. Walker's Texas Division. This brigade was led by Brigadier General William Scurry. The other brigades of the division were the First Brigade under Brigadier General Thomas N.

Waul and the Second Brigade under Brigadier General Horace Randal. Polignac and Colonel Henry Gray commanded brigades under Brigadier General Alfred Mouton's Louisiana Division. See Appendix 1.

37. See chap. 1. This was Sergeant James A. Jarratt's company. This account corroborates Jarratt's version with few exceptions.
38. This was Major Cyrus Dickey. Jim Huffstodt, *Hard Dying Men: The Story of General W.H.L. Wallace, General T.E.G. Ransom, and Their "Old Eleventh: Illinois Infantry in the American Civil War (1861–1865)* (Bowie, MD, 1991), 177; Gary D. Joiner, *One Damn Blunder from Beginning to End: The Red River Campaign of 1864* (Wilmington, DE, 2003), 100.
39. See chap. 1.
40. Reid.
41. See chap. 1. Jarratt's account differs slightly. Jarratt, an eyewitness, places Mouton's death on the south side of Honeycutt Hill, but near the road. The difference in the two accounts is possibly less than fifty yards. Jarratt's is probably correct.
42. Contact. This is a recurring typographical error.
43. Bee's Cavalry Brigade commanded by Brigadier General Hamilton P. Bee. The regiments were the 1st Texas Cavalry, commanded by Colonel Augustus C. Buchel; the 26th Texas Cavalry, under Colonel Xavier B. Debray; and possibly Terrell's Texas Cavalry, under Terrell's Texas Cavalry commanded Colonel Alexander W. Terrell. See Appendix 1.
44. Dudley's Brigade. There were no Kansas cavalry units in it. The overall commander, Albert L. Lee, however, was from Kansas.
45. Randal's Brigade of Walker's Texas Division.
46. First Division of the 19th Corps Commanded by Brigadier General William H. Emory. See Appendix 1.
47. See chap. 4.
48. Hewitt is referring to Lieutenant Colonel James W. Raine of the 12th Texas Infantry Regiment (also known as the 8th Texas Infantry Regiment), part of Walker's Division, First Brigade commanded by Brigadier General Thomas N. Waul. Stewart Sifakis, *Compendium of the Confederate Armies: Texas* (New York, 1995), 124.
49. Colonel Wilburn H. King commanded the 18th Texas Infantry Regiment.
50. See chap. 5, unnumbered general order by Major General Richard Taylor.
51. Frank Moore, ed., *The Rebellion Record: A Diary of American Events* (New York, 1862–71), 8:548.
52. Horace Greeley, *The American Conflict: The American Conflict: A History of the Great Rebellion in the United States of America, 1860–65* (Washington DC, 1898).

53. Lieutenant Colonel Franklin H. Clack.
54. Major Mercer Canfield.
55. The church stood northeast of the northern end of North Jefferson Street and backed up to a steep ravine. The Baptist Tabernacle has been destroyed as well.
56. Captain J. H. Garrett, Company K, 27th Louisiana Infantry Regiment. Booth, *Records,* 1:977. This company was known as the McLaurin Invincibles and was from Natchitoches Parish. Arthur W. Bergeron, *Guide to Confederate Units, 1861–1865* (Baton Rouge, 1989), 137. Garrett may have been one of hundreds or thousands of Confederates who may have illegally fought at Mansfield. If unparoled, unexchanged, and captured, he could have been hanged by Union forces.

The Battle of Mansfield Song

Edited by Marilyn Murrell Segura Joiner

The Battle of Mansfield was commemorated in a song composed by Mansfield residents Margaret and Charlotte Pegues.[1] Family legend has noted that the spinster ladies were so aware of the historical significance of their writing about the battle that their original document included footnotes. The version from which this transcription was made was copied in pencil by their niece, Laura Cale,[2] a Mansfield resident whose niece, Mittie Laura Cale Murrell,[3] preserved it in her papers. The handwritten copy is in the collection of the editor. Mittie Murrell recalled the words from memory and frequently sang them to the editor. Her father, John Evander Cale, born in 1856, was a boy at the time of the battle. He recalled sitting on the steps of the Cale family home and watching soldiers come into town following the battle. One stopped and asked him for whiskey.

For more than 100 years, "The Battle of Mansfield" was passed down through the family and was familiar to the members of the Kate Beard Chapter of the United Daughters of the Confederacy in Mansfield. During planning of the 100th anniversary of the battle, the editor was a member of the Mansfield High School band and suggested that the song be played at the celebration. Hugh Hardin, the band director, was not familiar with the tune and asked her to provide both the words and the music. The words came from family records, while the tune was written on staff paper from memory. Special guest at the anniversary celebration was Victor Mansfield, the son of the Prince de Polignac, a French general who fought for the Confederacy and a hero of the Battle of Mansfield. A photo of the centennial celebration hangs in the foyer of the Mansfield State Historic Site.

Later in life, as a more mature musician, the editor heard a familiar melody and her research indicated the tune was "Kingdom Coming." While not a note-for-note match, it would be obvious even to the untrained ear that this is the period tune that was used for "The Battle of Mansfield."

Throughout history, popular tunes have taken on new life as writers appropriated the familiar music for use with new words. It is not surprising that "The Battle of Mansfield" borrowed the popular song of the Civil War era, "Kingdom Coming," written by Henry Clay Work.[4] Yet, there is some irony to the Confederate sisters' choice of music. Work was the son of an abolitionist whose family assisted slaves escaping to the North. While in the printing trade, he began to write songs with encouragement from E. P. Christy.[5] Work was under contract to Root and Cady, music publishers. He has been compared to Stephen Foster[6] and George Frederick Root.[7] Among his other noted songs are "Marching through Georgia" and "Grandfather's Clock."[8] "Kingdom Coming" was written in dialect, which was common at that time.

The Battle of Mansfield

Oh, come good folks while I sing you a ditty of the year of sixty four
When Gen'ral Banks[9] marched out of the city with thirty thousand or more
He swore he'd capture Shreveport[10] town or else know the reason why
For he'd bring old Steele[11] with his army down and just make rebels fly

Chorus: Old Banks, he run a ha,[12] the Rebels chased a ho
And such a hot race you never did see since the year of sixty-four.

The Mansfield people were very much frightened when they heard that the Yanks had come
But their hearts grew lighter and their faces grew brighter when they heard Dick Taylor's[13] drum
Old Dick was there and Mouton[14] too and Green's[15] Val Verde Boys
And Walker's Texans[16] were not so very few for they kicked up a terrible noise
Chorus

They soon used up the thirteenth corps[17] and the nineteenth[18] had to run
And the way they double-quicked[19] twenty miles or more I'll tell you boys 'twas fun!

They fought mighty hard we will not deny at the town of Pleasant Hill[20]
But Missouri[21] boys gave them a try and they more than got their fill.
Chorus

They marched away in the middle of the night to retreat to Grand Ecore[22]
For they heard General Churchill[23] had joined in the fight and they didn't know how many more
When Churchill's men were in the line who came from Arkansas
And when they charged I'll tell you what the Yanks they knew 'twas war
Chorus

Early next morning our cavalry started in pursuit of the fleeing[24] Yanks
When Walker's Texans marched away to cure old Steele of his pranks
And thus did end the Mansfield Battle and the fight at Pleasant Hill
'Tis said to this day old Banks hears the rattle of the Mansfield muskets still.
Chorus

The original song, "Kingdom Coming," is also known as "The Year of Jubilo," taking this phrase from the chorus. The meter of these lyrics reinforces the origin of the tune.

Original Song

Kingdom Coming
(Year of Jubilo) [25]

1. Say, darkies hab[26] you seen de massa[27],
Wid de muffstash[28] on his face,
Go long de road some rime dis mornin';
Like he gwine[29] to leab[30] de place?
He seen a smoke way up de ribber,[31]
Where de Linkun[32] gunboats lay;
He took his hat and lef' berry[33] sudden,
An' I 'spec he's run away!
Chorus:
De massa run, ha! ha!
De darkey[34] stay, ho! ho!
It mus' be now de kingdom comin', an' de year of Jubilo![35]

2. He' six foot one way, two foot t'udder[36]
An' he weigh t'ree hundred pound,
His coat's so big he couldn't pay de tailor
An' it won' go half way 'round.
He drill so much dey calls him Cap'n,
An' he gets so mighty tanned,
I 'spec he'll try to fool dem Yankees
For to tink he's contraband.[37]
Chorus

3. De darkeys got so lonesome libin'[38]
In de log hut on de lawn,
Dey move dere[39] t'ings into massa's parlor,
For to keep it while he's gone.
Dar's[40] wine an' cider in de kitchen
An' de darkeys de'll hab some;
I 'spose dey'll all be confiscated
When de Linkun sojers[41] come.
Chorus

4. De oberseer[42] he make us trouble,
An' he dribe[43] us 'round a spell;
We lock him up in de smoke-house cellar,
Wid de key t'rown in de well.
De whip is los', de han'-cuff broken,
But de massa'll hab his pay;
He's ole enough, big enough, ought to know better
Dan[44] to went an' run away.
Chorus 1.

Notes

1. Daughters of Anne Lindsay and Malachi Pegues of Mansfield. Charlotte Pegues, born 1839 in Loundes County, Alabama; died 1910 in Mansfield, Louisiana. Mary (Margaret) Pegues, born 1838 in Loundes County, Alabama; died 1905 in Mansfield, Louisiana. Also known as "Tolly" and "Molly." Neither married. Cale family papers in the collection of Annie Laurie and Harvey Samuels Jr., Mansfield, Louisiana.
2. Laura Cale, born February 5, 1865, in DeSoto Parish, Louisiana, daughter of Sarah Ann Pegues and Evander McIver Cale; died January 13, 1949, in Mansfield, Louisiana. Also known as "Honey." She never married. Cale family papers in the collection of Annie Laurie and Harvey Samuels Jr., Mansfield, Louisiana.
3. Daughter of Sallie Waters Richardson and John Evander Cale of Mansfield, born February 25, 1894, and died July 5, 1991, in Mansfield. She was the wife of Joseph Warren Murrell and the grandmother of Marilyn Murrell Segura Joiner. Cale family papers in the collection of Annie Laurie and Harvey Samuels Jr., Mansfield, Louisiana.
4. Born October 1, 1832, in Middletown, Connecticut; died in Hartford, Connecticut, June 8, 1884.
5. Minstrel, founder of the Christy Minstrels.
6. Prolific American composer of popular music of the nineteenth century.
7. American composer and publisher of music in the mid-nineteenth century; partner in Root and Cady.
8. http://eir.library.utoronto.ca/rpo/display/index.cfm Representative Poetry On-line (RPO), prepared by the members of the Department of English, University of Toronto, published by the University of Toronto Press from 1912 to 1967. RPO Edited by Ian Lancashire, Department of English, University of Toronto, 2003.
9. Union General Nathaniel Prentiss Banks, from Massachusetts, commander of Union forces at Mansfield.
10. Confederate capital of Louisiana; in 1864 the nexus of the Texas Trail by which the Confederacy received supplies from Texas and Mexico.
11. Union Major General Frederick Steele, commander of Federal forces in Arkansas.
12. In some versions, the song was sung "he ran a ha ha," which more closely follows the beats in the music that inspired the melody.
13. Confederate general with strong ties to Louisiana. Son of former U.S. President Zachary Taylor, brother-in-law of Jefferson Davis through his first wife, Sarah Knox Taylor, sister of Taylor.
14. Confederate Brigadier General Jean Jacque Alexandre Alfred Mouton, commander of the Louisiana Division.
15. Confederate Texas cavalry corps commander General Tom Green.

16. Troops of Confederate Major General John George Walker's Division.
17. Union 13th Corps, commanded by Brigadier General Thomas E. G. Ransom.
18. Union 19th Corps, commanded by Major General William Buel Franklin.
19. Speed of marching.
20. Battle of Pleasant Hill fought April 9, 1864, a day after the Battle of Mansfield. The second engagement was considered a tie.
21. The division commanded by Brigadier General Mosby M. Parsons.
22. High vantage point on the Red River, just north of Natchitoches, Louisiana.
23. The Arkansas Division led by Brigadier General Thomas James Churchill. Parson's command was part of this division.
24. Some versions of the song refer to "flying Yanks."
25. Denes Agay, *Best Loved Songs of the American People* (New York, 1975).
26. Have.
27. Master.
28. Mustache.
29. Going.
30. Leave.
31. River.
32. Lincoln.
33. Left very.
34. Slave, person of dark complexion.
35. Joy or Jubilee.
36. The other.
37. Fugitive slave.
38. Living.
39. They move their.
40. There's.
41. Soldiers.
42. Overseer, the person who runs a plantation.
43. Drive.
44. Than.

ORDERS OF BATTLE FOR THE RED RIVER CAMPAIGN

Operations in Louisiana, March–May 1864

CONFEDERATE FORCES

GENERAL EDMUND KIRBY SMITH COMMANDING THE ARMY OF THE TRANS-MISSISSIPPI

Maj. Gen. Richard Taylor commanding the District of Western Louisiana
    Headquarters Escort Company (Louisiana Cavalry)—Capt. Joseph Benjamin
Unattached—2nd Battalion Louisiana Reserves

FIRST INFANTRY DIVISION

Maj. Gen. John G. Walker

First Brigade—Brig. Gen. Thomas N. Waul
    12th Texas Infantry—Col. Overton C. Young
    18th Texas Infantry—Col. Wilburn H. King
    22nd Texas Infantry—Col. Richard B. Hubbard
    13th Texas Cavalry, Dismounted—Col. Anderson F. Crawford
    Haldeman's Texas Battery—Capt. Horace Haldeman

Second Brigade—Col. Horace Randal (promoted brigadier general April 13)
    11th Texas Infantry—Col. Oran M. Roberts
    14th Texas Infantry—Col. Edward Clark
    28th Texas Cavalry, Dismounted—Lt. Col. Eli H. Baxter Jr.
    6th (Gould's) Texas Cavalry Battalion—Lt. Col. Robert S. Gould
    Daniel's Texas Battery—Capt. James M. Daniel

Third Brigade—Brig. Gen. William R. Scurry
- 3rd Texas Infantry—Col. Phillip N. Luckett (attached about April 15)
- 16th Texas Infantry—Col. George Flournoy
- 17th Texas Infantry—Col. Robert T. P. Allen
- 19th Texas Infantry—Col. Richard Waterhouse Jr.
- 16th Texas Cavalry, Dismounted—Col. William Fitzhugh
- Edgar's Texas Battery—Capt. William Edgar

First Division Artillery
- Haldeman's Texas Battery—Capt. Horace Haldeman
- Gibson's Battery
- Daniel's Texas Battery—Capt. James M. Daniel
- Edgar's Texas Battery—Capt. William Edgar

Second Infantry Division

Brig. Gen. Jean Jacque Alexandre Alfred Mouton (killed April 8), Brig. Gen. Camille Armand Jules Marie, Prince de Polignac

First Brigade—Col. Henry Gray
- 18th Louisiana Consolidated Infantry—Col. Leopold L. Armant (killed April 8), Lt. Col. Joseph Collins (promoted colonel)
- 28th Louisiana Infantry—Lt. Col. William Walker (killed April 8), Maj. Thomas W. Pool (promoted colonel)
- Consolidated Crescent Regiment—(Louisiana) Regiment—Col. James Beard (killed April 8), Col. Abel W. Bosworth, Capt. William C. C. Claiborne, Jr.

Second Brigade—Brig. Gen. Camille J. Polignac, Col. James R. Taylor (killed April 8), Lt. Col. Robert D. Stone (killed April 8), Co. James E. Harrison
- 15th Texas Infantry—Lt. Col. James E. Harrison (promoted colonel April 15), Maj. John W. Daniel (promoted lieutenant colonel April 15)
- 17th Texas Consolidated Cavalry, Dismounted—Col. James R. Taylor, Maj. Thomas F. Tucker
- 22nd Texas Cavalry, Dismounted—Lt. Col. Robert D. Stone, Maj. George W. Merrick
- 31st Texas Cavalry, Dismounted—Maj. Frederick J. Malone
- 34th Texas Cavalry, Dismounted—Lt. Col. John H. Caudle
- Artillery—Maj. Thomas A. Faeries
- Confederate Regular Battery, Capt. John T. M. Barnes
- Bell (La.) Battery—Capt. Thomas O. Benton
- Boone's Louisiana Battery (siege guns)—Lt. Maunsel Bennett

St. Mary (La.) Cannoneers—Capt. Florian O. Cornay (killed April 26), Lt. John B. Tarleton.

Second Division Artillery—Maj. Joseph L. Brent (promoted lieutenant colonel)
Reserve Battalion—Maj. Charles W. Squires
West's Arkansas Battery—Capt. Henry C. West
Pelican (La.) Battery—Capt. B. Felix Winchester

Detachment, District of Arkansas

Brig. Gen. Thomas James Churchill

First Division

Brig. Gen. James C. Tappan

Tappan's Brigade—Col. H. L. Grinstead
19th (Dawson's) and 24th Arkansas Infantry—Lt. Col. William R. Hardy
27th and 38th Arkansas Infantry—Col. R G. Shaver
33rd Arkansas Infantry—Col. Hiram L. Grinstead
Etter's Arkansas Battery—Capt. Chambers B. Etter

Gause's Brigade—Col. Lucien C. Gause
26th Arkansas Infantry—Lt. Col. Iverson L. Brooks
32nd Arkansas Infantry—Lt. Col. William Hicks
36th Arkansas Infantry—Col. James M. Davie
[? 39th Arkansas Infantry—Col. James W. Rogan?]
Marshall's Arkansas Battery—Capt. John G. Marshall

Second Division

Brig. Gen. Mosby M. Parsons

First Brigade—Brig. Gen. John B. Clark Jr.
8th Missouri Infantry—Col. Charles S. Mitchell
9th Missouri Infantry—Col. Richard H. Musser
Ruffner's Missouri Battery—Capt. Samuel T. Ruffner

2nd Brigade—Col. Simon P. Burns
10th Missouri Infantry—Col. William M. Moore
11th Missouri Infantry—Lt. Col. Thomas H. Murray
12th Missouri Infantry—Col. Willis M. Ponder
16th Missouri Infantry—Lt. Col. Pleasant W. H. Cumming

9th Missouri Battalion Sharpshooters—Maj. Lebbeus A. Pindall
Lesueur's Missouri Battery—Capt. Alex A. Lesueur

Cavalry Corps

Brig. Gen. Thomas Jefferson Green (killed April 12), Brig. Gen. Hamilton P. Bee, Maj. Gen. John A. Wharton

First Division

Brig. Gen. Hamilton P. Bee (relieved May 14), Brig. Gen. Arthur P. Bagby

Debray's Brigade—Col. Xavier B. Debray (promoted brigadier general)
23rd Texas Cavalry—Col. Nicholas C. Gould (arrived April 9–10)
26th Texas Cavalry—Lt. Col. John J. Meyers
36th Texas Cavalry—Col. Peter C. Woods (arrived April 9–10)

Buchel's Brigade—Col. Augustus C. Buchel (mortally wounded April 9), Col. Arthur P. Bagby (promoted brigadier general April 13), Col. Alexander W. Terrell
1st Texas Cavalry—Lt. Col. William O. Yager
35th (Likens') Texas Cavalry—Col. James B. Likens, Lt. Col. James R. Burns (arrived April 9–10, detached to Sub-District of North Louisiana)
Terrell's Texas Cavalry—Col. Alexander W. Terrell

First Division

Brig. Gen. James P. Major

Lane's Brigade—Col. Walter P. Lane (wounded April 8), Col. George W. Baylor
1st Texas Partisan Rangers—Lt. Col. R. P. Crump, Maj. W. P. Saufley
2nd Texas Partisan Rangers—Col. Isham Chisum, Lt. Col. Crill Miller
2nd Regt., Arizona Brigade—Col. George W. Baylor, Lt. Col. John W. Mullen
3rd Regt., Arizona Brigade—Lt. Col. George T. Madison

Bagby's Brigade—Col. Arthur P. Bagby, Col. William P. Hardeman, Lt. Col. George J. Hampton, Lt. Col. Edward Waller Jr.
4th Texas Cavalry—Col. William P. Hardeman, Lt. Col. George J. Hampton, Maj. Charles Lesueur
5th Texas Cavalry—Maj. Hugh A. McPhaill
7th Texas Cavalry—Lt. Col. Philemon T. Herbert Jr. (promoted colonel; mortally wounded April 8), Lt. Col. Gustave Hoffman

13th Texas Cavalry Battalion—Lt. Col. Edward Waller Jr., Capt. W. A. McDade

Vincent's Brigade—Col. William G. Vincent (operated independently)

2nd Louisiana Cavalry—Col. William G. Vincent, Maj. Winter O. Breazeale

4th (7th) Louisiana Cavalry—Col. Louis Bush

Horse Artillery—Maj. Oliver J. Semmes

Grosse Tete (La.) Flying Artillery Battery—Capt. John A. A. West

Gibson's Texas Battery—Capt. William E. Gibson (arrived about May 10)

McMahan's Texas Artillery Battery—Capt. Martin Van Buren McMahan

Moseley's Texas Artillery Battery—Capt. William G. Moseley

Valverde (Tex.) Artillery Battery—Capt. Thomas D. Nettles

Louisiana State Guard

1st Louisiana Battalion Cavalry—Lt. Col. Benjamin W. Clark, Maj. Thomas J. Caldwell

2nd Louisiana Battalion Cavalry—Lt. Col. Henry M. Favrot

Miscellaneous

Harrison's Louisiana Cavalry Battalion—Lt. Col. William Harrison

Red River Scouts (La.) Cavalry Battalion (two companies)—Capt. Willis A. Stewart

1st Trans-Mississippi Cavalry Battalion—Maj. Thomason J. Bird

King's Louisiana Battery (siege guns)—Capt. Edward T. King

Crescent Artillery (Company A)—Capt. T. H. Hutton

Sub-District of North Louisiana—Operating East of Red River

Brig. Gen. St. John R. Liddell (relieved May 10), Col. Isaac F. Harrison

Harrison's Brigade—Col. Isaac F. Harrison

3rd Louisiana Cavalry—Lt. Col. Francis W. Moore

4th Louisiana Cavalry—Col. A. J. McNeill

5th Louisiana Cavalry—Col. Richard L. Capers

8th Missouri Cavalry (detachment)—Lt. Col. Samuel J. Ward

35th (Likens') Texas Cavalry—Col. James B. Likens, Lt. Col. James R. Burns

Artillery—Capt. T. Kinlock Fauntleroy

2nd Louisiana Heavy Artillery Battalion (siege guns)—Lt. Col. George W. Logan, Capt. Daniel Scully

Cameron's Louisiana Battery (one section)—Lt. T. Jefferson Key

Battery H, 1st Mississippi Light Artillery Regiment (one section)—
Lt. J. Wood Coleman

Union Forces

Major General Nathaniel Prentiss Banks, Commander Department of the Gulf

13th Army Corps (Detachment)

Brig. Gen. Thomas E. G. Ransom

Third Division

Brig. Gen. Robert A. Cameron

First Brigade—Lt. Col. Aaron M. Flory
46th Indiana Infantry—Capt. William M. DeHart
29th Wisconsin Infantry—Maj. Bradford Hancock

Second Brigade—Col. William H. Raynor
24th Iowa Infantry—Maj. Edward Wright
28th Iowa Infantry—Col. John Connell
56th Ohio Infantry—Capt. Maschil Manring Artillery
1st Missouri Light Artillery, Battery A—Lt. Col. Elisha Cole
Ohio Light Artillery, 2nd Battery—Lt. William H. Harper

4th Division

Col. William J. Landram

First Brigade—Col. Frank Emerson
77th Illinois Infantry—Lt. Col. Lysander R. Webb
67th Indiana Infantry—Maj. Francis A. Sears
19th Kentucky Infantry—Lt. Col. John Cowan
23rd Wisconsin Infantry—Maj. Joseph E. Greene

Second Brigade—Col. Joseph W. Vance.
130th Illinois Infantry—Maj. John B. Reid
48th Ohio Infantry—Lt. Col. Joseph W. Lindsey
83rd Ohio Infantry—Lt. Col. William H. Baldwin
96th Ohio Infantry—Lt. Col. Albert H. Brown Artillery

Indiana Light Artillery, 1st Battery—Capt. Martin Klauss
Chicago Mercantile Battery—Lt. Pinkney S. Cone

19th Army Corps

Maj. Gen. William B. Franklin

First Division

Brig. Gen. William H. Emory

First Brigade
Brig. Gen. William Dwight
29th Maine Infantry—Col. George L. Beal
114th New York Infantry—Lt. Col. Henry B. Morse
116th New York Infantry—Col. George M. Love
153rd New York Infantry—Col. Edwin P. Davis
161st New York Infantry—Lt. Col. William B. Kinsey

Second Brigade—Brig. Gen. James W. McMillan
15th Maine Infantry—Col. Isaac Dyer
160th New York Infantry—Lt. Col. John B. Van Petten
47th Pennsylvania Infantry—Col. Tilghman H. Good
13th Maine Infantry—Col. Henry Rust Jr.

Third Brigade—Col. Lewis Benedict
30th Maine Infantry—Col. Francis Fessenden
162nd New York Infantry—Lt. Col. Justus W. Blanchard
173rd New York Infantry—Col. Lewis M. Peck
165th New York Infantry—Lt. Col. Gouverneur Carr Artillery
1st Delaware Battery—Capt. Benjamin Nields
Battery L, 1st U.S. Artillery—Lt. Franck E. Taylor
1st Vermont Battery—Capt. George T. Hebard

Cavalry Division

Brig. Gen. Albert L. Lee

First Brigade—Col. Thomas J. Lucas
14th New York Cavalry—Maj. Abraham Bassford
16th Indiana Mounted Infantry—Lt. Col. James H. Redfield
2nd Louisiana Mounted Infantry—Maj. Alfred Hodsdon

Third Brigade—Col. Harai Robinson
- 1st Louisiana Cavalry (U.S.)—Maj. Algernon S. Badger
- 87th Illinois Mounted Infantry—Lt. Col. John M. Crebs

Fourth Brigade—Col. Nathan A. M. "Goldlace" Dudley
- 2nd Illinois Cavalry—Maj. Benjamin F. Marsh Jr.
- 3rd Massachusetts Cavalry (31st Massachusetts Mounted Infantry)—Lt. Col. Lorenzo D. Sargent
- 2nd New Hampshire Cavalry (8th New Hampshire Mounted Infantry)—Lt. Col. George A. Flanders

Fifth Brigade—Col. Oliver R Gooding
- 18th New York Cavalry, Companies K and D—Capt. William Davis
- 3rd Rhode Island Cavalry (detachment)—Maj. George R Davis
- 2nd New York Veteran Cavalry (?)—Col. Morgan H. Chrysler

Artillery
- Rawles's Battery (Battery G, 5th U.S. Light Artillery)—Lt. Jacob B. Rawles
- 6th Missouri Cavalry, Howitzer Battery—Capt. H. H. Rottakan
- 2nd Battery (B) Massachusetts Light Artillery—Capt. Ormand F. Nims

16th Army Corps, Army of the Tennessee

Brig. Gen. Andrew J. Smith

Also under Smith's command was the Provisional Division of the 17th Corps and the Mississippi Marine Brigade.

First Division

Second Brigade—Col. Lucius F. Hubbard
- 47th Illinois Infantry—Col. John D. McClure
- 5th Minnesota Infantry—Maj. John C. Becht
- 8th Wisconsin Infantry—Lt. Col. John W. Jefferson

Third Brigade—Col. Sylvester G. Hill
- 35th Iowa (nonveterans 8th and 12th Iowa attached)—Lt. Col. William B. Keeler
- 33rd Missouri (nonveterans, 11th Missouri attached)—Col. William H. Heath

Third Division

Brig. Gen. Joseph A. Mower

First Brigade—Col. William F. Lynch
58th Illinois Infantry—Maj. Thomas Newlan
119th Illinois Infantry—Col. Thomas J. Kinney
89th Indiana (nonveterans, 52nd Indiana attached)—Col. C. D. Murray

Second Brigade—Col. William T. Shaw
14th Iowa Infantry—Lt. Col. Newbold
27th Iowa Infantry—Col. James J. Gilbert
32nd Iowa Infantry—Col. John Scott
24th Missouri (nonveterans, 21st Missouri attached)—Maj. Robert W. Fyan

Third Brigade—Col. Risdon M. Moore
49th Illinois Infantry—Thomas W. Morgan
117th Illinois Infantry—Lt. Col. Jonathan Merriam
178th New York—Col. Edward Wehler

Artillery
3rd Indiana Battery—Capt. James M. Cockefair
9th Indiana Battery—Capt. George R. Brown

17th Corps

Detached to Brig. Gen. A. J. Smith (16th Corps)

Second (Provisional) Division

Brig. Gen. Thomas Kilby Smith

First Brigade—Col. Jonathan B. Moore
41st Illinois Infantry—Col. John M. Nale
3rd Iowa Infantry—Lt. Col. James Tullis
3rd Wisconsin Infantry—Maj. Horatio H. Virgin

Second Brigade—Col. Lyman M. Ward
81st Illinois Infantry—Lt. Col. Andrew W. Rogers
95th Illinois Infantry—Col. Thomas W. Humphrey
14th Wisconsin Infantry—Capt. Carlos M. G. Mansfield

Artillery
1st Missouri Light Artillery, Battery M—Lt. John M. Tiemeyer

Mississippi Marine Brigade

Brig. Gen. A. W. Ellet

Infantry Regiment—Col. Charles R. Ellet
Cavalry Battalion—Maj. James M. Hubbard

Corps d'Afrique—U.S. Colored Troops

First Division

First Brigade—Col. William Dickey
73rd Regiment USCT—Col. Chauncey J. Bassett, Maj. Hiram E. Perkins
75th Regiment USCT—Col. Henry W. Fuller
84th Regiment USCT—Col. James H. Corrin
92nd Regiment USCT—Col. Henry N. Frisbie, Lt. Col. John C. Chadwick

Engineer Brigade—Col. George D. Robinson
97th Regiment USCT—Lt. Col. George A. Harmount
99th Regiment USCT—Lt. Col. Uri B. Pearsall

Garrison Troops holding Alexandria that did not actively participate in the campaign farther north but were sent to Grand Ecore as reserves after the battles of Mansfield and Pleasant Hill:

19th Army Corps

Maj. Gen. William B. Franklin

Second Division

Brig. Gen. Cuvier Grover

Second Brigade—Col. Edward L. Molineaux
13th Connecticut Infantry—Col. Charles D. Blinn
1st Louisiana Infantry—Col. William O. Fiske
90th New York Infantry (three companies)—Maj. John C. Smart
159th New York Infantry—Lt. Col. Edward L. Gaul

Third Brigade—Col. Jacob Sharpe
38th Massachusetts Infantry—Lt. Col. James P. Richardson
128th New York Infantry—Col. James Smith
156th New York Infantry—Capt. James J. Hoyt
175th New York Infantry—(three companies) Capt. Charles McCarthey

Artillery
7th Massachusetts Battery—Capt. Newman W. Storer

26th New York Battery—Capt. George W. Fox
Battery F, 1st U.S. Artillery—Lt. Hardman P. Norris
Battery C, 2nd U.S. Artillery—Lt. John I. Rodgers

Cavalry
3rd Maryland Cavalry—Col. C. Carroll Tevis

Reinforcements ordered to Alexandria from Texas following the battles of Mansfield and Pleasant Hill. They did not actively participate in the campaign farther north and did not participate in the battles of Mansura and Yellow Bayou.

13th Army Corps

Maj. Gen. John A. McClernand

First Division

Second Brigade—Brig. Gen. Michael K. Lawler
49th Indiana— Lt. Col. James Keigwin
69th Indiana—Lt. Col. Oran Perry
34th Iowa—Col. George W. Clark
22nd Kentucky—Col. George W. Monroe
16th Ohio—Lt. Col. Philip Kershner

Operations in Arkansas, April–May 1864

Confederate Forces

Lt. Gen. (later Gen.) Edmund Kirby Smith, Department Commander and Commander of the Army of Arkansas

District of Arkansas—Maj. Gen. Sterling Price

Escort—14th Missouri Cavalry Battalion—Maj. Robert C. Woods

Fagan's Cavalry Division

Brig. Gen. James F. Fagan

Cabell's Brigade—Brig. Gen. William L. Cabell
1st Arkansas Cavalry—Col. James C. Monroe
2nd Arkansas Cavalry—Col. T. J. Morgan

4th Arkansas Cavalry—Col. A. Gordon
7th Arkansas Cavalry—Col. John F. Hill
Trader's Regiment of Arkansas State Troops—Col. W. H. Trader
Gunter's Arkansas Cavalry Battalion—Lt. Col. T. M. Gunter
Blocher's Arkansas Battery

Crawford's Brigade—Col. William A. Crawford
2nd Arkansas Cavalry—Capt. O. B. Tebbs
Crawford's Arkansas Cavalry Regiment—Col. William A. Crawford
Wright's Arkansas Cavalry Regiment—Col. J. C. Wright
Poe's Arkansas Cavalry Battalion—Maj. J. T. Poe
McMurtrey's Arkansas Cavalry Battalion—Maj. E. L. McMurtrey

Dockery's Brigade—Brig. Gen. Thomas P. Dockery
18th Arkansas Mounted Infantry
19th Arkansas (Dockery's) Mounted Infantry—Lt. Col. H.G.P. Williams
20th Arkansas Mounted Infantry
12th Arkansas Mounted Infantry Battalion (Sharpshooters)

Artillery
Hughey's Arkansas Battery—Capt. W. M. Hughey

Marmaduke's Cavalry Division

Brig. Gen. John S. Marmaduke

Greene's Brigade—Col. Colton Greene
3rd Missouri Cavalry—Lt. Col. L. A. Campbell
4th Missouri Cavalry—Lt. Col. William J. Preston
8th Missouri Cavalry—Col. William L. Jeffers
10th Missouri Cavalry—Col. Robert R. Lawther
Harris's Missouri Battery—Capt. S. S. Harris

Shelby's Brigade—Brig. Gen. Joseph O. Shelby
1st Missouri Battalion Cavalry—Maj. Benjamin Elliot
5th Missouri Cavalry—Col. B. Frank Gordon
11th Missouri Cavalry—Col. M. W (or V). Smith
12th Missouri Cavalry—Col. David Shanks
Hunter's Missouri Regiment—Col. DeWitt C. Hunter
Collins's Missouri Battery—Capt. Richard A. Collins

Maxey's Cavalry Division

Brig. Gen. Samuel B. Maxey

Gano's Brigade—Col. Charles DeMorse
- 29th Texas Cavalry—Maj. J. A. Carroll
- 30th Texas Cavalry—Lt. Col. N. W. Battle
- 31st Texas Cavalry—Maj. Michael Looscan
- Welch's Texas Company—Lt. Frank M. Gano
- Krumbhaar's Texas Battery—Capt. W. Butler Krumbhaar

Second Indian Brigade—Col. Tandy Walker
- 1st Choctaw Regiment—Lt. Col. James Riley
- 2nd Choctaw Regiment—Col. Simpson W. Folsom

First Infantry Division—Department of Arkansas

Brig. Gen. Thomas James C. Tappan

Tappan's Brigade—Col. Hiram L. Grinstead
- 19th (Dawson's) and 24th Arkansas Infantry—Lt. Col. William R. Hardy
- 27th and 38th Arkansas Infantry—Col. R. G. Shaver
- 33rd Arkansas Infantry—Col. Hiram L. Grinstead
- Etter's Arkansas Battery—Capt. Chambers B. Etter

Gause's Brigade—Col. Lucien C. Gause
- 26th Arkansas Infantry—Lt. Col. Iverson L. Brooks
- 32nd Arkansas Infantry—Lt. Col. William Hicks
- 36th Arkansas Infantry—Col. James M. Davie
- [? 39th Arkansas Infantry—Col. James W. Rogan?]
- Marshall's Arkansas Battery—Capt. John G. Marshall

Second Division

Brig. Gen. Mosby M. Parsons

First Brigade—Brig. Gen. John B. Clark Jr.
- 8th Missouri Infantry—Col. Charles S. Mitchell
- 9th Missouri Infantry—Col. Richard H. Musser
- Ruffner's Missouri Battery—Capt. Samuel T. Ruffner

Second Brigade—Col. Simon P. Burns
- 10th Missouri Infantry—Col. William M. Moore
- 11th Missouri Infantry—Lt. Col. Thomas H. Murray
- 12th Missouri Infantry—Col. Willis M. Ponder
- 16th Missouri Infantry—Lt. Col. Pleasant W. H. Cumming
- 9th Missouri Battalion Sharpshooters—Maj. Lebbeus A. Pindall
- Lesueur's Missouri Battery—Capt. Alex A. Lesueur

Walker's Texas Division

Maj. Gen. John G. Walker

First Brigade—Brig. Gen. Thomas N. Waul
- 12th Texas Infantry—Col. Overton C. Young
- 18th Texas Infantry—Col. Wilburn H. King
- 22nd Texas Infantry—Col. Richard B. Hubbard
- 13th Texas Cavalry, Dismounted—Col. Anderson F. Crawford
- Haldeman's Texas Battery—Capt. Horace Haldeman

Second Brigade—Brig. Gen. Horace Randal
- 11th Texas Infantry—Col. Oran M. Roberts
- 14th Texas Infantry—Col. Edward Clark
- 28th Texas Cavalry, Dismounted—Lt. Col. Eli H. Baxter Jr.
- 6th (Gould's) Texas Cavalry Battalion—Lt. Col. Robert S. Gould
- Daniel's Texas Battery—Capt. James M. Daniel

Third Brigade—Brig. Gen. William R Scurry
- 3rd Texas Infantry—Col. Phillip N. Luckett
- 16th Texas Infantry—Col. George Flournoy
- 17th Texas Infantry—Col. Robert T. P. Allen
- 19th Texas Infantry—Col. Richard Waterhouse Jr.
- 16th Texas Cavalry, Dismounted—Col. William Fitzhugh
- Edgar's Texas Battery—Capt. William Edgar

Union Forces

Maj. Gen. Frederick Steele, Commander, Department of Arkansas and the Army of Arkansas

Headquarters Escort
- Co. D., 3rd Illinois Cavalry—Lt. Solomon M. Tabor
- Co. H., 15th Illinois Cavalry—Capt. Thomas J. Beebe

Third Division

Brig. Gen. Frederick Salomon

First Brigade—Brig. Gen. Samuel A. Rice
- 50th Illinois Infantry—Lt. Col. Thomas H. Benton Jr.
- 29th Iowa Infantry—Col. Thomas H. Benton Jr.

33rd Iowa Infantry—Maj. Hiram D. Gibson
9th Wisconsin Infantry—Col. C. E. Salomon

Second Brigade—Col. William E. McLean
43rd Indiana Infantry—Maj. Wesley M. Norris
36th Iowa Infantry—Col. Charles W. Kittredge
77th Ohio Infantry—Col. William B. Mason

Third Brigade—Col. Adolph Engelmann
43rd Illinois Infantry—Lt. Col. Adolph Dengler
40th Iowa Infantry—Col. John A. Garrett
27th Wisconsin Infantry—Col. Conrad Krez

Artillery—Capt. Gustave Strange
Battery E, 2nd Missouri Light Artillery—Lt. Charles Peetz
Springfield Illinois Light Artillery (Vaughn's Illinois Battery)—Lt. Charles W. Thomas
Company F, 9th Wisconsin Infantry (Voegele's Wisconsin Battery)—Capt. Martin Voegele

Frontier Division

Brig. Gen. John M. Thayer

First Brigade—Col. John M. Edwards
1st Arkansas Infantry—Lt. Col. Elhanon H. Searle
2nd Arkansas Infantry (eight companies)—Maj. Marshall J. Stephenson
18th Iowa Infantry—Capt. William M. Duncan
2nd Battery, Indiana Light Artillery—Lt. Hugh Espey

Second Brigade—Col. Charles W. Adams
1st Kansas Colored Infantry—Col. James M. Williams
2nd Kansas Colored Infantry—Col. Samuel J. Crawford
12th Kansas Infantry—Lt. Col. Josiah E. Hayes
1st Battery, Arkansas Light Artillery—Capt. Denton D. Stark

Third (Cavalry) Brigade—Lt. Col. Owen A. Bassett
2nd Kansas Cavalry—Maj. Julius G. Fisk
6th Kansas Cavalry—Lt. Col. William T. Campbell
14th Kansas Cavalry—Lt. Col. John G. Brown

Cavalry Division

Brig. Gen. Eugene A. Carr

Co. B., 13th Illinois Cavalry—Capt. Adolph Bechand
3rd Iowa Cavalry (detachment)—Lt. Franz W. Arnim
1st Missouri Cavalry (eight companies)—Capt. Miles Kehoe
2nd Missouri Cavalry—Capt. William H. Higdon

3rd Brigade—Col. Daniel Anderson
10th Illinois Cavalry—Lt. Col. James Stuart
1st Iowa Cavalry—Lt. Col. Joseph W. Caldwell
3rd Missouri Cavalry—Maj. John A. Lennon

Garrison Troops at Pine Bluff

Col. Powell Clayton
18th Illinois Infantry—Lt. Col. Samuel B. Marks
1st Indiana Cavalry (eight companies)—Maj. Julian D. Owens
5th Kansas Cavalry (ten companies)—Lt. Col. Wilton A. Jenkins
7th Missouri Infantry—Maj. Henry P. Spellman
28th Wisconsin Infantry—Lt. Col. Edmund B. Gray

Mississippi Squadron Vessels Deployed in the Red River Campaign, March–May 1864

THE FOLLOWING UNION VESSELS PARTICIPATED IN THE RED RIVER CAMPAIGN. The list includes U.S. naval vessels, U.S. Army Quartermaster Corps vessels, and those of the Mississippi Marine Brigade. An asterisk indicates the vessel was lost during the expedition.

VESSEL NAME	TYPE
Benton	Converted Ironclad
Choctaw	Converted Ironclad
*Eastport**[1]	Converted Ironclad
Essex	Converted Ironclad
Lafayette	Converted Ironclad
Carondelet	Ironclad
Louisville	Ironclad
Mound City	Ironclad
Pittsburg	Ironclad
Chillicothe	Ironclad
Neosho	River Monitor
Osage	River Monitor
Ozark	River Monitor
Black Hawk	Large Tinclad
Ouachita	Large Tinclad
Lexington	Timberclad

Argosy	Tinclad/Stern-wheeler
Avenger	Tinclad/Side-wheeler
*Covington**[2]	Tinclad/Side-wheeler
Fort Hindman	Tinclad/Side-wheeler
Gazelle	Tinclad/Side-wheeler
Cricket	Tinclad/Stern-wheeler
Forest Rose	Tinclad/Stern-wheeler
Juliet	Tinclad/Stern-wheeler
General Bragg	Tinclad/Side-wheeler
Naiad	Tinclad/Stern-wheeler
Nymph	Tinclad/Stern-wheeler
*Signal**[3]	Tinclad/Stern-wheeler
Saint Clair	Tinclad/Stern-wheeler
Tallahatchie	Tinclad/Stern-wheeler
General Sterling Price	Ram/Armed Supply Vessel
New National	Mail/Supply/Receiving Vessel
General Lyon	Ordnance/Stores, Dispatch Vessel
Benefit	River Service Vessel Side-wheeler
William H. Brown	River Service Vessel Stern-wheeler
*Champion No. 3**[4]	Tug/Pump boat/Side-wheeler
*Champion No. 5**[5]	Tug/Pump boat/Side-wheeler
Dahlia	Tug
Fern	Tug
Thistle	Tug
Judge Torrence	Ordnance Boat
Samson	Floating Machine Shop
Alf Cutting	Mississippi Marine Brigade/Tug
Autocrat	Mississippi Marine Brigade/Transport
Baltic	Mississippi Marine Brigade/Transport
Cleveland	Mississippi Marine Brigade/Tug
Diana	Mississippi Marine Brigade/Transport
John Raine	Mississippi Marine Brigade/Transport
Lioness	Mississippi Marine Brigade/Ram
Little Rebel	Mississippi Marine Brigade/Gunboat
T. D. Horner	Mississippi Marine Brigade/Transport
*Woodford**[6]	Mississippi Marine Brigade/Hospital Boat
Bell Darlington	Mississippi Marine Brigade/Tug
Adriatic	U.S. Army QMC Transport Vessel
Alice Vivian	U.S. Army QMC Transport Vessel
Any One	U.S. Army QMC Transport Vessel

Arizona	U.S. Army QMC Transport Vessel
Bella Donna	U.S. Army QMC Transport Vessel
Belle Creole	U.S. Army QMC Transport Vessel
Black Hawk	U.S. Army QMC Transport Vessel
*City Belle**[7]	U.S. Army QMC Transport Vessel
Clarabell	U.S. Army QMC Transport Vessel
Colonel Cowles	U.S. Army QMC Transport Vessel
Des Moines	U.S. Army QMC Transport Vessel
Diadem	U.S. Army QMC Transport Vessel
Emerald	U.S. Army QMC Transport Vessel
*Emma**[8]	U.S. Army QMC Transport Vessel
Gillum	U.S. Army QMC Transport Vessel
Hamilton	U.S. Army QMC Transport Vessel
*Hastings**[9]	U.S. Army QMC Transport Vessel
Henry Chouteau	U.S. Army QMC Transport Vessel
Iberville	U.S. Army QMC Transport Vessel
Ike Davis	U.S. Army QMC Transport Vessel
Illinois	U.S. Army QMC Transport Vessel
J. C. Lacy	U.S. Army QMC Transport Vessel
James Battle	U.S. Army QMC Transport Vessel
Jennie Rogers	U.S. Army QMC Transport Vessel
John H. Groesbeck	U.S. Army QMC Transport Vessel
*John Warner**[10]	U.S. Army QMC Transport Vessel
Kate Dale	U.S. Army QMC Transport Vessel
*La Crosse**[11]	U.S. Army QMC Transport Vessel
Laurel Hill	U.S. Army QMC Transport Vessel
Liberty	U.S. Army QMC Transport Vessel
Louisiana Belle	U.S. Army QMC Transport Vessel
Luminary	U.S. Army QMC Transport Vessel
Madison	U.S. Army QMC Transport Vessel
Mars	U.S. Army QMC Transport Vessel
Meteor	U.S. Army QMC Transport Vessel
Mittie Stephens	U.S. Army QMC Transport Vessel
Pauline	U.S. Army QMC Transport Vessel
Polar Star	U.S. Army QMC Transport Vessel
Red Chief No. 2	U.S. Army QMC Transport Vessel
Rob Roy	U.S. Army QMC Transport Vessel
Sallie Robinson	U.S. Army QMC Transport Vessel
Shreveport	U.S. Army QMC Transport Vessel
Silver Wave	U.S. Army QMC Transport Vessel

Sioux City	U.S. Army QMC Transport Vessel
South Wester	U.S. Army QMC Transport Vessel
Starlight	U.S. Army QMC Transport Vessel
Superior	U.S. Army QMC Transport Vessel
Texas	U.S. Army QMC Transport Vessel
Thomas E. Tutt	U.S. Army QMC Transport Vessel
Universe	U.S. Army QMC Transport Vessel
W. L. Ewing	U.S. Army QMC Transport Vessel

U.S. Navy	42
Mississippi Marine Brigade	11
U.S. Army QMC	51
Total Vessels	104

Notes

1. Sunk April 16, 1864, by Confederate torpedo.
2. Destroyed by Confederate artillery at Dunn's Bayou, twenty miles below Alexandria on May 5, 1864.
3. Destroyed by Confederate artillery at Dunn's Bayou, twenty miles below Alexandria on May 5, 1864.
4. Destroyed by Confederate artillery and infantry at mouth of Cane River on April 26, 1864.
5. Destroyed by Confederate artillery and infantry at mouth of Cane River on April 26, 1864.
6. Ran aground and burned at Alexandria prior to March 27, 1864.
7. Captured by Confederate artillery at David's Ferry (Snaggy Point), thirty miles below Alexandria on May 5, 1864.
8. Destroyed by Confederate artillery at David's Ferry, on May 1, 1864.
9. Snagged and lost at Alexandria April 23, 1864.
10. Destroyed by Confederate artillery at Dunn's Bayou, twenty miles below Alexandria on May 4, 1864.
11. Destroyed by Confederate artillery at Egg Bend April 12, 1864.

RED RIVER CAMPAIGN TIME LINE

March 7	Lead elements of the U.S. 13th and 19th Corps assemble in and near Brashear City (Morgan City). They are five days behind schedule. These troops are to meet the navy in Alexandria on March 17.
March 8	The advance of the column, led by the Cavalry Division of the 19th Corps heads west from Brashear City toward Opelousas.
March 10	U.S. Brigadier General A. J. Smith of William T. Sherman's command (13th, 16th and 17th Corps) leaves Vicksburg aboard transports.
March 11	Evening—Army transports and Mississippi Squadron under Rear Admiral.
	David Dixon Porter rendezvous at mouth of the Red River.
March 12	Combined fleet enters Red River.
	Simmesport secured as bridgehead.
March 13	Advance units of Mississippi Squadron move upriver.
	A. J. Smith moves inland to Marksville after taking four unfinished Confederate forts at Yellow Bayou, two miles from Simmesport.
March 14	Admiral Porter clears piling dam and Smith's forces take Fort DeRussy with support from USS *Eastport.*

	CSA First (Texas) Division under Major General John G. Walker withdraws to Bayou de Glaize.
March 15	Admiral Porter orders USS *Osage* to demand surrender of Alexandria. The town surrenders without firing a shot.
March 15–16	A. J. Smith's men attempt to destroy Fort DeRussy and USS *Benton* and USS *Essex* pound the fort and fail to destroy it.
March 16	CSA Major General Richard Taylor orders forces to gather west of Alexandria and for all Confederate vessels and army units to evacuate the town.
	3rd Division of 16th Corps under Brigadier General Joseph Mower takes control of Alexandria.
	Admiral Porter enters Alexandria with the fleet minus the USS *Benton* and USS *Essex*.
March 16–24	The fleet and Sherman's men at Alexandria stealing 3,000+ bales of cotton from surrounding area.
	Porter monitors the river falling and does understand why it should not be rising following the spring rains.
March 17	Arkansas—Union Major General Frederick Steele orders Brigadier General John Thayer of the Frontier Division to lead a force from Fort Smith to Arkadelphia and link up with him for the drive on Shreveport. Steele, coming from Little Rock is the senior Union commander in Arkansas. His two columns are to join and draw off Confederate forces against Banks.
March 18	CSA Trans-Mississippi Department commander Lieutenant General Edmund Kirby Smith orders a huge transport, the *New Falls City* to be removed from Coushatta Chute (Bayou Coushatta) and to be taken to the foot of Scopini's Cutoff (near the village of Robson in southern Caddo Parish) and to be wedged across the River to block it.
	A chain forged at a local plantation is being strung across the river upstream from the *New Falls City*.
	Smith also orders a dam (the Hotchkiss Dam) at Tone's Bayou (about two miles south of LSU-S on the Port of Shreveport-Bossier property) to be blown up and water diverted from Red River into Bayou Pierre, thus starving the river of water and hopefully trapping the Union fleet.
March 21	CSA 2nd Louisiana Cavalry Regiment under Colonel William Vincent captured at Henderson Hill near Boyce. The Confederates have no reconnaissance arm.

	Union Major General Nathaniel Prentiss Banks, the senior Union army commander leaves Baton Rouge after installing the new governor in office. Rather than march with is men, he ascends the river aboard the *Black Hawk,* a U.S. Army quarter-master vessel. He has with him several cotton speculators.
March 23	Arkansas—Steele leaves Little Rock with his column.
March 25	Lead elements of the 19th Corps Cavalry Division encamp outside Alexandria, seven days late. The Union column extends behind the lead units for about twenty-five miles.
	Banks arrives at the wharf in Alexandria late in the day and is thwarted in cotton stealing by the navy.
	Arkansas—Confederate Brigadier General John Marmaduke sends out units to find the Union columns. Marmaduke is at Camden.
March 26	The last regiments in Banks's column march into Alexandria.
	2,500 African American troops of the Corps d'Afrique arrive by steamboat.
	Banks now has 32,500 combat troops in Alexandria.
	Banks orders the Cavalry Division to advance up-stream to Grand Ecore, the port of Natchitoches. The column follows.
	Porter leaves about half the fleet at Alexandria due to low water. The remainder accompanies the army up the river.
	Banks receives a letter from Lieutenant General U.S. Grant informing him that Sherman's 10,000 veterans must be returned no later than April 15 and that Banks is not to enter Texas.
	Arkansas—Steele reaches Arkadelphia. Thayer is not there.
March 28	The last of the army's column leaves Alexandria that morning.
	Banks stays behind to organize elections.
March 30	Cavalry division arrives in Natchitoches. No Confederates are there.
April 1	Banks holds elections in Alexandria.
	First U.S. infantry units arrive in Natchitoches.
	Banks sends a letter to army Chief of Staff Henry Halleck stating that he would be Shreveport by April 10 and would chase the Confederate army into Texas if needed, ignoring Grant.

	Porter anchors his fleet at Grand Ecore, four miles from Natchitoches.
	Richard Taylor orders the brigades from the Louisiana and Texas Divisions to meet at Mansfield. He also requests that the Texas Cavalry Corps be released for action in Louisiana and that the Arkansas and Missouri Divisions in southern Arkansas be moved to Shreveport and then Mansfield.
	Arkansas—Steele leaves Arkadelphia for Washington, Arkansas, the Confederate provisional capital.
April 2	Banks leaves for Grand Ecore aboard an army transport vessel.
April 3	Banks arrives at Grand Ecore.
April 4	Porter sends a raiding party up stream to Campti where two Confederates are captured.
	Banks decides to hold an election in Grand Ecore.
	Banks receives bad advice about roads and determines to move his army inland away from the protecting guns of the navy.
	Porter and Banks have a conference in which they determine to meet at Springfield Landing (on Smithport Lake in northern DeSoto Parish) on April 10.
	Porter pleads to wait until he can perform an armed reconnaissance along the river, but Banks refuses.
April 5	Banks holds elections at Grand Ecore.
	The Confederate commander of the District of Texas, Major General John B. Magruder, releases the Texas Cavalry Corps under Brigadier General Thomas Jefferson Green, for operations in Louisiana. The cavalrymen leave camp in Hemphill, Texas, and ride toward Logansport.
April 6	The Union Cavalry Division takes the lead west out of Natchitoches along the old Spanish Royal Road (LA Hwy. 6). They turn northwest at White's Store (Robeline) and continue north at Crump's Corner (Bellmont). They then head north on the Natchitoches-Shreveport Stagecoach Road (LA Hwy. 175).
	Green's Texas cavalry reach Keachi where they bivouac for the night.
	The Union Cavalry Division beds down at Pleasant Hill (then in southern DeSoto Parish).

Arkansas—Marmaduke receives reinforcements from the Indian Territory (Oklahoma).

April 7 — Porter selects six gunboats to escort twenty transports up-river for the final push on Shreveport. The river level is too low for his largest vessels.

Green meets Richard Taylor at Mansfield and is ordered to range forward to slow down the Union column.

Taylor picks a large field three miles south of Mansfield to lay his trap for the Federal column.

Green blocks the road at Wilson's Farm, about three miles north of Pleasant Hill. A short fight ensues, delaying the Union column.

Green harasses the Union cavalry for another seven miles until the Federals stop for the night at Carroll Jones's mill, about halfway between Pleasant Hill and Mansfield.

April 8 — Green slows the Union column down for about four hours until they reach Honeycutt Hill, three miles south of Mansfield.

Taylor positions his two divisions of infantry across the road in a giant "L" shape and waits for Banks to attack him.

The Union cavalry Division supported by the small Union 13th Corps prepares a smaller "L" line to respond to the Confederates about noon.

Banks is seven miles behind the forward units. He begins to move forward after reinforcements are requested.

A small division of infantry in the Union 19th Corps is brought up behind the forward line and sets up at Sabine Crossroads (today at the intersection of DeSoto Parish Addison Road and LA Hwy. 175).

Another division is brought forward to the ridge south of Chapman's Bayou.

Kirby Smith refuses to allow the Arkansas and Missouri divisions to come to the battlefield before the battle.

At 4 P.M. the Confederates attack.

The wagon train of the Cavalry Division blocks the road from Honeycutt Hill back more than three miles, keeping adequate reinforcements from coming forward and blocking the retreat of the Union forces.

	Within an hour and a half the initial Union line is destroyed.
	The second Union collapses about 5:30.
	The third Union line is pushed back across Chapman's Bayou and darkness ends the fighting about 7 P.M.
	Confederate casualties are about 1,000 men including 11 field commanders.
	Union casualties are about 2,500 including the commander of the 13th Corps and two of the brigade leaders.
	Arkansas—Steele bridges the Little Missouri River during torrential spring rains.
	Banks leaves the field during the night and withdraws his army to Pleasant Hill.
April 9	At 1:30 A.M. Taylor lays out his plans for the next day's battle.
	At dawn Taylor gives chase and catches Banks army at Pleasant Hill.
	The battle began at 4 P.M. with the Confederates using Taylor's plan of the night before.
	The Arkansas and Missouri divisions attack through the woods on the Confederate right but wheel too soon and enter the battlefield in front of Sherman's men. Taylor did not believe Sherman's men were there, but on the river guarding the fleet. They had always been at the back of the column.
	The Louisiana and Texas divisions attack down the road and the battle ended with darkness as the day before, but this time in a tactical tie.
	Arkansas—Steele and Thayer join. Thayer's column is low on supplies, as is Steele's. Steele sends an empty supply train back for supplies.
April 10	Arkansas—Steele pushes the Confederates back at Prairie d'Ane.
	Kirby Smith removes the Texas, Arkansas, and Missouri divisions from Taylor's command, sends them to Shreveport and prepares for operations in Arkansas.
	Admiral Porter, with six gunboats and twenty transports reaches what he thinks is the mouth of Loggy Bayou. He is in fact four to five miles north of it, one mile south of Tone's Bayou. His progress is stopped by the *New Falls City*.

	A Union cavalry unit finds Porter and tells the army escort of the 17th Corps to return to Grand Ecore, that Banks has met "with a reversal."
	The fleet begins the retreat.
April 11	Arkansas—Confederates abandon Camden and gather at Old Washington.
April 12	Tom Green and 2,500 Texan cavalry attempt to trap the fleet at Blair's Landing (now in southern Red River Parish). Green fights a two and a half battle against the USS *Osage*, the USS *Lexington*, and a transport. There are very few casualties, except Green, who was decapitated by a canister round from the *Osage* in the first use of a periscope in battle.
	Banks's column arrives at Grand Ecore after a three-day retreat. Banks begins to fortify the bluffs.
April 12–13	Arkansas—Steele's combined column enters Camden.
	Kirby Smith sends the Texas, Arkansas, and Missouri divisions to Arkansas via separate routes. The units are to rendezvous at Calhoun, Arkansas.
April 13	Porter's fleet anchors at Grand Ecore at 1 A.M.
April 16	The *U.S.S. Eastport* is sent down river from Grand Ecore before the fleet. Two miles downstream it strikes a mine laid by the CSS *Missouri*, based in Shreveport, before the fleet reached Grand Ecore. Efforts to refloat the vessel take several days.
April 18	Arkansas—Marmaduke destroys Steele's supply train at Poison Spring.
	Arkansas—Steele receives a message from Banks to join him at Grand Ecore. Steele does not comply as he has no supplies and believes there is no way to get them to the South.
April 19	Arkansas—Kirby Smith arrives at Calhoun, Arkansas, with the Arkansas, Texas, and Missouri divisions.
April 21	The *Eastport* is refloated and begins her trek downstream. Efforts to raise the vessel from the shallow river are successful, but the gash in her hull proves a problem. She will almost trap the fleet behind her on several occasions as she makes her way downstream. She will travel another forty miles and become wedged in a logjam near the village of Montgomery (in Grant Parish). All efforts to extricate the vessel are in vain.

Banks moves the column away from Grand Ecore and the river at 5 P.M. A. J. Smith's men torch the buildings of Grand Ecore.

Through the night the column covered twenty miles. They did not torch Natchitoches because Confederate cavalry, now under Brigadier General Major, harasses the rear units.

Banks makes another large tactical error. He moves the column onto Cane River Island, the land between the Cane and Red rivers. He hugs the western road away from the fleet and finds that there are no exits except far to the south at Monett's Ferry (Bluff).

Taylor dispatches cavalry under Brigadier General Hamilton Bee to block Monett's Ferry. The Louisiana Division, under the Prince de Polignac, is sent south to cover any possible crossing north of the ferry. Taylor pleads for the Texas, Arkansas, and Missouri divisions to be returned.

April 23 — Bee fails to stop the Union column from exiting Cane River Island. An African American runaway slave leads the Union troops to a ford behind the Confederates and Bee is outflanked. This is the last great chance to capture Banks's column.

April 25 — The lead elements of Banks's column enter Alexandria.

Arkansas—A second Union supply train is ambushed at Marks' Mill ending hopes of reinforcements for Steele.

April 26 — Arkansas—Steele abandons Camden heading for Little Rock.

Porter decides to destroy the *Eastport* by putting a ton of black powder aboard and detonating it. The fleet loses its most powerful warship.

April 27 — Arkansas—Confederate enter the abandoned Camden.

Confederate cavalry and infantry attack the fleet near the mouth of Cane River. Porter loses the *Champion No. 3* and *Champion No. 5*. The *Cricket* and *Juliet* are heavily damaged.

Porter's fleet limped into the area just above Alexandria in the evening. He finds the river so low that the rocks forming the falls, or rapids, are clearly visible. His fleet is now trapped in two groups, those above the falls and those below. His most heavily armed vessels are above the town.

April 28 — Porter begins to remove guns from the armor plating from ironclads to lighten the vessels.

April 29	Porter and Banks accept a plan by Lieutenant Colonel Joseph Bailey to construct a dam to raise the water level in the Red River and allow the fleet to pass into the deeper water downstream. Construction begins using African American engineering troops of the Corps d'Afrique and Maine troops who were lumbermen.
	Arkansas—Kirby Smith catches Steele's column trying to cross the Saline River at Jenkins' Ferry. Most of the Union column had crossed. Smith makes an ill-fated frontal attack reminiscent of Pickett's Charge at Gettysburg in 1863 and wastes large portion of his three divisions. Two of the three Texas Division brigade commanders are mortally wounded.
	Arkansas—Steele crosses the river and burns his bridges. Kirby Smith has no pontoon bridges and cannot follow. Steele returns to Little Rock.
May 1	Confederate artillery sinks the transport *Emma* at David's Ferry (near Echo).
May 2–9	Bailey's dam is constructed. On May 9, the large dam gave way due to excess water pressure, the device worked too well. Bailey begins to reconstruct the dam and adds two wing dams a short distance upstream to ease the water pressure on the main dam.
May 3	Arkansas—Smith releases the three divisions for operations with Richard Taylor, but they will return too late to have any effect on fighting in Louisiana.
May 4	Confederate artillery sinks the transport *City Belle* at David's Ferry.
May 5	Confederate artillery sinks the *John Warner, Signal,* and *Covington* at Dunn's Bayou.
May 10	The *Lexington,* the monitors *Osage* and *Neosho,* and the iron-clads *Mound City, Carondelet,* and *Pittsburg* cross the falls.
May 13	The first troops of Banks's column leave Alexandria at 7 A.M.
	The *Ozark, Louisville,* and *Chillicothe* cross the falls.
	Union troops set fire to Alexandria and burn most of the business district and downtown residences.
May 15	The *St. Clair* engages Confederate artillery at Eunice's Bluff below Alexandria.
May 16	Richard Taylor attempts to block the Union column at Marksville. The two armies side step each other and the two forces fight an artillery duel at Mansura.

Backflow water from the Mississippi River extends up the Red River to near Alexandria and increases the depth to the extent that the Mississippi Squadron steams downstream and out into the great river without difficulty.

May 18 — The Confederates make a final attempt to halt the retreat of the Union army at Yellow Bayou, two miles west of Simmesport. They fail to stop the Union column.

Union Major General E.R.S. Canby arrives at Simmesport and notifies Banks that he has been fired, the command has been reorganized, and that Banks is now working for him in an administrative capacity.

May 19–20 — High water almost traps the army, but Lieutenant Colonel Bailey again rescues the troops by building a bridge by lashing the army's steamboats together and building a plank road across them. After the last units cross the Atchafalaya River, the steamboats are separated and the Confederates cannot follow. This ends the campaign.

JULIUS L. KNAPP DIARY, JANUARY AND FEBRUARY 1864

Year's diary of 1864 commencing Jan. 1st

At this time the 116th Regt. N.Y.V.[1] are in camp at newtown or more frequently called New Iberia Louisana. the weather being remarkable cold for this climate there is an inch of snow on the ground the most snow seen in this state for fifteen years. we have a fine camp on the banks of biyou[2] Teche a fine country for foraging and handy to our base of supplies[3] and properly speaking everything is handy to accomodate the wants of a soldier and as a person would naturally suppose the time a soldier passes in such a camp as this moves off as rapidly as a pleasant dream the first day of the new year many of the boys in the regiment wanting some amusement indulged rather freely in wines & had as a natural consequence before all was over there was one or two black eyes in the regt. there was a little incident occured which I deam worthy of mention although the weather was freezing cold one of the boys to avoid punishment swam the biyou with his clothes all on a distance of two hundred feet and remained with his clothes on for nearly an hour. when he was brought back with a boat and the next day was ready for duty feeling as well as ever.

On the 2nd there was nothing of importance going on in camp the boys taking this day to get over NewYears.

3RD

Some talk of a move in the morning but proves not true. inspection in the morning by Major Sentell on general Fmmorys Staff.[4]

4TH

a very rainy and dull day in camp the boys go across the biyou and kill a beef in the afternoon and we had a beef steak fly in the evening in generally

5TH

cloudy and dull in the morning and at night commences raining and freezes as it falls and the next morning everything is icy around camp

6TH

we have orders to break camp at daylight and after our tents are all taken down we recieve orders to put them up and the move is postponed until tomorrow another dissappointment for a soldier but being use to it we take it all in good humor and go to work putting up our tents again although many of the men slept without a bed being so confident of moving that they burned up their straw and boards (alas what an unfortunate being a soldier is)

7TH

we break camp again at daylight form line at 7 A.M. and march 12 miles towards the village of Franklin[5] and bivouac for the night in a large sugar mill although the mill was a very large one with the whole regiment we had to sleep as I used to hear the expression three in a bed and two in the middle.

8TH

we woke early in the morning and cooked our cup of coffee took our piece of Salt Pork and hard Tack. And took an easy position on the ground and eat our breakfast, but I will assure you that what little we had for breakfast did not take us long to dispense of. and in a short time we were all ready for a start, but no sooner ready than the order came to fall in when we shouldered our knapsacks and were soon upon the road we marched ten miles and halted for the night within 4 miles of Franklin the boys confiscating honey and chickens enough upon the march to have a gay supper.

9TH

we renew the march at 7 A.M. and arrive in Franklin about 10 A.M. and commence stealing boards to build our tents but our fun was stopped about noon by the guards.

10TH

myself and tentmate make a raft and go across the biyou[6] after a load of lumber and have a very good sucess but not being sailers our raft near drowns us on the way back but after a desperate time we succeed in getting the rest of our lumber across, with a wet shirt as compensation for stealing the lumber from a loyal Secessionish.

11TH

Hearing we were to stay in this camp we busy ourselves all day in bringing brick and lumber across the biyou, Just across from our camp there was a large brick Kiln which supplied the whole army for material for chimneys, but we had to bring our boards about a mile on our backs and then raft them across the biyou the best way we could. Our mode of taking brick across was to fill a sugar tub full and then paddle them across with a piece of board for in this country canoe or boat was all out of fashion.

12TH

We commence putting up our tents and get them pretty well started when we hear we are not to stay in this camp, we then conclude to fix up for a few days and let the tent go

13TH

very rainy and muddy we amuse ourselves by laying in our tents and read novels smoke our pipes and talk over old times, hardly willing to go out for our grub,

14TH

we hear we are to move only a short way and our things are to be carried we go over and get another load of brick in the forenoon, in the afternoon four companies move over to the new camp our company one of them

15TH

The rest of the regiment moves over in the morning we commence building our tent and work hard all day and are very tired at night.

16TH

we finish the tents. the most of them and commence ditching and grading the company streets we are in a very nice grove and the men are resolved to have a fine camp.

17TH

all quiet in camp no drill on account of the streets not being finished I go on a foraging in the afternoon and get a good amount of sweet potatoes.

18TH

There is a large detail out of each company to police the entire camp which occupies the most of the day.

19TH

Mail arrives in the morning with letters the boys take most of the day in Reading and answering them, nothing special going on in camp.

20TH

Inspection in the morning at ten o'clock the regiment is inspected by Luient Clark[7] our Col. leaves Staf, they are pronounced in good Style.

21ST

Regiment commences drilling for the first time in this camp. Sutlers arrives from New Orleans

22ND

Company drill in the forenoon and are ordered to get ready in the afternoon for Sundays inspection the boys all busy in washing and cleaning their things.

23RD

the inspection is postponed the 26th company drill in the forenoon the rest of the day spent in cleaning camp.

24TH

Inspection in the morning at ten o'clock the regiment pronounced in very good condition.

25TH

the regiment company drill in the forenoon and in the afternoon prepare for a review on Tuesday

26TH

The regiment form line at 9 A.M. and at ten are upon the review ground received by General Emmery

27TH

Mail arrives from home in the morning I receive a letter from brother henry, weather extremely warm.

28TH

the rest of the brigade moves their camp there is prospects of rain. Company drill in the forenoon and afternoon.

29TH

Rainy and muddy in the morning so there is no regular guard mounting but clears away and the sun comes out warm in the afternoon

30TH

This is a rainy and muddy day and there is nothing of importance going on in camp

31ST

Inspections in the morning at ten o'clock the wind blows like a hurricane in the afternoon this ends the month of January 1864

FEBRUARY 1864

The second month of the year

first day finds the camp of the 116th N.Y.V. in a State of for nothing exciting going on. Company drill in the forenoon, Battalion drill in the afternoon.

2ND

We awake in the morning and find a rather Sudden change in the weather. the day before being a most remarkable pleasant one it commences to rain about 8 A.M. and forces a very uncomfortable day in camp.

3RD

Weather more agreeable company drill in the forenoon and in the afternoon we prepare for a parade on the ? we are now in camp within one half mile of the village of Franklin and about once a month it is our misfortune to have a parade down town and back with our gayest uniform Shining boots black big thing you must fix up gay boys for you are going to parade by the Generals Head quarters.

4TH

Every thing checks charmingly we form line at 9 A.M. and are soon upon the march. pass through town and back arrived in camp about 1 P.M. and the rest of the day is to our own pleasure.

5TH

Company drill in the forenoon also in the afternoon Capt. having arrived to the regt also Capt Clark[8] having been home on a furlough.

6TH

Company drill in the forenoon and the afternoon is taken for getting for inspection on Sunday.

7TH

Regimental inspection at ten A.M. and the company Streets are inspected at 12 A.M. the regiment is pronounced in fine condition.

8TH

A general review at 11 in the fornoon on the old review ground we are reviewed by Major General Chamberlin[9] return to camp about 8 P.M.

9TH

the regiment goes on a foraging expedition with two days rations but having good Success we return the Same evening about nine oclock.

10TH

there is no drill today the boys have chickens the most of them for dinner having gobled them the day before a foraging. I got Seven chickens and make a coop and keep 5 of them about a month. three of the hens lays every day which of course gives me Eggs for breakfast every morning.

11TH

Company drill in the forenoon and also in the afternoon Some of the boys being detailed in erecting Ornaments this being a fine camp the men are erecting Ornaments at the end of each company Street

12TH

Weather fine and in the forenoon there is company drill but no drill in the afternoon the boys have a match game of base ball.

13TH

Drill in the forenoon but the camp is policed in the afternoon Capt Morgan[10] Starts for Baton Rouge for the knapsacks at night.

14TH

Brigade review at 10 A.M. and after review we go down town on parade and arrive back to camp about 3 P.M.

15TH

Rainy and muddy in the forenoon the boys having the day to themselves it clears away in the afternoon and the prospects are good at night for a fine day tomorrow

16TH

Weather fine but rather cool the officers of our regiment have a match game of ball with the officers of the 30th Mass.[11] Battalion drill in the afternoon

17TH

Nothing of importance going on in camp drill in the forenoon and the afternoon is given to the boys for their own amusements.

18TH

30th Mass Regt. departs for home our Brigade escorts them down to the boat also the third Brigade extremely cold for this country.

19TH

Company drill in the forenoon and dress parade at 5 P.M. General Enmmbry [*sic*] Franklin and McMellan[12] there to it also many other officers from the 19th corps. they pronounced it the best drilled regiment in the 19th Army Corps.

20TH

company drill in the forenoon and the afternoon taken up in policing the camp and cleaning up for inspection.

21ST

Inspection in the morning at ten A.M. preaching in camp in the evening by the chaplin of the 30th Mass. my first day with the fever and ague,[13]

22ND

Washington birthday a Salute of the guns fired at Sunrise all the troops of Emmorys command Stand under arms during the firing of the Salute at 12 A.M. the third Salute at Sundown

23RD

Nothing of importance going on in camp mail arrives from the north a Small one I have the Second attack of the ague weather very fine

24TH

Captain Seymore[14] arrives from home being absent on a furlough Company drill in the forenoon and Battallion drill in the afternoon.

25TH

Leiut Morgan returns from Baton Rouge with the knapsacks. the men busy all day in examing them and cleaning their clothes.

26TH

Inspection in the morning at ten oclock we are inspected by Col. Dwight. pass a very rigid inspection Dolan[15] and myself busy the rest of the day fixing drums,

27TH

Regiment goes on a foraging expedition and return about 9 A.M. with rather poor success I did not go not being very well.

28TH

The regiment being out late the night before there is no inspection as usual there is nothing Special going on in camp Dress Parade at 5 P.M. with the usual amount of Spectators.

29TH

Company drill in the forenoon. and in the afternoon we are mustered for pay now having four months pay due us and the prospects are good for us to wait two months more. Monthly Inspection is the close of Feburay 1864.

Diary Entries commencing April 23, 1864

23D

All quiet in camp the boys fix up their tents expecting to Stay here a Spell they go to the woods and cut Brush and make Shades for their tents Orders for to turn in all the wagons except two weather very fine.

24TH

The Officers commence making out new Pay Rolls to fill the Place of Some lost on a boat coming down from Alexandria five new recruits arrive to the regiment, every thing quiet along the river large amounts of Supplies arrive from New Orleans

May 25th

We draw full rations of every thing the first time we have done it in a long time. one Brigade of the 13th Army Corps takes transports and go down the river their destination Supposed to be Carlton.[16]

26th

I go to the Division comisaries and get rations in the morning every thing quiet in camp the only excitement going on is fishing in the missippi river and this is rather to Slow work for any amusement

27th

Another Brigade of the 13th Army Corps takes transport for the lower part of the Missippi River. we Practice two hours in the course of the day mail arrives in the afternoon weather very warm

28th

Every thing quiet in camp I write four letters which Ocupy the most of the day. 29th Maine Sutter arrives from New Orleans with a large Supply of Sutler Stores.

29th

three Brigades of the 13th Army Corps moves their camp from about two miles up the river down oposite us and go into camp. they rally on Some of the barns and fendes belonging to the old Farmers near by and put up comfertable quarters. three boats come down the river from Vicsburg Loaded with commisary Stores. weather very fine but warm.

30th

The 13th Army Corps goes on a reconnoisance with two days rations with the cavalry intending to capture two thousand Rebels. but this reconnoisance like many others proves to be a failure we have a heavy thunder Shower in the afternoon.

31st

We draw rations of flour for two days in the morning, Capt. Cerpenteris on pickett Frank Bartell goes back to Stay the Colonel as Orderly, the 13th Army Corps returns to camp at night being perfectly worn out from their march in persuit of the Rebels. they go into camp Just across the road from our Brigade.[17]

Notes

1. New York Volunteer Infantry Regiment.
2. Bayou.
3. The supply base was at Breashear City, today Morgan City, in St. Mary Parish, Louisiana.
4. This is Major W. H. Sentell, of 160th New York Volunteer Infantry. Brigadier General William H. Emory commanded the First Division of the 19th Army Corps.
5. Franklin, the parish [county] seat of St. Mary Parish, is located to the west of Morgan City.
6. Bayou Teche.
7. Unless this is Captain Orton S. Clark (see note 9), which it does appear to be, this Lieutenant Clark is unknown in the roster of the 116th New York and is not mentioned in Richard B. Irwin's *History of the Nineteenth Army Corp* (Baton Rouge, 1985).
8. This is Captain Orton S. Clark. Clark entered service as a sergeant and rose to the rank of captain. See Record Group 04, Microscopy 551, Roll 25, National Archives and Records Administration. After the war, Clark published a history of the regiment. See *The One Hundred and Sixteenth Regiment of New York Volunteers* (Buffalo, NY, 1868).
9. This is possibly Brigadier General (later Major General) Augustus Louis Chetlain, who at that time was based in Memphis.
10. There is no Captain Morgan on the rolls of the 116th New York. This officer may be a staff officer of the brigade or division. The closest name in Irwin's *History of the Nineteenth Army Corps* is Major Morgan Morgan Jr. of the 176th New York Infantry Regiment.
11. The 30th Massachusetts Infantry Regiment was part of the First Brigade, First Division, of the Nineteenth Corps. It was sent back for duty at Galloupe's Island in Boston Harbor prior to the Red River Campaign.
12. Brigadier William H. Emory, commander of the First Division of the 19th Army Corps, Major General William Buel Franklin, commander of the 19th Army Corps, and Brigadier General James W. McMillan, commander of the Second Brigade of the First Division of the 19th Army Corps.
13. Ague is the common name given to a form or stage of malarial disease; the ague fit is the cold, shivering stage, and hence the word is also loosely used for any such malady.
14. This is Captain Elisha W. Seymour, who commanded Company D of the 116th. He entered service as a 2nd Lieutenant and achieved the rank of Captain. See Record Group 94, Microscopy 551, Roll 126, National Archives and Records Administration.

15. This is John Dolan of Company C of the 116th. He is listed as a drummer and rank of musician. See Record Group 94, Microscopy 551, Roll 37, National Archives and Records Administration.
16. Carollton, near New Orleans.
17. During June, the 116th New York remained in southern Louisiana. In July, the 19th Corps was ordered to Virginia and embarked for Washington. Upon its arrival there it marched through Maryland and participated in Sheridan's campaign in the Shenandoah Valley. The regiment was heavily engaged at the Battle of the Opequan, was present at Fisher's Hill, at New Market, and at Cedar Creek.

Sidney Harding Diary Entries before March 1864 and after the Campaign

July 1863–Thursday 21st

Left home this evening. Johnny Peters in the carriage with us. Got here late. W.F. not home yet. Follow on horse back. 18 Miles from home. prarie house.

Friday 22nd

W. F. got here early. Cousin M.,[1] Lefy, Ma and myself Went to New Town[2] to auction. Capt. Gouds[3] left the young soldiers here. Everyone up in arms about my hair. Bought nothing at the auction. Everthing this morning went up large quantities. Merchants bought open for Ladies at B.[4] Capt. Barnes,[5] Leut Morse,[6] Cos.[7] Alfred's family dined at Aunt M's. All made such a fuss at the loss of my hair that I felt like sticking my poor head in some porch hole. All said I looked ugly. Lut. M.[8] tried to console me. I only regret because Ma does so much. Went again to auction. So crowded-things so dear we soon came back. Liked Leut. M. very much. Thought he sat up to me. Aunt M. gave ma a dress. Got to the P.'s house late.[9] Lt. L. much amused. The sick mouths ate five water melons. Start on our weary journey in the morning.

Saturday 23rd

Started this morning sick. Two sick boys passed all artillery. Saw Capt. Fries.[10] Could not get any of these miserable arcadians,[11] only people living along here, to take us in. Young men very angry. We slept in car—they on the ground.

Sunday 24th

Travelled on slowly. Came near being upset. Boys very uneasy about furlough. Fraid they cant get out of going to Mrs. Offutts. Met Capt. Furman[12] at gate. Glad to see him. Three miles of boys gone there. Capt. P[13] came to the gate to meet us. Oh, so handsome. All seemed glad to see us. Both captains staid had a pleasant evening. Louis talked till late. Capt. F. Left. Louis[14] is too handsome. Mary P's[15] very pretty. All quite a very pleasant family. Aaron[16] got home from V's. David Magill[17] killed. Poor fellow, no one to grieve. I do not know what I feel while talking to L.P.[18] Oh, I fear to say that I think too much of him.

Monday 25th

Left Mrs. O's[19] this morning for Col. Ash's[20] on the wayside. Rained, obliged to stay. Very kind. All plain people. Am disappointed at not returning this evening. L. said he would try to get off from camp and be there.

Tuesday 26th—Washington

Here we are again. Got here this morning. Had a delightful day. Plaiting a palmetta hat for Base.[21] After dinner Mrs. F. O., S. O, E.P and myself took a ride to camp. [Colonel William] Vincent[22] rode right to Capt. P's tent. He came up called Capt. F. Capt. Barrow,[23] then L. said he didn't know whether could go home, unless I asked the Col. Oh no Col. V. will think it strange. No, he said. I said, now would you like your sisters to do so.—Yes you know me so well and Cos.[24] too, but I did not go. Begged me to stay tomorrow and he and Capt. F. would get off to see me. They kept up till late. would not let us go. Saw all my friends., Lt. Kelly,[25] Mr. Labarre, L. Willy M. and B. Marshall.[26] Said he would try to get off to go with us tomorrow. Hope he can. Lt. K did not want to see me. My hair cut. They all will never cease talking about it. I told them they were the most impolite set in the world, to make remarks about it. Capt. F and L. said they, regretted the pretty hair, not my good looks, for I had then still. But I disliked to tell them all goodbye. L said he would try to steal off. Which he did after supper. Made himself agreeable as usual. Told me to beg Ma[27] to stay. Oh, what makes me write of him so much. I hope I am not in love.

Wednesday

Left the Offertts before breakfast. Sissy[28] and Mrs. O up. had nice coffee and biscuits. Nice lunch put up. Oh what kind people. Passed by Camp Bayou between. Benny Marshall did not come. I am so sorry. A nice pleasant soldier to protect us would be Pleasant indeed.

Stopped to rest. Gentleman sent nice piece of watermelon. Servant said name Co. Moss. Packing house man very common looking. Sent him some lunch. Was giving us peaches. Seemed to take us under his wing. Mended the carriage. I was anxious to get rid of him. Rode till late. Stopped near Mr. Prescott's. Sent to ask if Mr. Willis would not let us stay. Came out and said certainly. L. told us to come here. W. was very kind. Sat up till late talking. Old servant going to put us up a lunch. Oh those peaches made me feel so badly. What if I should be sick here. No one but a young man. Well, we will start at daylight on our weary way.

THURSDAY 28TH

Got up very early. Had a nice cup of coffee. Willis kept us talking till after sunrise. Very pleasant. Not handsome like L. Oh no, but all so good and frank and kind. Met with old Moss again but we stopped and he rode before us. Stuck in the mud. Hope old black taken sick. Ma's. old net stopped miles below Chennyville[29] to eat dinner. Looked up and who should I see but Willis['] brother Loloy [?]. Yes Mas. L. in C.[30] Waiting for us. Moss told him we were coming. All well at home. We went near C and sent for him. Dear old fellow, we've not seen him for three months. Looks very rough-Texas. Going to join Louis Prescott's company. We only saw him half an hour. Had to go. Horses little gall been splendid. Pony dead. Stopped at Mr. G's to stay all night. Old lady was very kind said yes. But the dyptheria and pneumonia was there, so we cam[e] on here to Mrs. Lloyds—Large home, rather common.[31] Gave us supper.

FRIDAY 29TH

Left Mrs. L's early. No lunch. Stopped bought some buttermilk, and bread from an old negro. Asked at Mrs. M. Stafford's for some peaches. Sent us a basket of splendid ones. Ate all the way

All the dinner we had. Stopped in the woods to rest and a man with a waggon stopped— Texan came to the carriage. I was frightened—thought how defenseless we were, but he was very polite I gave him some peaches, and he moved off. Oh what beautiful places on Bayou B.[32] —The M's, Mrs. F's Gen. B's, Mr. W's, S's and lastly Mrs. A. Prescott's, where we stopped. The ladies all gone to their cousins who has died. The old gentleman so kind and polite. The young misses there, Rosa and Georgie Villain. Went in the-room to change my dress. Mrs. John Prescott came back. The others staid all night. She is a nice little thing, quite pretty. Mr. J. P.'s[33] cordial. I like the rest. The little V's, 15, 8, 13 are great talkers. We have had a very pleasant evening. Will stay here tomorrow. Old black came—the carriage broken.

SATURDAY AUGUST 1ST

Mr. & Mrs. Prescott went off early today—at daylight to the funeral. Old Mr. P. entertained us very pleasantly till eleven or twelve when Mrs. P and Mrs. Griffin, the governess, came for Mr. P has the dropsy[34] very badly and is very large. He is in very delicate health. They lost their only daughter nineteen years old, three years ago. Poor things, they have her rooms just as she left it. No one ever occupies it since. Her graveyard beautifully fixed. Miss G.—her governess always to live with them. She took me in her room— beautifully furnished. They idolize her. Mrs. P is a splendid ho[u]se keeper Everything so nice on the table and house handsomely furnished. Old Mr. P. commodore, big general and the like says I have such a commanding appearance and my hair short I ought to get up a brigade of bloomers and go to the war. He is so kind.

Sunday August 2nd 12 O'Clock

Left Mr. Prescott's this morning. Sorry to leave. Never saw a Prescott I did not like. All have the same kind friendly manners. Perhaps it is because I like one so much. Mrs. P. put up a nice lunch of ham, mutton, biscuit and butter and a nice watermelon, which we have just broken on the ground and eaten some. Waiting here for the horses to rest. Will go to Judge B's or Mr. Bowles this evening. Got here at Judge Boya's[35] late this evening. Heard his daughters were here. Hated to get out, knowing them. The Judge not in, Mrs. Clark very kind. Judge came in. Changed dresses, saw Mr. & Mrs. Lindsey very crosseyed, hair short, very ugly Young White ugly but very kind.

Tuesday Aug. 4th

Left early through pine woods. Very steep places Get in and out all the time. Cross the ferry Asked several places if we could stay. Refused. Did not know what to do. Got to Chaucheville.[36] Afraid to go to hotel. Asked nice house. Very kind indeed—french—several ladies. Leave soon in the morning. Name Benor

Wednesday Aug. 5th

Left very early. Went through the cut-off. Crossed the ferry early. Intended going to the Paud home. Stopped and changed dresses in the carriage. Got there just at twelve. Very warm. Ma said she hated to stop. I said, well don't let's stop when she go[t] provoked. We drove past her she said we had made her dress uselessly and she had rather go. She got in one of her contrary humors, but it ended in our going. Received very kindly. Asked us to stay to dinner, which we did. Very agreeable time. Much more so than waiting ender the trees. Miss Hattie P and Miss Archinard are very pleasant girls. Left after dinner. Old gentleman invited us to stay several days, but did not. Wanted to get to Mrs. Hiams early so as to go on if not invited to stay. Horses gave out before we got near Natch[itoches]—would not go dark mile from there. Stopped to stay. Young men came out said he did not live there but knew we could not get accomodations. Said he would lend us his mules. Leave the horses to be sent for. Exceedingly polite. Said he would ride there with us. Oh, no too much trouble, but he insisted Very nice young man. Had some trouble finding Mrs. H's.[37] Hotel not fit for ladies. Hated to go to Mrs. H's. Had not called before, but had to get there. All cried out there. Aunt Emily received us kindly, Chauncey and Henry there. Jill not go very early.

Friday Aug. 7th

Left Mrs. H's after breakfast. L.H. a very sweet girl. C. very sweet face. Henry a perfect monkey. Red headed, freckled face. Mrs. H. quite handsome. Went to all the stores. Did not buy much. Caught in a rain. Hills very slippery, hard to travel on. [A]Bout three miles in pine woods, soldier asked to let him ride. Afraid to at first, but at last let him drive. Crippled, can't walk. At last he got an ambulance. Stopped out, the rain started. Had to get out and walk up a steep slippery hill. Oh how I disliked it. The first thing I did was to come down sprawling fast filled with this horrid mud. Delightfu[l] situation. Well we got up that one but had to undergo the same thing every half mile. Expected to get to Mrs. Elzie's boarding house by night, but dark caught us out in the pine woods. These miserable woods. Horses almost given out. Oh me, I was so disgusted, but no[t] much frightened. Tho heard there were 4 diserters. Every-thing seemed so quiet. Came to a steep hill when not another step would old black-Dave[38] take Whipped and coaxed but no use. Put S. In but there we stuck. Took all the things out. We all got out. Ma led, D. pushed, I whipped. Anyone coming up would have enjoyed the scene. At last poor Ma. mounted the box, but no use.

At last we gave it up and got in the carriage to sleep. Oh how miserably I felt.— So defenseless. I thought I would stay awake and think over our misfortunes, but "Nature's sweet restorer" came to my assistance and all was sunk in oblivion till "crack", something went in the woods. Oh Lord I thought we were gone, but only some tree Did not sleep after that. Tried to get up about daylight, but just as bad as ever. Horses would not budge. We sat down in despair, when a man drove up in a waggon. Sent Dave off for assistance. When the wagonner came back to us Ma says "He is coming to rob us". Oh no, "I don't think so, Ma. He came to offer to take the car up with his mules" Which he did. Stopped at Mrs. E. Never asked us to breakfast. The meanest people in these pine woods, I ever saw. We started off on our weary travels once more— tired enough. Had not gone far when another steep hill. We got out. I had on a pair of India rubbers—not tied.[39] When down I went in the mud. Left shoes had to pull off my stockings and take it barefooted. Oh, I wish you could have seen me trailing up this steep assent barefooted—dressed up and a chock in my hand. Did I ever expect to be so situated. Just got into the carriage. So muddy but I almost cried I was so outdone. Had not come much further when old Smith was found too sick to travel. When here we have to stop with the most miserably poor people I ever knew. Quite a nice house, but nothing in it but two or three poor looking beds, two chairs, knives and forks, three or four plates a dirty woman, five dirty little children (always eating raw onions) one table and that is all. Their few clothes piled up on bed or floor. I never dislike anything as much as staying here.

Saturday August 8th

Here we are at Dr. Wilson's. Left Mr. Blakinchip[40] early. She put us on a mattress but so dirty, we put shawls and skirts on the floor, but so hard and bed bugs so bad, I couldn't sleep. Sat up on the floor and actually cried. Never felt so miserable, Old Smith died. Had no breakfast. Intended getting to Mrs. Glassell's[41] but it rained. Stopped at Mrs. Wilson's.[42] Quite nice people. Everything very nice and clean here. We will stay till morn. Had a very nice supper.

SUNDAY AUGUST 9TH

Had a very fatiguing trip today. Found them all at prayers. House full of company. Went right into Cos. Maggie's room. Another outcry about my having cut off my hair. I get sick and tired of hearing of it. Dressed for dinner. Cos. M. very anxious that I should make a good appearance among the Mansfield folks. Introduces to Major Ashton.[43] quite handsome. Mrs. Ashton not pretty, Black hair, grey eyes. Two Maj[or]s. Gibbs,[44] ugly. Light hair,— eyes. Major Triom[45]— same. Did not have much idea of entertaining. Went off to themselves. I read my prayers and a sermon.

None of the young folks ready for prayers. Major A.[46] slept in the parlor so it is well we were not. Most of the girls went off to themselves again. Major A. read some beautiful pieces of poetry written by himself-really pretty. Reads them so well, I would give, oh so much to be able to produce rhyme. He read some time to Meta, Thom and me. Then a great waiter of peaches came in. I peeled some for poor Major. They were soon all eaten. They're such plain country ways of doing everything here. No order, not much comfort, no pretension, but every kindness. Everyone does as he pleases at Liberty Hall. Going home to Moskow.[47] Maj. A. going with us on way to Monroe.

Had a very gay evening. Sloppy Gibbs sang. then we had a dance. Maj. A. asked me. He is very graceful. Does not miss his arm. Is as active as a two arm man. Then he sang several songs. The gayest young man I ever saw. Reminded me of Lewis C.—more gentlemanly and polite. The prayer bell rang in the midst of it all. Oh what reading and prayers Mr. G.[48] does make.— So stupid.[49]

TUESDAY AUG. 11TH

Here we are at old Keachie place.[50] Really delighted to get back and such a trip up as we had. We started about nine o'clock with mules that stopped at the first hill. When out we had to come and this it was nearly all the way. It was so warm but the Major was so polite and entertaining. Such a time as we had. So relieved when we saw the old dark looking log house. Had quite a nice dinner. I cut up his meat, poor fellow. I feel so sorry for him. Ma, of course never could remember his name. It was Mr. Major all the time. Amused us very much. Sister A.[51] gone to the Marshall's.[52] Well I am really glad to be back again like the place so much. Spent a very pleasant evening.

THURSDAY OCT. 7TH

Ma., Sis A. gone to Shreveport. Had a quiet day. Sewed and tried to draw. Succeeded quite well. Would give anything to do it well.

FRIDAY OCT 8TH

Busy as usual sewing, reading, drawing. Cos. Charley came in this eveing en route to Shreveport. Got a note from Maj. A. saying the Prescott's had left Mrs.

G's and we must come. Cos. C. came back in evening. Said we had whipped the Yanks near Franklin. Took 400 prisoners.[53]

Saturday Oct 11th

Just returned from Mrs. Glassel's. Had a pleasant trip, but got tired and homesick. Arrived there Monday night after they had all gone to bed. I wished to sleep in the carriage instead of distrubing them, but Sis. A. said that would not do. Maj. A. and Julia A. soon came out. Had not gone to bed. Then Cos. M[54] and Mrs. G. got supper for us. Sat an hour or two talking. Then retired. Cos Mag staid in our room till late talking. Tuesday we got up very early. Knitted, talked and layed till after dinner when Mrs. G., Miss J. A and M. T. went to see the Prescott girls at their camp. Had a fine dinner. Johnny's birthday. A terrible road. I said I bet A. P[55] would run if he saw us. Sur[e] enough we saw him running off to the woods. The girls seemed very glad to see me. Said they could not come home with me now but would come to see me soon. Felt like meeting home folks. Different from the people up here. Said, they would to Mrs. G's the next day to see the Yankee prisoners who were coming up to Mans.[56] 400 of them. Did not stay long. Maj. A and Sis A. set up right smart to each other. I was in hopes she would be more dignified than other widows, but she does not mind being plagued, about a man so much younger than herself and so dissipated. We had a nice dance after super Cos. M. played. Sis A. danced the wild irishman. J.A. is very lively. Not pretty. Very indifferent. Says just what she has a mind to, whether she hurts their feelings or not. M.T. is a very nice girl. Quiet, very ugly. Not very smart.

Wednesday .

The Prescott girl came early, but ? had gone up. They looked so pretty. M particularly. So different from the girls up here. I felt like being with home folks with them. They seemed to feel the same with us. Just as they were going away in the evening, Audrey said the Y.[57] had passed. It was too late to go tho. Made an arrangment to meet them in Mansfield. Mary does look so much like L. Perhaps that is why I like her so much. I hope not. I allow myself to think too much of him. They promised to pay me a visit soon. Took a ride with J.A and M. T. Met a handsome stranger.

Thursday

Got up at daylight to go to M's. Would have prepared to continue on home but thought we would have to carry some of the ladies back to Mrs. G's. Sis Aand self went to see some of the 2nd La.,[58] who they said were guarding them. J. A and Miss Page did not get up to go. M. T. Nelly, Maj. A and myself went in our carriage. Sis A., Cos. M. the children in the other. Maj. A. told me he would not ride in Cos. M's carriage as she had talked about him. Got to town.[59] Found the prisoners would be there all day. Went out to the shoe store. The others went up. M. and myself stayed in carriage. A soldier passed whom I addressed very politely thinking him to be ours. When to our horror found him to be a Yankee. Said no more to him. As we were going to camp, met Maj. Cushmere,[60]

Miss Gibbs, Capt. Morehead.[61] They got in and went down with us. I was dreadfully disappointed at finding none of the 2nd La. there. Did not address any of the wretches— miserable looking creatures.

Also Omitted at the End of Diary in 1864

SOMETIME IN JUNE OR JULY
DATE ?

? went below today. No one sorry. Some servants came for milk for wounded soldiers at Parson's camp, three miles below. Told us when they were wounded who they were and everything. We felt so sorry concluded to ride down and bring them up—The soldiers were surprised when we asked. Said none had been there. All a story of negroes. The Maj. spent evening with us again. Sang many songs oh so beautifully. I never had anything give me more pleasure.

AUGUST OR SEPTEMBER?
THURSDAY ?

Mr Crawford came today. Said the prisoners would be in Shreveport tomorrow. Mr Edwards, one of them, sent word. Oh what an excitement for us. Ma imagines that L. will not be on the boat.[62] Is afraid to hear. Fears that he is left in the city dead or sick. But Oh, I know he is there and am impatient for tomorrow.

FRIDAY ?

Anxious and excited all day. Heard nothing more. Mr. E did not come home. I've been busy tying a straw bonnet. It is very troublesome . . . particularly at this time. I do not like sewing and wish very much that I had someone to do it for me. I always get out of patience. Oh me, I wish I had more.

SATURDAY ?

This morning Mrs. C sent us word that Mr. E. had come. We wrote a note immediately. Oh we waited so breathlessly for the boy's return. I was anxious then, so afraid he would say Lyman was not there. But Oh joy, ? brother is at Mrs. Watsons. Will be down this evening. Such the ? of his note. Who can tell our joy. I took a bath, and dressed for him. Then he rode up, looking so handsome. We showered him with questions.

SUNDAY

Ma and myself persuaded L to go to church today. I was so proud walking in with him. He had a very hard time of it. Our Lady friends in the city were so friendly to him. . . . God bless them for it. Poor S. Frerman left in N. O. with smallpox. I feel so sorry for them. How will I ever be able to thank God enough. Took communion for the first time.

DATE (CHRISTMAS?)

Was waked up early by Base. running or dancing in to show the contents of his stocking. Poor little darling. We always manage to get something for him. Went to church. Heard a splendid sermon, but when did Mr. Sandal give any other. The rest of the day spent exactly like any other. We invited the little Couriers to dine with us. They did not come. Oh if we could only have had the boys with us.

DATE ?

I cannot tell what it is that oppresses me so, I felt bowed down with low spirits most all the time. Feel perfectly miserable at times, so homesick and tired of this miserable place. When will we ever leave it. And then I think so much of the sinful usless life I am leading.

DATE (NEW YEARS EVE?)

Here is the end of 64. No changes for us in the Confederacy. Was still going on. No chance of peace. Oh how it sickens the heart to begin another year with this terrible cruel war still raging. Young men still in the field from their homes and undergoing the hardships of war. Parents and friends still anxious and grieved and poor refugees still away from their loved homes. God grant that it will not be so another year. And myself I think some improved but alas it is very little. I hope and pray that this time next year that there will be a very perceptable change in my poor sinful self. I am more, yes much more homesick and gloomy than last year. Then I looked forward to returning home soon. Now there seems no hopes of it. God help me to bear it patiently, but my heart feels often as if it would break with longing for home.[63]

Notes

1. Sidney's cousin Maggie.
2. The town of New Iberia. In 1863 the name was in transition from New Town.
3. This was possibly a First Lieutenant Goode of the St. Mary's Cannoneers.
4. Probably the town of Berwick in St. Mary Parish.
5. This was possibly First Lieutenant John W. Barnes, Company E, 28th Louisiana, Infantry (Gray's).
6. This was possibly Third Lieutenant A. W. Morse, Company C, 4th Regiment, 3rd Brigade, 1st Division, of Louisiana Militia.
7. Cousin.

8. Lieutenant Morse.
9. Peters.
10. No records of an officer by this name were found in Andrew B. Booth's *Records of Louisiana Confederate Soldiers and Louisiana Confederate Commands,* 3 vols. (Spartanburg, SC, 1984).
11. Acadians or Cajuns.
12. This is Major S. C. Furman of the 2nd Louisiana Cavalry Regiment.
13. This is Captain Louis Prescott of Company A, 2nd Louisiana Cavalry Regiment.
14. Louis Prescott.
15. Mary Prescott.
16. Aaron Prescott.
17. This was possibly Lieutenant D. W. Magill, of the Washington, Louisiana, Heavy Artillery.
18. Louis Prescott.
19. Mrs. Offutt or Offert.
20. No records of an officer by this name were found in Booth's *Records.*
21. This was one of the Harding family slaves, apparently a child house servant.
22. Colonel William Vincent commanded the 2nd Louisiana Cavalry Regiment.
23. No records of an officer by this name were found in Booth's *Records.*
24. Her cousins.
25. No records of an officer by this name were found in Booth's *Records.*
26. Willy Marshall and Benny Marshall. Willy was Private William Marshall, Company E, 2nd Louisiana Cavalry. The Marshall family was among the elite families of South Carolina who migrated to Louisiana prior to the Civil War. Henry Marshall Sr. was a Confederate Congressman from Louisiana and had been an officer in the South Carolina militia prior to his move. When war broke out, the plantation known as "Land's End" began to prepare for battle activity. Private William "Willie" Marshall joined the 2nd Louisiana Cavalry and rode with it through much of the war. During the Red River Campaign he was captured at Henderson Hill and sent as a POW to New Orleans. He died in the prison camp on May 13, 1864. His family received the body and buried him on the plantation.
27. Elizabeth Harding.
28. Sissy Offutt or Offert.
29. Cheneyville is located in Rapides Parish, Louisiana.
30. Cheneyville.
31. Loyd Hall. This home still exists.
32. This is probably Bayou Beouf, one of many such named streams in Louisiana. This Bayou Beouf runs parallel to Bayou Rapides northwest of Alexandria.

33. John Prescott.
34. An edema, swelling from excessive accumulation of serous fluid in tissue.
35. This is probably Judge Henry Boyce. The plantation was located north of Alexandria and is the site of the Town of Boyce today.
36. Cloutierville in Natchitoches Parish.
37. Hiams.
38. An elderly slave.
39. Boots.
40. Blankenship. The family stills lives in the Pleasant Hill area.
41. The Glassells owned a farm south of Sabine Crossroads, three miles southeast of Mansfield.
42. Dr. Wilson owned a farm three miles north of the village of Pleasant Hill. The following April a sharp skirmish would be fought on this property as the Union forces marched to Mansfield.
43. This is James S. Ashton Jr., Captain of Company D, 11th Louisiana, Infantry. He was wounded at Battle of Manassas, August 30, 1862. Booth's *Records* states "Arm Amputated on Furlough."
44. This was Surgeon R. T. Gibbs of the 2nd Louisiana Cavalry Regiment. Surgeons typically held equivalency ranks of captain or major. Gibbs was captured at Natchitoches, March 21, 1864, at Henderson Hill. He was taken to New Orleans and placed in the Federal holding compound, perhaps at the Bellville foundry, on March 26, 1864. Booth's *Records* states: "Released as surgeon and sent through the lines in April, 1864, by order Gen. Banks."
45. No records of an officer by this name were found in Booth's *Records.*
46. Ashton.
47. This was probably a cotton plantation, although no local records exist of it.
48. Gibbs.
49. Sidney used the word "stupid" consistently for anything she deemed boring, frustrating, or in any situation in which she did not want to participate.
50. This is the village of Keachi or Keachie, northwest of Mansfield about twenty miles by road at the time.
51. Sidney's sister Anne (or Annie).
52. Land's End Plantation, located north of Keachi near the Caddo Parish boundary with DeSoto Parish.
53. These prisoners were taken at the Battle of Stirling Plantation on September 29, 1863.
54. Maggie.
55. Aaron Prescott.
56. Mansfield.

57. Yankees.
58. 2nd Louisiana Cavalry Regiment.
59. Mansfield.
60. No records of an officer by this name were found in Booth's *Records.*
61. This is Captain E. F. Morehead of Company E, 28th (Thomas's) Louisiana Infantry Regiment. Booth's *Records* states: "Federal Rolls of Prisoners of War, Captured Pt. Coupee Par., March 30, 1864. Recd. New Orleans, La., April 5, 1864. Paroled New Orleans, La., _, 1864. Exchanged Red River Landing, July 22, 1864."
62. Lyman, Sidney's favorite brother, was apparently accompanying Confederate exchanged prisoners from New Orleans. She expected him to appear daily.
63. Sidney Harding's diary ends with this passage.

Bibliography

Primary Sources

Manuscripts

Bounds, Steve. Unpublished casualty lists of the Battle of Mansfield. Mansfield State Historic Site, Mansfield, LA.

Dearman, Scott. "Order of Battle of the Confederate Army at the Battle of Mansfield, Louisiana. Major General Richard Taylor, April 8, 1864." Mansfield State Historic Site, Mansfield, LA.

Hall, Louis. "The Battle of Mansfield: The Experience of a Veteran." TS. Mansfield Public Library, Mansfield, LA.

Harding (Miss Sidney) Diaries, 1863–64, 1865. Louisiana and Lower Mississippi Valley Collections, Manuscript Group #721, Hill Memorial Library, Louisiana State Univ., Baton Rouge. Also in *Records of Ante-Bellum Southern Plantations from the Revolution through the Civil War, Series I, Selections from the Louisiana and Lower Mississippi Valley Collection, Louisiana State University Libraries, Part 1, Louisiana Sugar Plantations* (Frederick, MD: University Publications of America, 1988).

Harris, F. B. 4th Texas Cavalry Regiment. Letter. Folio 6 of the Aimer Collection, Cammie Henry Research Center, Northwestern State Univ., Natchitoches, LA.

Jarratt, James A. Consolidated Crescent Regiment. Self-published MS. Copy in the collection of Russell and Mary Margaret Schulze, Houston.

Joiner, Gary D. "A Place Name Geography of Union Parish, Louisiana." Louisiana Tech Univ., Ruston. Copy in the Union Parish Library, Farmerville, LA.

Lale, Max S. "New Light on Battle of Mansfield." N. S. Allen Collection, Noel Memorial Library, Louisiana State Univ., Shreveport. Favrot family diaries and letters. Semmes Favrot personal collection, New Orleans.

Pegues, Margaret, and Charlotte Pegues. "Battle of Mansfield." Handwritten transcription by Laura Cale in the collection of Marilyn S. Joiner, Shreveport, LA.

"The Red River Expedition to Shreveport and Back." Mss. 83422, Louisiana and Lower Mississippi Valley Collections, Louisiana State Univ. Libraries, Baton Rouge.

Smith, Kirby. Papers. Southern Historical Collection, Wilson Library, Univ. of North Carolina, Chapel Hill.

Tate, Mrs. Claude B. Papers. Barker History Center, Univ. of Texas, Austin.

Walker, John G. Papers. Southern Historical Collection, Univ. of North Carolina, Chapel Hill.

Whitney, William H. 38th Massachusetts Infantry Regiment. Letters. Mss. 1043, 1046, Louisiana and Lower Mississippi Valley Collections, Louisiana State Univ. Libraries, Baton Rouge.

Diaries and Letters

Ballard, B. E. 36th Texas Cavalry Regiment. Letter, May 20, 1864. Original in the collection of Duval Beatty, Port Neches, TX.

Beard, James H. Consolidated Crescent Regiment. Letters, April 1864. Originals in the collection of Nancy Beard Wilson, Kentfield, CA.

Camille, A.J.M., the Prince de Polignac. Letter to General Sterling B. Hendricks, Oct. 28, 1863. Original in the collection of Dr. Thomas Pressly, Shreveport, LA.

Causland, D. E. Company H, 4th Confederate Engineers. Letter, Mar. 4, 1865. Original in the collection of Dr. Thomas Pressly, Shreveport, LA.

Couthouy, Joseph Pitty. U.S. Navy. Letters. Originals in the collection of Jimmy H. Sandefur, Shreveport, LA.

"Delamaster." Letter, May 27, 1864. Original in the collection of Gary D. Joiner, Shreveport, LA.

Fullilove, Lizzie. Diary. Samford C. Fullilove Collection, Archives and Special Collections, Noel Memorial Library, Louisiana State Univ., Shreveport.

Goss, Mrs. Mary Porter. "Information on Big Battle Recalled." TS. Mansfield State Historic Site, Mansfield, LA.

Halbert, Joshua L. 15th Texas Cavalry Regiment. Letter, Apr. 13, 1864. Original in the collection of Jimmy H. Sandefur, Shreveport, LA.

Hayden, Thomas. 38th Massachusetts Infantry Regiment. Letter, May 4, 1864. Original in the collection of Jimmy H. Sandefur, Shreveport, LA.

Howell, Zach. Papers. Archives and Special Collections, Noel Memorial Library, Louisiana State Univ., Shreveport.

Jim ——. 30th Maine Infantry Regiment. Letter, May, 1864. Otherwise unidentified soldier. Original in the collection of Jimmy H. Sandefur, Shreveport, LA.

Kemp, Rufus C. Company D, 165th New York Infantry Regiment. Letters. Originals in the collection of Jimmy H. Sandefur, Shreveport, LA.

Knapp, Julius L. Company I, 116th New York Volunteer Infantry Regiment. Diary, Mar.–Dec. 1864. Original in the collection of Jimmy H. Sandefur, Shreveport, LA.

Knox, R. A. Company H, 2nd Texas Cavalry Regiment. Letter, Apr. 21, 1864. Original in the collection of Jimmy H. Sandefur, Shreveport, LA.

Maedgen, Moritz. Company D, 4th Texas Cavalry. Letter, June 24, 1864. Original in the collection of Bryan James Maedgen, Houston.

Morgan, Jefferson. Company E, 35th Texas Cavalry Regiment. Letters, 1863–64. Originals in the collection of Ann Turk, Arlington, TX.

Novyus, Wilson. 161st New York Infantry Regiment. Letter, Apr. 15, 1864. Original in the collection of Jimmy H. Sandefur, Shreveport, LA.

Pearce, F. W. Company A, 2nd Maine Cavalry. Letter, Apr. 21, 1864. Original in the collection of Jimmy H. Sandefur, Shreveport, LA.

Scarborough, William H. Company B, 96th Ohio Infantry Regiment. Letter, Mar. 27, 1864. Original in the collection of Jimmy H. Sandefur, Shreveport, LA.

Shaw, W. T. Texas cavalry. Letter, Apr. 13, 1918. Original in the collection of Molly Wiggins, Covington, LA.

Stinson, Lillie Dandridge. "Reminiscences of the Battle of Pleasant Hill." Mansfield State Historic Site, Mansfield, LA.

Thomas ——. Letter, Apr. 9, 1864. Otherwise unidentified soldier's letter (possibly 19th Corps). Original in the collection of Jimmy H. Sandefur, Shreveport, LA.

Voigt, Hugo. Company C, 29th Wisconsin Infantry Regiment. Letter, May 4, 1864. Original in the collection of Jimmy H. Sandefur, Shreveport, LA.

Government Documents

Jarratt, J. A. Application for Confederate Veteran's Benefits. Louisiana State Archives Microscopy CP1.72.

Massachusetts Adjutant General's Office. *Massachusetts Soldiers, Sailors and Marines in the Great Civil War.* Vol. 4. Norwood, MA: Norwood Press, 1931.

National Archives and Records Administration. RG 94, Microscopy 378, Roll 15. Confederate service records.

———. RG 94, Microscopy 543, Rolls 1, 13, 16, 17, 19, 21. Union service records.

———. RG 94, Microscopy 544, Roll 18. Union service records.

———. RG 94, Microscopy 551, Rolls 22, 25, 37, 42, 51, 64, 78, 85, 104, 105, 113, 126, 129, 133, 150. Union service records.

———. RG 94, Microscopy 552, Rolls 94, 75. Union service records.

———. RG 94, Microscopy 559, Roll 31. Union service records.

State of Louisiana. Louisiana Dept. of Natural Resources, Bureau of State Lands, Louisiana Land Records, 1852.

———. Secretary of State, Division of Archives, Records Management, and History. *Vital Records Indices.* Baton Rouge, Louisiana, Death records for Orleans Parish, 1919.

State of Louisiana (C.S.A.). *Official Report to the Conduct of Federal Troops in Western Louisiana, during the Invasions of 1863 and 1864, Compiled from Sworn Testimony under Direction of Governor Henry Watkins Allen.* Shreveport: Confederate State of Louisiana, 1865.

U.S. Congress. *Report on the Joint Committee on the Conduct of the War, 1863–1866.* Vol. 2, *Red River Expedition.* Millwood, NY: Krauss Reprint, 1977.

U.S. Dept. of Commerce. 7th Decennial Census (1850), Pike County, Georgia. Unpublished tabulations in the National Archives and Records Administration, Washington, DC.

———. 8th Decennial Census (1860), Caddo Parish and Bossier Parish, Louisiana. Unpublished tabulations in the National Archives and Records Administration, Washington, DC.

———. 8th Decennial Census (1860), Middlesex County, Massachusetts, Series M653, Roll 508. Unpublished tabulations in the National Archives and Records Administration, Washington, DC.

———. 8th Decennial Census (1860), Sabine Parish, Louisiana. Unpublished tabulations in the National Archives and Records Administration, Washington, DC.

———. 8th Decennial Census (1860), St. Mary Parish, Louisiana. Unpublished tabulations in the National Archives and Records Administration, Washington, DC.

———. 14th Decennial Census (1920), Caddo Parish, Louisiana. Unpublished tabulations in the National Archives and Records Administration, Washington, DC.

U.S. Dept. of the Interior. Louisiana Land Records, 1852. Bureau of Land Management's General Land Office (GLO), Washington, DC.

U.S. War Dept. *Atlas to Accompany the Official Records of the Union and Confederate Armies.* Washington: U.S. Government Printing Office, 1891–95.

———. *Official Army Register of the Volunteer Force of the United States Army for the Years 1861–65.* 8 parts. Washington, 1865.

———. *Official Records of the Union and Confederate Navies in the War of the Rebellion.* 31 vols. Washington, DC, 1895–1929.

———. *War of the Rebellion: The Official Records of the Union and Confederate Armies.* 128 vols. Washington, 1880–1901.

Maps

U.S. Geological Survey. 7.5 minute topographic quadrangle map, Leola, Arkansas.

———. 7.5 minute topographic quadrangle map, Mansfield, Louisiana.

———. 7.5 minute topographic quadrangle map, Trenton, Louisiana.

Venable, Maj. Richard, C.S.A. "Map of the Battlefield at Mansfield," 1864. Jeremy Gilmer Papers, Southern Historical Collection, Univ. of North Carolina, Chapel Hill. Also a copy in RG 77, folio Z 34-2, National Archives and Records Administration, Washington, DC.

———. "Shreveport and Environs," 1864. Jeremy Gilmer Papers, Southern Historical Collection, Univ. of North Carolina, Chapel Hill.

Newspapers and Periodicals

Cambridge (MA) Chronicle, May 8, 1909

Galveston (TX) Weekly News, Apr. 20, 1864

Houston Daily Telegraph, Apr. 1864

Mid-America 40 (Jan. 1958)

New Orleans Times, May 4, 1864

(New York) Daily Tribune, Mar. 28, 1864

(Saint Louis) Daily Republican, Mar. 26, 1864

Shreveport (LA) Times, Apr. 15, 1921; Oct. 30, 1944

Southwestern Historical Quarterly 34 (Oct. 1930)

Washington (AR) Telegraph, May 1864

Other Printed Primary Sources

Bartlett, Napier. *Military Record of Louisiana: Including Biographical and Historical Papers Relating to the Military Organization of the State.* New Orleans: L. Graham and Co., 1875.

Bearss, Edwin C., and Willy H. Tunnard. *A Southern Record: The Story of the 3rd Louisiana Infantry, C.S.A.* Dayton, OH: Morningside, 1988.

Bee, Hamilton P. "Battle of Pleasant Hill—An Error Corrected." *Southern Historical Society Papers* 8 (1880): 184–86.

Beecher, Harris H. *Record of the 114th New York N.Y.S.V. Where It Went, What It Saw, and What It Did.* Norwich, NY: J. F. Hubbard Jr., 1866.

Benson, S. F. "The Battle of Pleasant Hill." *Annals of Iowa.* Des Moines, IA: Henry H. English, 1906.

Biographical and Historical Memoirs of Northwest Louisiana. Chicago and Nashville: Southern Publishing Co., 1890.

Blessington, J. P. *The Campaigns of Walker's Texas Division.* Austin: State House Press, 1994.

Bonner, T. R. "Sketches of the Campaign of 1864: Walker's Division—Retreat up Red River—Battle of Mansfield." *The Land We Love* 5 (Oct. 1868): 459–66.

Botkin, B.A., ed. *Lay My Burden Down: A Folk History of Slavery.* Chicago: Univ. of Chicago Press, 1945.

Childers, Henry H. "Reminiscences of the Battle of Pleasant Hill." *Annals of Iowa.* Des Moines: Henry H. English, 1906.

———. "Reminiscences." In *DeSoto Parish History: Sesquicentennial Edition, 1843–1993,* 514–16. Mansfield, LA: DeSoto Historical and Genealogical Society, 1995.

Clark, Orton S. *The One Hundred and Sixteenth Regiment of New York Volunteers.* Buffalo: Printing House of Matthews and Warren, 1868.

Couthouy, J. P. "Descriptions of New Species of Mollusca and Shells, and Remarks on Several Polypi Found in Massachusetts Bay." *Boston Journal of Natural History* 2 (1838): 53–111.

———. "Remarks upon Coral Formations in the Pacific; with Suggestions as to the Causes of Their Absence in the Same Parallels of Latitude on the Coast of South America." *Boston Journal of Natural History* 4: 66–105, 137–62.

———. *San Pedro's Treasure: Exploring Scheme to Visit Cumana Harbor: Believed to Be a Waste of Time and Money, as Captain Joseph B.* [sic] *Couthouy of Boston Went There in 1856 and Found the Spanish Ship's Hulk, but Only a Few Scattered Coins.* Boston: n.p., n.d. Copy in the Boston Athenaeum.

Cuccia, Phillip. "'Gorillas' and White Glove Gents: Union Soldiers in the Red River Campaign." *Louisiana History* 36 (1995): 413–31.

Dall, W. H. "Some American Conchologists." *Proceedings of the Biological Society of Washington* (1888).

Dorsey, Sarah H. *Recollections of Henry Watkins Allen, Brigadier General Confederate State Army, Ex-Governor of Louisiana.* New York: M. Doolady, 1866.

Dyer, Frederick H. *A Compendium of the War of the Rebellion.* 3 vols. Dayton, OH: Morningside, 1979.

Edwards, John N. *Shelby and His Men: or, The War in the West.* Cincinnati: Miami Printing and Publishing Co., Print, 1867.

Ewer, James K. *The Third Massachusetts Cavalry in the War for the Union.* Maplewood, MA: Historical Committee of the Regimental Association, 1903.

Flinn, Frank M. *Campaigning with Banks in Louisiana in '63 and '64 and with Sheridan in the Shenandoah Valley in '64 and '65.* Lynn, MA: Thomas. P. Nichols, 1887.

Fox, William F. *Regimental Losses in the American Civil War.* Dayton, OH: Morningside Books, 1985.

Gould, John Mead. *The Civil War Journals of John Mead Gould, 1861–1866.* Baltimore: Butternut and Blue, 1997.

———. *Directory of the First-Tenth-Twenty Ninth Maine Regiment Association, Compiled for the Use of the Association.* Portland, ME: Stephen Berry, 1889.

———. *History of the First-Tenth-Twenty-Ninth Maine Regiment, in Service of the United States, from May 3, 1861, to June 21, 1866.* Portland, ME: Stephen Berry, 1871.

Greeley, Horace. *The American Conflict: A History of the Great Rebellion in the United States of America, 1860–65.* Washington DC: National Tribune, 1898.

Harrell, J. M. *Arkansas.* Vol. 10, *Confederate Military History.* Atlanta: Confederate Publishing Co., 1899.

Heartsill, W. W. *Fourteen Hundred and 91 Days in the Confederate Army: A Journal Kept by W. W. Heartsill for Four Years, One Month, and One Day or, Camp Life; Day by Day, of the W. P. Lane Rangers from April 19th, 1861 to May 20th, 1865.* Edited by Bell Irvin Wiley. Wilmington, NC: Broadfoot Publishing Co., 1992.

Hewitt, Jane B. *Texas Confederate Soldiers, 1861–65.* Wilmington, NC: Broad-foot Publishing Co., 1997.

Hewitt, J. E. *The Battle of Mansfield.* Mansfield, LA: Enterprise Publishing Co., 1925.

Irwin, Richard B. *History of the Nineteenth Army Corps.* Baton Rouge: Elliott's Book Shop Press, 1985.

Jarratt, J. A. *Reminiscences of a Great Struggle Told by Heroes of the Confederacy.* Mansfield, LA: By the author, 1907.

Johnson, R. I. "Occasional Papers on Mollusks, Museum of Comparative Zoology." *Harvard University* 1, no. 5 (1946).

Jones, S. C. *Reminiscences of the 22nd Iowa Infantry Giving Its Organization, Marches, Skirmishes, Battles, and Sieges, As Taken from the Diary of Lieutenant S.C. Jones of Company A.* Iowa City: Camp Pope Bookshop, 1993.

"Keatchie College Organized." In *DeSoto Plume Digest.* Vol. 1. Mansfield, LA: DeSoto Parish Historical Society, 2000, 137–89.

"The Last of the Mohicans." Unidentified article in the archives of the Mansfield State Historic Area, Mansfield, LA.

Lewis, W. H. "Mansfield's Newspaper Story." In *DeSoto Plume Digest.* Vol. 1. Mansfield, LA: DeSoto Parish Historical Society, 2000, 158–61.

Lubbock, Francis Richard. *Six Decades in Texas; or Memoirs of Francis Richard Lubbock, Governor of Texas in War Time.* Edited by C. W. Raines. Austin, TX: B. C. Jones & Co., 1900.

Marshall, Thomas B. *History of the Eighty-Third Ohio Volunteer Infantry, the Greyhound Regiment.* Cincinnati: Eighty-Third Ohio Volunteer Infantry Association, 1913.

Maury, D. H. "Sketch of General Richard Taylor." *Southern Historical Society Papers* 7 (1879): 343–45.

Medford, H. C. "The Diary of H. C. Medford, Confederate Soldier, 1864." Edited by Rebecca W. Smith and Marion Mullins. *Southwestern Historical Quarterly* 34 (Oct. 1930): 220–21.

Moore, Frank, ed. *The Rebellion Record: A Diary of American Events.* New York: Putnam (Vols. 1–6) and Van Nostrand (Vols. 7–12), 1868.

Northup, Solomon. *Twelve Years a Slave: Narrative of Solomon Northup, a Citizen of New-York, Kidnapped in Washington City in 1841, and Rescued in 1853.* Auburn, NY: Derby and Miller, 1853.

Paris, Compte de [Louis Philippe Albert d Orléans]. *History of the Civil War in America.* Vol. 4. Philadelphia: Porter and Coates, 1875–88.

Pitts, Florison D. "The Civil War Diary of Florison D. Pitts." Edited by Leo M. Kaiser. *Mid-America* 40 (Jan. 1958): 22–63.

Poe, Clarence, ed. *True Tales of the South at War: How Soldiers Fought and Families Lived, 1861–1865.* Chapel Hill: Univ. of North Carolina Press, 1961.

Powers, George W. "Bitter and Sweet." *Bivouac* 3 (1885): 342–45.

Reid, John B. *Civil War Letters of John B. Reid.* Greenville, IL: Bond County Historical Society, 1991.

Rigby, Alfred A. *Union Soldier's Diary.* N.p.: Tortoise Press, n.d.

Scott, John. *Story of the Thirty Second Iowa Infantry Volunteers.* Nevada, IA: By the author, 1896.

Sherman, William T. *Memoirs of General W. T. Sherman Written by Himself.* 2 vols. New York: D. Appleton and Co., 1875.

Shorey, Henry Augustus. *The Story of the Maine Fifteenth: Being a Brief Narrative of the More Important Events in the History of the Fifteenth Maine Regiment, Together with a Complete Roster of the Regiment.* Bridgton, ME: Press of the Bridgton News, 1890.

Sprague, Homer B. *History of the 13th Infantry Regiment of Connecticut Volunteers, during the Great Rebellion.* Hartford, CT: Case, Lockwood, 1867.

Stanyan, John Minot. *A History of the Eighth Regiment of New Hampshire Volunteers, Including Its Service as Infantry, Second N.H. Cavalry, and Veteran Battalion in the Civil War of 1861–1865.* Concord, NH: Ira C. Evans, 1892.

Taylor, Richard. *Destruction and Reconstruction: Personal Experiences in the Civil War.* New York: Da Capo, 1995.

"Three Women of DeSoto Parish, Who Helped the Cause of the Confederacy, and the Battle of Mansfield, April 8th, 1864." *DeSoto Plume Digest.* Vol. 1. Mansfield, LA: DeSoto Parish Historical Society, 2000, 137–39.

Van Dyke, Ben. "Ben Van Dyke's Escape from the Hospital at Pleasant Hill, Louisiana." *Annals of Iowa.* Des Moines: Henry H. English, 1906.

Walters, Nannie Townsend. "Walter Bailey Townsend." In *Father Wore Gray,* edited by Lela Whitton Hegarty. San Antonio: Naylor, 1963.

Whitney, William H. *A Watertown Farm in Eight Generations: A Memorial of the Whitney Family.* Cambridge, MA: New England Historic Genealogical Society and Watertown Historical Society, 1898.

Woods, Joseph T. *Services of the Ninety-sixth Ohio Volunteers.* Toledo: Blade Printing and Paper Co., 1874.

Yeary, Mamie, comp. *Reminiscences of the Boys in Gray, 1861–1865.* Dallas: For the author by Smith & Lamar, 1912.

Secondary Sources

Agay, Denes. *Best Loved Songs of the American People.* Garden City, NY: Doubleday & Co., 1975.

Andrews, J. Cutler. *The North Reports the Civil War.* Pittsburgh: Univ. of Pittsburgh Press, 1983.

Bearss, Edwin C. *Steele's Retreat from Camden and the Battle of Jenkins Ferry.* Little Rock: Eagle Press of Little Rock, 1990.

Belisle, John G. *History of Sabine Parish Louisiana.* Many, LA: Sabine Banner Press, 1912.

Bergeron, Arthur W., Jr. *The Civil War Reminiscences of Major Silas T. Grisamore, C.S.A.* Baton Rouge: Louisiana State Univ. Press, 1993.

———. "A Colonel Gains His Wreath: Henry Gray's Louisiana Brigade at the Battle of Mansfield, April 8, 1864." In *The Red River Campaign: Union and Confederate Leadership and War in Louisiana.* Shreveport, LA: Parabellum Press, 2003, 1–25.

———. "General Richard Taylor as a Military Commander." *Louisiana History* 23 (Winter 1982): 35–47.

———. *A Guide to Confederate Military Units, 1861–1865.* Baton Rouge: Louisiana State Univ. Press, 1989.

Booth, Andrew B. *Records of Louisiana Confederate Soldiers and Louisiana Confederate Commands.* 3 vols. Spartanburg, SC: Reprint Co., 1984.

Brooksher, William Riley. *War along the Bayous: The 1864 Red River Campaign in Louisiana.* Washington: Brassey's, 1998.

Brown, Norman D., ed. *Journey to Pleasant Hill: The Civil War Letters of Captain Elijah P. Petty, Walker's Texas Division, C.S.A.* San Antonio: Univ. of Texas Institute of Texan Cultures, 1982.

Burgess, Lauren Cook. *An Uncommon Soldier: The Civil War Letters of Sarah Rosetta Wakeman, Alias Pvt. Lyons Wakeman, 153rd Regiment, New York State Volunteers, 1862–1864.* Pasadena, MD: Minerva Center, 1994.

Chrysler, Liz . "The Battle of Pleasant Hill—From a Boy's Viewpoint." *Mansfield Enterprise,* May 17, 1977.

Costello, Brian J. *A History of Pointe Coupeé Parish Louisiana.* New Roads, LA: B. J. Costello, 1999.

DeSoto Parish History: Sesquicentennial Edition, 1843–1993. Mansfield, LA: DeSoto Parish Historical Society, 1995.

Dimitry, John. *Louisiana.* Vol. 10 of *Confederate Military History.* Atlanta: n.p., 1899.

Dollar, Susan E. "The Red River Campaign, Natchitoches Parish, Louisiana: A Case of Equal Opportunity Destruction." *Louisiana History* 43, no. 4 (2002): 411–32.

Edmonds, David G. *Yankee Autumn in Acadiana: A Narrative of the Great Texas Overland Expedition through Southwestern Louisiana: October through December, 1863.* Lafayette, LA: Acadiana Press, 1979.

Faulk, Odie B. *General Tom Green: A Fightin' Texan.* Waco: Texian Press, 1963.

Freeman, Douglas Southall. *R. E. Lee: A Biography.* 4 vols. New York: Charles Scribner's Sons, 1934–35.

Gallaway, B. P. ed. *Texas, The Dark Corner of the Confederacy: Contemporary Accounts of the Long Star State in the Civil War.* Lincoln: Univ. of Nebraska Press, 1994.

Huffstodt, Jim. *Hard Dying Men: The Story of General W.H.L. Wallace, General T.E.G. Ransom, and Their "Old Eleventh": Illinois Infantry in the American Civil War (1861–1865).* Bowie, MD: Heritage Books, 1991.

Johnson, Ludwell H. *Red River Campaign: Politics and Cotton in the Civil War.* Kent, OH: Kent State Univ. Press, 1993.

Joiner, Gary D. "Confederate Encampments Prior to the Battle of Mansfield." *DeSoto Plume* 39, no. 4 (2005): 9–10.

———. "The Congressional Investigation Following the Red River Campaign." *North Louisiana History* 35, no. 4 (Fall 2004): 147–67.

———. *40 Archaeological Sites in the Red River Campaign* (1997). Archives of the Division of Archaeology, State of Louisiana, Baton Rouge.

———. "I Will Fight Banks If He Has a Million Men." *DeSoto Plume* 37, no. 3 (2002): 2–10.

———. *One Damn Blunder from Beginning to End: The Red River Campaign of 1864.* Wilmington, DE: Scholarly Resources, 2003.

———. "Up the Red River and Down to Defeat." *America's Civil War* (Mar. 2004): 22–29. This was also published in *Pivotal Battles and Campaigns of a Decisive Year—1864: Grinding, Relentless War* (Leesburg, VA: Primedia Publishing, 2004), 11–17.

Kinard, Jeff. *Lafayette of the South: Prince Camille de Polignac and the American Civil War.* College Station: Texas A & M Univ. Press, 2001.

Lowe, Richard. *Walker's Texas Division, C.S.A.: Greyhounds of the Trans-Mississippi.* Baton Rouge: Louisiana State Univ. Press, 2004.

———. *The Texas Overland Expedition of 1863.* Fort Worth: Ryan Place, 1996.

Mills, Gary B. *The Forgotten People: Cane River's Creoles of Color.* Baton Rouge: Louisiana State Univ. Press, 1977.

Parks, Joseph Howard. *General Edmund Kirby Smith, C.S.A.* Baton Rouge: Louisiana State Univ. Press, 1954.

Parrish, T. Michael. *Richard Taylor: Soldier Prince of Dixie.* Chapel Hill: Univ. of North Carolina Press, 1992.

Power, Sally. "The Red River Expedition to Shreveport and Back." *Louisiana History* 40, no. 2 (1999): 355–64.

Reid, John B. *The Civil War Letters of John B. Reid.* Greenville, IL: Bond County Genealogical Society, 1991.

Riffel, Judy, ed. *A History of Pointe Coupeé Parish and Its Families.* Baton Rouge: Comité des Archives de la Louisiana, 1983.

Savas, Theodore P. "A Death at Mansfield: Col. James Hamilton Beard and the Consolidated Crescent Regiment." in *The Red River Campaign: Union and Confederate Leadership and War in Louisiana* (Shreveport, LA: Parabellum Press, 2003), 68–103.

Sifakis, Stewart. *Compendium of the Confederate Armies: Louisiana.* New York: Facts on File, 1995.

———. *Compendium of the Confederate Armies: Texas.* New York: Facts on File, 1995.

Warner, Ezra J. *Generals in Blue: Lives of the Union Commanders.* Baton Rouge: Louisiana State Univ. Press, 1993.

Whittington, G. P. "Rapides Parish, Louisiana—A History." *Louisiana Historical Quarterly* 18 (1935): 26–28.

Winters, John D. *The Civil War in Louisiana.* Baton Rouge: Louisiana State Univ. Press, 1963.

Wooster, Ralph A. *Civil War Texas.* Austin: Texas State Historical Association, 1999.

Zeitlin, Richard H. *Old Abe the War Eagle: A True Story of the Civil War and Reconstruction.* Madison: State Historical Society of Wisconsin, 1986.

CONTRIBUTORS

GARY D. JOINER, Ph.D., serves as the director of the Red River Regional Studies Center at Louisiana State University in Shreveport, where he is also an assistant professor of history. He is coeditor of *No Pardons To Ask, Nor Apologies to Make: The Journal of William Henry King, Gray's 28th Louisiana Infantry Regiment* and author of *Through the Howling Wilderness: The 1864 Red River Campaign of 1864 and Union Failure in the West;* both were published by the University of Tennessee Press in 2006. An earlier book, *One Damn Blunder From Beginning to End: The Red River Campaign of 1864* (Scholarly Resources, 2003), won the Albert Castel Prize in 2004 for best historical book on the Western Theater and the A. M. Pate Award for excellence in research and writing in the Trans-Mississippi Theater in 2005. He is also coeditor of and a contributor to *The Red River Campaign: Union and Confederate Leadership and the War in Louisiana* (Parabellum Press, 2003), coauthor of *Historic Shreveport–Bossier City* (Historical Publishing Network, 2000) and *Red River Steamboats* (Arcadia Tempus Publishing, 1999), and author of several articles.

MARILYN MURRELL SEGURA JOINER is a native of Mansfield, where she was instilled with an interest in the war and its participants. As an undergraduate, she focused on English, journalism and history. She left a journalism career to enter marketing and public relations and is a marketing executive. She is married to the senior editor.

TARA Z. LAVER serves as assistant curator for manuscripts in Special Collections, Louisiana State University Libraries, in Baton Rouge, Louisiana.

Bryan James Maedgen is a native of Houston, Texas. Among the items in his personal collection of family papers are those of his great uncle, Moritz Maedgen. One of them is included in this volume.

Steven M. Mayeux is a graduate of Louisiana State University and a former U.S. Marine Corps officer. He works as an agricultural consultant in central Louisiana, and is president of Friends of Fort DeRussy, Inc. His forthcoming book on the history of Fort DeRussy is currently under contract with the University of Tennessee Press.

Dyson Nickles is a graduate student majoring in history at Stephen F. Austin University in Nacogdoches, Texas. A serious living historian, he participates in battlefield reenactments and bivouacs, portraying a member of the 3rd Texas Cavalry.

Monica R. Pels is a student majoring in history at Louisiana State University in Shreveport.

Thomas A. Pressly III, M.D., is both an accomplished physician and a student of the Civil War in the Trans-Mississippi. He owns an extensive collection of documents, letters, and images from the period.

Allan C. Richard Jr. is a graduate of Louisiana Polytechnic Institute (now Louisiana Tech University). He has been employed in construction management all his working life but is also an avid historian. A member of several historical organizations, he has served as both president and symposium chairman of the North Louisiana Civil War Round Table. Allan and his wife, Mary Margaret, are the authors of *The Defense of Vicksburg: A Louisiana Chronicle* (Texas A&M University Press, 2004). Allan found the Lucien Flournoy letter while researching another project, the history of Greenwood, Louisiana.

Jimmy H. Sandefur of Shreveport, Louisiana, is a long-time collector of Civil War letters and manuscripts, several of which appear in this volume. He permitted the use of the Joshua Halbert and R. A. Knox letters; the Julius Knapp diary; the letters of "Jim," "Thomas," Thomas Hayden, Wilson Novyus, F.W. Pearce, William H. Scarborough, Rufus Kemp, and Hugo Voigt; and the letters concerning the death of Joseph P. Couthouy.

Ann Turk of Arlington, Texas, is a graduate of the University of North Texas at Denton and a retired mathematics teacher. She grew up in Waxahachie, Texas, near the family homestead in Ellis County. She is a great-granddaughter of Jefferson Morgan and has spent much time seeking to "know and understand" the lives of Jefferson and his wife, Amanda Morgan.

CHERYL WHITE, Ph.D. teaches history at Louisiana State University in Shreveport. Her areas of expertise include nineteenth-century American history, British history, and religious studies. While she has written extensively on other historical subjects, this is her first foray into Civil War history.

MARY (MOLLY) WALLACE STUART-MCASKILL WIGGINS, is the great-great-granddaughter of General Tom Green, CSA. She a registered-nurse graduate of Emory University in Atlanta and holds a master's degree in education from the University of New Orleans. She is married to Judge R. G. "Bob" Wiggins, justice of the peace in St. Tammany Parish, Louisiana. She is past president of the Louisiana Division, United Daughters of the Confederacy, and member of the Daughters of the Republic of Texas. Her collection of General Green's papers and memorabilia contains the letter from W. T. Shaw.

NANCY BEARD WILSON is a native of California but descended from two early Louisiana families, the Beards and Scogins. She graduated from Stanford University with a B.A. in journalism and has written several articles about different aspects of Louisiana history. She is a member of many local historical organizations, including Keachi Heritage Foundation, Kate Beard Chapter of the United Daughters of the Confederacy, and the DeSoto Parish Historical Society. She was instrumental in obtaining the James A. Jarratt pamphlet.

Index

Page numbers in boldface refer to illustrations.

Little to Eat and Thin Mud to Drink was designed and typeset on a Macintosh computer system using InDesign software. The body text is set in 9.75/13 New Baskerville and display type is set in Baskerville Old Face. This book was designed and typeset by Stephanie Thompson.

www.ingramcontent.com/pod-product-compliance
Lightning Source LLC
Chambersburg PA
CBHW020253120726
47904CB00001B/189
* 9 7 8 1 6 2 1 9 0 1 9 5 2 *